C0-BJJ-487

WITHDRAWN
UTSA LIBRARIES

100 Years of Child Protection

RENEWALS 458-4574

DATE DUE

GAYLORD			PRINTED IN U.S.A.

WITHDRAWN
UTSA LIBRARIES

100 Years of Child Protection

Edited by Stan Meuwese, Sharon Detrick
and Sjaak Jansen et al.

This book contains contributions from the International Conference *100 Years of Child Protection – Recommendations for the Future*, which was held on 28-30 November 2005 in Amsterdam, The Netherlands. The involved organisations were the Amsterdam Center of Child Studies (Vrije Universiteit, Amsterdam), Defence for Children International Netherlands, the Dutch Association for Family and Youth Law, the Dutch Child Protection Board, the Dutch Ministry of Health, Welfare and Sport, the Dutch Ministry of Justice, the International Association of Youth and Family Judges and Magistrates, and the International Society of Family Law.

The publication of this book was made possible by a financial contribution from the Dutch Council for the Judiciary.

Library
University of Texas
at San Antonio

Editors:
Stan Meuwese
Sharon Detrick
Sjaak Jansen
Masha Antokolskaia
Corinne Dettmeijer - Vermeulen
Judith Masson
Paul Vlaardingerbroek

Editing Assistants:
Marlijn Lelieveld
Pooja Patel

ISBN 978-90-5850-294-0

Published by: Wolf Legal Publishers (WLP)
P.O. Box 31051
6503 CB Nijmegen
The Netherlands
Tel: +31 24-3551904
Fax: +31 24-3554827
E-Mail: wlp@hetnet.nl
Http://www.wolflegalpublishers.com

All Rights Reserved
© 2007 Wolf Legal Publishers

No part of this work may be reproduced, stored in a retrieval system, or transmitted in any form or by any means, electronic, mechanical, photocopying, microfilming, recording or otherwise, without written permission from the Publisher, with the exception of any material supplied specifically for the purpose of being entered and executed on a computer system, for exclusive use by the purchaser of the work.

Contents

Preface

Willibrord Davids, President of the Dutch Supreme Court

At all times, in all places, there have always been children, or haven't there? There are times, and situations, where children are not seen as independent beings with their own intrinsic personalities and perceptions but, rather, as not yet fully grown-up adults, who should be taught as early as possible to carry all the demands put on adults.

Indeed, the most remarkable thing about the developments since the turn of the 19th century has been the breakthrough of a widely accepted realisation that children have the right to protection of their own values as such and – on the other side of the same coin – others have the obligation to ensure this protection. In this light, charity for children seems too non-committal, however beautiful, honourable and well-intended it has been in past centuries. And thus the development from social to legal, with all the shifts of emphasis described by Stan Meuwese in his introduction. In the Netherlands, when preparing the new children's laws which came into force on 1 December 1905, much attention was already paid to the obligation to carry out parental authority in the best interests of the child. And with that, the authority of the legal order, this is to say of the governmental power, to interfere in cases where parental authority is used for other purposes, or for other consequences, than those which are in the best interests of the child. Foreign jurisdictions preceded the Dutch jurisdiction with such reasoning. Now, the different national legal systems can be distinguished from each other, but not separated. Child protection must not allow itself to be limited by national borders. International instruments such as treaties, conventions, and written standards and guidelines have also entered into this field. Those who strove to bring about these instruments deserve our great respect.

But however necessary these instruments may be, the final piece must be formed by the worldwide protection of children. Worldwide protection of children must be achieved, particularly protection against the most immoral and unjust kinds of exploitation, such as heavy physical labour, the use of children in the sex industry or in warfare, or for criminal activities committed by their parents or other adults.

It might be an illusion to think that the final piece will ever be achieved in practical and concrete terms.

Let me conclude this preface not only by thanking the organisers and everyone else who has contributed to the success of this conference, but also, and especially, by expressing this wish: that all persons, governments and institutions involved with children shall comply with all of the recommendations resulting from this international conference.

Even if only a part of this wish comes true, the conference may already be regarded as a success.

This book contains contributions from the International Conference '100 Years of Child Protection – Recommendations for the Future', which was held on 28-30 November 2005 in Amsterdam, the Netherlands. The involved organisations were the Amsterdam Center of Child Studies (Vrije Universiteit, Amsterdam), Defence for Children International Netherlands, the Dutch Association for Family and Youth Law, the Dutch Child Protection Board, the Dutch Ministry of Health, Welfare and Sport, the Dutch Ministry of Justice, the International Association of Youth and Famaly Judges and Magistrates, and the International Society of Family Law.

Contributors

George Oppong, Youth Development Foundation, Chief Executive Officer, Defence for Children International – Ghana (DCI-Ghana), Executive Secretary, Rapid Results International School, Neo-Caste Enterprise and Managing Proprietor, Ghana

Marjan Boertjes, William Schrikker Group, Expertise Centre Youth Care – Disability Care, Director, the Netherlands

Julia Brophy, University of Oxford, Centre for Family Law and Policy (OXFLAP), Senior Research Fellow, Oxford, United Kingdom

Willibrord Davids, Dutch Supreme Court, President, The Netherlands

Piet Hein Donner, (former) Minister of Justice (27 May 2003 – 21 September 2006), the Netherlands

Ruth Farrugia, University of Malta, Faculty of Law, Senior Lecturer, Advocate, Malta

Caroline Forder, University of Antwerp, Professor, Senior Lecturer, Family Property Law, Gifts and Inheritance, Antwerp, Belgium

Danya Glaser, Great Ormond Street Children's Hospital, Doctor for Child Protection, Consultant Child and Adolescent Psychiatrist, London, United Kingdom

Wiebina Heesterman, University of Warwick, School of Law, (former) Information Systems Manager, Ph.D., Visiting Fellow

Herman Klein, Child Protection Board (*Raad voor de Kinderbescherming*), Project Manager, Zwolle, the Netherlands

Carine Le Borgne, CINI ASHA, (former) Child Participation Adviser, Calcutta, Bangladesh

Marcia Lever, William Schrikker Group, Expertise Centre Youth Care – Disability Care, Staff Functionary, the Netherlands

Judith Masson, University of Bristol, Professor of Socio-legal Studies, Bristol, United Kingdom

Aukje Mens, University of Groningen, Private International Law Section, Ph.D. Student

Stan Meuwese, Defence for Children International – the Netherlands (DCI-Netherlands), Director, Amsterdam, the Netherlands

Beatriz Monje-Barón, ATD Fourth World, Coordinator of Family Support Projects, United Kingdom

Anna Catharina (Nanneke) Quik-Schuijt, (former) Judge Family and Youth Law, the Netherlands

Kirsten Scheiwe, University of Hildesheim, Faculty of Social and Pedagogical Sciences, Professor of Law, Germany

Julia Sloth Nielsen, University of the Western Cape, Professor, Children's Rights Law and Juvenile Justice, South Africa

Velina Todorova, Plovdiv University, Faculty of Law, Lecturer, Family and Inheritance Law, New Bulgarian University, Lecturer, Child Protection, Sofia, Bulgaria

Carol Van Nijnatten, Radbound University Nijmegen, Professor, Social Work, Utrecht University, Associate Professor, Social Studies, Developmental Psychologist, the Netherlands

Irvin Waller, University of Ottawa, Professor, Criminology, International Centre for Prevention of Crime, (previously founding) Executive Director, Ottawa, Canada

Annemieke Wolthuis, Defence for Children International – the Netherlands (DCI-Netherlands), Section Youth Law, Project Coordinator, Amsterdam, the Netherlands

Part I

Introduction

100 Years of Child Protection

Piet Hein Donner, Minister of Justice

It is an honour and a pleasure to welcome you here at the Free University. A university that was dedicated to the idea that schooling and knowledge are not neutral, but in the end are oriented by our fundamental beliefs about man, society and their destiny. Hence the conviction that parents, and not the state, are responsible for the schooling and academic development of their children.

These days we commemorate and celebrate the enactment in the Netherlands, a century ago, of a number of fundamental legislative rules concerning the protection of children and their development. A century has passed. The world has changed in the meantime. Our feelings towards children and youth still remain somewhat ambiguous. The general feeling still associates youth with the future, but that is stating the obvious. The question of course is whether we can rest assured of a better future if we have to confide in present-day youth. There have always been dissident sentiments on the subject, like George Bernard Shaw, who thought that, "Youth is wasted on the young," and Oscar Wilde, who said, "I am not young enough to know everything." We therefore have to take stock, and draw up a balance of our achievements and failures with regard to our ambitions, in order to move forward. Four aspects deserve our special attention in that respect:
  - Child protection by means of mandatory interventions
  - Juvenile delinquency
  - Organisation of youth care services
  - Multiculturalism in youth care.

I would not have dared to offer you an in-depth analysis of these aspects in this opening speech. If the Minister knows best, than we would not have organised a congress with all kinds of experts and expertise. I would, however, like to take the opportunity to reflect on a number of developments and aspects, both in the Netherlands and elsewhere.

A first question is whether we have really improved. If you look at certain aspects of modern life, the French saying, '*plus que ca change, plus que ca reste la même chose*', the more it changes, the more it remains the same.

One of the more abhorring aspects of Roman law with regard to the young was the *ius vitae ac necis*, which implied the right of a Roman father to take a child his wife had given birth to and, if it displeased him, throw it into the Tiber river, or, less 'definitively', to sell it to the highest bidder. To our modern minds, it is astonishing to accept that such a practice was legitimised by law. And yet, perhaps just as strange as the fact that, even today, children are sold, also in Western countries. Because that is what inter-country adoption sometimes amounts to.

Rules of parental discipline also stem from the Roman period and, in those days, were referred to as *ius castigandi*. Today, parents still have an incontrovertible right pertaining to their child. But there are huge drawbacks attached to it, for instance, the alarming increase in the number of cases of child abuse. Estimates indicate that each year in the Netherlands, there are between 50,000 and 80,000 cases of abused children.

Recently I submitted a bill to prohibit parental violence, whether physical or mental, or any other form of humiliation brought to bear in child-rearing. It is often ridiculed as a proposal to prohibit a so-called 'corrective slap'. It is not. Practically, it is intended as a warning to parents that parental correction cannot be an excuse for domestic violence. Judicially, it is an attempt to reverse the burden of proof in cases of child abuse, and thereby contribute to a more effective prosecution.

Though in some respects we can ask what is new, we must admit that the education and protection of children has improved a lot over the past century. It started in 1905. Child labour had been abolished a mere 30 years previously. The act obliging children to attend school had only been in force for a couple of years. In 1905 three important acts aimed at child protection were added: the Civil Law Children's Act, the Criminal Law Children's Act and the Administrative Law Children's Act, which set out the principles for the organisation of child protection. We are here to celebrate this milestone today.

In subsequent years, until 1955, the emphasis was on child protection. In 1922, the juvenile court and supervision orders came into being. Other new developments followed. From 1955 to 1980, adoption became a key feature. Adoption of course was familiar to the Romans, but in the Netherlands it was only introduced in 1956. Paternal authority was another subject of development. Though paternal authority had been replaced in 1905 by parental authority, the father's opinion remained decisive up until 1970. Yet another point of change was the right of access of both parents after divorce, which only took shape from 1971 onwards.

Another important aspect of the development since 1905 is of course the introduction of international instruments of protection. The Convention on the Rights of the Child entered into force in the Netherlands in 1995. It establishes a worldwide standard with a broad field of application. Though some think that the Convention is more about the rights of parents and only offers measures to protect the child, and not the child's rights, there is an authoritative Committee on the Rights of the Child, which is clear in its conviction that a child is more than simply the object of protection. The Committee has made numerous states aware of this fact, including the Netherlands.

The position of children in the world is influenced by many factors besides upbringing, legislation and policy. Culture, prosperity, education, and so on all play a role. And in our rapidly changing world, new issues are constantly presenting themselves.

In the light of a number of alarming developments that I have outlined, such as child abuse, in the Netherlands we are beginning to ask who is largely responsible for the upbringing of children. Recently, there has been a trend to place responsibility specifically with educational institutions, supervisory bodies and organisations rather than with the parents. These agencies are made responsible for duties that used to lie within the province of the parents.

As far as I am concerned, there should be no misunderstanding. Parents are responsible for bringing up their children. The state may unreservedly and compulsorily regulate a number of matters but, in the main, parents have a prime responsibility. And the state can and should appeal to its citizens' sense of any responsibility.

This does not mean that we should not prevent failing parents from having a negative impact on their child's development at an early stage. As far as this is concerned, Article 3 of the Convention on the Rights of the Child is the key. If choices have to be made, the interests of the child come first! Parents must be given the opportunity to shoulder their responsibilities, to which the state can contribute. Parents experiencing problems raising their children can receive state-funded professional help and, not to forget, the intervention of a mediator who can also offer parenting support.

If married parents are on the verge of a divorce, the state should assume that, even after the divorce, the parents continue to be responsible for their children. It is up to the parents to make suitable arrangements, naturally in consultation with their children. Parliament is on the verge of adopting proposals that will introduce the obligation of a so-called 'parent plan'.

At the same time, if a child lives with a foster family for a long time and returning to the parental family is not longer a realistic prospect, the child and its foster parents should be given more assurances about continued foster care, and we should consider whether the natural parents should continue to exercise parental authority.

The child is increasingly being recognised as a person with legal rights, and is also recognised as such in international legislation and policy. However, it is not easy to say how the relationship between parent and child, and their relationship with the state, should develop in the future. It seems clear to me that it will not simply be a case of personal legal rights. Some children will primarily need protection, particularly in view of their age and the miserable material conditions in which in certain countries they still live. The aspect of protection will therefore continue to be topical. There should also continue to be no less attention, in my opinion, for the responsibilities of the child itself. This is, I feel, one way of taking children seriously.

Over the coming days, you will discuss the past but, more importantly, the future. The goal of your congress is to draft recommendations for the future. I have attempted to go a little way towards that. And I would like to say at the outset that a child does not only deserve protection, but must also be acknowledged as a unique individual. Likewise, I feel that the function of the family cannot be emphasised enough. Bringing up children is mainly the task of the parents. The state should offer the necessary facilities, such as education and health care, and draw up legal frameworks. There must be a safety net to compensate for parents' structural shortcomings in the interests of the child. And for those cases where there is really no other option, the effect of juvenile criminal law can and may be stepped up.

'Implement' is indeed a verb. Making children's rights concrete is not something that happens automatically. I wish you luck in your work on this over the next few days.

This is the Opening Speech of the International Conference '100 Years of Child Protection – Recommendations for the Future', which was held on 28-30 November 2005 in Amsterdam, the Netherlands.

One Century of the Child Not Enough

Stan Meuwese

1.   Is a century 100 years?

The 20th century was supposed to be the Century of the Child, so proclaimed the Swedish educationalist Ellen Key in '*Barnets arhundrade*'. This was a romantic discourse, based on the French philosopher Jean-Jacques Rousseau ('discoverer of the child'), to think and act more from the perspective of the child in the upbringing of children. It was meant to counterbalance the morality at the turn of the century that children were threatened and governed by badness and sinfulness.

The 20th century was short, according to some historians. The 19th century went on until 1914, when the Great War – as World War II was long referred to – broke out. And the new millennium had an early start, when the Berlin Wall fell in 1989. The course of history does not always keep to our schematic division of time into years, decades and centuries.

1.1   The beginning is the end of olden times

Did the Century of the Child last only 75 years? Or was it longer? In the context of the Netherlands, the new era in the field of child protection began with the first law prohibiting child labour that was passed in 1874. This law – always referred to in the diminutive as 'Van Houten's little law for children' ('*Van Houten's Kinderwetje*') – was named after a conservative member of parliament, who hoped to prevent that the Netherlands, by permitting child labour in factories, would be unable to compete with the other previously industrialised countries because of having too many illiterate labourers.

The Century of the Child actually began in the Netherlands with the introduction of the Compulsory Education Act ('*leerplichtwet*'), a law compelling all children who were too young to be allowed to work to attend school. This law flanked and complemented the legal prohibition of child labour. The Compulsory Education Act was established more than 20 years before political agreement could be reached on the (financial) equalization of public schools and Protestant and Catholic schools . A number of other European countries had preceded the Netherlands in introducing compulsory education, including England in 1870, France in 1881, and Germany – though only in Prussia – as early as 1763.

The Compulsory Education Act of 1900 obligated parents to register their children at a school and to send them to school. The government thus gave a direct order to parents and introduced therewith a (limited) encroachment upon the parental authority.
Not allowing children to work, but making them go to school, was only the first step towards government protection of children. For 'scoundrels and orphans',

thus children who have problems, more needed to be done. The system which had – mainly on the basis of charity – come into existence in the course of the 19th century had no basis in law, nor financial support from the government. This situation changed through the Child Acts of 1901-1905, not one 'little law for children' but three substantial acts. The laws were established in 1901 and their implementation followed four years later, in 1905, in order to open the possibility to free the budget for the construction of a number of orphanages, such as Eikenstein in Zeist, the Heyacker in Breda and the Hunnerberg in Nijmegen.

It was in exactly this same period that the Convention Governing the Guardianship of Infants was adopted internationally, and ratified by the Netherlands in 1904. This convention confirmed that, in questions of guardianship and other child protection matters, the nationality of the child determined which law should be applied.

For the Netherlands, which had been able to preserve their neutral status in World War I, the 20th century in child protection began, not in 1914, but in 1901.

1.2   The end as a new beginning

And the end of the century? Was the fall of the Berlin Wall on 9 November 1989 the moment when a new era began? The chopping of holes in the cement wall, the abolishment of Checkpoint Charlie, the mass entry of 'Ossies' into West Berlin. In short, the downfall of what Churchill once had referred to as the Iron Curtain rang in the end of the dominance of communist ideologies of a number of East European countries, and the introduction of a market economy based on capitalism.

Eleven days after the fall of the Wall, in New York, the General Assembly of the United Nations adopted the Convention on the Rights of the Child. This covenant was the product of ten years of negotiations by diplomats and civil servants in Geneva, which had begun on the eve of the International Year of the Child (1979). The proposal to transform the United Nations Declaration of the Rights of the Child (1959) into a children's rights treaty was made by the Polish government. The first draft of the proposal referred only to the social, cultural and economic rights of children, i.e. fundamental (social) rights that contain a government responsibility of care. This approach was strongly supported by the governments of East European countries with centrally regulated economies. In that sense, the proposal strongly reflected the content of the International Covenant on Economic, Social and Cultural Rights (1966), and not that of the other major human rights treaty of that same year, the International Covenant on Civil and Political Rights. For this reason, an open-ended working group was appointed that received a broad mandate to formulate a children's rights covenant, under the auspices of the UN Human Rights Commission. The negotiators were critically observed by representatives of a small group of non-governmental organisations, the pioneers and quartermasters in the field of children's rights.

While in Berlin government intervention was smothered under the Wall's rubble to pave the way for the market, the Member States of the United Nations were putting their seal on a document in which, well considered, not the rights of children but the responsibilities of the government were formulated with regard to the protection and development of children, and the provision of services.

Future historians will probably not have the 20th century end in 1989 but in 2001, with the attack on the Twin Towers. Not the downfall of the communist system but the rise of Islamic activism will be the break off point, not only of two centuries but of two millennia. The destruction of the two skyscrapers in New York on 11 September 2001 had a dramatic effect on everyone's life ('Where were you when you heard about the attack on the Twin Towers?'). But it also had a less important side-effect, namely that the UNGASS, the UN Children's Summit, which had been planned for 20-22 September 2001, was postponed until more than half a year later. Is its final document, *A World Fit for Children*, adopted on 10 May 2002, the introduction to the new Century of the Child?

The Century of the Child stirs between 1900, with the beginning of government encroachment upon parental authority, and 2000, with the adoption of international norms and agreements on children's rights.

2.   Looking back 100 years
What do we see when looking back at the history of child protection? What developments can we distinguish?

2.1   From charity to governmental care
Child care was – and is – the business of parents. But what if the parents are incapable or unwilling? Who will stand up for children without parents and children who have problems? The oldest beginnings of child protection in Europe were to be found in monasteries and churches in the Middle Ages, where they were willing to take in needy children. Since the Holy Ghost was considered the inspirer of charity, child care was in the hands of the Holy Spirit Tables ('*Tafels van de Heilige Geest*'). Somewhat later on, city governments became involved in matters of child protection, in the form of Municipal Orphanages, which were established in a great number of cities starting in the 15th century. The age-old discord between government and charity/private initiative was already rearing its head. In the 16th and 17th centuries, the Reformation contributed to this discussion. The almighty Catholic Church lost influence and power in Northwest Europe. Reformed congregations founded their own poor-relief boards, some for the benefit of needy children.

These provisions, differing per city, including contributions by both municipal governments and religious charities, lasted until the formation of the unitary state, until the French Revolution and the reign of Napoleon.

In the meantime, Rousseau, in his '*Discourse sur l'origine et les fondements de l'inegalité parmi les hommes*' of 1755, had written that human beings in their natural thus primitive state, preceding any education, are (as '*bon sauvage*') good, and that they only are spoiled by exposure to society. The age of Napoleon was marked by much centralist regulation, which in turn was abolished by the newly established Kingdom of the Netherlands. There was a return to municipal orphanages and religious charities, supported by city governments according to national laws. In particular, the 19th century's industrialisation and accompanying changes in family structure were a huge source of worry to notables. This concern led to all sorts of new initiatives in child protection. Some ideas wafted over to the Netherlands from other countries, such as the orphanage-cum-agricultural-colony in the French village Mettray, near Tours. And so there came to be an 'archipelago of children's homes' in Europe, in the words of the Dutch historical educationalist, Jeroen Dekker. The word archipelago is well chosen, as the homes were like small islands, isolated from the bad influence of the big cities. The increased social responsibility of the government resulted in government regulation, and ultimately subsidisation, of these charity/private initiatives. Government involvement developed from a supervising role to an ordaining, from following to initiating. In the end, a stage was reached in the Netherlands in which private institutions carry out government policies. This goes hand in hand with numerous regulations for implementation, which affect internal organisation, methods applied and the treatment of the children. In the Netherlands, institutions narrowly miss being placed under the umbrella of the government; they remain private institutions with quite a number of foundations and an administrative legal capacity (as independent administrative bodies).

One hears the expression QUANGOs, quasi non-governmental organisations. This process has not yet fully crystallised. Some decennia ago, the children's homes that had been founded after the war, especially for children weakened by wartime hardship, were privatised. The closed youth detention facilities, at this time, are of various kinds, including both government and private institutions. On the one hand, it is not unusual that a minister gets blamed for an incident in a facility. On the other hand, there is a limit to what policy makers can do from behind their desks in the practical implementation of child protection measures in a small group unit.

2.2   From volunteers to professionals

The charitable impulse expressed in private donations to orphanages and children's homes has also been expressed in another type of involvement in the care of neglected children, that of volunteer work. Much work in homes is prescribed and carried out by volunteers. Of course there have always been many people who had regular jobs as caretaker, cook or teacher in an institution. But then the management consisted of notables who formed a board which presided over these institutions. There was not yet such a profession as 'pedagogue'. The Century of the Child showed an increasing professionalism in child protection. Higher Vocational Education for Social Work, which originated in the first half of the last century, naturally contributed much to this development. Those schools ultimately evolved into the present colleges for social-pedagogic workers.

Volunteers have now disappeared almost completely from the world of child care; foster parents being the last non-professionals to play a role. Child protection work has become a profession, which does not mean that the professionalism of child care is not still in its infancy. Child protection has not professionalised to the same degree as health care or education. Much energy is being invested in the development of new methods, including an evaluation system entitled *What Works*.

While personal involvement had been the main factor in voluntary child care, expertise plays the greatest role in professional youth work. But the challenge remains to reach a proper balance between 'commitment' and 'expertise'.

2.3 From non-regulation to over-regulation

The proliferation of new legislation in our society has not left child care untouched. Starting with the three children's laws, only a few loose-leaf binders represented the legal state of affairs at the turn of the century. Relatively simple and clear laws with few sub clauses have now developed into executive legislation on which masses of stipulations and regulations are based. There are very precise systems determining the responsibilities of institutions, detailed terms of employment for the workers, and elaborate laws on legal status, personal participation and privacy of both young people and their parents.

This also goes for the work itself. In courts, formal written reports have replaced the statements by guardians. An approach governed by rules and budgets is winning more and more ground from the simple approach, namely the question: 'What must be done for this child?'. Diagrams, protocols and budgets have become the very foundation of the organisation of child welfare. Particularly, the new Child Care Act, created 100 years after the first three children's laws were implemented, has the reputation of being unnecessarily bureaucratic. When it took effect on 1 January 2005, a child welfare brigade was immediately organised for the purpose of combating excessive bureaucracy.

Obviously, a sector such as child care and protection, in which important decisions and drastic interventions in the lives of families are unavoidable, cannot do without rules. Legal protection needs to be regulated by law.

2.4 From denominational to secular

There used to be numerous organisations and institutions in the area of child care, with fine names like Roman Catholic Virgins House, Protestant-Christian Child Care and Humanistic Orphans Fund. This was the sign of '*verzuiling*' in the Netherlands, which means 'a society based on the pillars of denominational groups'. It suggests, on the one hand, that the upbringing and education of children should be based on a religious or ideological conviction and, indirectly, that there should not be a state based education system. Together with this social fragmentation into religious groups goes the subsidiarity principle: anything that can be realised by one's own group need not be organised at public level (now, *mutatis mutandis*, a much heard point of discussion in the European Union). The '*verzuiling*' is also often defended from the standpoint of emancipation: first strength within one's own group and only then contact with other denominations.

Although the first half of the 20th century showed a steady increase in this '*verzuiling*' (e.g. in education, trade unions, culture and the media), in the second half of the century this phenomenon was definitely on the decrease. This was also evident in the area of child care. Education is the one area in which '*verzuiling*' has largely survived. New groups, particularly Hindustani and Islamic, are developing, particularly where creation of new schools is concerned. In child and youth care, there remain practically no institutions based on religious conviction, and the new religious groups have not manifested themselves in the child care system.

Article 15 of the Child Care Act of 2005 states loosely that a provincial youth care agency which coordinates and adjudicates should consider the religious, cultural and ideological background of clients in its decision-making. A hundred years ago, the religious component of child protection was more highly valued.

2.5 Distinction civil-penal not clear-cut

The batch of laws made at the beginning of the 20th century showed a distinction between an approach based on penal law and one based on family law. However, this distinction does not imply a complete separation of the two. However different procedures may be, the same provisions will be used in their implementation. In both cases, the Child Protection Board, originally called the Guardianship Board, plays an important role. Children are separated from adults in the closed institutions, but for over 100 years no distinction has been made between child detainees referred by penal law and those placed on civil grounds. The basic reasoning is that there is little difference in the backgrounds and problems of these groups of children. Those who cause trouble, in the form of juvenile delinquency, are children with problems in their home environment. Inappropriate, antisocial and delinquent behaviour all overlap. This way of thinking is starting to change. This is happening because the punitive character of Dutch law applying to juvenile offenders has grown stronger. Sentences to detention have become more numerous, and longer. And, at the same time, starting in the 1960s, a whole new future has been developing for the (legal) child protection system: (voluntary) day care, ambulatory care, family therapy methods.

As far as the closed youth facilities are concerned, the decision has been made to segregate children placed there on grounds of civil law (children who have problems) from those placed there under penal law (children who cause problems).

2.6 The role of child protection in socialisation of the working class

It cannot be denied that child protection has always had to do with a strong class element. It was actually the upper class which was and is concerned about how children are cared for in the lower class. Poverty can be a strong factor in child neglect. It goes without saying that the lack of sufficient financial means can have all sorts of negative consequences on people's ability to rear their children. This can lead to forms of child neglect that exceed socially permissible limits. Child abuse is not found exclusively in the lower classes. Juvenile delinquency is to a great degree, but not exclusively, the domain of poor youngsters. The 20th century shows a high degree of emancipation of the working class in many areas, the necessities of life, social security, education and working conditions.

In recent decennia the class element has been coloured by the element of ethnicity. The number of youngsters with an immigrant background has grown disproportionately. It seems to prove that some groups of immigrants are the new marginalized groups in our society.

3.   A glimpse into the future
Making predictions is difficult, especially about the future.

3.1   Children's rights as basis
The Convention on the Rights of the Child (CRC), the result of one century's discussion on the position of children, is the starting-point for child protection in years to come. The CRC is the product of development in the concepts of both child protection and human rights, the essence being that the child is not seen as the object of care, but as the subject of rights.

The subject of children's rights is not yet closed, all the more because minors have only a limited say in the pursuit of their rights. Parents are still the legal representatives of their children, and it is they who are entitled to represent their children in legal matters.

The holistic character of the CRC is crucial: basic social rights (claims on the government), the right to liberty (safeguard from government interference), and Protection, Provision and Participation, the famous '3 Ps' of the CRC.

One central concept of the Convention on the Rights of the Child is 'the best interests of the child'. The CRC does not specify further, but leaves the interpretation to judges, policy makers, educationalists and other professionals. Since 'the best interests of the child' sounds much the same as the expression 'for your own good', there is some risk that an opening in the CRC, which could offer a youngster optimum chances for development, might backfire if used as a new way to patronise instead.

3.2   Three trends: internationalisation, information technology and individualisation
Trying to describe the character of this current era as a base for predictions of future developments is a risky undertaking. It cannot be much more than a cautious extrapolation on some obvious trends of the moment, internationalisation, computerisation and individualisation.

3.2.1   Internationalisation
'Global in reach, local in touch' and 'think globally, act locally' are two slogans which attempt to put the immediate environment of citizens (therefore also of young citizens) in an international context. Globalisation of markets and conflicts, regional (EU) legislation and internationalisation of (legal) norms – all of this caus-

es, and is caused by, the enormous mobility of goods, of relations, work and recreation. Worldwide migration is another symptom. International mobility results in international relationships, international marriages and divorces, and sometimes international abduction. Adoption, intended as a kind of child protection, seems to be preponderantly family planning via the international market. Migration of millions of people all over the world creates opportunities as well as problems in countries of both origin and destination. Labour migration and refugee movement occur on a worldwide scale. This has caused the need for a series of new approaches in family and children's law. International children's law encompasses both the aspect of international civil law (international family law) and that of public law (the human rights conventions). One need not be clairvoyant to predict that an intensification of the international framework for child protection, in the broadest sense of the word, is to be expected.

This globalisation also leads inevitably to internationalisation of legislation. The Convention on the Rights of the Child is significant, as a blanket treaty in relation to other treaties on subjects like child labour, kidnapping, adoption and maintenance.

3.2.2 Information technology
Information and communication technologies have been introduced with dizzying speed into our way of life. Adults have experienced the age before computers, as well as the computer era. Children take the world they have come into for granted, including television, computers and mobile telephones, in short, the whole gamut of today's technology. It is inevitable that the arrival of information and communication technology has enormous consequences, affecting acquisition of knowledge, educational methods and social communication. In general, children are way ahead of most adults when it comes to managing these innovations. Moreover, many parents have little control over what their children are seeing. As in so many matters, information technology has, along with its advantages, negative aspects: child pornography on internet, bullying via text messages. The distinction 'the haves and the have-nots' is aggravated by the new division into 'the knows and the know-nots'. One the one hand, modern communications offer unlimited possibilities to underdeveloped countries and peoples. On the other hand, lack of access to information amounts to social exclusion at both local and global levels.

3.2.3 Individualisation
One of the most important kinds of individualisation, which has a direct effect on child rearing, is the emancipation of women, particularly the increased participation of women in paid employment. Not having to work used to be a sign of prosperity for married women, with or without children, in the first half of the last century, as was the end of child labour. All this was viewed as accomplishments of the welfare state. The heightened participation in the job market during both World Wars was considered a necessary evil.

3.3 A sharper distinction between civil-penal

At the start of the Century for the Child, a distinction was made between children who have problems and those who cause problems, but there was no difference in approach or facilities for these groups. To this day there is still doubt as to whether the legal distinction between civil-penal is actually artificial, or can be traced back to the true nature of the problems.

In the meantime, the decision to change the distinction to a division between these two groups has been taken and put into practice. Not only has the number of youngsters placed in closed institutions increased threefold in the last 15 years, the number within this group placed on civil grounds has doubled, while four times as many youngsters have been placed under penal law. This is a considerable shift.

One may hope that the separate status will result in a considerable reduction of the number of penal placements. This could be done by taking child protection measures sooner and, hopefully, more effectively (e.g. by placing youngsters under supervision, with a legal order for placement outside the home), and by reacting differently to juvenile delinquency, with less emphasis on punishment and more on rehabilitation.

3.4 Child protection as acculturation of immigrants

Anyone looking around a Dutch juvenile prison is sure to see more dark-skinned youngsters than white ones. It seems as though white youths who go astray are more often sentenced to a psychiatric or psychological rehabilitation programme, while dark ones are most often condemned to imprisonment. This could have to do with prejudice. It might also suggest that 'western' methods of treatment work less well when applied to youths of Mediterranean or tropical origin or, better said, 'have even less effect' on immigrant youths than on Dutch ones.

4. In conclusion: doom or dream?

Besides all the changes in relationships within society and within families, there are also a number of constant factors. It is unimaginable to think that parents have loved their children less and less as the centuries passed. And it is unfortunately just as unimaginable that there are no parents who deprive their children of love, and neglect and abuse them. It could be that violence between parents and children is on the decrease. Just as masters once beat their servants, sergeants their soldiers, jailers their prisoners, men their wives and teachers their pupils, so it might be that, in the future, the beating of children by their parents will also become illegal and socially unacceptable.

During the Annual Youth Lecture of 2005, organised by the *Jantje Beton*, Humanitas and the daily newspaper *Trouw*, the Dutch demographer Jan Latten gave a description of future developments which he called inevitable:
- Children will become scarce
- There will be more single-parent families
- The role of mothers will become more important and that of fathers less important

- More people will be rich and more will be poor
- The division between white and people of colour will grow.

Few children, raised by their mothers, rich white people and poor black ones – that's it in a nutshell. Professor Latten sketches a picture of the future in which social differences will be greater, in which no tears or laments can turn the tide, and no course of action either. Some plan might be able to take the sharp edges off these developments, but the government will be unable to prevent them.

From the standpoint of children's rights, I cannot add much to this. I can only hope it is not a self-fulfilling prophecy, and offer my own vision of scenarios for the future.

The doom scenario for children's rights in the coming decennium contains the following elements:
A.   At government level:
- The state leaves, after 100 years, the rearing of children to free marker forces
- Young people will be the economic victims of the financial profit made off the elderly
- The approach to governing youth will degenerate to policies of repression, discipline and sanctions.
B.   At the level of jurisprudence:
- The battle against terrorism will cost loss of human rights
- The rights of children will get pushed to the background.
C.   In the processes of upbringing and growing up:
- Children's rights will be experienced egocentrically
- Children will be merely consumers of 'fun'.

The dream scenario for children's rights in the coming decennium contains these elements:
- At government level: The concept of children's rights will be embraced as the basis of child protection policy.
- At the jurisprudence level: The CRC will be just as important in jurisprudence as the European Convention on Human Rights.
- In the processes of upbringing and growing up: Youth workers will truly get the spirit of children's rights in their hearts and minds, and know how to act on it.

Doom or dream, who can say what is to come? The Century of the Child has brought us children's rights. In the new century steps must be taken to ensure that they are also enforced.

Part II

Contributions

Sustainable Protection of Delinquent Children

A Case of Defence for Children International Ghana

George Oppong

1. Introduction

Juvenile delinquency is a common phenomenon in Ghana. The juvenile delinquents end up in police custody, remand homes and borstal institutions (i.e. corrective institutions for convicted juveniles). There are national laws, however, to protect children who offend and victims of offences in Ghana.

2. Legal reforms related to juvenile justice

Ghana ratified the UN Convention on the Rights of the Child (CRC) in 1990. Ghana's Children's Act 560 (1998) incorporates the CRC into the national legislation. The government of Ghana has set up a Women and Juvenile Unit (WAJU) of the police to handle all criminal cases involving women and children.

The Constitution of Ghana (1992) states that a juvenile who is kept in lawful custody or detention shall be kept separately from an adult offender. It further prohibits children from being subjected to torture or other cruel, inhuman or degrading treatment or punishment.

The Criminal Code (Amendment) Act 554 (1998) increases the age of criminal responsibility from seven to 12 and the age of sexual consent from 14 to 16. It also revises provisions on sexual offences against juveniles. A new Juvenile Justice Act 653, 2003 was passed by parliament in October 2003. It provides for a juvenile justice system, protects the rights of juveniles, and ensures appropriate and individual responses to juvenile offenders.

3. Judicial procedures

There are juvenile courts in Ghana, which are special courts of summary jurisdiction. They exercise such jurisdiction as the Chief Justice may confer upon them in relation to the hearing of charges against juveniles or the disposal of other matters affecting juveniles.

Under the rules governing juvenile courts, a panel is appointed for each area for which a juvenile court is constituted. It is made up of three members. The court follows an informal procedure, which involves the juvenile or his/her parent or guardian in the trial of the case. At this court, the consequential orders are designed to correct rather than to penalise the offender.

19

In Ghana, the practice has been that, even where a juvenile and an adult commit an offence together, they are both tried by the regular courts and where the juvenile is found guilty of the offence he/she is remitted to the juvenile court for sentence.

Apart from the juvenile courts that operate in Ghana, the Children's Act of 1998 (Act 560) also empowers District Assemblies to establish Child Panels. The non-judicial function of these Child Panels is to mediate in criminal and civil matters which concern children. Under its civil function, the Child Panel mediates in civil matters concerned with the rights of the child and parental duties. The function of the child panel in criminal matters is to assist in victim–offender mediation in minor criminal matters involving a child where the circumstances of the offence are not aggravated. The essence is to facilitate reconciliation between the child and any victim of the action of the child.

4.   Alternatives to deprivation of liberty

The first alternative to deprivation of liberty related to juvenile justice is, as referred to above, the establishment of the Child Panels at District levels to perform non-judicial functions, including mediation in criminal and civil matters affecting children outside the juvenile justice system. The Child Panels mediate, reconcile, caution, impose community guidance orders or propose an apology, or restitution to the victim.

The family Tribunal, which has the jurisdiction to try juvenile cases, may upon the investigative report and recommendation by probation officers of the Department of Social Welfare, place the juvenile offender under community probation. In this case the child lives with the family in the community where his/her conduct is followed up and supervised by a probation officer of the Department of Social Welfare for a period of six months to one year, after which the behaviour and conduct of the child are reviewed for consideration by the court.

The court may send a juvenile convicted of an offence to the Borstal or Industrial Institute for reformation and rehabilitation. A juvenile offender may also be granted a police or court bail signed by a bona fide family pending investigation or trial of the case.

5.   Problems of the juvenile justice system in Ghana

The juvenile justice system in Ghana cannot be said to be better. It is a system bedevilled with many problems, some of which are created by the law enforcement agencies.

There are situations where juveniles are tricked to inflate their ages so as not to be sent to a borstal home. The rationale is that he/she may get his/her freedom earlier by going to prison rather than by being sent to a borstal home, which normally takes up to three years.

There are situations where these juveniles are not represented by counsel and, where the panel is not conversant with the rights of the child, injustice may be done to the child.

Since the coming into force of Act 560, i.e. the Children's Act of 1998, the District Assemblies have failed to establish the Child Panels and, even where they have been established, they are dormant.

6. Innovative ways of protecting children in Ghana

Defence for Children International Ghana is one of the few organisations providing innovative ways of protecting the rights of children in Ghana. DCI-Ghana has been operating a socio-legal centre for children since 1998. Among the services provided by DCI-Ghana are training, education, referrals, legal defence and representations.

A study was conducted on protecting the rights of children in conflict with the law in Kumasi, Ghana, that was aimed at finding out what works best for juvenile delinquents in a developing world. DCI-Ghana was used as a case study for a period of six months, from October 2004 to March 2005. The study's main objectives were:
  – To examine the factors affecting children in conflict with the law in Ghana
  – To find out the strategies for defending the rights of children in conflict with the law in Ghana
  – To recommend ways of improving upon child protection in developing countries.

The study employed quantitative and qualitative methods of interviews, discussions, in-depth interviews, observations and review of records. A questionnaire with open-ended questions and a question guide were used to interview the respondents in this study. Four group discussions of four remanded juveniles each were held to elicit qualitative information for the study. One-on-one in-depth interviews were also held with the juveniles, their families and personnel at the remand home to obtain deeper insights into the data collected. Observations during monitoring visits and follow-ups as well as review of records kept by DCI-Ghana on detained juveniles were also analysed for the study.

Data on the ages, sex, family background, causes of delinquency, period of arrest and detention, conditions of detention, services received from DCI-Ghana, post detention status, and views on reformation and rehabilitation were collected and analysed for the study.

Sixteen juveniles between 12 to 17 years were purposely sampled for the study. These included juveniles who committed offences, got arrested and detained at the Kumasi Juvenile Remand Home pending trials of their cases. As personnel of DCI-Ghana went on monitoring visits, juveniles who were met at the Juvenile Remand Home were selected to participate in the study.

The study was thoroughly explained to the respondents for their full understanding and their consent was sought to participate in the study. Confidentiality was assured, meaning that all information provided would be used for the study and not for any other purposes without their prior knowledge and consent. Since the study involved juveniles, personnel of DCI-Ghana sought consent from their families during tracing before including any juvenile.

The findings as regards age distribution were as follows: 25% of the juveniles in conflict with the law were between the ages of 12-14 and 75% were between 15-17 years.

Age Distribution

Source: *Results of a study conducted in 2005*

As regards gender composition, the study revealed that almost all (100%) the juvenile delinquents were males. This is also due to the fact that more boys are involved in delinquency than girls, and girl delinquents are not usually remanded except of high degree cases.

As regards family background, the study showed that the delinquents came from poor families due to death, disease and unemployment of their families. These conditions partly push them into the streets to fend for themselves. Since there are no meaningful livelihoods in the streets, the juveniles resort to all forms of coping mechanisms to survive. These include violence, stealing, rape, bully, drugs, etc.

The offences committed by the juveniles included stealing (82%), defilement (6%), murder (6%) and drug peddling (6%). They were arrested by the police, charged to court and later remanded pending trial of their cases.

Offences Committed

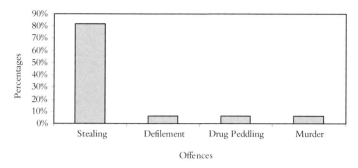

Source: Results of a study conducted in 2005

As regards the period of detention, the juvenile who committed murder spent almost three months in the remand home, the rest spent an average of two weeks in the remand home.

They all (100%) lacked information about their rights and legal aid while in custody since few programmes in the country target them. These juveniles were normally nomadic and therefore did not have access to information and education on their rights.

The conditions of custody were deplorable. Their accommodation was not well ventilated and untidy. Families of 80% of the detained juveniles did not visit them regularly to maintain the family bond and contact, as against 20% who did.

Familly visit to Juvenile Detainees

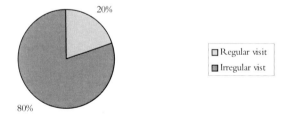

Source: Results of a study conducted in 2005

They had no beddings and had to sleep on bare ground while exposed to mosquitoes. They were not properly fed, as they were fed twice a day with relatively less nutritious food. They did not have access to games and play, which is vital for their rehabilitation and development.

The socio-legal services provided by DCI-Ghana to protect the rights of the detained juveniles includes monitoring the situation of their custody, offering suggestions to the personnel of the institutions and to the government, tracing of

23

families of the detained juveniles, counselling of the juveniles and their traced families, legal advice, defence and representations at the law courts, and follow ups.

DCI-Ghana conducts monitoring visits to the Police Stations, Prisons, Remand Homes, Borstal and Industrial Institutions to assess the situation of juvenile in-mates through interviews with personnel and in-mates as well as observations. DCI-Ghana has developed a record form to guide collection of information/data on the children in conflict with the law for analysis and records keeping.

DCI-Ghana undertakes tracing of families of children in conflict with the law to educate and counsel the families to visit and aid their children in detention and to help seek juvenile justice for them.

DCI-Ghana provides legal defence and representations for children in conflict with the law for bail, hearing, release, discharge or probation and reintegration. It conducts follow ups to children on bail, probation, release or discharge to further educate and counsel the former children in conflict with the law and their families to prevent further delinquency and ensure rehabilitation of the children concerned.

DCI-Ghana also educates and sensitises children, families, other stakeholders and the public on children in conflict with the law through outreach to schools, homes, communities, detention centres, reformation/rehabilitation institutions. Materials like Conventions, Acts, Constitutions, Rules, posters, flyers, leaflets and reports are used to support the educational programmes on children in conflict with the law.

Through the socio-legal aids by DCI-Ghana, 94% received court bail and were released to their families for good behaviour, whilst 6% refused bail and is still in custody pending trial. Of this, 60% and 20% were reintegrated into society through schooling and vocational training respectively. Twenty per cent were reunited with families in their home villages.

Post Detained Status

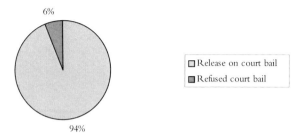

Source: Results of a study conducted in 2005

7.   Conclusions and recommendations

An integrated approach to protecting delinquent children is sustainable in the developing world.

Inter-sectoral collaboration using a holistic approach to child protection is appropriate. This should span through prevention to rehabilitation of child victims and offenders.

Education, including peer education, should be an integral part of child protection to prevent delinquency among children, especially street children.

Rigorous follow ups and monitoring of child offenders ensure protection against recidivism.

Parents and Children with Disabilities within the Youth Care System

The Dutch Perspective

Marjan Boertjes and Marcia Lever

1.   Summary

If child raising and pedagogical problems arise, then both parents and children are entitled to a well functioning system of youth care. However, the existing youth care system is not self-evidently equipped to meet the special needs of this target group of children with disabilities. The current method of working in youth care is coloured by the emphasis on demand-oriented care and the strong appeal to the client's own responsibility. In many cases, this working method does not dovetail the request for care where a disability is concerned. This paper argues that when a (mental) disability is evident in pedagogical problems, a 'different' working method is required. This working method is characterised by directive as well as emphatic and dialogical conduct. A proactive and outreaching basic attitude is required in order to organise a lifelong and life-wide support when necessary. Care workers with specific expertise and skills are needed. The care worker has to be nurtured and supported by an organisation, in which expertise in the field of disabilities is self-evidently available. Recognition and acknowledgement of the fact that 'different' youth care is needed is a prerequisite to safeguard the right to proper care.

2.   Preface

Youth care is liable to big changes. Improvements on care for youths and their parents and the strengthening of their position receive much attention. The client should be paramount in a system that is reorganised to be more transparent and simple. The care discipline has to transform from supply-oriented to demand-oriented. Besides this, the right to youth care is embedded in the law. Youths are entitled to care once they have been assessed. Care should be organised as closely to home as possible, as short and as light as possible, and realised as quickly as possible (in the Netherlands, this is referred to as the so-called 'as-as-as-policy'). All youth care is arranged via one central gateway, the Youth Care Agency. This comprises regular youth care, mental health care, judicial youth care and youth care for children with a (mild) mental disability.[1]

A transparent system, a recognisable gateway, the right to care and the client's demand paramount, who could be opposed to that? This paper explores whether enough space is built into this renewed system for children with a disability and children of disabled parents. The focus aims at the largest group, namely the (mildly) mentally disabled children and parents. But children with a physical handicap or multiple complex handicapped children also need special care. Is the right to different youth care guaranteed to them? First of all, three tendencies that influence the contemporary field of care and welfare – youth care included – are described. These tendencies interrelate and somewhat overlap and together they give insight into the way in which child care and disability care are grafted on at the moment. Subsequently, 'one's own responsibility', 'full citizenship' and 'demand-oriented care' are under discussion. Next, these three tendencies are juxtaposed to show the need of care for children with a disability and children of disabled parents. Finally, this paper argues for the importance of specialised care when special care demands are concerned.

3.   One's own responsibility

Until recently, many western societies called their well oiled social machine 'the welfare state'. The unemployed, the ill and single mothers almost automatically received their welfare benefits. People who could not afford their rent could claim their housing benefit. Community centres were established for youngsters who would hang out on the streets, and help was arranged for anyone experiencing difficulty in running the household. De Swaan has referred to, "an extended conglomerate of nation-wide collective and compulsory arrangements to remedy and moderate the external factors of scarcity and misfortune."[2]   As a consequence, according to de Swaan, the state has become the abstract, universal and anonymous caretaker of all members of society and people have less direct obligations to their fellow men.

However, a recent shift can be observed. The notion that the welfare state will ultimately become unaffordable has gained increasing recognition, while the notion of the desirability of a protective government receives less and less support. Since the last few years, a movement has been initialised by which the welfare state is either modernised (according to one), or deconstructed (according to the other). Many community centres have been closed and social grants are subject to discussion. Some refer to the transformation from the welfare state into a society of participation.[3] Everybody has to join in. A strong appeal is made to the citizen's own responsibility, for instance, to carry out paid employment despite a chronic illness, to provide informal care to an ill or elderly family member, to live a healthy life, and to account for the consequences of one's own actions. People who misbehave, or call down misfortune on themselves (criminals, addicts) are being held responsible for their own actions and are disciplined through policy. Solidarity disappears and makes room for individuality. De Vries describes the emergence of 'meritocrisation', which means people conceive their course of life and that of others as a reward according to personal achievement and individual talents, and not as a consequence of their descent (aristocracy).[4] The downside of the meritocratic ideology exhibits a danger, namely the emergence of prejudice based on human genes.   People who indulge in risky habits (smoking, for instance) and people with a disadvantageous social or genetic background (for example migrants and people with a handicap) run the risk of being excluded from employment or care, based upon their risk status. To put it bluntly: whoever is stupid or unhealthy can thank himself. It is here where the danger of 'racism based on intelligence', and also 'racism based on health' start to rear their head.

In the field of youth care, the tendency to acknowledge one's own responsibility is recognised in the as-as-as policy referred to in the preface. Assistance should in principle be short-termed. The goals are sharply formulated at the start of the assistance and, as soon as these goals are realised, the assistance is concluded. Residential care frequently makes room for ambulant care, and the social network of the family is often mobilised as a source of support. The increasing intolerance with regard to juvenile delinquency is another expression of the emphasis on one's own responsibility. Public opinion and a hardened climate concerning juvenile criminal law both emphasise punishment, while the pedagogical perspective is pushed into the background.[5] More youngsters are locked behind bars of judicial juvenile penitentiary institutions, while recidivism statistics paint a not too rosy picture of its efficiency. Moreover, an increasing amount of juvenile court cases are transferred to adult court.

Altogether, the notion of one's own responsibility has become an important cornerstone on which the system of care and welfare rests. We shall later illustrate what this means for parents and children with a disability. First, we will describe the second tendency, namely that of full citizenship.

4. Full citizenship

Full citizenship is a tendency that aims to give all citizens the opportunity to participate at all social levels. The term is used to refer to the inclusion of immigrants, for example, but is mostly used in the context of care given to people with a mental disability. Slowly but surely, the emphasis in disability care shifts from segregation and protection to integration. The movement of people with a mental disability from big institutions to community based housing can be observed. More and more often, children with a handicap attend a regular school. The objective is that people with a mental disability can participate fully and without any restraints in community life, and have a visible and rightful place in society. Person-bound budgets make it possible to make choices in the way support and help is organised. The care delivery aims to accomplish 'quality of life', which is a subjective measure.

Crucial in the approach to full citizenship is the understanding that a disability is not so much a consequence of injury or defect, but rather a consequence of social norms and values. To elucidate on this: a lower intelligence is a disability because intelligence is of high importance in our society. The need for support is elemental in the newest definitions of the notion of a 'disability'. A disability is characterised as a social given. As a rule, a disability has as a consequence a disadvantageous place in society, and it is therefore a social problem. The solution to this social problem should primarily be found in society itself. Disabled people should not conform to the rules of society. Rather, society should make room for people with such a disadvantageous position. Assistance in the form of support should supersede the traditional care model.[6]

However, some critical notes can be made about the ideal of citizenship. In practice, it shows that true inclusion is realised extremely slowly. Living in a normal neighbourhood does not automatically imply contact – let alone friendship – with neighbours. Most people are not waiting for a handicapped neighbour. Besides, the organisation of the social care system is insufficiently equipped to realise true inclusion. But above all, stories about people with a mental disability who are not able to make it on their own in daily life make the frayed edges of the ideal of citizenship visible. There is an increasing number of reports on problems connected with crimes committed by mentally disabled people. Parenting of people with a mental disability, and especially failed parenting occur more often.[7] An important condition for full citizenship is a balance between the demands that are made by the environment to people with a mental disability on the one hand, and the factual competences of that person on the other. This balance is clearly and poignantly destroyed for people with a mental disability who come into contact with the law (either criminal law or civil law). Before we explore these issues further, we will first throw light on a third tendency, that of demand-oriented care.

5. Demand-oriented care

In the last decades, social developments, for example the increasing empowerment and emancipation of civilians, and also market forces in the field of care have sharpened the attention to the client's demand and position concerning all forms of care. More and more, civilians' wishes form the starting point for the work that is carried out by social workers, care providers and service providers. Different terms (demand-oriented, demand-directed and dialogue-oriented) refer to this developmental direction. Central to this is the notion that care should not only meet professional standards, but should above all meet the wishes and expectations of the client.[8]

In this policy, Tonkens' ideal of "the self-sufficient, enterprising, assertive, responsible civilian" resounds.[9] People ought to know what they want, and it is assumed that they can stand up for themselves. Tonkens criticises the one-sided ideal of the empowered civilian and the expansion of freedom of choice as a normative starting point:

> *Since the reform of the welfare state, the empowered citizen that can make his own choices and can look after his own interests is paramount. No policy document or this heroic figure – no matter how handicapped, homeless or lonely – determines the general view.*[10]

According to Tonkens, the ideal of empowerment deprives us from noticing all those others who are not (and will never be) empowered and mainly rely on care. She signals overvaluation of evolvement and improvement, and misjudgement of value of content. Knorth and Ruijssenaars query the assumption that a mildly retarded person is capable of verbally formulating his own need and request for assistance.[11] 'Demand- oriented care' is of primary importance to this target group. The 'need' for care and assistance should be leading in the work of professionals, rather than mainly the request for assistance.

The increasing attention to the citizen's own responsibility, the ideal of full citizenship and demand-oriented care serve as important beacons for social and welfare policy. In order to consider the influence of these three tendencies on children and parents with a disability, it is necessary to form a notion of the influence of a mental disability on daily life. How can the disability be characterised?

6.   People with a mental disability
People with a mental disability are characterised by a lower level of functioning and a limited adaptive ability. Mentally disabled people often do not reach the developmental phase of formal operational thinking. This causes problems with abstract, principal-logical and hypothetical thinking. A consequence of this is that people with a mental disability have great difficulties with abstract reasoning. Experiences are less well generalised to other situations. The 'red thread' of situations and events is often not fathomed and picked up. It is usually difficult to see their own experiences in perspective and to relate them to other situations. They often think in terms of black and white. Their problem solving skills are limited, and they may have angry or aggressive reactions, so inadequate problem solutions may be observed. The knowledge base for problem solutions is limited. The development of the self is not fully reached. The phase of consideration of social norms and adjustment to the behaviour of others is only partly reached, and with great difficulty. The experience is usually self-centred and the level of functioning is strongly self-directed. Empathic skills are underdeveloped and the ability to imagine is restricted. Self-concept and self-identity are weakly developed, which results in insecurity and negative self-experience. There is a lack of ability to reflect upon one's own behaviour. The ability to reason morally is weakly developed, which influences the conscience function.[12]

Mentally disabled persons show a complex pattern of seemingly minimal limitations, which together lead to serious consequences for daily functioning. In case of a 'mild' mental disability, the handicap is in many cases not directly identifiable. There are no outward characteristics. Use of language and contact establishment seem to be normal at first instance. Nevertheless, what appears to be anti-social or unadjusted behaviour, unwillingness or impulsiveness can be a direct effect of a mild mental disability. When a mental disability is not distinguished, over-expectation forms a real danger that can result in severe behavioural problems.

If we revert back to the three aforementioned tendencies, we could define a mental disability from the care perspective as follows:

> People with a mental disability are people:
> – who are not capable to carry full responsibility for their own existence
> – for whom full citizenship is not self-evident, and
> – who are not, or to a lesser extent, capable to formulate their request for assistance.

People with a mental disability need assistance in order to maintain themselves in society. Their strive for full citizenship reaches its limits when environmental demands (burden) can no longer be balanced out against the possibilities that the person – despite all support – has resilience. And once the balance between burden and resilience is distorted, the mentally disabled cannot be expected to verbally give expression to their request for assistance. Therefore, it can be stated that people with a mental disability run the risk of becoming a victim of a system that is not designed to recognise their request for care. The less visible the handicap, the bigger the risk is, especially to the group of people with a mild mental disability.

7.   (Judicial) youth care when a disability is present

The right of the disabled child to special care is laid down in Article 23 of the Convention on the Rights of the Child. In Article 25 of the Universal Declaration of Human Rights, the right of mother and child to special care and assistance is established. When these rights are jeopardised, (judicial) youth care comes into action. We shall now sketch a few examples of common problems that occur when a disability is present and where (judicial) youth care needs to be called in. First, we will consider child raising problems with disabled children. Next, we will dwell on the problems of juvenile delinquency among youths with a handicap. Thirdly, we will pay attention to the possibilities that arise when we consider parenthood for people with mental disabilities.

Parenting a disabled child is usually a very demanding task. The child's limitations put high demands on parenting skills. Children with a handicap make a stronger and frequently a longer appeal to their caregivers. Nakken mentions an 'unusual' upbringing. Raising a child with a handicap (or preparing the child for an independent life in society) is less self-evident, and is often a more difficult and longer process. It is a bumpier road. From the moment that it becomes apparent that a disability is present, acceptance and consciousness of that fact usually comes as a shock to the caregivers. Their creativity and endurance can be affected. The need for long-term care and intensive support is a burdening task to them. Sometimes their upbringing skills are insufficient, for example when there is evidence of lack of patience or responsiveness. Insecurity about the long-term perspective can have a discouraging effect. It is not surprising that the upbringing situation of a disabled child bears many risks of becoming a 'problematic' upbringing situation. The problems that arise in this unusual upbringing situation generally cannot be solved with traditional knowledge and means.[13] An extra risk factor is that disabled children are likelier to become the victim of (sexual) abuse.[14] When a problematic upbringing situation arises or threatens to arise, then it is necessary to start assistance appropriate to the nature of the problems. A thorough problem analysis and correct referral to other professionals are prerequisite. Assistance should be provided for by professionals who have knowledge of the interference between handicap and upbringing. If the parents cannot carry the weight of the burdening upbringing (any longer), being raised in a family environment is the most desirable option, especially for children with a handicap. In many cases, foster care can offer a good alternative upbringing situation for disabled children. In such cases of placement in foster care, professional and specialised support for the foster parents, who take over this 'unusual' upbringing, is necessary.

Besides the upbringing problems of disabled children, juvenile delinquency often occurs. These youths are, even more so than their normally gifted contemporaries, easily influenced by their peer group and more susceptible to environmental influences and pressure. Because of their weakly developed self-identity, their ability to reason morally and their limited conscious function, they are at high risk of committing crimes.[15] In the Netherlands, people with a mental disability are tried within the regular judicial system if they have committed a crime. Counselling and treatment in order to prevent recidivism require special assistance and support in certain respects. Assisting the youth through legal proceedings is necessary to explain the implications of the verdicts and events. Otherwise, the trial will escape the youth's attention and no learning effect will occur. More so than with normally gifted youths, it is necessary to involve parents in the counselling or to build a supporting network in another way. Given their limited learning ability, preparing these youths for an independent life is a long-term process.

Independent living assistance and finding suitable housing and day care demand attention. These mentally disabled youths face an added problem because many forms of youth care have adopted the age limit of 18. Due to their slow development, it is desirable for most of these youths to receive extended pedagogical assistance, at least until the age of 25.

A third common form of (judicial) youth care in case of mental disability is assistance of mentally disabled parents with the upbringing of their (disabled) children. Parenting of people with an intellectual disability occurs increasingly.[16] Falling in love, living together, getting married and sexuality, with childbirth as a consequence, whether desirable or not, are the apparent results of the fact that mentally disabled people take part in society. There is evidence of problematic and failing parenthood in many cases. A combination of multiple factors lies at the root of this.[17] Parent factors, child factors, family factors and factors on meso- and macro-level play a role in this. The parent, child and family factors are exemplified here. Frequently, parents cannot adjust their behaviour and parental style of upbringing to the needs of the child. Parenting requires adjustment to the specific needs and characteristics. Parents must possess the ability to step away from their own needs and interests in order to focus on the child's interest. A lack of adaptability can easily lead to escalation. The correlation between the parents' and the child's characteristics plays a significant part in this. A permissive parenting style does not automatically lead to problems in the life of a quiet and obedient child, but it can lead to problems in the life of an active and adventurous child. The IQ level is not a direct predictor of the quality of parenting. What is more important is the adaptability, the willingness and the ability to learn. Due to the limited ability to generalise, some parents are continually confronted with questions, which cannot be answered from the previously learned information. Sometimes, parents show insufficient insight into their own conduct and actions.

Confidence in the provided care and motivation are then vital to make the assistance effective. The child's behavioural and medical problems can be a burden for parents. Age also seems to act as a factor: the older the child, the more difficult. A child with a high IQ or with a difficult personality or temperament adds extra risk. Enough structure, rest and order are often absent. Having children is a risk factor. The assistance to these mentally disabled parents should be focused to all the factors that play a role in these problems. It is necessary to have an integral care supply, in which good structuring and communication between all care workers involved are arranged. The assistance needs to be practical and can last for years, if required. It is important that the care workers are equipped with necessary expertise in order to work with this group.[18]

From the examples we have presented, it becomes clear that a handicap has a specific influence on the request for assistance made to youth care. A specific request for assistance requires specific youth care, 'different' youth care. Different youth care implies recognition of the fact that assistance might be needed lifelong and life-wide. In different youth care, the demand-oriented approach does not entail addressing an articulated request for care, but the objective is to give fulfilment to a carefully determined need for care. Different youth care also pays attention to the achievement of full citizenship, but does not lose sight of the limits. The next paragraph will discuss the application of different youth care in practice.

8. Different youth care

When a child's development is jeopardised, intervention is necessary. When the parents or the child do not seek care, compulsory care within a legal framework (either civil or criminal law) must be carried out. The practice of 'different' youth care that is needed in case of a disability can be illustrated by the means of the following six themes.

8.1 Strictness

One important aspect of the way in which care is delivered is that conduct stems from a strict basic attitude. The law provides a moral framework. The protection of the child and the prevention of a further downslide postulate clear limits that are set and monitored. Because reduced moral awareness often goes hand in hand with a mental disability, an external conscience is of great importance. The caregiver sets the limits and is the personification of these limits, for example hitting a child is not allowed, neither is stealing a CD. Being strict manifests itself in the caregiver's control function and leadership or guidance. The strictness is also apparent from directive conduct, when necessary. For instance, a caregiver will dissuade mentally disabled parents or youths from a (subsequent) pregnancy.[19]

8.2 Carefulness[20]

Carefulness is the indissoluble and self-evident counterpart of strictness, and an essential condition. Carefulness implies empathy and solidarity. It means approaching each family, each child, each youth with an open mind, every time again. It means listening with respect and consideration. It means having patience and perseverance, adjusting to the client's level of understanding, having an eye for the possibilities within the client's network, and focussing on what does work and what is accomplished. Carefulness implies the awareness that mentally disabled people are and remain dependent, to a more or less extent. Working with the client's self-insight does not always suffice to solve the problems. The care worker is aware that, in many cases, it is necessary to take over (or delegate) the client's responsibilities for a long-term or even permanently. Carefulness presumes empathy. Empathy requires an intrinsic motivation of the care worker to search for the meaning of quality of life for every child, every youth, every family and, moreover, the determination to contribute to that.

8.3 Communication

In the execution of every form of care, constant attention to good communication is needed. Adaptation is a prerequisite here. In the communication with a mentally disabled client, this adaptation demands extra effort. The transition that needs to be made is larger, and the communication demands extra attention. The caregiver is constantly focusing on understanding the parent, the child and the youth in their situations. The care worker tries to obtain insight into the client's perception of reality in order to understand him or her. Time and again, he invests in adaptation of communication, and sees to the comprehensibility of the communication on one side, and understanding the client's perspective on the other side. In this way, a circular process of understanding and being understood is established. This requires a constant dialogue. Pace, timing and use of words are adjusted to the client's comprehension. Sometimes visual aids are used to stimulate communication. The care worker is directive in discourse and in formulating the goals.

8.4 Outreaching

The care worker uses an outreaching method of work by visiting the child, youth and family in their own environment. Hereby, an insight is gained into the possibilities and restrictions of the environment. An outreaching method of work also includes pro-active conduct when the situation calls for it. One should not wait until the client makes his request for assistance. Intervention care is often indicated for mentally disabled parents and children, and the care worker does not shrink back to substantiate this.

8.5 Lifelong and life-wide

The care provision involves all spheres of life. After all, a handicap affects all spheres of life. The care worker organises assistance as long and intensively as may be required. He does not cut the child, youth or family loose, but instead ensures a lifelong and life-wide system of support, if necessary. The care worker is considerate about the fact that the client's capability to generalise is impaired and that he will experience difficulty with the transition from one situation to another. Every new situation and change therefore require appropriate assistance. In organising this assistance, the care worker focuses on every resource of support that can be found within the network and fills in gaps with professional care. In this manner, an integrated supply of care is established. The care worker is well informed about the social map of disability care. Both care coordination and case management give shape to the client's perspective. The care worker ensures that all parties involved cooperate well and coordinate their contributions.

8.6   Ethical conduct

Care for clients with a mental disability brings along an asymmetrical balance of supervisory relationships. People with a mental disability are a vulnerable group. They are less capable of effectively standing up for their own interests and opinions. The care worker is aware that he has an advantage, an advantageous point of departure based on his authority, and with respect to pace, language, abilities and knowledge. Reflection on ethical aspects of conduct and learning from feedback are basic conditions to perform this – by nature unequal – position truthfully and respectfully. This asks for a constant consideration of the care worker's own conduct, openness to compare one's own conviction to that of others, and the willingness to change one's conviction.

9.   Conclusion

This paper sketches the need for 'different' special care in (judicial) youth care when a disability is present. When the balance between environmental demands and the disabled person's competences is disturbed, youth care must formulate an answer that meets the special need for care of this target group. Care workers need specific expertise with respect to disabilities, social maps, aspects of communication, adaptation problems and suchlike. Care workers are expected to adopt an attitude that is directive as well as emphatic and dialogic. A pro-active and out-reaching method of working is required, and assistance needs to be organised life-long and life-wide.

The more complex society becomes, the bigger the actual implications of a mental disability become, and therefore the bigger the necessity to provide special care. The more severe the problems are, the bigger the need for special care. The quality of care begins with the quality of the care worker. 'Different' care requires care workers who are willing to carry out their profession in a 'different' manner.

Both the care worker's expertise and professionalism are determining factors that safeguard the care for disabled parents and children. This expertise should be grafted on the motivation to wilfully work for this particular target group. In youth care practice, there are many people who do that with their heart and soul and with expertise. 'Different' youth care demands a 'different' organisation, where expertise on disabilities is self-evidently available. It demands an organisation in which the necessary specific knowledge is embedded (knowledge here is to be understood as both 'knowing' and 'acting'). It demands that the existing knowledge is transmitted to new employees. It is necessary to promote inter-collegial consultation, to share knowledge, to spread new knowledge and to act with a shared vision. It is necessary that the focus on ethical conduct is regarded as a collective responsibility. A collective breeding ground is needed to equip all individual care workers to carry out their functions for this particular target group in a 'different' manner. Without the central anchor of a specialised youth care organisation, there is the danger that knowledge disappears, vision dilutes and expertise is lost.

The right to special care is not anchored in the new Dutch Youth Care Act (2004). Awareness and, above all, recognition of what is needed on an individual and an organisational level, in order to provide adequate care to parents and children with mental disabilities, are prerequisite to safeguard the quality of care for this vulnerable target group.

Endnotes

[1] Ministerie van Welzijn, Volksgezondheid en Sport (2005), *Informatiebrochure Wet op de jeugdzorg*, The Hague.

[2] Swaan, de, A. (1989), *Zorg en de staat. Welzijn, onderwijs en gezondheid in Europa en de Verenigde Staten in de nieuwe tijd*, Amsterdam: Bert Bakker.

[3] *Inleiding van minister-president mr. dr. J.P. Balkenende, Bilderbergconferentie van Stichting NCW, Op eigen kracht; van verzorgingsstaat naar participatiemaatschappij*, 22 January 2005, Oosterbeek.

[4] Vries, de, G. (2000), *Nederland verandert. Maatschappelijke ontwikkelingen en problemen in het begin van de eenentwintigste eeuw*, Amsterdam: Het Spinhuis.

[5] See for example Dr. Junger-Tas, Het belang van het kind is in wezen ook het belang van de samenleving (The Best Interest of the Child is Essentially Also the Interest of Society), *Perspectief* 13e jaargang nummer 8 (December 2005).

[6] Gennep, van, A. & Steman, C (1997), *Beperkte burgers. Over volwaardig burgerschap voor mensen met een verstandelijke beperking*, Utrecht: Nederlands Instituut voor Zorg en Welzijn.

[7] Nakken, H. (2004), De invloed van meningen op opvoeden en ondersteunen van personen met beperkingen, in: *Wie maakt de dienst uit? Macht en onmacht in opvoeding en hulpverlening*, Utrecht: Agiel.

[8] Steege, M. van der (2003), *Gewoon goed hulpverlenen. Over de cliënt centraal, vraaggericht werken en cliëntparticipatie in de jeugdzorg*, Utrecht: Nederlands Instituut voor Zorg en Welzijn.

[9] Tonkens, E. (2003), *Mondige burgers, getemde professionals*, Utrecht: Nederlands Instituut voor Zorg en Welzijn.

[10] *Ibid.*, p. 69.

[11] Knorth, E.J. & Ruijssenaars, A.J.J.M. (2005), Jeugdigen tussen wal en schip?, in: Ploeg, J.D. van der & Goudena, P.P. (Eds.), *Verwaarlozing. Een kwestie van urgente individuele en maatschappelijke verantwoordelijkheid*, Utrecht: Agiel.

[12] Landelijk Kenniscentrum LVG (2005), *Beoordeling beperkingen in de sociale aanpassing bij LVG-jeugd ten behoeve van indicatiestelling (voor jeugdigen van 4-23 jaar)*, Utrecht: Landelijk Kenniscentrum LVG.

[13] Nakken, H. (2000), Het opvoeden van kinderen met een verstandelijke beperking, in: Gemert, G.H. van & Minderaa, R.B. (Eds.), *Zorg voor mensen met een verstandelijke handicap*, Assen: Van Gorcum. See also Nakken, H. (2003), Professionals moeten opvoedingsondersteuning serieus nemen, in: *Recht op zorg van het gehandicapte kind*, Amsterdam: William Schrikker Stichting.

[14] See Belie, de E., Lesseliers, J., Ivens, C. & Hove, van G., (Eds.) (2002), *Seksueel misbruik van mensen met een verstandelijke handicap, handboek preventie en hulpverlening*, Leuven/Leusden: Acco.

[15] Marle, van, H. (2004), Hulpverlening of justitie: keuzes in de zorg voor verstandelijk gehandicapten, in: *Verstandelijk gehandicapten in aanraking met politie en justitie*, Utrecht: NIZW/Aveleijn.

[16] Booth, T. & Booth, W. (1993), Parents with learning difficulties: lessons for practicioners, *British Journal of Social Work* 23, 459-480.

[17] Vries, de, J.N., Willems, D.L., Isarin, J. & Reinders, J.S. (2005), *Samenspel van factoren. Inventariserend onderzoek naar de ouderschapscompetenties van mensen met een verstandelijke handicap*, Amsterdam: Universiteit van Amsterdam.

[18] Reinders, J.S. (2000), Zorg voor mensen met een verstandelijke handicap en ethiek, in: Gemert, van, G.H. & Minderaa, R.B. (Eds.), *Zorg voor mensen met een verstandelijke handicap*, Assen: Van Gorcum.

[19] Fulpen, van C.A.M. (2005), *Vision of the William Schrikker Group on undesired pregnancy: 'Pregnancy undesired'*, Diemen: William Schrikker Group

[20] Tonkens (2003) describes how Swedish youth care workers succeed in being both strict and careful. On the one hand, these youth care workers intervene on (sometimes implicit) questions and needs of these youths. On the other hand, they sometimes counteract the questions of these youths. The law provides them with a moral framework from which they can derive support and inspiration. In judicial youth care for parents and children with a handicap, we also encounter this combination of being strict and careful, of listening and counteracting.

Child Maltreatment in Diverse Households

Challenges to Child Care Law, Theory and Practice in Diverse Settings

Julia Brophy

1.   Introduction

The research outlined below comes from a stream of work in England on issues of 'race', ethnicity, religion and linguistic and cultural diversity in care proceedings.[1] I would however like to preface discussion with some points about 'law' and child maltreatment in diverse households – not simply in European communities but also internationally.

First, it must be acknowledged that states within the European Community may have different approaches to what might be termed 'multi-culturalism', and issues of integration/'assimilation' of new and long-established 'immigrant' communities. Moreover, addressing variability in approaches to diverse populations is made more complex by recent demographic and political changes, shifts in immigration policy and notions of what constitutes 'citizenship' in member states.

Second, outside of Europe we know comparatively little about child care law practices and indeed, so far as issues of diversity are concerned, we have yet to address comparative practices through detailed research.[2]

The practices discussed below therefore represent one jurisdiction and it may well be that England and Wales have taken a different approach to this area compared with their European neighbours. Nevertheless, I hope the law and the practices discussed below will find resonance – and raise questions – about approaches to minority ethnic children and parents across jurisdictions.

Many European states have to address populations where lifestyles, values and attitudes towards children and family life may differ. The degree of variability within and between communities regarding core child protection issues in particular, and aspirations for children more generally remain debatable. Nevertheless, professionals and courts address domestic thresholds of harm and risk within the framework of Human Rights legislation, and try to get the balance right according to Article 6 (rights to a fair trial) and Article 8 (rights to family life), while at the same time prioritising the needs of *all* children to be protected from maltreatment within households.

European law also makes it clear that removing a child from a parent must be the last resort; the aim of such action, wherever possible, should be his/her eventual return. That framework places a responsibility on states to work with parents to see if changes to parenting can be achieved so that children may be safely returned to their care.

I begin below therefore with the concerns underscoring my research in this field. I will then briefly outline the relevant statute and Guidance to demonstrate how concerns about 'race', ethnic, culture, religion and linguistic diversity have informed policy in England and Wales.

I will then discuss findings from two recently completed studies on care proceedings in diverse settings in England.[3] Finally, I will explore the implications I think this work has for thinking about 'law', notions of multi-culturalism and issues of racism.

2. Background to the studies: disparate discourses

One concern in this area in the United Kingdom (UK) has been whether black children are over-represented in the number of children in the care of the state.[4] One of our early studies – at least with regard to the national picture – lent support to that concern (Brophy, Wale and Bates 1999).[5] However, exploring ethnic representation is complex and obtaining robust data by geographical area has been greatly hindered because courts do not currently collect data on ethnicity from family courts.

Second, some concerns have been expressed about whether professionals misunderstand childrearing practices in certain minority ethnic households, and whether there are attempts to impose Eurocentric/Americo-centric models of parenting on families who do not necessarily share *all* the practices/beliefs associated with Western European lifestyles/parenting. These concerns also raised questions about whether diverse contexts are routinely addressed by professionals in assessments of harm/risk to minority ethnic children and potential for change in parents.

Third, there are international debates about 'culturally bound' definitions of child 'abuse' and whether it is possible or indeed desirable to have a 'transcultural' definition of abuse, this agenda having its foundations in the seminal work of cultural anthropologies and others such as: Korbin 1980; Finkelhor & Korbin 1988; Korbin 1991; Korbin et al 1998; Elliott et al. 1997; Segal 1992; 1995; 2002.

To these groups must be added the work of writers exploring social work practices with black and Asian families, and those addressing the legacy of colonialism and slavery on the formation and functioning of black families – and on the thinking, practices and theorising taught in family studies.

An international review of research and writing in this field (Brophy 1999; 2003b; 2005)[6] demonstrated that concerns arose from disciplines with little history of interdisciplinary dialogue or research. In broad terms I think this is because one group – the family law specialists – has been seen as too deeply embedded in a legal discourse which others have found difficult to penetrate. Other groups, such as cultural anthropologists, transcultural psychiatrists, psychologists and sociologists have explored cultural contexts to 'childhood' and parenting – but this work is seldom located within a legal framework about definitions of harm/risk to children. Thus, in short, respective texts 'fail' because one group is too embedded in 'law', the other failing to engage with 'law'.

A further issue raised the profile of 'law' and race relations in the UK. This was the murder of a black youth, Stephen Lawrence, in London, and a failure by police to obtain a prosecution against white youths. An Inquiry by Lord Macpherson (Macpherson 1999) raised concerns about institutional racism in the police force and a lack of confidence in the criminal justice system by minority ethnic communities. That report resulted in a research programme on Diversity and the Courts by the Department of Constitutional Affairs.[7] Two of the studies on which I draw were funded under that programme.

Those issues and concerns form a backcloth to work on care proceedings concerning minority ethnic families. But as the array of discourses imply, the field is complex, drawing on a wide range of thinking, concepts and theories with little discussion or agreement about definitions and a limited history of robust empirical data.

3.   Law and Guidance related to issues of diversity

Aspects of the Children Act 1989 and relevant Guidance[8] highlight the importance of attention to diversity when working with minority ethnic families. Indeed when the relevant sections are pulled together, there is an array of directions about the importance of attention to race, ethnicity, religion, culture and language in a range of settings.

Guidance directs the local authority to the importance of attention to diverse backgrounds when commissioning or providing a range of services to families, and during decision-making processes. For example, in the recruitment of day carers and foster carers, local authorities must give attention to the ethnic mix of local populations and with regard to placement decisions, minority ethnic children should where possible be placed with matched carers. Also, where there are concerns about harm/risk, the framework for the assessment of parents highlights the need to consider issues of diversity during the core assessment exercise (see Table 1). Once in the care of the local authority (whether voluntarily or as a result of statutory intervention), Part III of the Act, s.22 (5)(c) places a duty on the authority to give due consideration to a child's religious persuasion, racial origin and cultural and linguistic background.

Where care proceedings are instigated under Part IV (s.1) of the Act, key principles guiding all courts[9] are:
- The welfare of the child is paramount, (s.1 (1))
- The welfare checklist, s.1 (a) – (g)
- Principle of non-intervention (s 1(5))
- Avoidance of delay in proceedings (s.1 (2)).

With regard to the welfare checklist, this specifies matters that must be considered when a decision is being made. It was intended to help courts but also parties and their legal advisers along with social workers and children's guardians. Included in the checklist at s.1 (3) (d) are the child's "...age, sex, background and any characteristics of his which the court considers relevant".

The incorporation of the European Convention on Human Rights into UK domestic law by the Human Rights Act 1998 requires the interpretation of the 1989 Children Act and Regulations in accordance with Convention Rights. Perhaps most relevant here are rights to a fair hearing (Article 6) and to privacy and respect for family life (Article 8). Local authorities and courts are not merely required to ensure that they do not breach these rights; they must take positive steps to ensure individuals obtain their rights.

As indicated in the Introduction, the European Court of Human Rights has repeatedly stated that taking children into care should generally be regarded as a temporary measure, the objective being the return of children to parent(s) to preserve their and their parents' rights to respect for family life. However, it is also accepted that parents are not entitled to decisions from the State that harm a child's welfare. The right to respect for family life is thus a qualified right. The State may intervene where the law permits if this is necessary to protect the child's rights and freedoms, for example, where it is necessary to protect a child from significant harm. Only action that is proportionate is accepted as necessary.

The right to respect for family life is also interpreted to require the involvement of parents and children in decisions that impact on their family life. Parents and children should be consulted throughout the process. If a local authority initiates legal proceedings, parents and children have a right to publicly funded legal representation and 'equality of arms' in that process.

An applicant for a care order must first establish that a child has/is likely to suffer *significant harm* as this is set out in s.31 of the Act. The focus of the criteria is on the child and the need for an evidence-based approach in establishing a child has suffered/is likely to suffer significant harm – as a result of parental attitudes/ actions/non-action. Harm must be *significant*; minor issues/lapses will not meet the criteria. Moreover, in the drafting of the Act 1989 Act there is a clear relationship between Part III (duties of the local authority to support and investigate) and Part IV (statutory intervention). Support and investigation precede most statutory intervention.

Despite that detailed reconstruction of the relationship between parents and the state where there are concerns about child maltreatment, there was no robust data about cases concerning parents and children from minority ethnic communities. For example, while we had concerns about issues of representation for some groups, we had no information about whether minority ethnic parents routinely contested cases on grounds of cultural/religious differences, and whether/how this might vary within and between groups.

We therefore addressed these issues in two empirical studies. The first study focused 182 completed court files in care proceedings in which cases were stratified by ethnic group[10] and randomly selected.[11] In addition we interviewed 25 court personnel (judges, magistrates and specialist (family) legal advisers) and observed at 36 hearings (Brophy, Jhutti-Johal and Owen 2003a/b). In a second study 45 solicitors and 12 parents/respondents from minority ethnic families were interviewed (Brophy, Jhutti-Johal and McDonald 2005).

4. Minority ethnic households and 'significant harm' in practice

In the first study court files were examined to determine whether issues of diversity are documented for courts.[12] Below I will address the extent to which issues of cultural/religious diversity were documented, whether reports from expert witnesses addressed these issues, role of 'cultural conflicts' with regard to allegations of child maltreatment and failures of parenting, and finally the degree to which parents included issues of cultural and/or religious contexts in their statements.

4.1 Descriptive and substantive information on diversity in court files

Two types of information on aspects of diversity were anticipated in court files: the first was descriptive information; the second substantive. All documents were therefore read and coded according to the range and type of information available to courts at each of four key stages in the process of preparing case for a final hearing.[13]

Descriptive information might specify the ethnic group of family, nominated religion and language spoken. However, this information could be extended. For example, a social work statement might describe a family as of 'South Asian/Pakistani origin' but the social worker may go on to say, "…the mother was born and raised in Pakistan and speaks little English; the father's family came from Pakistan but he was born and educated in the UK and thus speaks English. The family is Muslim…" This latter information may be followed by further information detailing the significance of the parents' cultural and religious background and beliefs for family lifestyles and living arrangements. Relevant religious rituals and festivals in the likely span of proceedings may be included. Information may also be provided on a parent's views regarding child care/maltreatment. It may also include more detail on the languages spoken in the home, for example that spoken adult to adult, and adults to children.

Thus, substantive information documented in statements/reports tells the court about the significance of cultural, religious and linguistic diversity for the family and perhaps with regard to any perceived relevance for the concerns/allegations of child maltreatment resulting in court proceedings.

Findings on the degree of *descriptive* information on diversity in documents were more encouraging than might have been anticipated. For example, for complex cases heard in the higher courts (44% of the sample),[14] a majority of cases (80%)

contained *some* descriptive information at each of the key stages in the legal process. Findings with regard to *substantive* information were much lower – especially in the early stages of cases. At the first hearing about half of cases (51%) contained some substantive information. That figure did however improve by the time cases reached a pre-trial review, at which point 83% of cases contained some substantive information.

Thus, with regard to questions about the information on issues of diversity available to courts, in most cases most judges in the higher courts had access to some information on some aspect of diversity at each of four key stages in proceedings. Nevertheless, findings leave little room for complacency, as they are based on a composite picture drawn from all the documents available at each stage. Some documents addressed diverse backgrounds, others did not; some contained descriptive information, others descriptive *and* substantive information. Moreover, the amount of substantive information in documents was lower at the start of proceedings (in the higher and lower courts).[15] Substantive information was also much harder to locate – it was not always in the same place in statements/reports and 'bits' of information were found in a wide variety of locations. Therefore, aggregating information at any one point in the process masks certain practices. This was, for example, evident from a detailed analysis of expert reports.

4.2 Experts reports and issues of diversity
In England research consistently indicates a high use of clinical evidence in care cases. The major disciplines instructed are paediatricians, child and adolescent/family psychiatrists, adult psychiatrists and psychologists (Brophy, Wale and Bates 1999; Brophy et al. 1999; Hunt et al. 1999). Research to date indicates these findings broadly hold across all ethnic groups (Brophy et al. 2003b).

In the court file study overall 89% of cases contained expert evidence (Brophy et al. 2003:46). Care must be taken once minority ethnic groups are 'disaggregated', because some numbers are small, but in this study findings demonstrate a focus on diversity in expert reports varied according to the discipline of the expert and with regard to the ethnic group of the child/parent.

Paediatricians were highly unlikely to include any descriptive or substantive on issues of diversity in reports. Child and adolescent/family psychiatrists were much more likely to address such issues – but this depended on the ethnic group of the family. For example, two-thirds of reports by child psychiatrists assessing families of South Asian origin contained descriptive *and* some substantive information, compared with under half of reports on black families. Moreover, if the black group is disaggregated, none of the reports based on families of African-Caribbean origin contained both categories of information.

This and other research (e.g. Brophy et al 2001) indicate there is a debate to be had about the significance of issues of cultural, religious and linguistic diversity for clinical work commissioned in proceedings. Such issues will not be relevant for certain types of assessments and for some families. However, it remains the case that some reports in this study were 'colour/culture blind'. These findings require further discussion with experts and with parents.

4.3   Grounds for care orders and 'cultural conflicts'

In this sample there were no 'single issues cases', that is, there were no cases where the dispute between minority ethnic parents and social workers about child ill treatment rested unequivocally on behaviours/attitudes defended by a parent as culturally acceptable but alleged as ill treatment by professionals. All cases were complex. Most contained allegations of more than one type of child ill treatment (i.e. more than one of sexual, physical and emotional ill treatment and neglect), with neglect and emotional abuse being the most common combination in aggregated groups.[16]

Moreover, most cases also contained multiple allegations of failures of parenting. For example, over 40% of all cases *included* concerns/allegations of failures of parenting resulting from mental health problems (and this finding has remained constant over several years of available data – see Brophy 2006). In over 70% of cases professionals also cited a failure of parent(s) to co-operate with health and welfare agencies, 51% of cases also included failures resulting from accommodation problems, 43% of cases included allegations related to disciplines problems at school, in over 60% of cases parents were unable to control children and 45% of cases included allegations about male violence to mothers[17] (Brophy et al. 2003b: 39).

Where cases did include evidence of 'cultural conflicts' between social workers and a parent(s), such conflicts were more evident in cases concerning parents of South Asian and African origin compared with cases concerning parents of African Caribbean origin. However, these conflicts were seldom pivotal by the time cases reached a pre-trial review hearing. Most parents in all groups – including white British – conceded the threshold criteria by that stage in proceedings.

Findings at that point should not however be 'read' as indicating there was little/no evidence of cultural conflicts in cases – rather, they were not usually relevant by the time advocates were ready to construct a threshold statement for the court. Two issues go some way to explaining this. First, the sheer range of problems resulting in failures of parenting in families – one-off events of ill treatment (with the possible exception of sexual abuse and serious non accidental injury to a baby) are unlikely to reach the courts.

Second, cases may not 'go to threshold' on all the initial allegations, rather professionals focus on those where the evidence is strongest and where, if parties cannot ultimately agree, the applicant is likely obtain a finding of fact from the court. This 'filtering process' can exclude examples of 'cultural conflict'. So for example, cases contained evidence of disagreements about the age at which children are considered old enough to be left home alone, in charge of younger siblings, or allowed to determine their own style of dress, circle of friends, etc. and how to deal with bad behaviour/truancy. Some parents had argued these issues were culturally determined and their views differed to values/practices in white British culture. However, such issues were not usually central to final debates about whether parents had breached the threshold criteria, rather they formed part of a pattern in which there were more serious attitudes/behaviours.

Equally, there were disputes between social workers and parents about 'physical punishment' and whether it was more/less acceptable in different cultural/religious contexts. In addition, parental motivation in using severe physical 'punishment' (e.g. whether a parent was motivated to harm or socialise a child according to cultural/religious traditions),[18] although important, was not pivotal in determining whether treatment resulted in significant harm to a child.

The study also indicated that families subject to proceedings share common socio-economic and psychopathological characteristics despite some diverse cultural, religious and linguistic backgrounds. Some of these characteristics – and how they are addressed – *may* be as important as perceived differences between groups. That hypothesis requires testing with a larger sample allowing for some multi-level modelling.

4.4 Coverage of diverse cultural/religious contexts in parents' statements

The study indicates there are gender but possibly also ethnic group differences in the likelihood of parents filing statements, and raising diverse backgrounds. The former was predictable given previous studies, but the impact of ethnicity on both counts is potentially interesting and requires further work.

In this study, overall, most mothers (just over two-thirds) but under half of fathers (47%) filed statements. When aggregated groups are compared some differing trends are suggested. Mothers of South Asian origin were more likely to file a statement (88% did so, compared with 50% of black mothers and 65% of White British mothers). However they may be slightly *less* likely to raise cultural/religious contexts (64% did so, compared with 71% of black mothers – and the majority of which were Black African).

Fathers of South Asian origin were also more likely to file statements (68% did so, compared with 32% of black fathers and 47% of white fathers). Moreover, slightly more fathers of South Asian origin raised cultural/religious contexts in their statements (71%, compared with 64% of fathers in the black groups).

The numbers for analysis by gender are small, therefore much caution and further work are necessary but, for example, all mothers of African origin and most mothers of Bangladeshi origin documented some issues of cultural/religious diversity in their statements compared with very few mothers of African Caribbean origin,

4.5 Reassessing 'law': 'significant harm' as a threshold

In summary, at the end of this study we could find no evidence that the law itself required re-assessment so far as parents and children from diverse cultural/religions are concerned. The research demonstrates that debates about whether a child had suffered *significant harm* did not usually 'turn' on fundamental differences between cultures/religions. Cases were complex with multiple allegations of child maltreatment and multiple problems of parenting. This applied to all groups. Neglect and emotional abuse were the dominant categories – this also applied to all (aggregated) groups. Where there were debates about whether physical mal-treatment was in fact acceptable physical 'punishment' in a minority culture, the maltreatment was severe, allegations were supported by medical evidence and physical maltreatment was not the only allegation in cases.

The study nevertheless raised concerns about aspects of the process and about variability and transparency in attention to issues of diversity. It resulted in atten-tion to this field of practice being included in major changes to the judicial man-agement of cases by courts (DCA 2003).[19] However, gaps in research evidence remained regarding, for example, the views of minority ethnic parents on these issues and also the views of solicitors representing such parents. It was hypothe-sised that the work of parents' solicitors was likely to be pivotal, since it is their task to translate the concerns and problems of parents into the language of law, courts and experts.

5.   The views of minority ethnic parents and their solicitors
In the second study therefore, 45 solicitors in three regions were interviewed about their views and experiences of taking instructions and advising parents from minority ethnic groups. Twenty-two additional court files were examined and interviews undertaken with 12 relevant minority ethnic respondents.[20]

Below I will focus on the solicitor's task in obtaining a parent's story and respon-sibility for broaching issues of diversity, decisions about including information on diversity in statements and cultural variation as an explanation for views/actions. I will also address solicitors' and parents' views about expert reports and, finally, whether parents received a fair hearing, and felt 'heard and understood' by courts, whether they had experienced anything in the court process that they considered to be racist.

The solicitor's task: getting a parent's story, explaining 'law' to parents and broaching issues of diversity. With regard to obtaining a parent's story, most solic-itors reported similarities between white British and minority ethnic parents, but also differences and some difficulties.

All parents seeking the help of a solicitor were reported as usually frightened and anxious. Getting their side of the story where the parent is from a minority eth-nic community can be difficult because in certain situations neither the solicitor nor the parent starts this exercise with much of a 'script'. The solicitor does not always know what he/she needs to ask a parent from a diverse background, equal-ly parents do not know what they need to tell their solicitor. Solicitors described two broad approaches.

For certain parents who are new/relatively newly arrived in Britain there may be substantial hurdles for a solicitor to overcome before getting a parent's story. Foremost can be a parent's total incomprehension at state intervention in parenting practices. Where parents originate from countries with corrupt state apparatus and/or no welfare or legal system, that background determines how a parent's story is told and how a parent responds to welfare, health and legal agencies – and this may include initial interactions with their solicitor.

In these circumstances, getting a parent's background and story about what has happened and how this resulted in proceedings takes longer – especially if using an interpreter. Interviews usually need to be shorter and it takes experience to judge how much information a parent can absorb in one session. It can remain difficult – even with an interpreter – to be sure some parents have fully understood issues.

With regard to representing second/third generation black/Asian British, for the most part, the task of getting a parent's own story started from a different place. Solicitors tended to make assumptions about parents' knowledge of welfare and legal systems and assumed a *degree* of integration or 'assimilation' into British society. In principle therefore, taking instructions was generally viewed as not very different from the task with white British parents. The task could however vary, for example, where a solicitor is jointly instructed by both parents but where one is relatively new to the UK and/or does not speak/understand much English. In these circumstances there may be some cultural mores, linguistic issues and inter-gender and inter-generational issues that need careful exploration.

When it came to explaining 'law' and care procedures to minority ethnic parents, most solicitors felt the language and terms used by professionals remained difficult for most parents – regardless of ethnic group. Some solicitors felt they were much better at getting a parent's story than explaining 'law' to parents. Interviews with parents confirmed that view: parents said solicitors were not very good at explaining law and procedures – although they acknowledged solicitors did try hard.

Solicitors were divided about responsibility for broaching areas of potential cultural variation with parents. Approaches could depend on whether parents were 'new arrivals' or second/third generation Black/Asian British. Some solicitors were extremely cautious about initiating discussion in this field – especially where they were unsure about how a parent might respond. They reported no knowledge/training on this aspect of their work and there were concerns about being viewed as racist – simply by raising the topic for discussion. Thus, unless it was obvious/unavoidable, some solicitors would leave it to parents to broach this area

Other solicitors however have developed methods of raising this area with parents – precisely because it was felt parents simply would not broach it 'uninvited'. For example, one solicitor with experience of a large Bangladeshi community tried to visited parents at home. This gave her a picture of the household and a framework from which to ask questions about how certain things might be done differently in families, perhaps using her own family/childhood as one example. Another solicitor reported being very straightforward with some parents acknowledging that he might need some assistance from them and others to enable him to better understand certain issues in diverse cultures/communities.

By comparison, some parents in this study at least were not clear why solicitors had wanted to discuss a parent's childhood. Other parents were happy to talk about their background, while yet others said their solicitor had not ventured much beyond questions about specific allegations and the parent had felt unable to initiate a discussion about 'how we do it', 'how it is in our family/culture' as framework to their 'way of life'.[21]

5.1   Parents' statements and information on diverse backgrounds

The first study identified considerable use of the 'rebuttal mode' as a format for parents' statements. Most solicitors in this sample, however, were highly critical of that approach. It was described as a 'lawyer's document', too easy to produce, not especially helpful to the court and problematic for parents in terms getting their story told.

Nevertheless, the question of whether to include information on 'cultural contexts' in statements raised issues of 'strategy' and whether solicitors felt information would help or hinder a parent's case. In the final analysis, however, most solicitors said the decision remained with parents. Some solicitors argued the importance of 'capturing the client' and would therefore include things which although 'culturally important, may not be legally relevant'.

In discussing the limited coverage of any aspect of diversity in statements from parents of African Caribbean origin, most solicitors interviewed reported limited experience of this ethnic group (and more research is required for this group). Most of the reasons these solicitors *suggested* might underscore limited coverage were based on the fact that African-Caribbean parents generally presented no obvious 'signifiers/triggers' of difference. Most parents were likely to have been born and educated in the UK, there were usually no language barriers, and styles of dress gave no obvious indicators of diverse values/lifestyles. It was therefore felt that solicitors might be very cautious of broaching this area with African-Caribbean parents for fear of being seen as racist.

As a 'launching pad' for further debate/research about parents' statements, it is worth noting over half the minority ethnic parents in this study at least were dissatisfied with their statements – because diverse backgrounds were not covered, statements were not in their own words and things were said differently. In cases where allegations included physical ill treatment of a child some parents were dissatisfied with the way in which this was addressed in their statement – for some it was in effect 'played-down'. In interviews they remained committed to the use of severe physical punishment and their right to do this without interference from the state.

5.2   Cultural variations in parenting and explanations for ill treatment

Solicitors reported *some* minority ethnic parents sometimes do defend certain views/practices by reference to different cultural/religious mores. Parents of African, South Asian and African-Caribbean origins have argued physical 'punishment' is sanctioned by their culture or religion. Equally, however, solicitors have also represented parents from these groups who have not considered it acceptable to beat or hit children.

We took the opportunity to ask this small group of parents whether they saw any differences in their approaches to parenting compared with white British parents – friends/neighbours they know. Most parents identified some differences. Some generalised their views to other parents in the same ethnic group, for example saying, 'Indians do it this way'. Other parents however distanced themselves from what they felt were stereotypes of parents of South Asian and African origin in British popular culture, especially with regard to the acceptability of hitting/beating children.

Some 'stereotypes' also emerged about what might be termed 'over-liberal' parenting in white British households. For example, some parents perceived a lack of discipline, boundaries and expectations of children regarding homework and household chores amongst their white British friends/neighbours. It must be noted this was very much a 'taster' question but responses indicate much research remains to be done identifying 'normative' practices in parenting within and across diverse ethnic groups in Britain.

5.3   Expert assessments and reports

Given variability in the focus on diversity in expert reports outlined above, we asked solicitors whether they felt issues of diversity were relevant for the major clinical experts instructed in proceedings. They generally felt issues of diversity were probably not relevant for the work of paediatricians, but highly relevant for the work of psychiatrists, psychologists and family centres. Moreover, some solicitors expressed concerns about experts who were not prepared to consider that people from other cultures might live and understand their lives differently.

We also asked parents about expert assessments and reports. For example, we asked whether they felt 'heard and understood' by doctors. Responses could depend on whether the clinician had actually raised issues of cultural/religious diversity with a parent, was then able to demonstrate some knowledge and understanding of different cultural contexts – or at least demonstrated an openness to discussing this area.

As with parents' experiences with their lawyers, if an expert did not raise issues of potential cultural/religious diversity with a parent, it was highly unlikely a parent would feel able to take the initiative. The reasons for this ranged from a lack of confidence about whether/how such issues might be relevant, doubts about whether the expert would understand and not wishing to be seen as 'foreign' or 'exotic'. As with ethnically matched solicitors, where a parent had been assessed by a 'matched' doctor, this did not necessarily resolve problems in this field.[22]

Solicitors in all regions expressed concern about the validity of psychometric testing on parents where there were language barriers and where parents came from countries where values and practices were likely to be different from those in which tests were developed. Parents were critical of psychologists who they felt failed to understand them, where personal histories were ascertained but then used in a crude/problematic way, or where psychologists simply failed to explore cultural contexts with parents.

5.4   Attending court

Solicitors said regardless of ethnic group, most parents were frightened and anxious about attending court. There are however additional issues for some groups. *Some* minority ethnic parents remain highly suspicious of state agencies. Where parents have no experience of state involvement in defining adequate parenting, many express total incredulity that courts should in any way be interested in their parenting. For some parents (newly arrived and second/third generation Black and Asian British), notions of pride and honour were important in understanding parents' views, courts remain associated with crime and punishment, attendance is thus a source of shame and damage to the honour and reputation of families.

Some solicitors felt that parents attending the few dedicated family courts probably had a better experience compared with those attending the majority courts which undertook a mixture of crime and family work.[23] Overall, County Court Care Centres were thought to provide a better experience than Magistrates' Family Proceedings Courts but this could depend on the particular judge. Some judges were regarded as particularly good with minority ethnic parents but in one region certain judges were avoided because approaches were thought to be racist, dismissive or disrespectful.

Overall, however, solicitors reported most care judges were generally good or excellent with most parents, judges with problematic attitudes could be dismissive and disrespectful of parents regardless of ethnic group. Some magistrates were also reported making great efforts with minority ethnic parents – some were described as excellent, others however have made inappropriate comments in court.

With regard to whether minority ethnic parents receive a fair hearing and felt 'heard and understood' by judges/magistrates, most solicitors felt parents probably did get a fair and just hearing. Nevertheless, substantial concerns were expressed about the *process*. Factors said to influence a parent's experience were the attitude of some judges, whether courts received a full picture of a parent's background including cultural contexts, whether parents instructed a specialist Children Panel solicitor, and the attitude of some experts to issues of diversity.

From *parents'* perspectives, a view that treatment by a court had been unfair resulted from a judge's comments to parents of African origin prior to hearing what parents had to say in oral evidence. The parents felt the judge's comments meant they were being pre-judged, the mother felt this was because, "…in Britain people think African parents are violent towards their children". However, most parents' views about unfair treatment focused on a lack of court time and judges for cases, being kept waiting for long periods then feeling proceedings were rushed once in court, and not being allowed to speak in court.

Thus, while some minority ethnic parents were indeed dissatisfied with their treatment by courts, most in this sample at least did not put this down to racism/discrimination based on the fact that they are Black or Asian. They felt most parents suffered similar insensitive and disrespectful treatment in court.

With regard to whether minority ethnic parents had been 'heard and understood' by courts, some solicitors in all regions were doubtful about this. It was felt that the response of certain courts to the detail of diverse cultural contexts was likely to make parents feel they were not understood. It was reported some judges and magistrates do *sometimes* fail to understand issues and thus misinterpret aspects of a parent's behaviour or attitude. For example, it was said that some judges fail to understand the complexities of domestic violence for some mothers of South Asian origin, their limited parameters of action and decision-making and the cultural and religious ramifications for a mother who leaves a violent husband/household taking her children.

Overall, however, most solicitors felt there had been substantial improvements by judges/magistrates in recent years. Most examples of problematic behaviour were felt to demonstrate insensitive or uninformed rather than racist attitudes (see below).

From the *parents'* perspectives, there were three categories of response to the question of whether they had felt heard and understood by courts. Some parents felt judges did not understand diverse backgrounds – either because the court simply did not get this type of information (it was not included in statements/reports), or because the court failed to understand information provided and/or there was a failure by judges/magistrates to talk directly to parents about these issues.

Some parents simply did not know whether they had been 'heard and understood'. They pointed out that the judge had not spoken to them in court, and where statements were poor on cultural contexts, they simply could not know whether they had been understood. Other parents felt the judge probably did understand them – even though they disagreed with his/her view.

As to whether the threshold criteria for a care order in any way discriminated against parents from diverse backgrounds, most solicitors thought that the 'significant harm' criteria were about right. No solicitor argued that findings of fact had been fundamentally unfair/unjust for a minority ethnic parent/carer. Equally, solicitors said in their experience cases do not usually 'turn' on culture/cultural conflicts. This view confirmed findings from the court file study discussed above.

Nevertheless, many solicitors felt the system 'left much to be desired'. It was argued a better understanding of diverse backgrounds may not change findings of fact so far as ill-treatment of a child is concerned, but many felt it could result in a better experience and less suffering for some parents during the process.

In all regions solicitors expressed concerns about the impact on parents of conceding the threshold criteria. Parents – especially those recently arrived in the UK –anticipated they would have an opportunity to 'have their say' in court, conceding the threshold thwarted that expectation. This was said to have a significant impact on parents' perceptions of having received a 'fair and just hearing'. Some concern was also expressed about the 'almost unimaginable' consequences for some mothers of South Asian origin: they could be rejected by families and ostracised by communities.

With regard to attempts to change aspects of parental care (through attending residential or non-residential family centres), a small number of solicitors were concerned about placing too much emphasis on cultural variation in this exercise and were also sceptical about its relevance to allegations of harm. Other solicitors, however, felt failures by social workers to 'engage' with some parents from diverse cultures meant parents never really understood what was required of them.

5.5   Parents' experiences of racism with the family justice system
In this study most parents did not experience attitudes/behaviours from their solicitor or barrister they considered racist. Most were, it appears, "…doing OK on that front". However, three parents reported disrespectful and uninformed comments from their advocates.

With regard to courtroom experiences, as indicated above, two black parents felt a judge had been racist and they had been stereotyped. But while most parents had not experienced anything they considered to be racist, more parents did experience treatment which they considered disrespectful or insensitive. As detailed above, not being acknowledged by the judge/magistrates once in court, being kept waiting for a judge, feeling things were rushed once in court, being seated at the back of the court (and thus feeling excluded), not being able to speak to the judge, and a judge behaving in an angry and arrogant manner.

6.   Conclusions
Three points require repeating. First, the court file study was based on a stratified random sample of 182 cases. It thus has strengths in terms of the robust nature of data. However, for some exercises disaggregated numbers (and questions relevant to gender) become small, and care is therefore necessary in generalising certain findings.

Second, the sampling framework for solicitors (see Brophy et al 2005:191) means that we have probably ascertained the views of some of the most experienced specialist child care lawyers in the three urban locations. It is likely therefore that we have identified 'best practice' in working with minority ethnic parents.

Third, with regard to parents' views, the sample was purposive and the method qualitative. It is *not* a study of ethnic groups per se but rather a study about 'difference' and its consequences as perceived by parents. It thus provides a framework from which to develop work on parents' experience in the family justice system.

6.1 Effective law and transparent practice

Overall, we found no evidence that the 'significant harm' criteria are in need of re-assessment. Cases reaching court in all ethnic groups containing multiple allegations of maltreatment and failures of parenting. Harm to children was serious, almost always supported by clinical evidence, and cases did not usually 'turn' on cultural conflicts.

Nevertheless, there was evidence that the process could be greatly improved. Some criticisms of the system apply equally to many white British parents (e.g. Freeman and Hunt 1998; Brophy and Bates 1998), but the studies demonstrate issues specific to some minority ethnic parents.

Where professionals do not explore and document diverse views and contexts (whether or not these are ultimately relevant to findings of fact), parents may feel misunderstood by a system promising fairness and justice regardless of race, creed or ethnic group. The studies indicate minority ethnic parents are unlikely to raise diverse backgrounds with solicitors or experts unless the professional initiates that conversation. The onus is thus on the professionals.

This does not however mean accepting a parent's initial view that the values/practices they subsequently describe are necessarily representative of a particular group, culture or sub-group within a culture. Nor is it to suggest that some parents will not on occasion 'hide' behind ill-treatment of a child by reference to culturally diverse values/practices. But it may be necessary to raise more questions and undertake wider research and discussion in coming to a view with and about a parent. In some cases it will be necessary to document a parent's cultural framework in more detail – whether or not in the final analysis their views, practices and values are legally relevant.

This is not to deny that a more systematic unpacking these issues will present dilemmas for lawyers in presenting a 'best strategy' for their client, or that some of these issues will require a re-appraisal of training. But both lawyers and parents argued training is necessary to improve the confidence and knowledge base of lawyers, experts and some judges working 'cross culturally'.

If the endeavour is to demonstrate to parents involved in the family justice system that it is indeed fair and transparent, then to quote the sentiments of Lord Macpherson: justice has to be done, but also seen to be done – by those parents involved in proceedings. That is arguably a challenge that applies to all member states.

6.2   Theorising 'law' in diverse settings

Finally, I want to turn to the implications of this work for thinking about the role of child care law in diverse settings. It should not be 'read' as a movement towards cultural relativism or cultural pluralism in the state's response to child maltreatment in diverse households. Advocates of cultural pluralism admit to no overriding values in this field, suggesting all values are conditional with a plurality of incompatible values. As a theory about sources of values, cultural pluralists tend to support the view that there are many reasonable values. As Freeman argued in this field political ethics needs to be able to surmount the difficulties caused by conflicting values: we need a measuring rod by which values can be compared (Freeman 1998). The rights of parents from diverse ethnic groups/cultures to use 'physical chastisement', and views about equality between women with men are often cited as examples of stumbling blocks.

Outside of 'law', in cultural anthropology, one early approach to determining whether actions constituted child 'abuse' was the 'emic' and 'epic' model (Korbin 1980). Here it was argued professionals should be familiar with the viewpoint of members within the culture in question (emic perspective) and those of people outside the culture (epic perspective). One must then distinguish child-rearing practices viewed as acceptable by one group but generally unacceptable by the other – and then determine 'idiosyncratic' departures from culturally accepted standards within a culture.

My concern with the above approaches is that they share some common problems. First, there is a tendency to view 'culture' as a static phenomenon, failing to look at how practices within and across groups change, how patterns in Diaspora along with more recent forced migration patterns influence views and practices. There is in effect a failure to address the dynamic nature of 'culture'.

Second, there is also a tendency to treat minority ethnic groups as homogeneous, and in the UK at least a tendency to revert to notions of 'country of origin' as a starting point for deciding whether behaviours/attitudes are generally acceptable. This approach fails to address that practices in a homeland are likely to have changed considerably from the period in which a parent/grandparent was resident – and that views and practices in a homeland may equally be varied and complex.

Third, approaches tend to ignore the impact of gendered relationships within households, and the influence of education, class and caste – and how certain community groups, especially some women's groups, are challenging certain ideas and practices. Equally, approaches do offer a mechanism to address the challenges generated by inter-racial, inter-ethnic and inter-religious partnerships or how cultural frameworks and identifies are negotiated by children/young people of dual heritage. And, finally, such approaches do not necessarily offer an analysis of power or a 'space' to examine issues of racism in professional practices.

6.3 Intersectionality in child care law

Where does this leave us – if not back to the 'silences' of current practice and the cul-de-sac of cultural relativism as theory – how can we progress? While research demonstrates that child maltreatment occurs across all ethnic and religious group-ings, as indicated in my introduction, discourses of cultural anthropology, psychi-atry and psychology and indeed law have not been terribly helpful in addressing the interdisciplinary nature of this field.

'Law' dictates that we start with the child and an evidence-based approach to exploring harm and possibilities for changes in parenting. Social research encour-ages us to recognise that 'culture' is a dynamic and negotiated territory. But research also identifies that racism remains a reality in the lives of some parents and young people, and in contemporary social and political economy it has a shifting agenda and 'agency'. Some racism is overt some is covert and more diffi-cult to unearth.

Within child care law, theory and practice therefore we may be looking at what might be called 'paradigms of intersectionality'. In sociological and cultural stud-ies literature important intersections are identified as 'race and social class', 'race and gender' and 'race and nationalism'. In the child protection arena the key ques-tions seem to me to be: what are the important stages – the important intersec-tions – informing this field, and how can 'law' access and facilitate their explo-ration?

In the UK at least, research suggests we should focus on key findings regarding the concerns and allegations resulting in failures of parenting, addressing intersec-tions of diverse culture/religious/linguistic frameworks at the juncture of:
- The delivery of family support services to minority ethnic families
- Non-cooperation of such parents with welfare and health professionals
- Parental mental health problems and support services for minority ethnic mothers[24]
- Assessments of potential for change and engaging in minority ethnic par-enting
- Male violence to mothers in minority ethnic households.

In the UK we have been slow to address 'theory' in the field of care proceedings and minority ethnic parents – not least because we have lacked empirical data. What I have aimed to demonstrate through new data in this field is: (a) the inter-relationship between Parts III and IV of the Children Act 1989 Act in the con-text of the provisions of the ECHR; (b) the benefits of a multidisciplinary approach to this field; but finally (c) a theoretical and practice 'space' in which the significance of cultural/religious diversity but also an agenda on racism can be retained addressed, and thus judged.

References

Brophy J (2006) Research Review: Child Care Proceedings under the Children Act 1989. Research Series 5/06. London: DCA.

Brophy J, Jhutti-Johal J and McDonald E (2005) Minority ethnic parents, their solicitors and child protection litigation. London: The Department for Constitutional Affairs.

Brophy J (2005) Building Bridges in changing Worlds: Messages from International Child Maltreatment Research, in *Representing Children*, Vol. 17, No 2, pp 116-130.

Brophy J, Jhutti-Johal J and Owen C [2003a] Child ill-treatment in minority ethnic households, *Family Law*, October, pp 756-764.

Brophy J, Jhutti-Johal J and Owen C (2003b) *Significant Harm: child protection litigation in a multi-cultural setting*. London: Lord Chancellor's Department.

Brophy J [2003c] Diversity and child protection, *Family Law*, September, pp 674-678.

Brophy J, Brown L, Cohen S and Radcliffe P (2001) *Child psychiatry and child protection litigation*, London: Gatskill/Royal College of Psychiatry.

Brophy J (1999) Child Maltreatment and Cultural Diversity: A critical review of 'race' and culture in clinical writing and research on child maltreatment (report for the Nuffield Foundation). Oxford Centre for Family Law and Policy, Department of Social Policy and Social Work, University of Oxford.

Brophy J, Wale C and Bates P (1999) *Myths and Practices: A national survey of the use of experts in care proceedings,* London: British Agencies for Adoption and Fostering.

Brophy J, Bates, P, Brown L, Cohen S, Radcliffe P and Wale C (1999) Expert Evidence in Child Protection Litigation: Where do we go from here? London: The Stationery Office.

Brophy J & Bates P (1998) The position of parents using experts in care proceedings – A failure of partnership? *Journal of Social Welfare & Family Law*, Vol. 1, No 1, pp 21-48.

Department for Education and Skills (DfES) Independent Reviewing Officers – Guidance – Adoption and Children Act 2002. London. www.dfes.gov.uk/adoption

Department of Health (DoH) (1991) The Children Act 1989: Guidance and Regulations Volume 2 Family Support, Day Care and Educational Provision. London: The Stationery Office.

Department of Health (DoH) (1991) The Children Act 1989: Guidance and Regulations Volume 3 Family Placement. London: The Stationery Office.

Department of Health (DoH) (2000) Framework for the Assessment of Children in Need and their Families. London: The Stationery Office.

Department of Health (2000) Assessing Children in Need and their Families – Practice Guidance. London: The Stationery Office.

Department for Constitutional Affairs (DCA) (2003) Protocol for Judicial Case Management in Public Law Children Act Cases. London: DCA.

Freeman M (1998) Cultural Pluralism and the rights of the child. In Eekelaar J and Nhlapo T *The Changing Family: Family Forms and Family Law*. Oxford: Hart Publishing, pp 289-304.

Freeman P and Hunt J (1998) Parental Perspectives on Care Proceedings. London: The Stationery Office.

Elliott J M, Tong C K and Tan P M E H (1997) Attitudes of the Singapore public to actions suggesting child abuse. *Child Abuse and Neglect*, 21, 5, pp 445-464.

Finkelhor D and Korbin J (1988) Child abuse as an international issue, *Child Abuse and Neglect,* 12, pp 3-24.

Hunt J, Macleod A and Thomas C (1999) The Last Resort: Child Protection, the Courts and the 1989 Children Act. London: The Stationery Office.

Korbin J E, Coulton C J, Chard S, Platt-Houston C and Su, M (1998) Impoverishment and child maltreatment in African American and European American neighborhoods. *Development and Psychopathology*, 10, pp 215-233.

Korbin J (1991) Cross-cultural perspectives and research directions for the 21st century. *Child Abuse and Neglect*, 15, (Supp.1), pp 66-77.

Korbin J (1980) The cultural context of child abuse and neglect, *Child Abuse and Neglect,* 4, pp 3-13.

Macpherson W (1999) *The Stephen Lawrence Inquiry,* London: The Stationery Office. (Cm 4264-1).

Segal U A (1992) Child abuse in India: An empirical report on perceptions. *Child Abuse and Neglect*, 16, pp 887-908.

Segal U A (1995) Child abuse by the middle class? A study of professionals in Indian. *Child Abuse and Neglect,* 19, pp 217-231.

Segal U A (2002) A Framework for Immigration. USA, Columbia University Press.

White R (1998) Significant Harm: legal applications, in White R and Adcock M (eds) Significant Harm: Its management and Outcome. Croydon: Significant Publications.

Endnotes

1   In the research programme funded by the Department for Constitutional Affairs, the term 'diversity' is used to encompass these issues. However, there are concerns that as shorthand the term is at risk of sidestepping issues of racism. In the work discussed here we have used the term as a general 'shorthand', but in terms of substantive issues we retained a focus on cultural and religious diversity and race and racism.

2   Based on an international review of research, writing and comment on issues of 'diversity' and child maltreatment, see: Brophy J (2005) Building bridges in changing worlds: messages from international child maltreatment research, *Representing Children*, Vol. 17, No 2 pp 116-130; Brophy J [2003b] Diversity and child protection, *Family Law*, September, pp 674-678.

3   I would like to acknowledge the significant contribution to aspects of this stream of work from Jagbir Jhutti-Johal, Charlie Owen and Eleanor Macdonald. Thanks are also due to members of the Advisory groups for the four studies on which I have drawn.

4   In England and Wales these children are referred to as 'looked-after'. They may be looked after by the state voluntarily, following agreement between parents and a local authority (under s.20 of the Children Act 1989), or as a consequences of statutory intervention (under s.31 or 44 of the Children Act 1989).

5   This work was based on a national random survey of care cases concerning just under one thousand children in the mid 1990s. It indicated that black children and children of mixed heritage were over-represented in the sample compared to their representation in the general population (see Table 4.2, Brophy, Wale and Bates 1999:20). However, as argued in the study, caution is necessary and work remains to be done exploring issues of ethnicity and representation by geographical area.

6   Funded by the Nuffield Foundation.

7   This programme included research on tribunals, housing and criminal proceedings.

8   In total, The Department of Health (DoH) issued nine volumes of Guidance to The Children Act 1989.

9   Historically in the UK family proceedings have been referred to as 'adversarial' (compared for example to the French system which is depicted as inquisitorial). In practice, care proceedings in England and Wales are a 'hybrid': part adversarial, in that if necessary evidence may have to be tested, but increasingly 'inquisitorial', with courts taking responsibility for the management and control of proceedings (e.g. see DCA (2003) Judicial Case Management in Public Law Children Act Cases).

10   It is important to note that white British is also an ethnic group – albeit the dominant group, thus, where I refer to 'all ethnic groups' or 'all groups in this sample', this includes the white British sample.

11   To gain access to a stratified random sample of cases, records from the children's guardian service were used. The 2001 Population Census was used to select groups with the highest representation in the urban setting for the study. Numbers and groups were: 33 Black children (these were children of African, African-Caribbean and other Black origins), 23 South Asian children (these were children of Indian, Pakistani and Bangladeshi origin), plus 32 children of mixed-heritage and 47 white British children (Table 1.1 Brophy et al. 2003).

12   Court files contain applications, interim orders, statements, expert reports, directions of the court and information involved in preparing cases for a final hearing (e.g. information on interim hearings, whether orders were contested, people attending hearings and outcomes etc.).

13   See Brophy et al. 2003, pp 48-51 and Tables 7.1 and 7.2.

14   Care applications in England and Wales usually begin in the Magistrates' Family Proceedings Courts (heard by a panel of lay magistrates supported by a legally qualified adviser). Complex cases are transferred to a County Court Care Centre or less usually the High Court (on both cases heard by specialist judges). In this sample 56 cases started and completed in the lower court, 44 cases were transferred.

15   See note 14 above.

[16] In the sample as a whole, emotional abuse featured 72% of cases, while neglect featured in 86% of cases (Brophy et al 2003:76).

[17] Drug and alcohol abuse featured in all aggregated groups but on both counts it was highest in the White British (Table 4.5 – Brophy et al. 2003).

[18] An argument which features in some of the anthropological literature (see Brophy 2005).

[19] The Protocol for Judicial Case Management in Public Law Children Act Cases (DCA 2003) includes the duties of parties, experts and courts to consider issues of diversity at key stages in cases.

[20] It is important to note the parent sample was a small highly detailed qualitative study exploring experiences and views about the process; it is not a study of ethnic groups per se. Selection issues and procedures are outlined in Appendix I, Brophy et al. 2005.

[21] Interviews with minority ethnic solicitors demonstrated that 'ethnic matching' between parents and solicitors is not necessarily a solution as to how to negotiate this sensitive area – both solicitors and parents who were matched according to ethnic group raised concerns – Brophy et al 2005.

[22] Parents had thought an ethnically matched doctor would automatically understand certain values/practices in the parent's household and were disappointed/angry when issues were not raised or included in reports. Research with child psychiatrists in this field indicated some clinicians felt minority ethnic parents would prefer a doctor from the same ethnic group (Brophy et al. 2001). What this research is beginning to suggest is that knowledge, understanding, confidence and a willingness to initiate discuss this area may be at least as important for parents as a racial or ethnic 'matching'.

[23] In practice there are only two courts dedicated to family proceedings in England. Both are in inner London.

[24] Including services for drug and alcohol abuse.

Protecting the Challenging Child

Ruth Farrugia

1.   Introduction

Child Protection issues usually focus on violence, exploitation and abuse with comprehensive literature identifying and detailing legal responses. The reality is often a far cry from the legal standard even where states have knowingly committed to the promotion and protection of children's rights. Within this small section of the population is an even smaller sample of children who exhibit challenging behaviour and who need protection because or in spite of this. As anyone who has worked with children knows, it is not always easy to provide such protection to children who constantly challenge carers, counsellors and the system itself.

My paper will highlight the situation of children who come into the care system because of challenging behaviour as well as those who start to demonstrate this behaviour as a consequence of the abuse, violence or exploitation to which they have been subjected. The distinction between these children is often irrelevant in responding to their needs and, unless a medical condition is present, challenging behaviour seems to be invariably linked to some breakdown with the development process where child protection is of the essence.

In Malta, work has recently started on a project on challenging behaviour intended to make recommendations for policy to address the challenge. Quantitative and qualitative research will be conducted with children and their carers in order to present a tangible backdrop for the study. Once the findings are collated by late September 2005, a start will be made to draft a realistic set of principles aimed at the better protection of children who often threaten the protection system itself.

Apart from sharing the findings of this work, this article also looks into comparative literature on the topic and relevant legislation at local, regional and international levels. It concludes with a set of recommendations and principles which could dovetail with a wider agenda of child protection.

2.   Raison d'être of the study

Issues relating to children with challenging behaviour have long been the subject of concern and debate both among professionals as well as within the general population. Recent events regarding violent behaviour of school children in schools have led to teachers seeking exclusion of these children from the school on the grounds of their having very challenging behaviour. There has been industrial action by teachers to raise awareness of the issue and to try to convince the authorities that suitable protection is required for teaching staff.

While this aspect is certainly a cause for grave concern and while it is true that all workers should be assured of a safe environment, a number of child rights professionals have countered by trying to identify the reasons for such behaviour and to address the root cause rather than manage the effects. It is felt that unless the motivation for such response is recognised these children will be condemned to a dubious childhood and an uncertain future.

Children who 'challenge' services come from a wide variety of backgrounds, circumstances and situations and may include those who have experienced bereavement or who are family carers, those with special educational needs or learning disability, those who have been diagnosed with autistic spectrum disorder, those with emotional behavioural or mental health difficulties.

Services for children with challenging behaviour have been set up and have come and gone over the years. Institutional care and a number of other responses have been tailored to meet the demands of these children but for a variety of reasons, most seem to have been stopped or come to an untimely end. The reasons for this will be referred to within this text in the attempt to identify a suitable reaction to children exhibiting this behaviour.

Early in 2005, the Commissioner for Children decided to address the issue by calling a national conference to debate the concern. She then invited a number of professionals to coordinate working groups addressing the salient components of the topic, namely the historical background, the statistical dimension, the current available services, alternative services available in other jurisdictions and what the children themselves had to say on the matter. Throughout the summer of 2005, all the groups met and worked hard to fulfil their brief until in October 2005 the findings of each working group were put to a co-ordinating group who deliberated on the results and drew up a final paper with recommendations.[1] These suggestions will be put to another national conference to be held on 28 May 2006, where the Prime Minister is to receive the proposals and, hopefully, put them into action.

3.   Definitions

Challenging behaviours are best thought of as being a way in which people communicate and try and gain control over difficult situations. Where this involves violence to themselves or to other people or breaking things, one might consider physically holding the person to limit the damaging consequences of their behaviour. Physical interventions are quite rightly a contentious issue. With the emergence of more positive approaches to the management of challenging behaviour, there has come a recognition that we all have a responsibility to do so much more than just try to eliminate the behaviour. This has been fuelled by a growing emphasis on the rights of people with learning disabilities, and on the ethical and moral considerations together with a real commitment to working together to improve people's quality of life through person centred approaches.

Alternative definitions vary in the detailed approach to the content of aggressive

behaviour: Excessively aggressive behaviours are behaviours that could harm your child, you or other people. Excessively aggressive behaviours include:
- harming others physically, using their physical strength, height or physical build to overpower and/or hurt others
- bullying siblings, schoolmates, and/or you – including using taunts, threats and intimidation to make other people fear them
- spreading damaging rumours about someone else
- purposely mutilating or killing a small living animal or pet
- purposely destroying someone else's property and belongings
- stealing and the destruction of public property
- harming her/himself with self-cutting, self-harm or a suicide attempt
- sexually abusing another child.[2]

Although there are a number of definitions regarding children with challenging behaviour for the purposes of the study, very challenging behaviour was defined as, "Behaviours of such intensity, frequency or duration that the physical safety of the person or others is placed in serious jeopardy, or behaviour which seriously limits the person's access to ordinary settings, activities and experiences."[3]

4.   Parental authority and the legal framework
Parents are bound to provide care and protection to their children. The law clearly sets out a responsibility on parents to, "look after, maintain, instruct and educate the children of the marriage taking into account the abilities, natural inclinations and aspirations of the children".[4]

"A child shall be subject to the authority of his parents for all effects as by law established".[5] The opening section in the Maltese Civil Code on parental authority sets the tone for all issues relating to conduct of the child. The child is expected to comply with the rules set by the parents and it is only when the child reaches the age of fourteen that s/he is deemed to be competent to make suggestions which must be taken into account by the court. Prior to this age, the court may act on its discretion in hearing children but the practice varies widely from one court to another so that the only enforceable rule is the age fourteen limit imposed by law.

Children are expected to obey their parents in all that is lawful so that when a child leaves the parental home without the consent of the parents, police assistance may be sought for his / her return.[6] This is in keeping with the notion of vicarious responsibility since the child is always deemed to be accountable to the parents and the parents in turn accountable for all actions of the child.

Where a child cannot be controlled by the parent or parents, the court may be petitioned to have the child removed from the parents' direct control. In this case the parents may place the child in alternative forms of care, "which the court will according to circumstances consider suitable, to be at the expense of the parents, cared for and treated in such manner as the court may deem conducive to the discipline and education of the child."[7]

Where parents are unable or unwilling to provide care, protection and control of their children and do not take steps to remedy the situation, the Children and Young Persons (Care Orders) Act[8] comes into action. This legislation enables the state to intervene in protecting the child from the inadequacies of the parents by placing him/her in alternative care subject to specific rules at law. Once a care order has been issued and confirmed by the court[9] the Minister for Family and Social Solidarity takes over the parental authority removed form the parents insofar as care and custody are concerned. In practice, this care is entrusted to the agency directing foster carers or a specific institution and the children are supervised by regular hearings held by the Children and Young Persons Board which keeps a record of each child's care plan and progress or deterioration as the case may be.

It should be pointed out that a Commissioner for Children was appointed in 2003[10] but to date there is no Children Act in Malta. All legislation relating to children is dispersed throughout other laws and codes and many sections require drastic amendment to bring them into keeping with modern basics in child law. A number of crucial issues such as fostering and institutional care are not even regulated at law and remain subject to practical *dicta* which leave much to be desired in terms of rights and obligations. This need for an adequate legal framework that supports and gives a legal backing to child-centred service delivery has been articulated since the fifties and continues to be a major lack in the system.

A comprehensive legal framework is needed to give legal backing to:
  - child-centred services and programmes
  - involuntarily admitting a child in care
  - outlining the responsibilities of parents, service brokers, providers and the State towards the more vulnerable of its citizens
  - action in providing for termination of parental rights when appropriate
  - legislating in favour of those providing foster care
  - regulation of international adoptions.[11]

The Care Orders Act has recently been impacted by the introduction of subsidiary legislation but this has in no way directly affected the fundamental legal issues of parental responsibility and child autonomy. There is still no possibility of judicial review for care orders and where the juvenile court is seized of a case, the alternatives are scant, mainly because there are no separate residences for children sentenced to a care order for control purposes.[12] Furthermore, the voluntary placement of children into care as prospected under Articles 134 and 96 means that the supervisory provisions of care orders do not apply to these children and there is no effective way to ensure their progress in the system or the contrary.[13] Finally, care orders can only be issued for children who have not attained their sixteenth birthday[14] and the gap in care for sixteen to eighteen year olds is an issue of concern.

The children interviewed in this study were unanimously clear in their appraisal of the care orders system and voiced the need for a renewed focused attention on the law and its regulations, particularly insofar as the modalities of contact with family are concerned. Although a number of issues should be easily attainable and identifiable, in practice the children felt that the Board was not timely in its responses and that the social workers frequently put off issues which the children deemed of importance because of delays in communicating with the Board. One of the conclusions is in fact to recommend that the roles of social workers and the Board should be clearly determined, training provided and that specific guidelines and procedures should be made available.

Furthermore, although the Children and Young Persons (Care Orders) Act makes direct reference to the provision of care for children in need of control, this provision has never been put into force because of the dearth of services available. The court faced with the alternatives offered has no option but to place the child in a custodial setting, to entrust him/her to an institutional home which is not equipped to respond to his/her needs or to return him/her to the parents who may have contributed directly to the situation pertaining. The final working group felt that community support services for children on care orders for control purposes should be made available. This would give young people a choice at present lacking and extend a legal obligation to ensure cooperation with the professionals involved. A widely felt recommendation concerned the issue that, "the whole care orders structure requires an overhaul, including amendments to effect a shift towards the increased role of the judiciary in issuing, monitoring and terminating a care order."[15]

With respect to children who exhibit challenging behaviour and fall foul of the law, the juvenile court also requires a number of substantial changes in order to render it better equipped to assist such children. The court should always have the authority to hear cases involving minors less than 18 years[16] of age since the present practice is to try sixteen to eighteen year olds with older persons where a crime is committed with an older person. Furthermore, the court should have access to trained personnel from various disciplines such as probation, police, psychology and education services which should complement the work carried out by the court and its personnel, although all these persons would greatly benefit from joint training in the area of children with challenging behaviour.

The common feeling among professionals involved in the study was that all efforts need to be made to avoid the need to exclude children and young people from schools. It was strongly felt that this exclusion is often the final straw that leads to truancy and antisocial behaviour and the lack of response to the child's special needs at that stage is seriously detrimental to his or her present and future well being. Interestingly, at the same time the concern was being raised in the British Parliament where regulations in the education sector, including exclusion measures were being debated: "The common characteristic among many young people in the criminal justice system is that they started by being excluded from school".[17]

5. Statistics

One of the most urgent recommendations to come out of this study was the need to address the compilation and storage of data related to children with challenging behaviour. The working group in this area found that recorded data concerning children was not kept in standardized format. Indeed, often this was misplaced or lost and at times not kept at all. The end result was that many services were not in a position to provide all or parts of the data requested. Moreover, some data is kept in such a way as to merge it into other statistical information whereby duplication of data and confusion with transitional movements between services follows.

Another interesting issue related to the interpretation of the Data Protection Act. The working group related that from the data collection process they carried out, it appeared that in most organisations, the Data Protection Act was not yet fully understood and was wrongly implemented. They were frequently provided with information which was not required or left without specific information they had requested. A number of organisations cited the Data Protection Act as their reason for failing to provide information, even though the Commissioner for Children Act specifically states that the office is empowered to access information and statistics when required for the purposes of an investigation.[18] As the covering letter which the group sent out made direct reference to this, the final working group echoed the concern at this reluctance to share valuable information which could serve the best interest of the children being studied. Perhaps the law should also include a clarification as to the term 'investigation' since it may have been the case that the study was not deemed to fall under the provisions of Article 15.

At the end of the day, the final working group felt that the lack of information available with regard to statistics was in itself significant and it was agreed that a strong recommendation should be made for a standardised legally enforced system in which data is stored and maintained across all services offering support to children.[19] It was suggested that such data should be available and accessible to the public utilising a format that meets the requirements of both the Data Protection Act and the right of citizens to freedom of information.

One major concern ensuing from the final observations of the working group on statistical collection emanated from their figure of 1.5% incidence of all children being considered as exhibiting very challenging behaviour. Instead of a sense of relief at the number, the unanimous feeling was one of apprehension since this was perceived to indicate that either a number of children are not receiving adequate attention for their behaviour or that the services concerned had simply failed to provide the real picture. In addition, the figure is low compared to the EU average and it was strongly felt that 1.5% does not represent the true situation due to lack of forthcoming information from existing services. Incidentally, it was suggested that gender difference in the way very challenging behaviour is exhibited may partly account for lower incidence in females since girls may not be as easily identified as boys.

The final working group made an additional recommendation to enable ongoing extensive research with sufficient legal backing to access existing and future data to compile the necessary statistics. This would serve to ensure that minimum standards of quality service provision are maintained as established and that they monitor the history of the children transiting from one service to another. This would also function to compile a history profile of each child accessing services in the effort to ensure that no child falls out of the service network and attempt to identify alternative service provision which is oriented towards the needs of the client.[20]

It was also deemed essential to focus on the shortcomings of the services provided and to carry out evaluations of programmes as an integral part of service delivery. Although the launch of new services is frequently viewed with great relief given the paucity of available programmes, it was strongly felt that pilot projects should first be carried out to ensure that the service provided is based on thorough research directly lined to the needs of the domestic realities. Weaknesses in ministerial co-ordination were also identified as crucial to the success of any initiatives in this field. Further research still needs to be undertaken to determine the extent of the problems and the effectiveness of the various interventions in the Maltese context.

6.   The children's position

6.1.   The research project
The children's ideas and words were gathered and presented in such a way that they provided information about the whole range of existing services and possible alternatives, rather than about any specific service. The group dealing with children's feedback spent considerable time narrowing down the focus of the study and drawing up the questionnaire administered to elicit responses. In the end, the group identified the main purpose of the study to listen to the perceptions of children about the services they were in and to record their ideas about other possible alternatives.

The underlying principle motivating the group was Article 12 of the United Nations Convention on the Rights of the Child:

> *States Parties shall assure to the child who is capable of forming his or her own views the right to express those views freely in all matters affecting the child, the views of the child being given due weight in accordance with the age and maturity of the child.*

One of the main questions of interest to the research group was to find out what the children's perceptions were relating to why and how they ended up where they currently were. They were asked whether they understood why they were in a particular service; were they aware that their behaviour was experienced as challenging at times; did they know what the aims and goals of being in the service were? The second research question was to elicit the children's experience of the service they were in. To this end they were asked how they felt about the service; what was their experience in it? Finally, the third question looked towards the future and asked the children: whether they had any suggestions; what did they feel would help them move on; what kind of help did they feel they needed?

The methodology chosen for this study was a qualitative one where a total of 27 children where chosen to be interviewed individually. The interviews were conducted by eight researchers. Much initial discussion took place prior to the interviews and was considered necessary so as to achieve consistency throughout the interviewing process.

A main bone of contention centred round the selection of the children to be interviewed. It was felt that the children should truly exhibit some form of challenging behaviour, but there was a marked reluctance in the group to depend on the professional workers' or on the parents' judgments. The research team agreed that doing so would allow for the possibility of bias and subjectivity in the selection procedure and thus reduce its validity. "Lack of agreed definitions of what constitutes challenging behaviour makes it difficult to gauge the full extent of it. Perception of poor behaviour is conditioned both by the context and by the observer's expectations."[21]

Eventually a decision was taken, together with the Child Commissioner, that the most objective way to carry out the process was to interview children who were currently in services and/or programmes that were addressing the issue of very challenging behaviour. The services chosen were Fejda, Suret il-Bniedem (Casa Spinelli and Casa Leopoldo), YPU, YOURS, and the special schools Mater Dei and St. Patrick's Craft Centre. A further decision was taken to limit the ages of the children interviewed to those between 10 and 18 years of age.

This decision effectively excluded the perspectives of children with challenging behaviour who were not currently, or who had never been, in those specific services. There was also the apprehension that it might also include children who, although using part of the service, did not exhibit challenging behaviour. Finally the research team opted for the pragmatic approach and interviewed children making use of services in the hope that this would reduce bias and ensure the validity of the study.[22]

6.2   What the children said

A number of initial questions to the children interviewed related to their concept of family. Most children were open and straightforward in their descriptions of their family. It was a salient element of the whole interviewing process to find that most of the descriptions children offered of their family and of past experiences were expressed with a major undertone of grief and loss. This was particularly apparent when the children recounted noteworthy memories, highlighting the death of a significant family member, the realisation that a parent was not biologically related or events in the family story such as illness and substance abuse.

A number of children highlighted their loss of innocence and their perception of life once removed from the family and on entering the service where this is residential. Many harked back to a happier childhood prior to entry in the service or the lack of any happy memories from home. It is worth pointing out that there were six different services observed in this research and each one is different in scope and application.

Having said this, when children were asked for their experiences in the service, most of the responses clearly illustrated the experience as negative with children strongly suggesting that they would advise against a hypothetical friend going there and with one child actually advocating that this friend should escape and run away. The children largely related feelings of lost freedom and the sensation of being cut off from family. A small number were deprecating of the care workers and of the chores they were forced to do and the lack of liberty in the residential service, with one respondent describing it as worse than her perception of being in a prison.

However, on the whole, the children responded that they related well with the professional staff, highlighting their need for significant relationships.[23] A recent British study[24] has found that for effective teaching and learning and improved behaviour, whether in mainstream, special or 'alternative' settings, children with challenging behaviour need to feel that they are wanted and valued by at least some of the professional staff.[25]

Children were interviewed about what they found most helpful in the service. They referred to the support they appreciate when they manage a significant relationship which is based on good communication and the ability to exchange views and ideas with someone who is ready to listen. They were largely grateful for the time most professional staff takes to give them attention and to validate their concerns.

It was also deemed important to clarify whether the children were aware of why they were in the service or programme and whether clear goals, guidelines and action plans within a timeframe had been specified. Several children explained that coming to the service was the result of a significant episode that led to a sequence of events. Two participants described how their behaviour changed greatly because of happenings at school. This could be somewhat related to research findings and namely to the observation that the challenging behaviour of many younger pupils arises mainly as a result of poor language, social skills and emotional development fitting to their age.[26] Other episodes related by the children included: being bullied; peer pressure; disobedience and risky behaviour; no longer fitting in a residential home; family difficulties, abuse; and dealing with death. The research group found it interesting to compare these factors to the definition of challenging behaviour.

Failure to obey authority both at school and at home was identified as a factor which led the child to begin using the service. Impulsivity was another factor, which emerged in two of the interviews. One person impulsively acted out in a way that could have caused seriously injury to herself and/or one of the professional staff. Her explanation for doing so was that during a session at the psychiatrist she felt that she had been the subject of the discussion to the exclusion of her input and that the carer had used the session to put her in a bad light. Another participant actually described the pattern of impulsivity detailing changes of mood and reaction and subsequent removal to a number of residential homes.

Most children related the service they were in to their 'challenging behaviour'. The children did understand that challenging behaviour was somehow connected to the service they were in. What differs across the interviews was their understanding of 'challenging behaviour' and their construct of the scope of the service. For some children, even though they were actually in the service, it was still somewhat unclear to them how the service was supposed to be helping and supporting them.[27] Only a few children were clearly aware that their behaviour was inappropriate.

The school experience was identified differently, with some children describing their experience in a very positive way and others perceiving it as a problematic time. Research shows that a significant proportion of pupils with challenging behaviour have poor language and social skills and limited concentration spans.[28] It was interesting to note that two respondents explained that they had had to change from one school to another several times. One of them, who was still in primary school (5-11 years of age), had already been to four different schools. While another participant, who was at the end of secondary school (11-16 years of age), had also been to four different schools.

A number of children described the transition from primary to secondary school as traumatic and listed a number of experiences which highlighted a drastic change in their experiences at school. Although many children had experienced a happy primary education, settling into a new school, making new friends and coping with a different curriculum posed problems for a number of others.

Finally, the interviews showed that children who had difficult, negative relationships with either their father or their mother were more likely to be anxious, depressed, worried or to be aggressive or have problems at school. Certainly, the home life that many children have to contend with did not make their behaviour any easier to cope with, particularly within a school setting which is largely intolerant of individuals who do not fit the mould.

The strongest message that emerged from the interviews was the children's wish to be heard and understood. Most of the children mentioned how important they felt it was to have someone who was ready to listen to them and value what they had to say. Two of the participants emphasised the importance of listening to both child and parent and felt aggrieved that many a time the parent's point of view or account of the story was give more credibility than their own. Issues relating to confidentiality were also raised with one child expressing regret at her feelings shared in confidence being relayed to others. Children also expected time and opportunity to make their comments about the service and for this feedback to be given due weight. Where residents' meetings were held, children expressed the wish for more regular occasions to exchange views and make proposals.

6.3 Recommendations

The research report's conclusions highlight the need for the needs of children to be understood before any service can hope to be effective. Services for children are to ensure that the child's right of a place in a family and forming secure lasting attachments is respected. It should be a *sine qua non* that before separating a child from the family, due regard is given to the child's ensuing anxiety and sense of loss and longing which can hardly ever be compensated for. Failing to validate this feeling and speak about it openly with the child has been shown to have negative effects so that relationships based on trust, respect, and good communication are essential to the transition into a care setting and fundamental if the child is perceive the staff positively.

Although it true that the child has a need and right to protection against harm, this should not come at the expense of the child's right to make his or her wishes known and voice heard. In the case of older children or young people, the possibility of choice when it comes to the decision of accessing and/ or selecting services should be offered as often as possible. While underlining the principle of best interests of the child, this should not be used as a pretext for making paternalistic decisions to the exclusion of children's wishes.

7. Responses to children with challenging behaviour

Children with challenging behaviour have been identified in a variety of settings. They may be present in the school system, residential care, mental hospitals, secure settings or in the privacy of the home. Responsibility to respond to the needs of children exhibiting challenging behaviour shifts constantly. The law places the initial responsibility directly on the shoulders of the parents, however where they decline or are deemed incompetent[29] such duty the state must take over. It is unthinkable that any child should be left without a competent adult or watch over, protect and care for him/her.

Irrelevant to state intervention, whether at the behest of the parents or of its own motion, the child is part of the education system. This prevailing party is present at all stages of the child's development and plays a massive role in the containment, reaction to and solution of the issue of challenging behaviour. To a large extent, it is immaterial who is entrusted with parental authority, be it the parents, the Minister in the guise of the residential home care team or foster carers. In the final analysis, children spend a huge portion of their daily life at school and their acceptance and adaptation within the school setting impact dramatically on their behaviour, rather than the other way round. This is why the issue of exclusion from school takes on such a powerful dimension in the life of any child but even more so in the case of a child who exhibits challenging behaviour.

Concrete measures advocated as a response to children who do not fit in at school and welfare needs in foreign counterparts, currently make a distinct move away from the medical model and opt towards the social model of resolving conflicts and finding adequate solutions. They also aim towards the rehabilitation of institutionalised persons back into the community.

Although what follows may be a somewhat harsh appraisal of affairs, the trend in Malta has generally been to attempt to solve the problem at source and when this fails to remove the problem and place it out of sight. For this reason, as in every other problematic social situation, the response should be veering away from the traditional method of attending to children who manifest very challenging behaviour. It needs to approach the issue from a lateral angle and think of it in terms of the child's needs rather than the more general impact on the environment, whether this is school or any other social setting. At present the response is to remove the child into residential care where a place is available.

While it is true that residential homes may always be needed and present as a possible option to tackle such behaviour, the profile of these homes may well deserve redefining. Services which are community based and therefore will not remove the child from his or her normal living environment should receive better investment in recognition of the trauma involved when removing a child from his or her family environment. Quite apart from the beneficial effects to the child where this is possible, there are also substantial financial savings to be made as the costs of residential care are frequently exorbitant. The savings could then be pooled into other support structures and services in the best interest of the child.

These community services would entail the joined forces of a number of professionals from varied backgrounds who together could address the invariably complex and critical situations faced by these children. Once appropriate training is provided and investment made into the setting up of such teams, early diagnosis and intervention could become the norm. It is true that such an initiative would entail substantial outlay in order to put it into action and to provide support for the child, family and community as a whole.

The recommendations of the final working group are that such a team service should be backed up by adequately resourced community support services. These should in turn be directed by an assessment team but this should follow in direct consultation with the family of the child, taking into consideration that such support package should be needs lead and not service provider lead. This final observation is perhaps the most crucial element of the recommendation, as the tendency in many areas seems to be the provision of a service with reluctance to make alterations to suit the user. Certainly this is the situation within the educational setting on the whole and undoubtedly contributes to some of the problem.

It is envisaged that there should be no preconceived support packages, forcing prospective child clients to fit into the support service. Instead, each support plan should be individualized and tailored to each specific child's needs:

Such a support package should be carried out by qualified and trained members of staff who are best suited for each task set out in the support plan. Furthermore medical and medication alternatives should only constitute a last resort to address such behaviours rather than being the primary solution as this in turn could create more far reaching negative effects on the child which would be carried throughout the child's life.[30]

The issue of exclusion from school has already been referred to in this paper. Certainly, as of right, children should be assured access to main stream services enjoyed by every other child living in the same community. It is unacceptable when children are precluded from main stream activities and establishments without being offered other alternatives suited to their needs. This could increase their sense of rejection and aggravate the challenging behaviour manifested. Indeed, such reaction could culminate in the necessitation of eventual residential placement later in life either in a correctional facility or a medical institution. The repercussions of these steps are commonly known to all in their damage to the person and to society.

In the case of a child taken into care under a care order, it is even more damning to note that the state which becomes responsible *in loco parentis* frequently carries out such exclusion with such deleterious effects on the child. Whereas a child in a family would have a parent or parents to plead his or her case and attempt to bring about acceptance into mainstream activity, in the case of a child under a care order such eventuality is infrequent and reliant upon the good will of the over-burdened social worker dealing with the case. Ironically the child who needs most attention may be most neglected. Issues relating to state responsibility and liability in this field are still in their infancy in Malta.

It is a matter for consensus that residential services should only be a last alternative and resorted to after exhausting all other possible remedies. Even in this case, these should always and also be community based. The introduction of specialised fostering would be beneficial to children with challenging behaviour, although this is dependent on suitable planning and support for prospective foster parents. This model would help to minimise the trauma children experience when entering into residential care. Again, in the current scenario where there is not even a legal framework to support standard foster care, this is a recommendation which requires a great deal of good will on the part of the authorities concerned.

Prospects realistically show that there will however remain the need for some residential service. Ideally this should be provided in a community based, home like environment consisting of a normal community dwelling with a very small number of children with substantial child staff ratios necessary to such an environment. One of the most negative effects of residential care perceived by the children was the continual turnover of staff who work in shift and who may leave the service after relatively short periods of employment. Links with the child's family, where this is possible, should be encouraged and supported and the numbers kept down to a small family setting in the effort to minimise the anonymity that comes with larger residential services and the ensuing feelings of loss and inability to bond.

Conclusions to the research report on children highlight the need for existing residential services based on regimental and rigid schedules and rules to evaluate their effectiveness. They pose a number of questions directly related to the well being of the child as a result of the practices operated within these institutions. The services are invited to evaluate whether the rigid rules they tend to apply help the individual child and whether there are alternative approaches which could help address the challenging behaviour. They ask whether the system itself might be making a contribution to the reactions displayed by the child, particularly in terms of aggression and rebellion.

This is not to say that all rules are to be removed. The child needs to know what is acceptable and what is not and that there are consequences for unacceptable behaviour. However, this needs to be clear to the child at the outset and the consequences proportionate to the deed, both from the child's and the adult's perspective. Any action taken should be placed within the aims of the service towards helping the child rather than as strictly punitive.

In the final analysis, no matter the service, the important thing is that it should have a pleasant environment which is warm and welcoming to the child or young person. All efforts should be concerted towards providing safety and comfort, together with respect for the child's personal and private space. In a country as small as Malta, issues related to stigmatisation are acutely felt and deserve priority. For children leaving a residential service, it may be further burden to face in integrating into society.

Prior to the Child Commissioner's intervention, evaluation of the system in Malta seemed more concerned with teachers' safety issues than with what was to become of children exhibiting challenging behaviour. Since the start of the project some incidents of violence in schools have cause the debate to escalate and the issue of exclusion has again come to the forefront of what has become a dispute.

It is a given that no worker should be exposed to violence and should be assured safety, dignity and respect so that all teachers are right to expect this from their students, superiors and co-workers. However, when a child does not conform to the general expectations of the education system, the alternative cannot simply be expulsion, particularly where the child does not have an alternative educational establishment to go to. The right of the child to receive an education is registered both under the United Nations Convention on the Rights of the Child and as part of the Education Act.

There seem to be numerous reasons for children exhibiting challenging behaviour and not one of them is the result of a wish to be a nuisance. Children who exhibit such behaviour need to be identified as such and to receive due support and assistance. The final responsibility to do this rests with the state. Although the balance between children, parents, and the state, shifts from time to time, "the state, in its various forms, must be able to intervene over an increased breadth of behaviour and to patrol public space. The 'community' gains a legal place, through new appeals to the state to control public space and to control the behaviour of children".[31]

In Scotland the introduction of antisocial behaviour legislation has come into conflict with the laws relating to children's welfare services. The Antisocial Behaviour etc. (Scotland) Act 2004 redefines distinctions between deserving and undeserving children, between good and bad parents, and between troubled and troublesome children. Malta is still at a stage where all these nuances could be taken into account in providing one coherent response to the challenging child. On 28 April 2006, a national conference is due to place the results of the research in the public domain and offer the Prime Minister a number of options in response. One can only hope that effective measures will be taken to address the issue as speedily as possible in the best interests of all children.

Endnotes

1. The author of this paper formed part of the working group listening to children and was a member of the final co-coordinating group making recommendations.
2. One Parent Families http://www.oneparentfamilies.org.uk/.
3. This was the definition agreed to within the launch conference chaired by the Commissioner for Children Mrs. Sonia Camilleri - Tfal u ˉghaẓagh b'Imgieba Difficli Hafna 2005.
4. Civil Code, Chapter 16 Laws of Malta, Article 3B. Although this article is directed to children in marriage, the sentiment is echoed in Article 7 which states: (1) "Parents are bound to look after, maintain, instruct and educate their children in the manner laid down in section 3B of this Code." Furthermore, amendments introduced by Act XVIII.2004 have removed any last vestiges of discrimination between children born within wedlock and those born outside wedlock.
5. Civil Code, Chapter 16 Laws of Malta, Article 131 (1)
6. Civil Code, Chapter 16 Laws of Malta, Article 132 (1) and (3)
7. Civil Code, Chapter 16 Laws of Malta, Article 134 (2). There still exists an element of discrimination in the treatment afforded to the child born out of wedlock who refuses to "follow the directions of the parent in regard to his conduct and education" without just cause. In this case, the parent is relieved from the obligation of maintenance (Article 96).
8. Chapter 285 Laws of Malta.
9. This is required in cases where there is opposition to the issue of the care order. The hearing is dealt with by the Juvenile Court (Chapter 287 Laws of Malta).
10. Chapter 462 Laws of Malta.
11. Report of the Final Working Group, unpublished document 2005 (to be published shortly).
12. At present YOURS which is the juvenile detention centre within the Correctional Facility is the only possibility.
13. Civil Code, Chapter 16 Laws of Malta, Article 134.
   (1) It shall be lawful for the parents, if they are unable to control the child, to remove him from the family, assigning to him, according to the means of the parents, such maintenance as is strictly necessary.
   (2) In any such case, the parents may also, where necessary and upon obtaining the authority of the court of voluntary jurisdiction, place the child, for such time as is stated in the decree, in some alternative form of care, which the court will according to circumstances consider suitable, to be, at the expense of the parents, cared for and treated in such manner as the court may deem conducive to the discipline and education of the child.
   (3) The demand for such authority may be made even verbally; and the court shall make the necessary order thereon without any formal proceedings, and without giving its reasons therefor.
14. The only exception to this rule is in the case of unaccompanied minors under the Refugees Act where a care order may be issued up until the age of eighteen years.
15. Report of the Final Working Group, unpublished document 2005 (to be published shortly).
16. In its concluding observations the United Nations Committee on the Rights of the Child, after considering Malta's initial report in June 2000, stated:
   Para 49. The Committee welcomes the establishment of a special rehabilitation programme for girls in conflict with the law (e.g. Fejda) and it is encouraged that a similar programme is being considered for boys. Nevertheless, concern is expressed at the low age of criminal responsibility (9 years); at the assumption, contained in the State party's legislation, that a child aged between 9 and 14 years could act with 'mischievous intent'; and at the exclusion of children aged between 16 and 18 years from the juvenile justice system.
17. Debate in the British House of Commons: Education (Pupil Exclusions) (Miscellaneous Amendments) (England) Regulations 2004 Fourth Standing Committee on Delegated Legislation Monday 10 May 2004 [Mr. Alan Hurst in the Chair] Education (Pupil Exclusions) (Miscellaneous Amendments) (England) Regulations 2004.
18. Article 15, Commissioner for Children Act, Chapter 462 Laws of Malta.
   Article 15: (1) For the purpose of an investigation the Commissioner may require any person who possesses documents or information relevant to the investigation to:
   (a) produce such documents; and, or
   (b) furnish the information in writing; and, or

(c)   attend at a specified time and place and give oral information on oath.

(2) The Commissioner shall have the power to summon witnesses and to administer an oath to any person concerned in the investigation and require them to give the relevant information.

(3) Notwithstanding the provisions of the preceding two sub articles, no person shall be compelled to give information or produce documents which such person could not be compelled to give or produce in civil or criminal proceedings before a Court.

[19]   Final Working Group report op.cit.

[20]   Final Working Group report, op. cit.

[21]   Ofsted report 2005: Managing Challenging Behaviour based on A study of children and young people who present challenging behaviour, directed by Dr John Visser, University of Birmingham, November 2003.

[22]   Unfortunately the worst fears of the research team were realised when one child interviewed was felt to be misplaced given that she was identified as not exhibiting any form of challenging behaviour. A referral was made to the Child Commissioner for action to be taken.

[23]   The term 'professional staff' refer to all the professionals involved in the children's lives and includes psychologists, social workers, occupational therapists, psychiatrists, care workers and so on.

[24]   Visser J., A study of children and young people who present challenging behaviour, November 2003 cited as part of the Ofsted report 2005 supra.

[25]   This has been emphasised in: published studies of the University of Birmingham's EBD Research Team Daniels et al (1998), Cole et al (1998); Visser, Daniels and Cole, (2001): and other researchers including Munn et al (2000).

[26]   Ofsted report 2005: Managing Challenging Behaviour based on A study of children and young people who present challenging behaviour, directed by Dr John Visser, University of Birmingham, November 2003.

[27]   Report of research group.

[28]   Ofsted report 2005: Managing Challenging Behaviour based on A study of children and young people who present challenging behaviour, directed by Dr John Visser, University of Birmingham, November 2003.

[29]   Civil Code, Chapter 16 Laws of Malta Article 154.

[30]   Final Working Group report.

[31]   Tisdall E.K.M., Antisocial behaviour legislation meets children's services: challenging perspectives on children, parents and the state, Critical Social Policy, Vol. 26, No. 1, 101-120 (2006).

Child Protection in Accordance with Human Rights and Children's Rights

Caroline Forder

1.   Introduction

This paper deals with the role of human rights and children's rights in private law mechanisms of child protection, and in this to engage in retrospection, reflection and the future. I shall pay particular attention to the interplay – and their interaction in positive and negative ways – of children's rights and human rights. The paper is divided into four parts: first, an overview of the relevant provisions of international law; second, the rules of international law regarding the sustaining of the parent-child relationship in the child protection context; third, the positive action required by international law to order to achieve adequate protection of children; fourth, the quality of care provided subsequent to initial intervention, discussed in the light of international law.

2.   An overview of the relevant provisions of international law

The key international law provision on child protection is Article 19 of the UN Convention on the Rights of the Child (hereafter CRC):[1]

> 1. *States Parties shall take all appropriate legislative, administrative, social and educational measures to protect the child from all forms of physical or mental violence, injury or abuse, neglect or ill-treatment, maltreatment or exploitation including sexual abuse while in the care of parent(s) or guardian(s), legal guardian(s) or any other person who has care of the child.*
> 2. *Such protective measures should, as appropriate, include effective procedures for the establishment of social programmes to provide necessary support for the child and for those who have care of the child, as well as for other forms of prevention and for identification, reporting, referral, investigation, treatment, and follow-up of instances of child maltreatment described heretofore, and, as appropriate, for judicial involvement.*

Article 19 CRC presents a full range of possible responses to child abuse and neglect. It calls for:
- Establishment of social programmes for the prevention of abuse and neglect in the family, including awareness-raising programmes amongst the population, including parents, teachers and children themselves;
- A system for reporting child abuse or suspected abuse;
- A system for responding to such reporting and establishing where help is needed;
- A judicial system which balances the conflicting interests between parent and child whenever compulsory intervention in the family is undertaken;
- A system for providing effective assistance and care to the children who

have suffered abuse and neglect, including, where possible, restoration to and reparation of the child's original family;
- A system for providing compensation (including financial) to the children damaged as a result of reasonably preventable child abuse and neglect;
- The undertaking of research regarding all or any of the above;
- Securing that, for the carrying out of all these missions, sufficient trained professionals are available;
- A clear mandatory norm in the legislation making clear that corporal punishment does not play a part in the upbringing of children at home or at school.

Article 19 may be the central provision on child protection in the CRC, but the duty to protect the child from abuse and neglect is present in many other articles of that convention, such as Article 3 (best interests of the child), Article 6 (right to life and survival and development), Article 16 (private life), Article 20 (right to special care in case of having no family), Article 21 (safe system of adoption), Article 23 (special care of disabled child), Article 24 (right to health), Article 25 (right to review of treatment), Article 27 (right to a minimum standard of living), Article 31 (right to rest and play), Article 32 (protection from economic exploitation), Article 33 (protection from drug abuse), Article 34 (protection from sexual abuse), Article 35 (protection from abduction), Article 36 (protection from other forms of exploitation), Article 37 (protection from torture or other cruel, inhuman or degrading treatment or punishment), Article 38 (protection from engagement in armed conflicts) and Article 39 (duty to promote recovery of child victims). Furthermore, one should not forget Principle 9 of the Declaration of the Rights of the Child:[2] "The child shall be protected against all forms of neglect, cruelty and exploitation. He shall not be subject to traffic in any form."

Apart from the conventions specific to children, there are other international instruments of importance. It is possible to divide the rights into human rights applicable to the child protection situation, and specific children's rights applicable to that situation. Children are protected by the human rights protection given by the International Covenant on Civil and Political Rights[3] (hereafter: ICCPR) and the European Convention on Human Rights[4] (hereafter: ECHR), with the attractive consequence that they are able to enjoy the more powerful enforcement mechanisms offered by the human rights conventions including, since the optional protocol of the Women's Convention came into force on 22 December 2000,[5] the right of minor men and women to petition for violation of the Women's Convention.[6] The right of individual petition includes, respectively, the right of bringing an individual complaint to the Human Rights Committee in Geneva, the European Court of Human Rights (hereafter: European Court) in Strasbourg, or the Committee for the Elimination of Discrimination Against Women (hereafter: CEDAW). The right of individual petition offers a more potent remedy in case of violation than the reporting procedure provided for under the Children's Convention.[7] Both the ECHR and the ICCPR provide, in Articles 3 and 7, first sentence, respectively, "No one shall be subjected to torture or to cruel, inhuman or degrading treatment or punishment." It is worth mentioning in particular that the ICCPR – a human rights convention – contains a specific provision on the rights of children. Article 24 reads:

> *Every child shall have, without any discrimination as to race, colour, sex, language, religion, national or social origin, property or birth, the right to such measures of protection as are required by his status as a minor, on the part of his family, society and the State.*

Also the Charter of Fundamental Rights of the European Union[8] contains a special provision – also Article 24 – on the rights of children. These two provisions embody the right of children to such protection and care as is necessary for their well-being. The Brussels II Regulation provides that the rules regarding the grounds of jurisdiction which the Regulation seeks to regulate are shaped in the light of the best interests of the child.[9] By contrast the ECHR contains no special provision on children's rights. However, it does contain a number of provisions of relevance to the human rights of children, of which particular mention should be made in the present context of child protection of Articles 3, 5, 6 and 8 ECHR. Article 3 states that, "No one shall be subjected to torture or to inhuman or degrading treatment or punishment." Article 6 ECHR provides that:

> *In the determination of his civil rights and obligations or of any criminal charge against him, everyone is entitled to a fair and public hearing within a reasonable time by an independent and impartial tribunal established by law.*

Article 8 ECHR states that, "Everyone has the right to respect for his private and family life." Article 5 ECHR provides that, "No one shall be deprived of his liberty save... (d) in the case of lawful detention of a minor by lawful order for the purpose of educational supervision..." However, it seems desirable that the ECHR, which is an older document than the two just mentioned, should also include a special provision on children's rights.

The European Court has in several cases strengthened the interaction between the human rights of children as protected by the ECHR and children's rights as prescribed in the CRC by referring in its decision to the latter. Most prominent is the milestone decision of *A v United Kingdom*,[10] in which the European Court held that the State was obliged under Article 3 ECHR to protect children against serious breaches of personal integrity by providing effective deterrence. In that case, in which a nine-year-old boy faced regular beatings with a garden cane by his stepfather, the Court in particular referred to the requirement of adequate protection of the criminal law and made specific mention of Articles 19 and 37 CRC.[11] In my view this link made by the European Court undermines the view held by many governments and judges that Article 19 CRC is purely programmatic and contains no provisions capable of being directly invoked by an individual in court. Account should be taken of the possibility that at least certain elements of Article 19 CRC may be directly binding and capable of successful invocation by individuals in national courts.

When one considers the list of objectives which I have suggested above need to be pursued in order to strive for compliance with Article 19 CRC, it must be apparent that countries will not be grappling with the same problems regarding child protection, and certainly will not be at the same level of protection. Whilst this difference is readily absorbed in the five-yearly reporting procedure provided for in Article 44 CRC, the different levels of protection are more problematic in the context of the European Court. There was a very disquieting report published in a Dutch newspaper in 2002 concerning the treatment of homeless children in Russia. According to that report, more than 4.3 million children in Russia are homeless and completely bereft of the most basic provisions.[12] What these reports tell us, insofar as accurate, is that there is a huge gap regarding the approach to children whose families have failed them, or who are not able to care for them, between the various countries in Europe and in the resources which those countries have at their disposal. This presents a problem for the European Court of Human Rights, which has the task of setting a minimum standard across Europe, from Vladivostok to Porto, also in case of child protection. Should the Court lower its standards to the level that is reasonable to expect the most impoverished countries to attain? Or should it be prepared to set different levels, depending on the resources and other circumstances? Regarding one aspect of child protection, the European Court has said (in considering whether the impugned measures were necessary in a democratic society):

> The Court will have regard to the fact that perceptions as to the appropriateness of intervention by public authorities in the care of children vary from one Contracting State to another, depending upon such factors as traditions relating to the role of the family and to State intervention in family affairs and the availability of resources for public measures in this area.[13]

This awareness of cultural difference should not lead to the tolerance by the Court of a first and second class level of protection of children in the child protection context. However, the situation described in Russia in the newspaper reports concerns Article 3 ECHR – inhuman and degrading treatment – not the protection of parental rights under Article 8 ECHR. Where a State Party has difficulty, due to lack of resources, in complying with the costly positive obligations arising under the European Convention on Human Rights (to be explained below), it should become the task of the Council of Europe to find ways of improving the situation. Finally, I would like to point out that these huge and very shocking differences regarding the level of child protection between countries even within Europe put the policies regarding child immigrants of certain European countries in a very cynical light. For instance, in the Netherlands, the Child Care Act which came into force on 1 January 2005[14] gives children without a residence permit and unaccompanied minors who are living in camps provided by the Dutch authorities only very restricted access to voluntary child care facilities (*Jeugdzorg*), and children without residence permit are excluded from the possibility of being placed in a foster family. Moreover, their entitlement to care is in both cases restricted in time. Other academics and I have argued that these provisions violate both the CRC (Articles 2, 3, 19 and

20) and Article 3 ECHR. These provisions are shameful and should be repealed.[15]

The Court of Human Rights has concerned itself with the question of child protection in a rather large number of cases. These will be discussed in the three following parts.

3. Rules directed to sustaining the parent–child relationship in the child protection context

The vast majority of the case law of the European Court of Human Rights is concerned with this aspect. It is also a setting in which there is quite readily a fundamental conflict between the human right of the parent in safeguarding the family against intervention and sustaining the parent–child relationship, and the child's right to protection from abuse and neglect. The general premise is that children are best off with their own parents and siblings. This principle is underwritten by Article 9, first paragraph CRC. The approach of the European Court is therefore that priority should be given to supporting the upbringing faculties of the parents, only taking the child into care when there is no other action possible, and ensuring that so far as possible the removal of the child remains a temporary measure. Once intervention has taken place, all measures should be consistent with the ultimate aim of reunification of the child and parent.[16] The European Court's approach differs depending on whether the initial decision to remove the child is at issue, or subsequent measures.

3.1 The initial decision to remove the child

Regarding the initial decision to take the child into care, which may take place in an emergency, the State enjoys a certain margin of appreciation, greater anyway than the margin applied to the decision to refuse to return the child to the family or to restrict or totally terminate contact between the parent and child.[17] Even in the emergency context, the Court must still be satisfied that, in the particular case, circumstances existed that justified the removal of the child. It is for the State to establish that a careful assessment of the impact of the proposed care measure on the parents and the child, as well as the possible alternatives to taking the child into public care has preceded the decision to intervene.[18] The European Court applies an extra strict scrutiny regarding the removal of a new born baby: 'extraordinarily compelling reasons' must be present (violations of Article 8 ECHR on this ground in *K and T v Finland*,[19] *P, C and S v United Kingdom*[20] and *Haase v Germany*[21]).

3.2 Subsequent decisions: restriction or termination of access; termination of parental rights; adoption

The State is in principle obliged to provide for access between parent and child. This principle applies with extra force if the intervention by the State has been the cause of separation.[22] In *Kutzner v Germany* a failure to safeguard access between parent and child was held to violate the rights, protected by Article 8 ECHR, of both the child and the parent, also including a violation of the children's rights to have contact with each other.[23] A total severing of all links between the child and the parents is only justified by the overriding requirement of the child's best interests[24] and must be based on valid reasons.[25] Furthermore, once the child has been removed, the State is under an obligation to take positive measures to sustain the parent–child relationship and to ensure that de facto relationship can be restored as soon as reasonably possible.[26] The State's duty to take measures to secure reunion requires that regular meetings are arranged. In the view of the European Court, regularity of meetings is more important than frequency. Moreover, given the disruption to the family, the State is obliged to ensure that the children are given proper preparation and support, in order to give the meetings a maximum chance of success.[27] The Court said in *K and T v Finland*, "The minimum is that the authorities should examine the situation anew from time to time to see whether there has been any improvement in the family."[28]

3.3   Procedural safeguards

Furthermore, the European Court requires that the national authorities safeguard the parent–child relationship through procedural safeguards, which the Court has deduced from Articles 6 and 8 ECHR. The first group of rules applies to the judicial decision and are founded on Article 6 ECHR:

- The judicial decision must be free from bias.[29]
- The parents have a right to an oral hearing.[30]
- The future of the parent–child relationship must not be determined solely by the duration of the proceedings.[31]
- The parents must be informed of the evidence relied upon by the authorities.[32]
- The parents have a right to legal representation in complex cases.[33]

Further rules apply to the procedure as a whole (i.e. including the pre-judicial phase):

- The length of proceedings can also violate Article 8 ECHR.[34]
- The parents must be adequately involved in the decision-making procedure.[35]
- The parent must be informed of the reasons for the decision. As the European Court said in *T P and K M v United Kingdom*:

> *This is relevant not only to the parent's ability to put forward those matters militating in favour of his or her capability in providing the child with proper care and protection but also to enable the parent to understand and come to terms with traumatic events affecting the family as a whole.*[36]

In *T P and K M* the decision to take the applicant's child into care was based on evidence acquired in an interview with the applicant's child. The interview was recorded on video, but the applicant (the child's mother) was not allowed to see it. Thus, she was deprived of access to material that formed the basis of the case for removal of her child into care. The procedural requirements of Article 8 ECHR apply even in case of emergency proceedings where the specific requirements of giving precise reasons and the parents' interests in such reasons has been amplified in recent case law of the European Court.[37] Furthermore, in case of emergency measures, the imminent danger and the necessity to exclude the parents from the information upon which the authorities rely in deciding to remove the child must be proven.[38] There may be instances where disclosure to the parents of the child's statements may place that child at risk. There can be no absolute right of the parent to view, for example, the videos of interviews conducted by medical professionals. However, responsibility for establishing whether the materials should be made available does not lie with the parent, but with the child welfare authorities who must bring their arguments in favour of non-disclosure before a court.[39] A striking case is *Venema v The Netherlands*, where the child was removed abruptly in emergency proceedings from the parent as the mother was suspected of suffering from the disorder Munchausen by proxy. The European Court found a violation of Article 8 ECHR. It was not explained to the Court's satisfaction why the doctors could not have discussed their concerns with the parents. The parents were at no stage in a position to contest the reliability of the information relied upon or to add information from their own sources.[40]

What is the relationship between the human rights of the parents to safeguard their private and family life (and thus prevent removal of the child or to secure recovery of the child once removal has taken place), and the right of the child who may be at risk of being exposed to abuse and neglect? The European Court has repeatedly stated that, when evaluating, for example, the parents' claim to reunification, the national authorities must make a fair balance between the rights of the parent and the child. In making this balance the European Court attaches particular importance to the rights of the child. Those rights, depending upon their nature and seriousness, may override those of the parent.[41] So far so good. So what are the situations in which the European Court (and the national authorities) might have difficulty in giving priority to a right of the child (human right or children's right) over that of the human right of the parent?

One situation concerns that of the unborn child. The most common situation that arises is that of an expectant mother who is engaging in drug abuse. During the pregnancy, help and treatment can be offered to the mother, but if she does not accept it, the mother cannot be forced to undergo treatment. The reason is that forced treatment is regarded as an unacceptable intervention in the mother's right of privacy.[42] In a case before the Canadian Supreme Court a couple of years ago, the child welfare authorities in Nova Scotia asked the courts to determine whether they were entitled to compel an expectant mother to submit to treatment for her addiction to glue sniffing. The negative answer of the majority of the Canadian Supreme Court[43] confirms that the mother's right to private life has priority over the rights of the child to protection.[44] Yet the damage to the child is severe. The child in this situation has a 60–80% chance of being born with a drug addiction. The child has to be treated in an incubator for several weeks and the contacts to the parents have to be strictly regulated. In very many cases the child is not allowed to leave the hospital with the parents and is placed with foster parents. Because there is a time-lapse whilst the authorities establish whether parental rights should be restricted and in arranging that restriction, the child is sometimes removed without notice by the mother from the hospital.[45] Certainly when the question is viewed from the perspective of the child, the level of protection is far from satisfactory. It is a matter of a finely balanced interest, but is the right balance being made?

The unfavourable balance between the rights of mother and child is underwritten by the unfortunate decision of the European Court in *Odièvre v France*.[46] In that case the European Court gave priority to the right of the mother to maintain secrecy regarding the birth of her child over the adult child's right to discover her identity. The arguments used in that case were, however, not convincing. The majority failed to decide whether Article 2 ECHR (right to life) was applicable to the unborn child, and peculiarly attached much weight to the risk that a mother, if not allowed to remain anonymous *vis-à-vis* her child, might choose for abortion or child abandonment.[47] The view of the dissenting judges, Wildhaber, Bratza, Bonello, Loucaïdes, Cabral Barreto and Pellonpää, that the French rule allowing anonymous birth and no possibility of disclosure against the mother's will did not make a fair balance of the interests of the mother and child, is therefore to be preferred.[48] The *Odièvre* case does not concern child protection, but covers issues very close to it. In my view the case is indicative of the tension between the parent's rights and those of the child, and the potential for movement in the balance of those competing rights. The current protection of the rights of the unborn child, even when not in conflict with the private life of the mother, is in any case far too weak. Consider for instance the European Court case of *V O v France*[49] and *Adelaide v France*,[50] in which a woman alleged violation of the right to life (Article 2 ECHR) due to the lack of possibility in French law to bring proceedings to recover damages for the unborn child she had been carrying and who had to be aborted due to a negligent medical intervention. The judgment of the majority of the European Court is very unsatisfactory. The court confounded the situation at hand with the cases – such as the abortion context – in which the interests of the child and the mother are in conflict. The Council of Europe instruments which touch on the rights of the child, like the Oviedo Convention on Human Rights and Bioethics,[51] are deliberately vague about the rights of the unborn.[52] Finally, I suggest it is necessary to consider whether it would be better to make an earlier intervention before the child is born, in order to prevent the need for a much more disruptive intervention after the child is born. Suffice it to say, I think there is room for progress in this unhappy compromise, in the circumstances in which the drug-abusing mother is not treated during pregnancy, but is then faced with a threat of removal of a child at birth. Not only legal research is needed, but also ethical and medical. Important research on these questions is presently being carried out in this institution.[53]

Another problematic area in the balance between the human rights of the parent and the rights of the child concerns the case in which the child has spent several years of his or her young life with foster parents. Sometimes in these cases the child has never actually lived with the parents at all, and only really knows the foster parents. In this situation all parties are losers. Often in these cases the birth parents are chronically unwell, often suffering from mental illness and/or drug addiction. They are constantly faced with the remote prospect that they might at some time in the future be able to care for the child, and their own feeling of inadequacy is recurrently reinforced by judicial review of the situation. Meanwhile, the foster parents are left in a situation of uncertainty regarding the child. Their substantive and procedural rights to defend their claim to the child are necessarily attenuated. The child is bonded to one group of parents through the love and care they have shown for him or her, but bonded in law – including human rights law – to the birth parents. The law does not safeguard to the child the security in his primary relationship which he or she so desperately needs.[54] The principle of the European Court of Human Rights that the authorities must strive for reunification of the child and birth parents plays an unhappy role. Whilst the case law of the European Court does leave room for the possibility that the goal of reunification does not have to be pursued where there is absolutely no prospect any more of re-establishing the relationship,[55] the principle in practice has a stagnating and paralysing effect.

The situation of uncertainty and indecision is often in practice prolonged beyond the time when there is any chance of restoring the child to the birth parents. Important work has been done on structuring this process by Bruning. Her work includes concrete proposals to try to make clearer when the duty to reunify is no longer operative.[56]

4. Positive action required in order to achieve adequate protection

I turn now to the case law of the European Court regarding the situation in which the authorities, being either aware or in such a position that it can reasonably be said that they should have been aware that children were being abused, have failed to take adequate action with the consequence that the children concerned suffered damage. This is, if you like, the flip side of the coin of the previous group of cases, in which the authorities are alleged to have been overactive by intervening too soon or by failing to timely discontinue measures or by using measures not justified by the circumstances. This development is also a logical consequence of the ruling in *A v United Kingdom*[57], in which the European Court held that States are obliged, on the basis of Article 3 ECHR – remember the Court also invoked Article 19 CRC – to provide adequate protection against child abuse. In that case the protection afforded by the criminal law was held to have fallen short. In subsequent cases, the failure to act or ineffectiveness of the actions of the child protection authorities were alleged to violate Article 3 ECHR. In *Z v United Kingdom*,[58] the national authorities were aware of abuse and neglect being suffered by four children, who had survived in circumstances described by a child psychiatrist as 'horrific', but the authorities had failed to take adequate steps to protect the children. In a landmark judgment the European Court held Article 3 ECHR to have been violated, i.e. the authorities were held responsible for the inhuman and degrading treatment to which the children had been subjected.[59] The Court held that 'no separate issue arises' under Article 8 ECHR.[60] This is presumably because the Court considered the violation of Article 3 ECHR to be sufficient to make the point. However, it must follow that Article 8 ECHR was *a fortiori* violated. This can be relevant in a later case in which the facts are not sufficiently severe to reach the high threshold required to cross in order to establish violation of Article 3 ECHR.

The State is not liable for inhuman and degrading treatment of which it is not aware and regarding which it cannot be said that the State should have been aware. In the *D P & J C* case,[61] the child welfare authorities were aware of multiple – especially financial – problems in the family, and also truancy and some incidental violence, but they were not aware of any sexual abuse. The European Court noted:

> *Social service records refer to the second applicant's problem of soiling which led to involvement by medics and a period as an inpatient... concerns about truanting by a number of children... Incidents of [sporadic] violence.*

The Court concluded:

> *These cannot be regarded as revealing a clear pattern of victimization or abuse. The Court is not persuaded therefore that there were any particular aspects of the turbulent and volatile family situation which should have led the social services to suspect a deeper, more insidious problem in a family which was experiencing financial hardship, occasional criminal proceedings and with a mother observed to be 'less caring' than she should be.*[62]

Accordingly, the European Court found no violation of the State's obligation under Article 3 ECHR. The same reasoning was applied to the complaint under Article 8 ECHR.[63] However, the State is liable under Article 3 ECHR for failure to prevent abuse of which it was not aware but as to which it can reasonably be expected to have made itself aware. In the case of *E v United Kingdom* the children's step-father had already been convicted for sexual abuse. Yet, after the conviction, he continued to visit the house. When social services called, the man always hid, and the children were hidden as well. But social services did nothing to follow up various signals which showed the children were not well.[64]

The European Court noted also the very poor coordination between school, police and social services, which meant that vital information about the condition of the children was not fed through to social services. Apart from extending the test of State liability from liability for abuse of which the State was actually aware to abuse of which the State should have been aware, the European Court also rejected an argument that the State could only be held liable if a causative link between the failure to act and the damage suffered could be proved. The United Kingdom government alleged that it should be proved that the abuse would have been prevented if the authorities had acted more effectively. In the case of failure to act the causative link is notoriously difficult to establish. The European Court rejected this argument with the statement:

A failure to take reasonably available measures which could have had a real prospect of altering the outcome or mitigating the harm is sufficient to engage the responsibility of the State.[65]

Whilst the European Court's approach to Article 3 ECHR is strident, its attitude to the complaint that Article 6 ECHR was violated is not. The children's action against the local authority for damages in negligence was struck out on the grounds of a rule in English law which protects local authorities against liability for damage caused by negligent performance of its duties regarding child care protection.[66] This meant the claim could not be heard or determined on its merits. The majority of the European Court held in *Z v United Kingdom*[67] that this rule did not constitute denial of access to court for determination of a civil right or obligation in breach of Article 6 ECHR.[68] The approach taken by the majority of the European Court is based on a fine and unconvincing distinction between the situation of child abuse and the case of liability of the police for their negligent actions[69] and upon the unrealistic assertion that the applicants were not in any practical manner prevented from bringing their action in tort. The majority asserted the rule entitling the striking out was not a rule of immunity but rather an integral rule of the substantive law of tort. This argument seems irrelevant to the question whether the applicants were denied an access to court within the meaning of Article 6 ECHR. The majority of the European Court allowed itself to be satisfied by the government's contention that the House of Lords had given very serious consideration to the balancing up of the policy arguments against liability and the claim of the applicants to a remedy in tort.[70] The views of the minority that the damage suffered was of sufficient gravity and seriousness that the applicants should have been entitled to bring their claim for damages to be heard by a court (Judges Rozakis, Palm, Thomassen, Casadevall, Kovler) are far to be preferred to the casuistic reasoning of the majority. The majority held, however, that there was a violation of Article 13 ECHR through the failure of the legal system to provide an effective remedy as an alternative to civil damages for negligence.

However, since that judgment the European Court has shown itself not easily satisfied under Article 13 ECHR by the alternatives to civil damages for negligence brought in a court. In *E v United Kingdom* the applicants concentrated on the allegation that Article 13 ECHR was violated. Article 13 ECHR says:

Everyone whose rights and freedoms as set forth in this Convention are violated shall have an effective remedy before a national authority notwithstanding that the violation has been committed by persons acting in an official capacity.

The government argued that the applicants already had an effective remedy through being able to make application to the Criminal Injuries Compensation Scheme and to the ombudsman. Moreover, the government insisted that there was, at least in some circumstances, a remedy in tort by action through the civil courts. Furthermore, the applicants also had the possibility of judicial review. In *E v United Kingdom* the European Court held that Article 13 ECHR was violated. At least at the time when the applicants withdrew their civil law action in damages in tort, the case law was such that they had no prospect of having their claim heard on the merits. (Admittedly, since then the law has developed, allowing for an action in damages in certain cases, but this did not apply to the situation at the time the applicants brought their proceedings). Moreover, the European Court did not find the damages granted by the Criminal Injuries Compensation Board a sufficient remedy in order to satisfy Article 13 ECHR. The Board was not able to provide compensation for any economic loss – such as loss of earnings - caused by the child abuse. Moreover, the ombudsman was not entitled to make a binding order; his statements of findings had only a declaratory character. Judicial review of the local authorities was also not a realistic remedy in the European Court's view. Due to the short time limits in administrative law actions and their function of controlling excess of power rather than providing damages, this remedy could only be used immediately after the actions or inactions by the local authority, and such action was not an option for these children.[71]

It should be noted that this case law provides no authorisation for preventative action. That is to say, measures applied to a group of people on the basis of a certain probability of damage occurring. Legal authorisation for such preventative action is to be found in Article 19 CRC. There is an obvious collision with parental human rights (see Part 2 above). The exploration of the precise limits allowed by the ECHR regarding preventative action is another area where future development seems desirable.[72]

5.   Quality of care provided subsequent to initial intervention

5.1   The case of the rescue by the Ethiopian lions
In the last section I consider the quality of care provided subsequent to initial intervention. On 22 June 2005 the Dutch newspaper *NRC Handelsblad* carried an unusual report in the 'international news'. A young girl aged 12 years was abducted from her home in Bita Genet, Ethiopia by some men. They held her for seven days, wanting to force her into a marriage. This terrifying ordeal was interrupted when the abductors were disturbed by three lions who drove the abductors away. It is most surprising that the lions did not kill the girl. According to expert advice, the lions most probably associated the pitiful crying of the girl with the cries of a lion cub. This brings me to the main point: the rescue, whether by lions or child welfare authorities, is only the beginning of the story. Unlike the lions, when the child welfare authorities with the sanction of the courts carry out a rescue, they have a responsibility to ensure that the care which is provided to the 'rescued' child complies with the standards of the CRC and the Human Rights Conventions.

It was mentioned above that Article 19 CRC requires that adequate help is offered following removal from the family. Also the European Court has given some indication in its case law of the quality of care to be expected once the authorities have intervened. In *Giunta and Scozzari v Italy*,[73] the European Court found a serious shortcoming in the quality of care provided subsequent to intervention. The children were removed from the care of their mother because they had been exposed to sexual abuse. Subsequent to removal they were placed in the institution called *El Forteto*, where two of the employees directly concerned with the children had convictions, admittedly 20 years earlier, for physical and sexual abuse of children.[74] In the words of Judge Zupanæiæ, who concurred with the majority:

> *When [the authorities] consider the possible legal interference in the family relationship, they must be certain that the care imposed by the State will be clearly and demonstrably better than the troubled situation the court is seeking to redress.*[75]

Notably, the European Court considered the rights of both the parent and the child, protected by Article 8 ECHR, to be violated. In paragraph 216 the European Court said:

> *Consequently, the Court considers that the authorities have failed to show the degree of prudence and vigilance required in such a delicate and sensitive situation, and have done so to the detriment not just of the first applicant's rights but also of the superior interests of the children.*

What is valuable about this case is that it sets a standard under Article 8 ECHR which can apply in a broad context. However, there is more case law of the European Court which specifically addresses the standards with which the State must comply if the child is removed from the home. These are the standards set by Article 5, first paragraph sub (d) ECHR and Article 37, preamble and sub-paragraph b CRC. For these provisions to apply, the measure must involve a deprivation of personal freedom. In *H L v United Kingdom*[76] the European Court held that whether a person is deprived of his liberty, in order to activate the safeguards prescribed by Article 5, first paragraph ECHR:

> *The starting-point must be the concrete situation of the individual concerned and account must be taken of a whole range of factors arising in a particular case such as the type, duration, effects and manner of implementation of the measure in question. The distinction between a deprivation of, and restriction upon, liberty is merely one of degree or intensity and not one of nature or substance.*[77]

It is not relevant whether the person originally voluntarily agreed to the regime, or whether the person is on a ward that is locked or lockable. Decisive in *H L* was the degree of actual control that was exercised over the person.[78]

Standards were set in the case of *Bouamar v Belgium*.[79] In that case the applicant complained that he had been detained in a remand prison on nine different occasions. In his view these detentions did not fulfil the requirements in Article 5, paragraph 1 ECHR of being detention of a minor for the purpose of educational supervision or for the purpose of bringing him before a competent legal authority. In the view of the Court, detention in a remand prison is not by definition in violation of Article 5, first paragraph ECHR, even if its purpose is not the immediate provision of 'educational supervision.' However the Court added:

> *In such circumstances, however, the imprisonment must be speedily followed by actual application of such a regime in a setting (open or closed) designed and with sufficient resources for the purpose.*[80]

In that case it emerged that the Belgian State had shuttled the applicant about and that it did not have any relevant facilities which could have helped the applicants with his problems, and which could thus be regarded as 'educational supervision' within the terms of Article 5, first paragraph ECHR. These requirements were further worked out in *D G v Ireland*.[81] In that case the placement of a minor in a youth prison was not regarded as educational supervision within the meaning of Article 5, first paragraph ECHR, even though the regime, regarding family visits and the actual educational and recreational programme which the applicant was allowed to follow, was more flexible than that applied to other inmates who had arrived via the criminal rote. The fact was that the applicant had no realistic hope of any provision which would fulfil the needs of the applicant, because there simply was no institution in Ireland suitable for the educational needs of children who had a criminal conviction and whom the court had judged were therefore in need of special supervision and training. The far-reaching consequences of these two decisions should be well-understood. A State which has educational or treatment facilities for children diagnosed to be in need of them, but which is unable to provide them without a long period of waiting, runs a serious risk of violating Article 5, first paragraph ECHR.[82]

6.   Conclusion and recommendations

- The ECHR should contain a specific provision on children's rights.
- At least certain elements of Article 19 CRC are directly applicable and capable of successful invocation by individuals in national courts.
- There should be no first and second class levels of protection of human rights regarding child protection.
- Discrimination on the basis of residential status regarding access to child care is unacceptable.
- The balance between the rights of the mother to protection of private life and the rights of the unborn child should stay under careful scrutiny. This is an area where the present preference for the privacy rights of the mother over those of the unborn child may be expected to change, especially in the light of increased knowledge about the unborn child.
- When a child has been in long-term foster care almost from the date of birth and has never lived with the natural parents, the European Court should give priority to the principle of continuity of care in preference to the claims of the natural parents.
- The precise limits allowed by the ECHR regarding preventative action require exploration.

- Children who have suffered damage through negligent failure of the public authorities should have the right to bring their claim to damages in a court of law, as protected by Article 6 ECHR, as explained in *Golder v. United Kingdom*.
- When the child welfare authorities with the sanction of the courts rescue a child from an unacceptable situation at home, they are obliged to ensure that the care which is provided to the child is an improvement upon the situation from which the child has been removed.

This article was prepared with the assistance of Linda Corvers and Joan Whittingham, student assistants in the department of Law at the University of Maastricht, respectively, in 2005 and 2006.

Endnotes

1   New York, 20 November 1989. Entry into force: 2 September 1990.
2   20 November 1959, Office of the United Nations High Commissioner for Human Rights, Geneva, Switzerland.
3   New York, 16 December 1966. Entry into force: 23 March 1976.
4   Rome, 4 November 1950. Entry into force: 3 September 1953.
5   New York, 10 December 1999. Entry into force: 22 December 2000.
6   New York, 18 December 1979. Entry into force: 3 September 1981.
7   Article 44 CRC.
8   Nice, 7 December 2000.
9   Brussels, 29 May 2000.
10 *A. v United Kingdom*, Eur. Court H.R. 23 September 1998.
11 *A v United Kingdom*, Eur. Court H.R. 23 September 1998 § 22 .
12 *NRC Handelsblad* 23/24 February 2002, C. van Zwol.
13 *Johansen v Norway*, Eur. Court H.R. 7 August 1996, § 64; *K and T v Finland*, Eur. Court H.R. 12 July 2001, § 154; *Kutzner v Germany*, Eur. Court H.R. 26 February 2002, § 66.
14 22 April 2004. Entry into force: 1 January 2005.
15 C. Forder, 'Over de kern en de grensgevallen van het familierecht', in: V. Van den Eeckhout, C.J. Forder, E. Hooghiemstra, E. Nicolaï & S.K. van Walsum, *Transnationale gezinnen in Nederland*, Nederlandse Gezinsraad/Meijers Instituut Leiden, Boom Juridische uitgevers, Den Haag, 2005, pp. 21-116; C. Forder, 'Basisvoorwaarden ter discussie: transnationale gezinnen versus andere gezinnen' in: Erna Hooghiemstra & Marjan Wijers (red.), *Allochtone Gezinnen, juridische positie*, Nederlandse Gezinsraad, Den Haag, June 2005; C. Forder, 'Family Rights and Immigration Law: a European Perspective' in: Hildegard Schneider (ed.) *Migration, Integration and Citizenship, A challenge for Europe's future, Volume II*, Forum Maastricht, 2005; C.Forder, 'Nederland is verplicht ook "illegale" kinderen te beschermen', *NJB* 2003 afl. 14 pp. 727-728.
16 *Olsson v Sweden (No. 1)*, Eur. Court H.R. 24 March 1988, § 78-81; *Eriksson v Sweden*, Eur. Court H.R. 22 June 1989, § 81; *Johansen v Norway*, Eur. Court H.R. 7 August 1996, § 64; *K and T v Finland*, Eur. Court H.R. 12 July 2001, § 178; *T P and K M v United Kingdom*, Eur. Court H.R 10 May 2001, § 71.
17 *Johansen v Norway*, Eur. Court H.R. 7 August 1996, § 64.
18 *P, C and S v United Kingdom*, Eur. Court H.R. 16th July 2002, § 116; *K and T v Finland*, Eur. Court H.R. 12 July 2001, § 166; *Kutzner v Germany*, Eur. Court H.R. 26 February 2002, § 67.
19 *K and T v Finland*, Eur. Court H.R. 12 July 2001, § 168.
20 *P, C and S v United Kingdom*, Eur. Court H.R. 16 July 2002, § 133.
21 *Haase v Germany*, Eur. Court H.R. 8 April 2004, § 101 .
22 *Eriksson v Sweden*, Eur. Court H.R. 22 June 1989, § 88-92.
23 *Kutzner v Germany*, Eur. Court H.R. 26 February 2002, § 79.
24 *P, C and S v United Kingdom*, Eur. Court H.R. 16 July 2002, § 118.
25 *Scozzari and Giunta v Italy*, Eur. Court H.R. 13 July 2000, § 177.
26 *K and T v Finland*, Eur. Court H.R. 12 July 2001, § 179; *K A v Finland*, Eur. Court H.R. 14 January 2003, § 144-146.
27 *Scozzari and Giunta v Italy*, Eur. Court H.R. 13 July 2000, § 175-177.
28 *K and T v Finland*, Eur. Court H.R. 12 July 2001, § 178.
29 *Buscemi v Italy*, Eur. Court H.R. 16 September 1999, § 68.
30 *L v Finland*, Eur. Court H.R. 27 April 2000 § 132.
31 *Paulsen-Medalen and Svenson v Sweden*, Eur. Court H.R. 19 February 1998, § 39; *Scozzari and Giunta v Italy*, Eur. Court H.R. 13 July 2000, § 173.
32 *Buchberger v Austria*, Eur. Court H.R. 20 December 2001, § 50 (equality of arms).
33 *P, C and S v United Kingdom*, Eur. Court H.R. 16 July 2002, § 99-100, also violation of Article 8, § 136.
34 *W v United Kingdom*, Eur. Court H.R. 8 July 1987, § 64.
35 *W v United Kingdom*, Eur. Court H.R. 8 July 1987, § 82; also in the pre-court phase: *McMichael v United Kingdom*, Eur. Court H.R. 24 February 1995, § 77.
36 *T P and K M v United Kingdom*, Eur. Court H.R 10 May 2001, § 80.
37 *Haasse v Germany*, Eur. Court H.R. 8 April 2004, European Human Rights Cases 2004, 46; Nederlandse Jurisprudentie 2005, 186 with annotation Jan de Boer.

38 *K A v Finland*, Eur. Court H.R. 14 January 2003, § 102-104.

39 *T P and K M v United Kingdom*, Eur. Court H.R. 10 May 2001, § 82-83; Buchberger v Austria, Eur. Court H.R. 20 December 2001, § 43; Haase v Germany, Eur. Court H.R. 8 April 2004, § 98.

40 *Venema v The Netherlands*, Eur. Court H.R. 17 December 2002, § 96-97.

41 *Olsson v Sweden (No 1)*, Eur. Court H.R. 24 March 1988, § 78-81; *Eriksson v Sweden*, Eur. Court H.R. 22 June 1989, § 81; *Johansen v Norway*, Eur. Court H.R. 7 August 1996, § 78; T.P. and K.M., Eur. Court H.R 10 May 2001, § 71).

42 R. Scott, *Rights, Duties and the Body*, Hart Publishing, Oxford, 2002.

43 *Winnepeg Child and Family Services (North West Area) v G.D.F.* (1997) 3 Supreme Court Cases 925.

44 See also my article on the unborn child's right to a healthy life: Forder, C. 'Het belang van het ongeboren kind: recht op gezond leven' in: E. Engelhard, T. Hartlief & G. Van Maanen (red.) *Aansprakelijkheid in gezinsverband*, Boom Juridische uitgevers Den Haag, 2004, pp. 189-219.

45 Vries de, M., 'Ethiek in de Stadskliniek: privacy beroepsgeheim en het belang van het kind' in: *Ned. Tijdschrift Geneeskunde*, 2004, 148 (40), pp. 1949-1952.

46 *Odièvre v France*, Eur. Court H.R. 13 February 2003.

47 *Odièvre v France*, Eur. Court H.R. 13 February 2003, § 45.

48 C. Forder, 'Accouchement sous X': annotatie bij het arrest van het Europees Hof voor de Rechten van de Mens, 13 februari 2003, Odièvre t. Frankrijk, *NJCM-Bulletin* 2003, pp. 774-784.

49 *V.O. v France*, Eur. Court H.R. 8 July 2004.

50 *Adelaide v France*, Eur. Court H.R. 6 January 2005.

51 Oviedo, 4 April 1997; Entry into force: 1 December 1999.

52 C. Forder, 'Bescherming van het ongeboren leven' (Protection of unborn life) *Nederlands Juristenblad* 2005, pp. 686-688.

53 Vries de, M., 'Ethiek in de Stadskliniek: privacy beroepsgeheim en het belang van het kind' in: *Ned. Tijdschrift Geneeskunde*, 2004, 148 (40), pp. 1949-1952.

54 C. Schuengel, W. Slot & R. Bullens (red.) *Gehechtheid en bescherming*, SWP Amsterdam, 2003.

55 *K and T v Finland*, Eur. Court H.R. 12 July 2001, § 155.

56 Bruning, M. & Steketee, M., 'Herziening OTS (nog) geen verbetering voor betrokkenen' in: *Tijdschrift voor familie- en jeugdrecht*, 2001, pp. 137-144; Bruning, M. 'Herziening kinderbeschermingsmaatregelen: over noodzaak en uitstel' in: *Tijdschrift voor familie- en jeugdrecht*, 2002, pp. 102-108.

57 *A v United Kingdom*, Eur. Court H.R. 23 September 1998.

58 *Z v United Kingdom*, Eur. Court H.R. 10 May 2001.

59 *Z v United Kingdom*, Eur. Court H.R. 10 May 2001, § 74.

60 *Z v United Kingdom*, Eur. Court H.R. 10 May 2001, § 77; *E v United Kingdom*, Eur. Court H.R. 26 November 2002, § 105.

61 *D.P. and J.C. v United Kingdom*, Eur. Court H.R. 10 October 2002, § 109-112.

62 *D.P. and J.C. v United Kingdom*, Eur. Court H.R. 10 October 2002, § 112.

63 *D.P. and J.C. v United Kingdom*, Eur. Court H.R. 10 October 2002, § 118.

54 *E v United Kingdom*, Eur. Court H.R. 26 November 2002, § 97.

65 *E v United Kingdom*, Eur. Court H.R. 26 November 2002, § 99.

66 House of Lords decision on 29 June 1995 in *X and others v Bedfordshire County Council* (1995) 3 All England Law Reports 353.

67 *Z v United Kingdom*, Eur. Court H.R. 10 May 2001, § 96-101; followed in T.P. and K.M. v United Kingdom, Eur. Court H.R. 10 May 2001, § 99-103 .

68 Based on the European Court's interpretation of Article 6 ECHR in *Golder v United Kingdom*, 21 February 1975, § 28-36, Article 6 ECHR, which includes the guarantee of access to court.

69 *Osman v United Kingdom*, Eur. Court H.R. 28 October 1998, § 115-116.

70 *Z v United Kingdom*, Eur. Court H.R. 10 May 2001, § 95-101.

71 *E v United Kingdom*, Eur. Court H.R. 26 November 2002, § 112-116.

72 Willems, J., The Children's Law of Nations: 'The International Rights of the Child in the Trias Pedagogica' in: J. Willems (red.) *Developmental and Autonomy Rights of Children*, Intersentia, Antwerp-Oxford- New York 2002, p. 69-102; Willems, J., 'Children's rights and the prevention of child abuse and neglect: the Quest for a trias pedagogica of children, parents

and society' in: I. Wolleswinkel & I. Westendorp (red.) *Violence in the domestic sphere*, Intersentia, Antwerp-Oxford 2005, pp. 151-182.

73   *Scozzari and Giunta v Italy*, Eur. Court H.R. 13 July 2000.

74   *Scozzari and Giunta v Italy*, Eur. Court H.R. 13 July 2000, § 202-216.

75   Concurring opinion Judge Zupanæiæ, p. 59.

76   *H.L. v United Kingdom*, Eur. Court H.R. 5 October 2004.

77   *Guzzardi v. Italy*, Eur. Court H.R. 6 November 1980, Series A no. 39, § 92; *Ashingdane v United Kingdom*, Eur. Court H.R. 28 May 1985, § 41; *H.L. v United Kingdom* Eur. Court H.R. 5 October 2004, § 89.

78   *H.L. v United Kingdom* Eur. Court H.R. 5 October 2004, § 90.

79   *Bouamar v Belgium,* Eur. Court H.R. 29 February 1988.

80   *Bouamar v Belgium,* Eur. Court H.R. 29 February 1988, § 50.

81   *D.G. v Ireland*, Eur. Court H.R. 16 May 2002.

82   Mariëlle Bruning, Ton Liefaard and Ludmila Volf, 'Rechtswaarborgen voor ots-ers in justitiële inrichtingen' in: *Tijdschrift voor familie- en jeugdrecht,* 2004, pp. 207-216, p. 211.

Child Protection and the Internet

A Comparative Analysis between the American and the Italian Legal Approach

Federica Giardini

1.   Introduction

The complexity of modern society means that legal protection of minors needs to be extended to every field where children operate and every field where they draw information that may be used for all kinds of purposes. Modern legislators seem to be aware of this, and for some time they have been seeking to enact forms of protection that take account of technological change and progress, covering all fields of communications, from traditional means, such as the press and television, to means that have spread more recently like the Internet.

Perhaps the Internet is one of the most delicate areas, taken from the angle examined here. The Internet, in effect, may be a valuable educational tool but, at the same time, it is a potential instrument for exposing minors to many of the dangers present in society. This ambivalence resides in the very nature of the Internet. To use a metaphor that captures the phenomenon of the Internet today, we may say that when a child uses the Internet, it is as if he or she looks onto the world, alone, suddenly opening a window onto global society.

The importance of the theme related to globalisation that is inherent in the phenomenon of circulation of information on the Internet translates, at legal level, into a need for protection that must involve both the international legal order and single national legislatures. The websites, which are the sources of information that people consult, are not necessarily located in the national territory of the user who gains access via his own computer.

Up to now, the problems concerning how and for what purposes protection of Internet users should be ensured, have been considered sector by sector, even with regard to adult Internet users. Current laws are directed at protection of economic transactions and computer security in general, rather than being directed at protection of the person.

Turning to the specific aspects peculiar to children, the problem today calls for urgent solutions. Children using Internet have many rights that require protection, ranging from the right to privacy or confidentiality and the right to training and education, to the right to personal security and freedom from psychological and even physical harm.

Here below an overview is given of the current legal position at international level, followed by an assessment of the positions adopted in this field by the United States and the Italian legal orders, leading to a number of conclusions as a basis for recommendations for the future in this field.

2. Protection at international level

Still today, at international level, there is no convention that specifically deals with the protection of minors and the Internet. In fact, the international legal order only indirectly provides significant elements relevant to the problem.

The protection of minors in Internet may somehow be brought under the provisions of the New York Convention on the Rights of the Child of 1989. Article 13 of the Convention protects the freedom of expression. In defining the ambit of this right, the Convention's text explicitly includes the freedom of the child, "to seek, receive and impart information and ideas of all kinds, regardless of frontiers, either orally, in writing or in print, in the form of art, or through any other media of the child's choice" (Art. 13(1)). The provision also establishes, in paragraph 2, the purposes for which the child's freedom of expression may be regulated by law, identifying limitations that may be set on the child's right in relation to respect of the rights or reputations of others, and also for the protection of national security, public order, public health or morals. Taken together, while on the one hand Internet may come within the scope of Article 13(1) – since it is one of the means through which the child may receive and impart information – Article 13(2) directs the Convention's protection towards rights different from those vested in the child and which justify the restrictions referred to above on his or her freedom of expression.

In Article 17, States Parties to the Convention recognise the importance of the function performed by the mass media and agree to ensure, "that the child has access to information and material from a diversity of national and international sources, especially those aimed at the promotion of his or her social, spiritual and moral well-being and physical and mental health." To this end, besides encouraging the mass media, "to disseminate information and material of social and cultural benefit to the child", and responding to the educational aims that the child's education must have under Article 29 of the Convention, States also encourage international co-operation in the production, exchange and dissemination of information and material of social and cultural benefit to the child, "from a diversity of cultural, national and international sources". States also favour, "the development of appropriate guidelines for the protection of the child from information and material injurious to his or her well-being, bearing in mind the provisions of Articles 13 and 18."

Finally, Article 18 imposes an obligation on States which have ratified the Convention to ensure, "the development of institutions, facilities and services for the care of children" for the purpose of guaranteeing and promoting the rights set forth in the Convention itself. It is precisely in this ambit that the systems of protection existing in Italy and in the United States of America are placed.

3.   Protection in Italy

Italy is an active participant in the Safer Internet Plus programme, launched by the European Commission as a multiannual Community action plan with the purpose of promoting safer use of the Internet by combating illegal and harmful content disseminated by means of global networks. The need and urgency for new legal measures directed at supporting safe use of the Internet, with special regard to protection of minors from the risks it may carry, has been repeatedly underlined at European level. Already at the end of 2004 a document, entitled *Proposal for a decision of the European Parliament and of the Council on establishing a multiannual Community programme on promoting safer use of Internet and new online technologies*, was drawn up by the European Economic and Social Committee – a body with advisory functions for the decision-making organs: the European Parliament, Council and Commission of the European Union. The Proposal stressed that two actions need to be undertaken: first, to impose a legal duty on Internet Providers to work positively for the protection of young users; and secondly, to put measures in place for the prevention of credit card use as a means of payment for the dissemination and distribution of child pornography over the Internet. The subject is extremely topical for the Italian legal order and has been addressed by legislation in recent years.

The protection granted in Italy today to children using Internet does not derive from a single, independent legislative provision, but stems from two types of sources, legislation and self-regulation. The legislation enacted covers both the civil and criminal spheres of action. The following provisions stand out: Legislative Decree No. 70 of 2003, implementing European Directive 2000/31 on certain legal aspects of information society services, in particular electronic commerce, in the internal market ('Directive on electronic commerce'); the Personal Data Protection Code (known as the 'privacy code'), which came into force in 2004; and most importantly, the Self-Regulation Code on Internet and Minors.

In the criminal sphere, besides the general provisions of the Criminal Code, another important enactment is Legislative Decree of 7 November 2003 (known as the anti-paedophilia decree), which adopts provisions to combat the sexual exploitation of children and child pornography, also through the Internet, and amends both the Italian Criminal Code and Law No. 269 of 1998 on the exploitation of prostitution, pornography and sex tourism causing damage to children, prohibiting them as forms of slavery. While it is true that Legislative Decree No. 70 of 2003 establishes some forms of responsibility of providers, and the privacy code extends the prohibition of the use of pictures or news relating to minors to cases where they are involved in legal proceedings, the legislature in Italy is definitely tending towards the use of the instrument of self-regulation in this area.

According to this logic, the Self-Regulation Code on Internet and Minors aims to protect children from contents that are unsuitable for young people, such as violence and pornography which may harm the physical or moral integrity of the minor. The Code was adopted at the end of 2003 by the major Associations representing Internet operators, in agreement with the Minister for Communications and the Minister for Innovation and Technology, based on the model of the Self-Regulation Code on TV and Minors. The Internet and Minors Code also aims: to help adults, children and families towards a correct and aware use of Internet; to offer equal and safe Internet access to children, in observance of national and international legal principles; to protect children's confidentiality and the correct treatment of children's personal information. Some of the most important provisions are briefly outlined below.

The use of a distinctive sign, *Internet e minori* (Internet and minors), testifies that the subject carrying on a business activity on the Internet adheres to the Code, and attests that the commitments undertaken by that subject are in conformity with adherence to the Code. In the home page of its services, the adherent to the Code visibly places a reference, *Tutela dei minori* (Protection of minors), leading to specific web pages containing information for a safe use of the Internet. Differentiated services for Internet surfing should be offered, depending on the available categories, such as for Families, Educators, Schools, Libraries, and so on. The Content Provider may apply systems for classifying contents that it thinks ought to be subject to conditional access, and may apply systems for identifying the user's age, which must respect the law on personal data protection.

In the logic of this framework, providers undertake to make Internet surfing safer for children, and to preserve information needed to identify the authors of illicit contents and to collaborate with security forces in the fight against child pornography online.

Disciplinary sanctions are provided for infringements of the code's provisions by adherents, and precise forms of responsibility are provided, distinguishing between the activities performed by Housing/Hosting Providers, Content Providers and Internet Point managers.

A final note concerns the current lack of specific protection of children against spamming, a phenomenon that is only regulated in general terms by the privacy code. By contrast, as described below, state legislation in some parts of the United States is orientated towards specific protection also in this field.

4.   Protection in the United States of America

In the United States legal order today, the legal protection of children as Internet users is complex, problematic and, as such, constantly evolving. The model of federal law has been preferred by the US legislator, with some single states enacting further laws. The noted complexity of legal protection granted in the United States to children using Internet can be traced to two distinct factors. The first is that the federal provisions enacted over a period of time have tended to regulate different areas of activity, ranging from the protection of children using Internet in general, to more specific spheres, such as Internet use carried on from schools or libraries, and from the protection of children's privacy online to protection against spamming. The second factor that still makes the American situation problematic today, as mentioned above, goes back to the end of the 1990s, and brings into play the power balance in relations between the legislative function, exercised by the federal Congress, and the judicial function, which in the United States system entrusts judicial precedent with the power to create legal rules. So, the dynamics of relations between Congress and the Courts are involved, particularly with regard to the need to reconcile the matter of child protection in Internet with the defence of the First Amendment.

In brief, the following cases have been fundamental in the development of United States law.

In 1997, in Reno v. American Civil Liberties Union, the Supreme Court struck down the Communications Decency Act (CDA), enacted in 1996 as part of the Telecommunications Act of 1996, and the first Statute approved by the Congress to regulate Internet pornography. The CDA, which seeks to protect minors from harmful material online by criminalizing Internet transmission of 'indecent' materials to minors, is held to be an unconstitutional restriction on Internet, because its reduces the materials available to adults, in breach of the protection granted by the First Amendment.

In October 1998, Congress approved the Child Online Protection Act, establishing criminal penalties for any commercial distribution of material harmful to minors. It also appointed the COPA Commission with the fundamental task of identifying support methods, including technological means, to reduce the possibility that a child using Internet is exposed to material harmful to him or her.

The constitutionality of COPA in relation to the restrictions it involves for freedom of speech has been evaluated by the courts on several occasions in recent years, between 1999 and 2004. The problem is that, given the protection of the First Amendment, free manifestations of thought should continue to be accessible to the adult public. Already in 1999, the Federal District Court of Philadelphia issued an injunction directed at preventing the enforcement of COPA by the government, based on the premise that preventing access to material harmful for minors would entail unconstitutional restrictions for adults, despite the fact that the provision itself contains some precautions intended to avoid this, such as requiring the number of a credit card or an adult access code for access reserved for an adult public. The results complained of include: discriminating against adults who possess and do not possess a credit card; making every interactive exchange on Internet subject to a check, including exchanges that are perfectly harmless for the minor; imposing extra, unjustified costs on adults for access to material that should be free; restricting privacy; and so on. In 2000, the Third Circuit of Appeals found the law to have unconstitutional elements on the basis of features characterising the very nature of cyberspace, considered as a geographically free entity.

In 2002, a case concerning these questions came before the Supreme Court, which did not, however, pronounce on the point of law, but ordered the lower

Court to decide the case on the basis of a wider range of First Amendment issues. In 2003, a new decision of unconstitutionality of the COPA was reached by the Third Circuit of Appeals, and in June 2004 came the Supreme Court decision in the case of Ashcroft v. American Civil Liberties Unions, confirming the injunction against the enforcement of the Child Online Protection Act on the grounds that the Government had failed to show that there were no alternative means less restrictive than the COPA.

The Children Internet Protection Act (CIPA), a federal statute passed by Congress in 2000 in relation to Internet access activity carried out by children from schools and libraries, has raised doubts linked to the same aspects of unconstitutionality for breach of the First Amendment envisaged for the COPA. The law, which was also enacted thanks to the work of the Federal Communication Commission, makes the award of federal contributions for schools and libraries subject to showing that security measures have been put in place for Internet use by minors by means of blocks or filters for material that is obscene, child pornography, or in any case harmful to minors. While the District Court held differently, in 2003 the Supreme Court found that the CIPA is not unconstitutional because it does not violate library patrons' First Amendment rights, since libraries are not public fora. At the same time, the Court held that the government is entitled to 'broad limits' when it attaches conditions to the receipt of federal funds, and that installing filtering software does not constitute an unconstitutional condition.

Some interesting interpretive aspects are still in question with regard to the Children's Online Privacy Protection Act (COPPA), a federal provision of 1998 enacted by Congress to prohibit unfair or deceptive acts or practices in connection with the collection, use, or disclosure of personally identifiable information from and about children on the Internet. The Federal Trade Commission has enacted a Rule to govern the online collection of personal information from children. The primary goal of the COPPA Rule is to give parents control over what information is collected from their children online and how such information may be used. The Rule applies to different types of operators, such as: operators of commercial Web sites and online services directed at children under 13 that collect personal information from them; general audience operators that knowingly collect personal information from children under 13; and the operators of general audience sites that have a separate children's area and that collect personal information from children under 13. The Rule requires operators to perform a series of steps: to post a privacy policy on the homepage of the Web site and a link to the privacy policy on every page where personal information is collected; to provide notice about the site's information collection practices to parents and obtain verifiable parental consent before collecting personal information from children; to give parents a choice as to whether their child's personal information will be disclosed to third parties; to provide parents access to their child's personal information and the opportunity to delete the child's personal information and opt out of future collection or use of the information; to maintain the confidentiality, security and integrity of personal information collected from children; not to condition a child's participation in a game, contest or other activity on the child's disclosing more personal information than is reasonably necessary to participate in that activity.

Spamming is another area that has recently prompted treatment specifically devoted to minors. Since 2003, spamming has been regulated at federal level by the CAN-SPAM Act (Controlling the Assault of Non-Solicited Pornography and Marketing Act of 2003), which came into force on 1 January 2004. On 1 July 2005, new child protection e-mail registry laws came into effect in the States of Michigan and Utah (www.protectmychild.com and www.utahkidsregistry.com). The goal of the laws is to prevent minors from being sent a message that advertises or otherwise links to a message advertising a product or service which a minor is prohibited by law from purchasing, viewing, possessing or otherwise receiving. The covered categories of messages include Alcohol, Tobacco, Pornography or Obscene Material, Gambling, Lotteries, Illegal Drugs, Fireworks and Firearms. Once an e-mail address has been registered, senders of e-mail messages that advertise or link to prohibited products or services are required to remove the address from their mailing lists within 30 days. The registrations are effective for two years in Utah and for three years in Michigan. Apparently CAN-SPAM cannot supersede these laws because they are worded as child protection laws and not as anti-spam laws.

5.   Conclusions and recommendations for the future

Today more than ever, progress in technology, and the speed with which technology is evolving, demand incisive action on the part of legal systems that is aimed at the protection of the fundamental rights of children. This necessarily requires coordinated action at international level which implicates national legislatures in a legally significant way, without neglecting the organisations that at every social and professional level are charged with disseminating information through means of communication.

At this moment in history, the Internet is evolving from the model of the past and, at the same time, interaction between the different means of communication is evolving inexorably. Traditional means of communication – that is to say the press, television, radio – and Internet are rapidly becoming one single means of communication that is able to provide users with every kind of information and to distribute not only information, entertainment and games, but also interactive services and tools for distance learning in every field of knowledge to all citizens, and therefore also to children. Today, information technology infrastructures such as Wi-Fi networks already guarantee broadband access in mobility.

Progress in communications together with this continuous and unstoppable interaction between the different means of communication call for a different sensibility on the part of legislators, and it should be stressed that this extends to the actual quality of legal technique used for drafting the law. Now, more than ever, approximation or lack of specific expertise also in the field of technology on the part of the legislator dealing with these matters may lead to legislative intervention with no force to protect children. For example, any picture of a child, taken as he or she plays, can instantly be transformed and used without difficulty for purposes of child pornography. It can be put on the Internet and transmitted directly to the homes of people who make use of pornography. When we talk about protection on the Internet, we must therefore refer to a complex reality that needs to take into account the fact that information travels today via the computer and reaches the mobile phone, the pc and the television.

Protecting children in Internet today means protecting them in every sphere of communications. Here it must be borne in mind that, on the one hand, children's needs are unchanged (that is the rights of children that need protection are above all those envisaged by the New York Convention of 1989) and, on the other hand, with specific regard to Internet and the communications system in all its complexity and interaction, the situations requiring protection for children must also be identified in the right to confidentiality of personal information about the child, the right to be free from contact with data and information that is dangerous or in any case harmful for the child's development, and the protection of the child's security as well as freedom from psychological and even physical harm.

It is to be hoped that an international legal instrument, such as a convention on the rights of children in communications, will soon come into existence and take all the above into account. Meanwhile, national legislatures must orientate themselves towards forms of protection that have the objective limit of territoriality.

In this complex logic, the forms of protection quickly need to be reviewed and updated in a common action that extends to international and national legal levels, as well as self-regulation of the professional categories involved at every level. In addition, technological mechanisms of protection must not be overlooked, through special protective filters and programmes. It is also indispensable to include a social and educational approach in this sphere.

From this last perspective, mention should be made of the admirable action carried out also in the social and educational spheres by organisations such as Save the Children (www.savethechildren.org, www.savethechildren.it, www.stop-it.org) and the International Crime Analysis Association (ICCA, www.criminologia.org).

To conclude, and to repeat a wish I already partly stated in Athens at the International Spam Congress organised by the American Hellenic Chamber of Commerce: the scope of the newly created European Network and Information Security Agency (ENISA), with its seat in Heraklion, should be extended to cover the protection of children in communications, in the knowledge that security in communications also means protection of young users.

Minimising the Effects of Child Maltreatment

Primary, Secondary or Tertiary Prevention?

Danya Glaser

1.   The cost of child abuse and neglect

The cost of child abuse and neglect is now well-established. For the maltreated child, it includes emotional distress, unhappiness, anxiety and trauma. The child may experience physical pain and injury, and occasionally a child is killed in the process. The child's developmental progress may be distorted and child maltreatment is strongly associated with disorganised attachment organisation. The pattern of brain development is significantly determined by the young child's experiences. Child maltreatment has been shown to be associated with changes in developing brain structure and function. Severe deprivation may lead to the failure of development of certain functions. Distorted experiences such as violence may be followed by the brain's selective attention to aggression. Much of child abuse and neglect is stressful, and repeated activation of the physiological stress response may be harmful to the brain.

The child is not only affected during the process of maltreatment, which may be prolonged and become an integral part of the child's experiences, especially in cases of neglect and emotional abuse. Many adolescents and adults continue to be affected by the after-effects of abuse and neglect, which may sometimes only emerge later (after the maltreatment has ceased). These after-effects include depression, deliberate self-harm, low self-esteem and antisocial behaviour.

There is also a considerable cost to society by way of wasted human potential, and the possibility of antisocial behaviour and poor parenting in the next generation. The economic cost of the resources needed for intervention is considerable. These resources include investigation, child protective intervention and therapy.

2.   Prevention

Prevention of child abuse and neglect is therefore highly desirable. Three forms of prevention can be distinguished: primary, secondary and tertiary prevention.

2.1   Primary prevention

Primary prevention is a universal action that is aimed and targeted at whole populations. It is the ideal form of prevention, and is designed to eradicate harm. An example of this form of prevention is immunisation of infants and children. In relation to child abuse and neglect, it has very limited applicability for two reasons:

- Child abuse and neglect affect a minority of the child population
- In order to eradicate it, a number of well-recognised social, adult and child risk factors, including poverty, parental substance abuse and child disability, would have to be eliminated.

However, there are some aspects of primary prevention that could reduce the prevalence of child maltreatment:
- Universal home visitation for infants
- Increasing children's awareness of sexual abuse (but not just teaching them and relying on them to protect themselves)
- Increasing public awareness of child maltreatment, and reducing the denial of its existence and perpetration within families.

2.2 Secondary prevention

Secondary prevention is intervention for selected groups considered to be at particular risk. This form of prevention has considerable applicability in this field and is a desirable approach to disseminate. Secondary prevention needs to be targeted at both adults and parents who are at risk of maltreating their children, and children who are particularly vulnerable to abuse.

2.2.1 Adults at risk of maltreating

Some adults are at risk of maltreating due to social adversity, which includes poverty, migration and being a young unsupported parent. Some adults will be personally vulnerable due to mental ill health, their own past abuse, their current substance (drug and alcohol) misuse, domestic violence and being a young unsupported parent.

2.2.2 Children vulnerable to maltreatment

Children with disabilities are recognised as a vulnerable group due to their high dependency on adults and their possible difficulty in communicating. Gene-environment interplay means that some children are genetically more vulnerable to the effects of maltreatment, whereas others are constitutionally resilient. This raises an interesting future ethical question regarding seeking ways of screening for vulnerability in young children in order to protect them preferentially.

2.2.3 Interventions within secondary prevention

One way of conceptualising secondary prevention is to regard it as working towards the protection of children. This approach allows for work with families where children are at risk of maltreatment, which attempts to achieve change within the family prior to considering the need to remove children from a situation of serious risk. However, such an approach bears the risk of 'drift', in which work continues with the family while sufficient change to ensure the children's safety within the family remains elusive. Such an approach therefore requires a clear plan of the changes aimed for, and the contingencies that would follow if sufficient change is not achievable after a trial of intervention. The risk of drift is especially present in families where maltreatment is an integral part of parent-child interaction, as occurs both in cases of neglect (lack of provision of care and supervision of the child) and emotional abuse where the maltreating parents are also the primary caregivers of the child.

A further aspect of secondary prevention is work with parents and other adults at risk of maltreating children. This includes social support as well as specific help for the adults' particular difficulties, which may include mental ill health, substance misuse, a capacity for sexually abusive behaviour and domestic violence.

Direct and specific help for the adult caregiver in caring for the child is another aspect of secondary prevention. This includes parenting work and helping to promote secure attachments by the child to the adult caregiver or parent. This requires:
- Responding to the child's attachment needs
- Not frightening the child
- Not expressing hostility towards the child
- Not interfering with the child's self-soothing
- Not interfering with the child's own exploration in a way that actually alarms the child in his or her exploration.

2.3 Tertiary prevention

Tertiary prevention is intervention which is intended to minimise the potential or actual effects of harm that has already occurred. Within the field of child maltreatment, tertiary prevention requires that the abuse and neglect are recognised and acknowledged, at least by professionals. In this field, an important principle of tertiary prevention is ensuring that maltreatment will be as brief as possible, which therefore calls for early intervention. This leads into the domain of child protection.

2.3.1 Child protection

For an individual child, protection from maltreatment may be also an aspect of secondary prevention, depending on whether the child is at risk of future maltreatment only or has already been harmed.

Immediate protection is required in cases of likely sexual abuse and serious non-accidental injury, often as an aspect of tertiary protection to avoid 'further' abuse. In theory, protection can be achieved in one of three ways:
- Bringing about change in the maltreating parent
- Supervising all interactions between the adult and the child
- Separating the child from the harmful persons or environment.

In practice, only the third option is a realistic immediate one. If the abuser(s), risky adult(s), or neglectful parent(s) are not the child's sole caregivers, then protection can be achieved by the departure of the risky adult. This is preferable to the alternative, namely the removal of the child and placing him or her with another family member, in another family, or in an institutional setting. This is, however, necessary if the child's needs cannot be fulfilled in his or her family and the child is not protected from abuse. Such an intervention may well require the sanction of a court of law, which will firstly decide whether the child is at sufficient risk of actual or further harm and secondly how the child is to be protected.

There are several reasons for the frequent need for involvement of the law for immediate protection of the child. Moving a child or requiring an adult to leave the home is a radical one, with considerable impact on the child and the family. Furthermore, the context for immediate protection is often denial (denial of the abuse or its harmful nature) and disbelief (disbelief in the child's allegations or in the medical findings, for instance, the evaluation of fractures in infants as non-accidental). Both criminal and civil child protection aspects of the law may become involved. With the alleged abuser as the focus of criminal law, it is doubtful that criminal law is the most appropriate option for the immediate protection of children. The guilt of a particular adult is not the main question at this point. The needs of the child are the paramount consideration, and a child may need protection from his or her family environment even if it is, at that time, unclear who abused the child.

Following the move of a child, it will, sooner rather than later, become necessary to make a decision about a permanent placement for the child. Uncertainty and frequent moves, both within alternative care settings and in and out of home, are harmful to the child's development. A rehabilitation home is, in theory, the preferred option. For this to be possible, changes in the behaviour of the parents and the home environment are necessary and need to be achieved within the child's time-scale. Effective intervention for drug and alcohol misuse, domestic violence and mental health problems are particularly important. In practice, they are not easily achievable and returning children home is associated with up to a 30% rate of breakdown of the placement.

For a minority of children then, a temporary change of home becomes a long-term or permanent change. If such a change becomes inevitable, delay in making the decision and in its implementation carries with it a poorer prognosis. There is much to commend about placing a child within kinship or extended family care. However, this option is not without its difficulties. The family is often the one in which the parents were, themselves, reared and may not therefore be trouble-free. It may be difficult for other family members, such as grandparents or aunts and uncles, to protect the child from further harmful contact with his or her parents. Professionals often overlook the fact that kinship carers require as much help and support as foster or adoptive parents.

While decisions are being made about the permanent placement of a child and during the period of uncertainty, it is important that the process is one of parallel planning, so that several pitons are explored simultaneously rather than sequentially. There is the possibility for some children to be placed with a family who could, if necessary, become the long-term, permanent parents of the child. Such an arrangement, termed concurrent planning, reduces the number of moves for the child. This is especially important for very young children.

108

2.3.2 Therapeutic work with the child's caregivers

The child's permanent caregivers, who may be the biological parents or alternative carers (foster or adoptive parents), require help and support in order to ensure that the child's placement and attachments become secure. The parents need help in:

- Understanding the troubled child's difficulties and experiences. The experiences of different children vary, as does the impact of the experiences on the particular child. For instance: telling lies may well indicate the child's inability and fear of owning up to his or her own misdeeds; stealing is often a sequel of deprivation; apparent lack of empathy is a reflection of the child's own experiences. In addition, the child may have his or her own innate difficulties such as, for instance, hyper-kinetic disorder or difficulties in the autism spectrum.
- Recognising sensitively the child's signals. Children may well not be able to express their reactions and feelings verbally. For instance, children may appear as rejecting affection, as a way of protecting themselves from disappointment, or may be frightened of reminders of past trauma that the caregiver may not recognise.
- Nurturing the child (including sensitive touch). Some children become very wary of touch, which they might misinterpret, or become avoidant of supportive contact as an aspect of disorganised attachment.
- Managing the child's behaviour. Some children who have been maltreated show oppositional, aggressive or anti-social behaviour. There are well validated ways of interacting with children who have these difficulties that lead to a significant reduction in these difficulties.
- Regulating the child's emotional arousal, and sleep and eating habits. Biological deregulation is one outcome of abuse and neglect, which started early in the child's life and requires particular attention.
- Following the child's lead. Given that many of the child's experiences, including moves, will have been imposed on the child, it is important to include the child in age-appropriate decision-making.
- Awareness of one's own reactions. Children who have been maltreated can evoke powerful and unexpected feelings in those who interact with them closely. These feelings include: compassion; sadness; anger with those who hurt the child, as well as sometimes with the child due to his or her behaviour; and a sense of helplessness or inadequacy in fulfilling the child's considerable needs. These feelings are all understandable but can be difficult to bear, and may impact adversely on the child and his or her placement. It is therefore important to work with the child's caregivers in dealing with their responses.

2.3.3 Therapeutic work with the child

Children who have been maltreated require help in a number of domains of their functioning:

- Depending on the nature of the abuse, a significant minority of children will suffer from post traumatic effects, including re-experiencing aspects of trauma, avoidance of reminders and general arousal. There are now

109

specific interventions for these difficulties, including Cognitive Behavioural Therapy (CBT), and Eye Movement Desensitisation and Reprocessing (EMDR).
- Children require specific help in coming to understand the nature of their abusive and neglectful experiences, as well as an opportunity to explore the impact and meaning of the experiences to them.
- Inappropriate sexualised behaviour is the most common sequel of sexual abuse and requires specific intervention in order to minimise the stigmatising effects on the child and possible harm to other children. Cognitive Behavioural Therapy has proven to be effective here.
- Older children require cognitive-directed help with their own difficult and antisocial behaviour (including a problem-solving approach, and work to help them develop an understanding of the effects of their behaviour on others and the consequences to themselves).
- Some children seem to lack empathy, and have difficulty in recognising others' and their own emotions, and in regulating their effect and arousal. They have frequent temper and angry outbursts. These difficulties require patient and skilled help.
- Many of these children show educational underachievement for a number of reasons. They require a careful analysis of the nature of their educational difficulties. Direct educational remediation, as well as attention to those factors which have contributed to the educational difficulties are necessary. This is one of the most important aspects of help for children who have been maltreated. It will enhance their self-esteem and contribute significantly to their social functioning.

The children clearly have a number of diverse needs that require attention. Different aspects of the work can be offered in individual, in group, or as part of parent-child or family settings.

2.3.4   The requirements and costs of tertiary prevention

The costs of tertiary prevention and child protection are considerable. It can only be effective if provided by a cooperative, multi-agency and multidisciplinary approach. It is neither appropriate nor efficacious for one agency to work in isolation. These agencies and professions include the legal profession, law enforcement, social care, various branches of medicine, psychology and mental health, and education.

Economically, it is very labour intensive. It requires constant communication between professions, skills by professionals, and supervision within professions and agencies.

3.   Conclusions

Child maltreatment is probably not entirely preventable. There is a place and need for all three forms of prevention. Inter-professional cooperation is essential to achieve any positive outcomes. In child protection, care must always be taken that no further harm is experienced by the child. Early intervention is essential in order to curtail the duration of the maltreatment, and to ensure that young children will enjoy the majority of their childhood free of abuse and neglect, and so that there is a prolonged opportunity for the sequels of maltreatment to abate. It is particularly important to attend to the needs of children after maltreatment has ceased, both in terms of treatment and attention for any remaining difficulties which the child may have and to the nature of any alternative placements. Permanency with sensitive and skilled care is vital with minimal number of moves.

'One Happy Island' Living Up to Its Name?

Comparison of Child Protection Policies in the Southern Caribbean

Wiebina Heesterman

1.   Introduction

When touching down on the Island of Aruba, one of the first things to strike the eye is a slogan on every number plate: 'One Happy Island'. Perhaps the island offers a happy experience to tourists, but the happiness certainly does not extend to all inhabitants. According to a recent report by the Dutch Social Economic Council (SER), the level of physical child neglect gives rise to concern and an estimated two per cent of children suffer serious abuse. These most alarming instances of lack of parental care are indicative of a more general 'affective neglect'. There is a shortage of after-school care in a society where many parents come home from work late and have difficulty communicating with their children.[1] A cause for concern is also the phenomenon of young people's sexual services to so-called 'sugar-daddies' and 'sugar-mommies'.[2] Recent developments of more coordinated procedures dealing with child abuse give some grounds for optimism.

We may ask whether awareness of conditions similar to those in Aruba on other islands in the southern Caribbean also gives rise to a more integrated approach to child abuse and neglect. This chapter examines the situation on three island territories: Aruba; the Republic of Trinidad and Tobago (T&T); and Curaçao, one of the Antilles Islands, which like the Island of Aruba is a semi-independent member of the Kingdom of the Netherlands. The chapter is based on interviews with key personnel of government child service departments and members of NGOs as well as recent publications.

In order to be able to comment on the effectiveness of child protection schemes in the different communities, the chapter begins by giving an outline of societal considerations. This is followed by an account of the history of child protection in the islands from the early 1900s onwards and a discussion of anticipated developments.

The three societies are multi-cultural and multi-lingual. Aruba displays these characteristics to the greatest extent, with as many as 79 different nationalities recorded in its population.[3] In addition, these islands attract large-scale immigration from both Latin America and other Caribbean islands due to their relative affluence.[4] In Aruba, children of undocumented families, estimated between 4000 and 8000 in 1996,[5] are particularly vulnerable, as their families live in constant fear of deportation.[6] These children are generally unable to attend school. Education is not compulsory and there is a shortage of teaching capacity.

Several factors contribute to a lack of family cohesion in Aruba and Curaçao, such as the steadily increasing number of one-parent families,[7] with many mothers still in their teens. In addition, parental alcohol and drug abuse threaten the fabric of family life.[8] Although Aruba is one of the more prosperous territories in the Caribbean, disparities in income give cause for further concern.[9]

All three communities attract mass tourism, which relies upon an imagery of exciting sexual encounters, while fuelling expectations of unattainable luxury lifestyles, particularly among young people.[10] In addition, the Carnival period, which begins several months before the date proper with the election of carnival queens and the creation of exciting and highly revealing female festival outfits, gives rise to an atmosphere of heightened sexuality. In particular in Aruba, female children may be drawn into a whirl of erotic excitement by being entered into girl queen elections, construing them as sex objects from an early age.[11] Here too the popular lyrics of a group called 'De Immoralen' link sex with violence directed at females, while in the English Caribbean, dance hall songs and calypso celebrate woman beating.[12] Also, domestic violence, which is often linked to child abuse and in any case negatively affects family members (even those who are not direct victims) is an all too frequent occurrence in much of the Caribbean.[13] Moreover, a firm belief in the benefits of corporal discipline ('spare the rod...') tends to be widespread in the Caribbean.[14]

2.   Geographical location and basic facts
Located between 11° and 12°N, near to the Venezuelan coast, outside the hurricane zone:

Aruba, Curaçao, Trinidad and Tobago

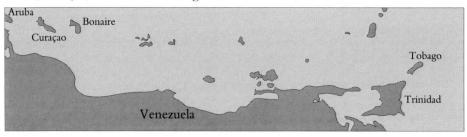

	Aruba	Curaçao	Trinidad and Tobago
Land surface	193 km^2	182 km^2	5,128 km^2
Population size	100,000	130,000	1,628,644
Under 18	15,474	44,958 below age 19	350,000 (1996 figures)
Ethnic composition	Mixed white/Carib Amerindian 80%, Latino, Chinese	Mixed black 85%, Carib Amerindian, white, East Asian, Latino, Chinese	Indian 40%, African 37.5%, Mixed 20.5%, Other
Language	Papiamento,[15] Dutch (official), English, Spanish	Papiamento 65.4%, Dutch 7.3% (official), English 15.9%, Spanish 6.1%, other 5.3%	English (official), Hindi, French, Spanish, Chinese
Religion	Roman Catholic 82%, Protestant 8%, Hindu, Muslim, Confucian, Jewish	Roman Catholic 72%, Protestant 3.5%, other Christian 16.8%, Jewish	Roman Catholic 26%, Hindu 22.5%, Anglican 7.8%, other Christian 23.8%, Muslim 5.8%
Economy	Tourism, offshore finance, oil refining	Tourism, oil refining, offshore finance	Petroleum – natural gas production, tourism
Legal system	Based on Dutch civil law with English common law influence	Based on Dutch civil law with English common law influence	Based on English common law
GDP per capita	$28,000 (2002 figures)	$11,400 (2003 est.)	$10,500

Based on CIA World Fact Book; Written replies to the Committee on the Rights of the Child, CRC/C/Q/NLD/2 and CRC/C/61/Add4; Government of Trinidad and Tobago (2003); Fundacion Telefon pa Hubentut Aruba (2005); Nieuws, September 21, 2005, http://www.arubaanse.com/Article5256.phtml.

3.   An overview of child protection procedures

One may divide a full sequence of procedures into four discrete phases: 1) abuse prevention; 2) procedures to deal with immediate risk or incipient maltreatment; 3) a post-abuse phase; and 4) re-integration. Elements of these phases can be found in all three societies. The different phases of a child protection framework in each of the three societies are shown in tabular form below. Institutions and programmes printed in bold focus on the well-being of children and young people, while those printed in bold italic are expected to become operational during the course of 2006.

4.   Phases of a child protection framework

	Aruba	Curaçao	Trinidad and Tobago
Abuse Prevention	• **Fundacion**[1] **Respeta mi** • **Child and Youth Telephone helpline** • **Fundacion pa nos Muchanan** (quality of childcare and education)	• SEDA,[16] FAJ[17] (Family support) • **Stichting Kinderbescherming Curaçao** • *Child and Youth Telephone helpline* (February 2006 start)	• Families in Action (Family support) • **YMCA** • **Child Telephone helpline** • **PLUS** (T&T Coalition Against Domestic Violence programme)
Immediate risk	• Juvenile Police and Vice Dept. • **Comiso di Abuso di Mucha** • *Sostenemi* (Advice and Reporting Centre) (March 2006 start) • **Child Protection Board** • Department of Social Affairs (voluntary assistance)	• **Werkgroep tegen kindermishandeling** • Juvenile Police and Vice Dept. • *AMK* (Advice and Reporting Centre) (Summer 2006 start) • **Child Protection Board** • Department of Social Affairs (voluntary assistance)	• Community Police • Rape Crisis Society • National Family Services Division (Ministry of Social Development) • *Children Authority* (To be established at an unspecified date)
Intervention	• Placement with relative, foster parents, children's home	• Placement with relative, foster parents, children's home	• Placement in Certified Industrial School/Orphanage
Rehabilitation	• Return to family/ under supervision by the **Child Protection Board/ Fundacion Guiami** & Dept. of Social Affairs	Return to family, supervision by the **Child Protection Board/ Fundashon PSI/Skutchami &** Dept. of Social Affairs	

5.   Criteria for the assessment of the efficacy of systems

In order to make an assessment of current policies on child abuse in three Caribbean societies by means of comparison, it is hard to think of more relevant criteria than those developed on the 'General Day of Discussion on Violence' of the Committee on the Rights of the Child.[18] Clearly, issues, such as appropriate legislation and adequate funding, are generally applicable to several of the phases outlined above. Also, additional questions need to be asked regarding the societal traditions and practices of the communities concerned.

6.   History of child protection – the twentieth century

6.1   Trinidad and Tobago

By the early 1900s the two islands formed a British colony. In 1962 they gained independence as the Republic of Trinidad and Tobago. The colony's delegated legislation reflected the law of the motherland. The Criminal Offences Ordinance No. 22 adopted in 1905, which criminalised sexual relations with girls under 16 and cruelty towards children, was based on the Offences Against the Person Act (1861) and the Criminal Law Amendment Act (1885).[19] Although the Protection of Children Ordinance was passed in 1919, the Corporal Punishment Ordinance (1905) was not abolished until 1940,[20] while the Children Act (1925), Chap. 46:01, which sanctions corporal punishment in the home, in schools, and institutions, was still in force in 2005.

The ethnic diversity led to the adoption of several parallel Marriage Acts, mostly dating from the 1920s and still in force today. The Marriage Act (1924), which requires parental consent for marriage of a person under 18, exists side by side with the Muslim Marriage and Divorce Act, by which a 12 year old female and a 16 year old male can marry with parental consent, the Hindu Marriage Act, with a minimum marriage age of 16 for girls and 18 for boys, and the Orisa Marriage Act (1999), where at least one of the parties professes the Orisa faith, the marriage age is 16 for girls and 18 for boys, unless one of the partners is a widow or widower, when couples can marry at a lower age.

The Family Law Act (1925) lays down the parental obligation to maintain their children, with failure to comply punishable by a fine of $1000 TT or two months imprisonment.

6.2 Post-independence legislation
The adoption of the Constitution of the Republic of Trinidad and Tobago (1976) heralded an era of home-grown legislation. The most important acts from our point of view are the Sexual Offences Act (1986), which sets the age of consent for sexual intercourse at 16, reconfirming the offences of rape, sexual relations with minors, incest, indecent assault and procuring of underage girls,[21] and the Domestic Violence Act (1991), which, in addition to protection for adult victims, provides for protection orders for children in respect of the whole range of physical abuse, from assault to reckless neglect. However, while several thousand cases of domestic violence are filed each year,[22] few child abuse cases are brought under the Act.[23]

6.3 Curaçao and Aruba pre-1986
The Antilles Islands, including Aruba, remained colonies until 1954, when the islands became semi-independent members of the Kingdom of the Netherlands.[24] Until 1986 when Aruba opted for separate status, legislation enacted for the Antilles applied to both Curaçao and Aruba. The first Criminal Code enacted for the islands received Royal Assent in 1913, was amended in 1960 and largely reflected the 1881 Dutch Criminal Code. Sexual Offences and Battery were covered in Titles XIV and XX. Other acts relating to young persons were Ordinances 1923, no. 37, and 1950, no. 35, concerned with corporal punishment and the conditions under which offenders under 16 could be manacled.

6.4 Child-related legislation post-1986
Criminal Codes, Titles XIV and XX, are still applicable to both islands. However, punishment tariffs differ, for instance, in the Sexual Offences Act.[25] Relevant are also Art. 1:356:1 BW (Civil Code) and Art. 1:359 BW, 'admitting minor into an institution' and 'suspension of parental authority'.

117

7. Awareness of child abuse

7.1 Trinidad and Tobago

It was not until the late 1980s that the Caribbean woke up to the endemic character of abuse of women and children. In 1987 a government report devoted exclusively to child abuse was published,[26] followed by a handbook specifying symptoms of physical abuse.[27] The Caribbean Regional Conference on Child Abuse & Neglect, October 10-13, 1989, in Port of Spain, Trinidad, was a major event calling attention to the phenomenon. Several papers respectively outlined the legal aspects,[28] Caribbean regional aspects[29], and different types of abuse[30] related to the Trinidadian situation. In 1989 the National Family Services Division of the Ministry of Social Development, which is responsible for the collation of cases of child abuse, was also established.

7.2 Curaçao

Before the mid-1980s child abuse did not receive any serious attention on the island, while the various agencies involved in child welfare operated with little in the way of coordination. Newspaper reports related to the issue tended to be sensationalist rather than informative.[31] In 1985 a meeting of welfare organisations, organised by the Guardianship Court, led to the creation of the 'Confidential Office for Child Abuse Cases', which unfortunately had to close after two years. Yet the enthusiasm to work towards the creation of an effective Advice and Reporting Centre did not abate. No fewer than ten delegates from Curaçao attended the 1989 Conference in Port of Spain, where Dr Jackson presented a paper, *Child Abuse – the experience of the Island of Curaçao*. Until the late 1990s the Foundation for Child Protection, established in 1947, mainly engaged in giving advice and practical help in educational situations. Since the mid-1990s the NGO has concentrated on the prevention of abuse through information and documentation. In the early 1990s young people also had access to a telephone helpline, which unfortunately was forced to cease operations due to financial irregularities.

7.3 Aruba

As in Curaçao, sexual child abuse has been far from people's thoughts until 1990, when the Department of Social Affairs organised a course on support for victims, leading to the establishment of *Fundacion Respeta Mi*, followed in 1997 by a Child Abuse Commission, appointed by the Minister of Social Affairs. The Commission has initiated projects relating to criminal procedures intended to facilitate cooperation with the Government and the Youth and Vice Police, for instance by making the hearing rooms child-friendly. In addition, it has developed a protocol for schools to draw the attention of teaching personnel to symptoms indicative of child abuse.

For both Curaçao and Aruba, accession to the Convention on the Rights of the Child (UNCRC) marked an important change. Accession took place in January 1998 for the Antilles, including Curaçao, and in January 2001 for Aruba. In both islands the Convention lies very much at the heart of the various organisations working on behalf of children.[32]

8.   The Twenty-First Century

8.1   Trinidad and Tobago

Although several acts relating to the welfare of children, including the Children's Authority Act No. 64, have been adopted in 2000, none of these were in force by late 2005. Neither had any official initiatives been formulated for a coordinated approach to the prevention of child abuse and/or the rehabilitation of victims. Yet violence in the home against children is widely reported in the media.[33] In addition, Trinidad's street children are seriously at risk of sexual and other violence.[34] According to a member of the Coalition against Domestic Violence, there is a great deal of misunderstanding concerning child sexual abuse, "People don't think that a thirteen year old girl having sex is being abused rather that she is hot or promiscuous." As violence at school and in the home tend to reinforce each other, the Coalition operates a programme 'Peace, Love and Understanding in Schools' aimed at the reduction of aggression and bullying. It also houses the T&T child helpline but this is rarely used to report violence or abuse.

Need for intervention: In many cases, taboos and fear of being accused of interfering prevent reporting of abuse.[35] On occasion, the response from the police may be seriously upsetting, as described by a YMCA outreach worker taking a 13 year old rape victim to the district police station. The circumstances, under which this particular instance of abuse took place, are all too common in the Caribbean: lone parents may encourage daughters to be 'kind' to men whose contribution to household expenses keeps the family afloat.[36] Recently there has been an unexplained reduction in numbers of the community police,[37] who provide a valued service, from 400 officers down to fewer than 80.[38] While counselling of abused children by NGOs has been known to lack professionalism,[39] psychological help may be provided to children placed by the National Family Services Division. However, provisions are acknowledged as being inadequate and limited.[40]

8.2   Curaçao

The main organisation engaged in preventative work is the *Stichting Kinderbescherming Curaçao*, which aims at educating and informing the public of abuse.[41] To that end, the Foundation issues publications and gives interviews in the media. Where intervention is required, it is the task of the Child Protection Board (an official body) to generate an order to remove children from abusive situations.

In 2001, the creation of an effective Advice and Reporting Centre against Child Abuse for Curaçao was raised again at the instigation of the Dutch Ministry of Health, Welfare and Sports, and the Antillian Department of Welfare, Family and Humanitarian Affairs.[42] An Action Plan was formulated on the basis of data obtained through fact-finding missions. Recommendations, such as the establishment of a National Steering Committee for central coordination and management, were set out in a subsequent report. This proposed a central role for the Foundation for Child Protection in conjunction with the Juvenile Police and Vice Department.[43]

Despite the publication of a further report, in 2003, which outlined practicalities for the envisaged Centre, like the creation of a reporting code similar to the one developed by the *Expertise-Centrum Kindermishandeling*,[44] by 2005 it had not been possible to establish an Advice and Reporting Centre due to financial constraints. However, new funding has been made available, and the new Centre is expected to be created by the end of 2006. Funding has also been made available for a new child helpline, to be operated by the Foundation for Child Protection and expected to become operational in early 2006.

8.3   Aruba

Two NGOs in particular should be singled out for their activities aimed at protecting children from abuse and neglect. The first one, *Fundacion Respeta Mi*, aims to make a contribution towards the prevention of child abuse by publicising new insights in the field. It operates an information centre, and organises lectures and workshops on subjects as diverse as sexual education, child violence and bullying. It also participates in TV programmes and publishes brochures in Papiamento, the language spoken by the majority of the population. It is intended to add a number of publications in Spanish in order to include the many immigrants from Latin America so as to try and reach out to more ethnic groups. This raises questions about differences in culture, expressed in child-rearing practices and in particular the punishment regimes practised in some immigrant communities.[45] It also conducts special campaigns, for instance on the prevention of physical punishment and parental behaviour at Carnival time. By late 2005 *Respeta Mi* was engaged in training professionals from a range of social sectors in gender issues and gender-specific assistance.

The other NGO is the Aruban Child and Youth Helpline, established in November 1999 on the model of the helpline then operated by Child Helpline Curaçao. It provides Aruban children with the opportunity to access information and talk about their concerns, which are essential in a society where there is a lack of communication within families. In the case of undocumented immigrant children, who may be locked in at home while parents are at work because they do not want to attract attention to their presence resulting in the family's extradition, non-communication is an even greater problem.[46] Aruba's toll-free helpline is staffed from 2-6 pm by trained volunteers, who assume a special helpline name and personality to ensure strict confidentiality, and are able to communicate in the four main languages spoken in Aruba, Papiamento, Spanish, Dutch and English. Several volunteers are still in their teens and closer in age to the target users. Whilst the majority of callers are desperate for a chat and some human contact, some ask questions concerning issues they are reluctant to discuss at home, such as sexuality, a topic that is still a societal taboo. The Helpline represents a sympathetic, non-judgmental response that stimulates young people to find a solution to their problems. Only two per cent of callers ring about violence,[47] mainly bullying and occasionally ill-treatment at home. Many children feel loyalty and love towards their parents despite any abuse, and are reluctant to expose them to punishment. To give an example, a seven year old told one of the helpline operators that her Daddy had a problem and that he needed help, as he wanted to do nasty things. She felt unable to confide in her mother, but the helpline volunteer encouraged her to think of relatives who could support her. Clearly a Child Telephone Helpline can act as a first line of support in abuse cases. The NGO celebrated its first five year anniversary by publishing a book on its work. Its continued operation is due to the support it has received from successive governments, secured by means of written agreements with Government Departments, the telecommunications industry, and business interests.[48]

Cases where intervention is required: Indication of a possible case of child abuse is reported to the police section Youth and Vice or the Child Protection Board.[49] If a child is in acute danger, the Board issues a child protection order,[50] later confirmed by the judge. If parents are implicated in the abuse, the person alerting the agency acts as the child's representative, and is encouraged to prepare her for an interview with the police and to reassure her. The police may refer the child to a gynaecologist if it is thought that there are internal injuries. In the event of prosecution, victims, who may be called as witnesses, are kept informed of the proceedings.[51]

The preferred solution is one which allows a child to remain in the community.[52] While social networks used to be more important in the past, relatives or friends may receive the child in their own family in the hope that counselling and support to parents and treatment of the child by a child psychologist will in due course allow family reunion. However, the large-scale immigration of the last 20 years has led to isolation of many migrant families, leading to placement in one of Aruba's children's homes.

The longest established children's home, *Fundacion Imeldahof*, founded in the 1950s by Catholic nuns, is able to accommodate children with social, emotional and behavioural problems, either on a voluntary basis or following referral by the Child Protection Board. Compared to the situation of five years ago, the level of general education of staff has increased, and training sessions are organised on a regular basis.

Although the majority of children in children's homes are native Arubans, undocumented immigrant children are also accommodated if their welfare is threatened. In that case special arrangements are required. Costs for medical care are reimbursed by the Child Protection Board, while state schools are generally prepared to admit undocumented children from the home.[53] Children who are removed from an abusing family are prepared for the judicial hearing by discussing the different stages of the judicial process. The homes are run on the principle that institutionalisation does not benefit young people and should be avoided if at all possible. As the preferred solution is to reintegrate children in their home environment, regular contact with parents and relatives is encouraged. When a young person goes back to her family, the situation is monitored by the social work team of the Department of Social Affairs or by *Fundacion Guiami*.

121

In November 2002, a member of staff of the Department of Social Affairs (also a member of the board of *Fundacion Respeta Mi*) attended the First Conference on Child Abuse Reporting & Advisory Centres in the Netherlands Antilles. Subsequently, Professor Hermanns also visited Aruba and presented a paper on the work of Reporting Centres. Soon afterwards, a Steering Group was appointed for the establishment of a Centre, consisting of professionals from Social Affairs and members of foundations, such as *Respeta Mi*, the Child Helpline and the Children's Homes. This resulted in the creation of an office to administer the future Centre, to be called *Sostenemi* ('Support me').[54] Staff, social workers, a part-time child abuse medical counselor and an administrator were appointed by Autumn 2005. The Centre will deal with all types of child abuse. Instead of multiple locations where abuse may be reported,[55] *Sostenemi* will provide a single referral point, intended to coordinate the activities of the different services,[56] with the emphasis on prompt response and strict confidentiality.

The four main tasks are envisaged as covering: 1) advice and consultation; 2) acceptance and processing reports of abuse; 3) coordination of support; 4) registration and referral to the organisation most suited to provide assistance.[57] Both child(ren) and parents should be kept informed throughout the procedures.

Independence from any existing services is regarded as an essential precondition for the Centre, in order to allow it to function on equal terms with other organisations. In addition, it should operate a low-threshold and provide a prompt response to referrals. It has been recommended that an organisation be created to provide support for *Sostenemi's* staff, possibly consisting of the members of the present Steering Group. A major difficulty is that currently care professionals are bound by a confidentiality code not to exchange client data with other organisations. This can work against the interests of clients. This complication gives rise to a need for research into the legal position regarding professional confidentiality and possible changes in the law. As the time to amend the law on issues such as confidentiality of medical practitioners would result in unacceptable delay, the intention is not to wait until amendments have been passed, but to rely instead on written protocols with various agencies, such as the Child Protection Agency, the Department of Youth Welfare, and the Youth and Vice Police. It is also proposed that Aruba adopt an Act of Youth Assistance in the near future on the lines of the recently enacted Dutch Act (*Wet op de Jeugd Hulpverlening*).

Without a low-threshold and well-known reporting point, the reporting situation has been something of a lottery. Few Arubans are aware that suspicious incidents can be reported anonymously, absolving them of the fear of being accused of interfering. As an additional safeguard, the new Reporting Centre will be authorised to involve the Child Protection Board without alerting the child's parents, in case this might compromise the informant's anonymity or increase risks to the child or her siblings. There are further recommendations concerning the need for written protocols on the various responsibilities of the different actors involved.[58]

9.   Conclusion

While it is not possible to discuss the full range of issues raised in the research on child protection in the three societies in a short chapter, several inferences can be drawn. In all three communities certain societal practices work to the detriment of children and young people. For instance, it is notable that violence against women and children is so widely accepted as to be celebrated in popular songs.

The expectations of mass tourism give rise to a skewed sense of the importance of youth, beauty and sexual gratification. In particular during the maelstrom of excitement of Carnival, it is unavoidable that young people are affected, whether neglected by parents, intent on enjoyment, or because they are drawn into the atmosphere of heightened sexuality which on that occasion intensifies to fever pitch. Whilst reporting of child abuse cases in the media still tends to be sensationalist, in T&T and Curaçao in particular, local television and newspapers have also been actively engaged in campaigns to raise awareness of the vulnerability of children to neglect and abuse.

While all three societies are multi-ethnic and multi-cultural, this has not resulted in any major confrontations. Apart from a number of preconceptions regarding specific ethnic groups, there is surprisingly little sign of inter-ethnic hostility or racial discrimination. In Trinidad, the different ethnic sections of the population largely live separate lives, although celebrating together on festive occasions. Perhaps there is a feeling that violence, robbery and gun crime in particular are the province of disaffected young Afro-Caribbeans. In Aruba, there is a certain tension between Arubans and the Latino immigrants, many of whom tend to be excluded from welfare services because of their undocumented status. The various social agencies and foundations are, however, well aware of the implications for children of this disadvantaged group and do their utmost to include these children in their programmes, treating them as children first and immigrants last, making no distinction between nationals and possibly undocumented children. In Aruba, the ability to speak several languages is taken for granted by the different agencies in the care sector.

In contrast to the lack of child sensitivity reported by several respondents in Trinidad, Aruba scores highly. The Helpline volunteers treat children with courtesy however rudely they behave, children are listened to and, above all, they are believed.

With regard to preventative measures, both NGOs and government social departments in T&T and Aruba are involved in programmes to assist and counsel dysfunctional families,[59] while NGOs on Curaçao engage with problem households through guidance and poverty relief.[60]

As to the creation of effective abuse reporting systems, the first precondition is the coordination of all agencies involved, recognised in recent project plans for centres in Curaçao and Aruba.[61] The latter began to form alliances at an early stage through written protocols and is well on the way to realising a high level of integration and coordination. In all three societies, social services departments and NGOs are aware of the need to improve record keeping. Trinidad's Family Services Division records statistical data. Aruba's children's homes were experimenting in Summer 2005 with a new computer system, intended to provide statistical information at the touch of a button, while the future Advice and Reporting Centres have budgeted for a proper record system.[62] However, a major difficulty is the failure of first-line recipients of reports of abuse to pass data to the agency charged with recording.

Although there is still a great deal of room for improvement, such as participation by children in decision-making in schools, advances since earlier visits to the Caribbean have been considerable. For example, there is more in service training and children's homes staff are now better educated.

Undoubtedly, there is a world of difference in attitude towards children between the early 1900s, when the law commanded special tariffs for whipping and manacling of children, and the present, with the partial abolition of corporal punishment and serious attempts to prevent the abuse of children at school and in the family. While all three islands have some elements in place that could form part of an effective child protection system, to date the territory with the most advanced preparations is undoubtedly Aruba. That the island appears to be on the point of adding an important link to its existing child protection system, is due to the enthusiasm and perseverance of the welfare workers and members of the various agencies involved and government support. However, there is still a great deal to accomplish.

Bibliography
CIA World Fact Book, http://www.cia.gov/cia/publications/factbook/index.html.
Committee on the Rights of the Child (2001), *Report of the Day of General Discussion on 'Violence Against Children within the Family and in Schools'*, *28th Session of the Committee on the Rights of the Child*, CRC/C/111, Geneva: UN Office of the High Commissioner for Human Rights.
Committee on the Rights of the Child (2002), *Concluding Observations of the Committee on the Rights of the Child: Netherlands Antilles*, CRC/C/15/Add.186, Geneva: United Nations.
Committee on the Rights of the Child (2004), *Concluding Observations of the Committee on the Rights of the Child: (Netherlands and Aruba)*, CRC/C/15/Add.227, Geneva: United Nations.
Daal, L.H. and Schouten, T. (1992), *Antilliaans Verhaal: Geschiedenis van Aruba, Bonaire, Curaçao, Saba, St. Eustatius en St. Maarten*, Zutphen: Walburg Pers.
Ferguson, J. (ed), (1997), *Caribbean Children's Law Project: Trinidad and Tobago: the law relating to children in Barbados, Jamaica, Guyana, Trinidad and Tobago*, prepared by F. Clift, London: Ackroyd, Hornby and Levy.
Ffolkes, S. (1997), 'Violence against women: some Legal Responses', *Gender: a Caribbean Multi-Disciplinary Perspective*, E. Leo-Rhynie, B. Bailey and C. Barrow. (eds.), Kingston: Ian Randle, Oxford: James Currey, pp. 118-130.
Forde, N.M. (1990), 'The Legal Aspects of Child Abuse in the English-speaking Caribbean', *Caribbean Regional Conference on Child Abuse & Neglect, October 10-13, 1989*, Port of Spain: Ministry of Social Development and Family Services.
Fundacion Telefon Pa Hubentud Aruba (2004), *Papia cu mucha*, Fundacion Telefon Pa Hubentud Aruba y Editorial Charuba.
Hermanns, J. (2001), *Towards Advice and Reporting Centres against Child Abuse*, Willemstad/Woerden: CO-ACT Consult.
Hermanns, J. and M. ter Meulen (2002), *Towards Advice and Reporting Centres against Child Abuse in the Netherlands Antilles; From Design to Implementation*, Willemstad/Woerden: CO-ACT Consult.
Inter-Agency Campaign on Violence Against Women and Girls (April 1999), *UNDP Regional Project RLA/97/014: National Reports on the Situation of Gender Violence Against Women: National Report Trinidad and Tobago*, http://www.undp.org/rblac/gender/trintobbigfile.pdf.
Jackson, D.H. (1990), 'Child Abuse – The experience of the Island of Curaçao, Netherlands Antilles', *Caribbean Regional Conference on Child Abuse & Neglect, October 10-13, 1989*, Port of Spain: Ministry of Social Development and Family Services, pp. 106-111.
Lazarus-Black, M. (2001), 'Law and the pragmatics of inclusion: governing domestic violence in Trinidad and Tobago', *American Ethnologist*, 28, pp. 388-416.
Le Franc, E. (2002), 'Child Abuse in the Caribbean; Addressing the Rights of Children', *Children's Rights, Caribbean Realities*, C. Barrow (ed.), Kingston: Ian Randle.
Mullings, B. (2004), 'Caribbean Tourism', *Introduction to the Pan-Caribbean*. T. Skelton (ed.), London: Edward Arnold, pp. 97-117.
Ministerie van Sociale Zaken en Infrastructuur (2003), *Gezin als pijler, Sociale sector van Aruba in perspectief*.
Ministry of Social Development and Family Services (1989), *Caribbean Regional Conference on Child Abuse & Neglect, October 10-13, 1989*, Port of Spain: Ministry of Social Development and Family Services.
Paynes, M. (1990), 'Child Abuse - a Caribbean Regional Perspective', *Caribbean Regional Conference on Child Abuse & Neglect, October 10-13, 1989*, Port of Spain: Ministry of Social Development and Family Services, pp. 51-99.
Rock, L. (2002), 'Child Abuse in Barbados', *Children's Rights, Caribbean Realities*, C. Barrow (ed.), Kingston: Ian Randle, pp. 305-345.
SER (2005), *Rapport: Veiligheid voor opgroeiende kinderen in Aruba*.
Sharpe, J. (1990), 'Child Abuse - The Trinidad and Tobago Perspective, *Caribbean Regional Conference on Child Abuse and Neglect, October 10-13, 1989*, Port of Spain: Ministry of Social Development and Child Services, pp. 99-105.
Stichting Kinderbescherming Curaçao (2005), Projectplan kinder- en jeugdtelefoon Curaçao. E. Hellinga (ed.), Stichting Kindertelefoon Curaçao.
Stichting Kinderbescherming Curaçao (2005), *Projectdossier Mucha t'ei … pa nos stima nan*.
Stuurgroep Advies- en Meldpunt Kindermishandeling (February 2005), *Sostenemi, Advies- en Meldpunt Kindermishandeling Aruba, Eerste Aanzet*, M. Hanegraaf (ed).

Stuurgroep Advies- en Meldpunt Kindermishandeling (May 2005), *Sostenemi, Centro pa conseho y coordinacion den caso di abuso y maltrato contra menor.*

Trinidad and Tobago Coalition on the Rights of the Child (2005), *NGO Comments on Trinidad and Tobago Second Periodic Report under the CRC,* http://www.crin.org/docs/resources/treaties/crc.40/Trinidad_ngo_report.pdf.

Werkgroep AMK (2003), *Projectplan advies- en meldpunt kindermishandeling (AMK) op Curaçao,* Curaçao, November 2003.

Yearwood, J.E. (1988), *Proceedings for dealing with child abuse and neglect, with special focus on non-accidental injury,* San Fernando: Medical Social Work Department.

Endnotes

1   SER (januari 2005), *Rapport Veiligheid voor opgroeiende kinderen in Aruba.*
2   *Ibid.,* p. 6.
3   Fundacion Telefon Pa Hubentud Aruba (2004), *Papia cu mucha,* Oranjestad: Fundacion Telefon Pa Hubentud Aruba y Editorial Charuba, p. 18.
4   Seven per cent of the Curaçao population is illegal (respondents from FAJ), eight to 20% per cent of Aruban inhabitants (several respondents).
5   Ministerie van Sociale Zaken en Infrastructuur (2003), *Gezin als pijler, Sociale sector van Aruba in perspectief,* p. 46.
6   A common occurrence (several respondents).
7   Over 40% of families on Curaçao and over a quarter of Aruban families are headed by a single parent, Stichting Kinderbescherming Curaçao (2005), 'Projectplan kinder- en jeugdtelefoon Curaçao', E. Hellinga (ed.), *Stichting Kinderbescherming Curaçao,* p. 7; Ministerie van Sociale Zaken en Infrastructuur, *Gezin als pijler,* p. 36.
8   Ministerie van Sociale Zaken en Infrastructuur, *Gezin als pijler,* p. 47.
9   SER, *Rapport: Veiligheid voor opgroeiende kinderen,* p. 33. Income of half of Aruban families is less than 2489 guilder, the official poverty line, Fundacion Telefon Pa Hubentud Aruba, *Papia cum mucha,* p. 21.
10 Mullings, B. (2004), 'Caribbean Tourism', T. Skelton, (ed.), *Introduction to the Pan-Caribbean,* London: Edward Arnold, pp. 103, 111.
11 Interviews 2000.
12 Ffolkes, S. (1997), 'Violence against Women: some Legal Responses', E. Leo-Rhynie *et al* (eds.), *Gender: a Caribbean Multi-Disciplinary Perspective,* Kingston: Ian Randle, p. 120.
13 Ffolkes, 'Violence against Women: some Legal Responses', E. Leo-Rhynie *et al* (eds.), *Gender: a Caribbean Multi-Disciplinary Perspective,* Kingston: Ian Randle, pp. 119-120; Jackson, D.H. (1990), 'Child Abuse - The experience of the Island of Curaçao, Netherlands Antilles', *Caribbean Regional Conference on Child Abuse & Neglect, October 10-13, 1989,* Port of Spain: Ministry of Social Development and Family Services; Le Franc, E. (2002), 'Child Abuse in the Caribbean, Addressing the Rights of Children', C. Barrow (ed), *Children's Rights, Caribbean Realities,* Kingston: Ian Randle, p. 288; Paynes, M. (1990), 'Child Abuse - a Caribbean Regional Perspective, *Caribbean Regional Conference on Child Abuse & Neglect,* October 10-13, 1989, Port of Spain: Ministry of Social Development and Family Services; Sharpe, J. (1990), 'Child Abuse - The Trinidad and Tobago Perspective', *Caribbean Regional Conference on Child Abuse and Neglect, October 10-13, 1989,* Port of Spain: Ministry of Social Development and Family Services, p. 101.
14 Interviews, also Sharpe, 'Child Abuse - The Trinidad and Tobago Perspective', note 13 above, p. 99.
15 A Spanish - Dutch - English - Portuguese - African language. Hermanns (2001), *Towards Advice and Reporting Centres against Child Abuse,* Willemstad/Woerden: CO-ACT Consult, pp. 61, 62.
16 Fundacion, Fundashon, Stichting = Foundation, NGO; Kinderbescherming = child protection.
17 Sentro pa Desaroyo di hende Muhé.
18 Federatie Antilliaanse Jeugdzorg.
19 Committee on the Rights of the Child (2001), *Report of the Day of General Discussion on 'Violence Against Children within the Family and in Schools', 28th Session of the Committee on the Rights of the Child (CRC/C/111)* , Geneva: UN Office of the High Commissioner for Human Rights.

20 S.2 of the Ordinance.

21 A male offender not above the age of sixteen years of age [. .] may in lieu of any other punishment be ordered to be whipped [. . .]. Where the offender is seven years of age, and not more than twelve years of age, the number of strokes shall not exceed six.

22 Rape, sexual relations with girl under 14 and buggery with male under 16 punished with life imprisonment.

23 Lazarus-Black, M. (2001) 'Law and the pragmatics of inclusion: governing domestic violence in Trinidad and Tobago,' *American Ethnologist* 28, p. 396.

24 Three cases of child abuse specifically (interview with the Director of the National Family Services Division).

25 Daal, L.H. en T. Schouten (1992), *Antilliaans Verhaal: Geschiedenis van Aruba, Bonaire, Curaçao, Saba, St. Eustatius en St. Maarten*, Zuthphen: Walburg Pers, p. 134.

26 Criminal Code, Aruba 1991, Title XIV Sexual Offences, AB 1991. Antilles: Art. 250 sexual relations with girl under 12, punishment up to 24 years imprisonment. Aruba: up to 12. However, promoting sexual relations with minor child, step-child, or foster-child, or young person to whom the culprit stands in a position of authority, Art. 258, four years in both jurisdictions.

27 Ferguson, *Caribbean Children's Law Project*, p. 75.

28 Yearwood, J.E. (1988), *Proceedings for dealing with child abuse and neglect, with special focus on non-accidental injury*, San Fernando: Medical Social Work Department.

29 Forde, N.M. (1990), 'The Legal Aspects of Child Abuse in the English-speaking Caribbean', *Caribbean Regional Conference on Child Abuse & Neglect, October 10-13, 1989*, Port of Spain: Ministry of Social Development and Family Services.

30 Paynes, *Child Abuse - a Caribbean Regional Perspective*, note 13 above.

31 Sharpe, *Child Abuse - The Trinidad and Tobago Perspective*, note 13 above.

32 Jackson, D.H. (1990), 'Child Abuse-the experience of the Island of Curaçao', note 13 above, p. 108.

33 Stichting Kinderbescherming Curaçao (2005), *Projectplan kinder- en jeugdtelefoon Curaçao*, note 13 above, p. 5; Fundacion Telefon pa Hubentud Aruba, *Papia cu mucha*, note 3 above, p. 14. Interview with office-worker of Fundacion Respeta Mi.

34 'Man gets 30 years for incest with girl, 12' and 'Baby doused with pepper sauce', pp. 3 and 7, *Trinidad Guardian*, August 30, 2005, also letter from Diana Mahabir-Wyatt, *Trinidad Guardian*, April 9, 2005.

35 YMCA outreach worker.

36 Interview with the Director of the National Family Services Division.

37 See Rock (2002), 'Child Abuse - a Caribbean Regional Perspective', *Caribbean Regional Conference on Child Abuse & Neglect, October 10-13, 1989*, Port of Spain: Ministry of Social Development and Family Services, pp. 334-335.

38 Such policing is representative of a strategy promoting cooperation between police and community to solve mutually defined problems, 'Inter-Agency Campaign on Violence Against Women and Girls (1999)', *UNDP Regional Project RLA/97/014: National Reports on the Situation of Gender Violence Against Women: National Report Trinidad and Tobago*, p. 46.

39 Interview with YMCA outreach worker.

40 As above. "The counsellor urged a girl rape victim to seek salvation in religion."

41 Interview with the Director of the National Family Services Division, also Ferguson, J. ed. (1997), *Caribbean Children's Law Project: Trinidad and Tobago: the law relating to children in Barbados, Jamaica, Guyana, Trinidad and Tobago*, prepared by F. Clift, London: Ackroyd, Hornby and Levy, p. 76.

42 295 cases between October 2003 and December 2004 (Stichting Kinderbescherming Curaçao (2005)), *Projectdossier Mucha t'ei … pa nos stima nan*, p. 9.

43 Hermanns, J. (2001), *Towards Advice and Reporting Centres against Child Abuse*, Willemstad/Woerden: CO-ACT Consult, p. 53.

44 Hermanns, J. and M. ter Meulen (2002), *Towards Advice and Reporting Centres against Child Abuse in the Netherlands Antilles; From Design to Implementation*, Willemstad/Woerden: CO-ACT Consult.

45 Werkgroep AMK (2003), *Projectplan advies- en meldpunt kindermishandeling (AMK) op Curaçao*, Curaçao, p. 18.

46 "Physical punishment is common in the Latino culture, while some immigrants from islands such as Haiti, have been known to burn a child's hand on the stove or touch them with a hot iron" (Helpline staff).

47 "Sometimes they ring out of boredom, having nobody to talk to", as above.

48 827 cases from 1999 to 2003.

49 Fundacion Telefon Pa Hubentud Aruba, *Papia cu mucha*, note 3 above, pp. 13, 14.

50 Shortly before the interview the Board received a phone call that a three year old was seriously abused by her mother, who kicked her in the stomach and head in the presence of a third party.

51 Civil Code, 1: 362.

52 Actiegroep inzake seksueel misbruik van minderjarigen, *Opvang, begeleiding en rechtsgang van minderjarigen bij sekseel misbruik*, pp. 1-12.

53 Acting Head of the Child Protection Board.

54 The Home's Director.

55 Stuurgroep Advies- en Meldpunt Kindermishandeling (February 2005), M. Hanegraaf (ed), *Sostenemi, Advies- en Meldpunt Kindermishandeling Aruba, Eerste Aanzet*, p. 4.

56 People have no idea whom to contact, and feeling embarrassed, ring nobody, or perhaps several agencies, leading to duplication (Acting Head of the Child Protection Board).

57 Stuurgroep Advies- en Meldpunt Kindermishandeling, *Sostenemi, Advies- en Meldpunt*, note 55 above, p. 4.

58 Stuurgroep Advies- en Meldpunt Kindermishandeling (2005), *Sostenemi, Centro pa conseho y coordinacion den caso di abuso y maltrato contra menor*.

59 Stuurgroep Advies- en Meldpunt Kindermishandeling, *Sostenemi, Centro pa conseho y coordinacion*, § 6.3

60 Representative of 'Families in Action', Director of the National Family Services of Division T&T, and social worker of Departments of Social Affairs of Aruba.

61 Office-holders of FAJ and SEDA.

62 Werkgroep AMK (2003), *Projectplan advies- en meldpunt kindermishandeling*; Stuurgroep Advies- en Meldpunt Kindermishandeling (May 2005), *Sostenemi, Centro pa conseho y coordinacion*, note 58 above.

63 Hermanns and ter Meulen, *Towards Advice and Reporting Centres against Child Abuse*; Stuurgroep Advies- en Meldpunt Kindermishandeling, *Sostenemi, Centro pa conseho y coordinacion*, note 58 above.

Participation of Ethnic Parents
by the Child Protection Board

Herman Klein

1.   Introduction

The *Participation of Ethnic Parents* is a project of the Child Protection Board in the city of Zwolle in the Netherlands. To better understand the project, an explanation is given here below of the legal tasks of the Child Protection Board. Secondly, some aspects of the juvenile criminal system are explained, followed by a description of the participation of parents.

2.   Legal tasks of the Child Protection Board

2.1   Mission Statement
The Child Protection Board (*Raad voor de Kinderbescherming*) represents the rights of the child whose development and upbringing are under threat. The Board creates conditions to remove or prevent this threat. The Board makes inquiries, provides advice in legal proceedings and can suggest measures or sanctions. The Board works in close cooperation with other agencies.

2.2   The right to care and protection
In the early 1900s Dutch law provided the country's first children protection legislation. As of 1995, the countries that enforce the UN Convention on the Rights of the Child (*Internationale Verdrag inzake de Rechten van het Kind*) include the Netherlands. Its premise is that a child requires special care and protection due to his/her vulnerable and dependant position. Evidently, the parents bear primary responsibility in this respect. They must provide care for their child, bringing him/her up and encouraging his/her development. If parents do not (cannot) assume their responsibility then the development of the child is put in jeopardy. In such situations, the authorities must provide support to the family and intervene if the situation of the child improves insufficiently. It is the Child Protection Board – a department of the Ministry of Justice – that performs these duties.

2.3   Inquiry and advice
Every child must be afforded the opportunity to develop into an independent and stable adult. This equally applies to children in trouble. The Child Protection Board represents the interests of these children by making inquiries into their (home) situation and by recommending professional help or imposing measures. All the Board's activities give priority to the interests of the child.

The Board itself does not provide assistance to families. The Board does ensure that, if necessary, professional help is called in.

The Board is a so-called second-line organisation. This implies that only a limited number of organisations are authorised to make direct contact with the Board, such as the Bureau Youth Care and Assistance / Child Abuse Counselling and Reporting Centre (*Bureau Jeugdzorg (BJZ) / Advies- en Meldpunt Kindermishandeling (AMK)*), the Police and the Courts. Other agencies and persons are permitted to call in Board assistance directly, but only in extremely grave situations. The AMK is notified when the Board accepts a crisis report as basis for an inquiry. This avoids a situation whereby both organisations work on the report.

2.4 The duties of the Board

The scope of activities of the Child Protection Board is broad. The Board:
- Is involved with families where upbringing has become a problem
- Is called in when divorcing parents are incapable of making arrangements concerning their children, such as arrangements regulating visitation rights or fixed abode
- Is involved in cases concerning adoption, ceding and descent
- Plays a role in criminal cases involving under-age children.

These duties are described below.

2.4.1 Protection

Sometimes the circumstances of the child and his/her family are so distressing that the professional help being provided is not adequate (any longer). Another possibility is that a family refuses to accept any help. The Bureau Youth Care and Assistance (*BJZ*) – or a section of it, the Child Abuse Counselling and Reporting Centre (*AMK*) – will then call in the Child Protection Board.

When the Board, having made its enquiries, decides that intervention is required, it will petition the Juvenile Court to order a so-called child protection remedy. The ruling of the Court will in part be based on the information provided by the Board. A remedy limits the authority of the parents, in whole or in part, until the situation of the child has improved. Moreover, professional help is (re-) initiated. The family is obligated to accept this help.

2.4.2 Divorce and visitation

The law provides that, after a divorce, parents in principle retain joint parental authority. The right to visitation of parents and children is regulated by law as well. It is important that both parents make effective arrangements about visitation, as they must about the fixed abode of their child. When parents are incapable of arranging these aspects themselves then they can petition the Court to rule on this. If necessary, the Court can request the Child Protection Board for advice.

2.4.3 Adoption, ceding and descent

When people wish to adopt a child then the Child Protection Board conducts a family home inquiry. This is a review of the family's suitability to bring up an adoptive child.

The Board is also engaged when parents wish to cede their child.

People may also apply to the Board when – after adoption or ceding – they have questions about their descent or want to get into contact with their biological parents or their child.

2.4.4 Punishment
When a minor is charged with an offence, or placed into custody, then the Police will notify the Child Protection Board. The Board will monitor this minor during his/her punishment, making sure that all activities of, for instance, the Board, the Police and the Prosecutor are properly coordinated. Moreover, the Board can make inquiries to inform the Prosecutor and the Court about the juvenile. Also, as a rule, the Board advises them on prosecution, punishment and professional help. In addition, the Board coordinates the enforcement of community service orders (see further below).

3. Juvenile criminal cases
When a child between the ages of 12-18 years is charged with an indictable offence, or is placed into custody, the police will notify the Child Protection Board. The Board will make inquiries to inform the public prosecutor and, if necessary, the court about the child. The Board also advises them about punishment and professional help, if applicable. The events that unfold when a child is suspected of an indictable offence are outlined here below. The Child Protection Board is involved in a number of the stages of the punishment.

3.1 Police questioning
When the child is suspected of an indictable offence, he/she will be questioned by the police. The police will want to hear from the child what he/she has done and why. In certain cases, for a minor offence for instance, the police can release the child with a caution.

3.2 Police report
In more serious cases the police will draft a police report. This relates what the child has told the police about his/her offence. This report also includes the statements of witnesses or victims, if applicable. The police will forward this report to the public prosecutor. The Child Protection Board is notified of the police report as well, upon which, as a rule, the Board starts an inquiry.

At least once a week, police, public prosecutor and Board meet to review all criminal cases of children in their district. During this so-called case review, they also discuss the child. They coordinate who does what and when this is done.

3.3 Public prosecutor and the court
The public prosecutor decides whether the child should receive punishment. The decision of the public prosecutor depends, among other things, on the seriousness of the matter. The public prosecutor can impose punishment but may also decide

that the child will appear before the court. In such cases, the court decides whether the child receives punishment.

3.4 Remanded in policy custody

Once the police report has been drafted, the child may be released. But if the offence is very serious or complex then the child is placed in police custody. He will then be required to remain at the police station to assist the police in its inquiries. In such cases, counsel is appointed to the child. Moreover, an associate of the Child Protection Board will visit the child to check on how he/she is doing.

3.5 Arraignment

In the course of his inquiries, the public prosecutor will question the child. The child will be arraigned before the public prosecutor for questioning. When the public prosecutor wants to prolong the custody period of the child, he must petition the court for permission. In this case also the court will hear the child. If the court rules that there is no longer any need for the child to be kept in custody, the child will (sometimes on certain conditions) be released. This does not mean, however, that the matter is settled.

3.6 Pre-trial detention

When the Court decides to prolong the custody period of a child, this means the start of the pre-trial period of detention (pre-trial detention). This has a maximum duration of 100 days: 10 days in police custody, 30 days imprisonment and two 30-day periods of extended imprisonment. These stages are consistently subject to an official court ruling. Duration of detention is subsequently deducted from the punishment.

3.7 Dismissal

When the public prosecutor decides against further prosecution of the child, he will dismiss the case. In such cases, the child is not required to appear in court. Another option is for the public prosecutor to decide against further prosecution of the child and instead impose punishment himself, for instance a penalty. This is called a *transactie* (discharge from liability to conviction by payment of a fixed penalty). The public prosecutor can attach one or several conditions to such a *transactie*, like counselling by the juvenile probation and after-care service. The case is dismissed when the condition(s) of the *transactie* have been fulfilled by the child. If not, then he/she will be required to appear before the court after all.

3.8 Court hearing

If a court hearing is decided then the child is appointed counsel. The child is ordered to appear in court by means of a written summons. This appearance is attended not only by the parents, the child and his/her counsel, but also by a judge and the public prosecutor. There may also be someone from the Child Protection Board. This is not a public hearing.

3.9   Decision

The courts will rule whether it has been proven that the child has committed the indictable offence. If this has not been proven then the child is acquitted. If the child is proven guilty as charged then the court will pronounce sentence for the indictable offence within two weeks.

Punishment ordered against the child may be a penalty, community service, imprisonment or treatment.

4.   The role of the Board

The role of the Child Protection Board in juvenile criminal cases consists of the following:
-   The Board makes inquiries into the background of the child, checking for the presence of, for instance, personal or family problems
-   The Board informs the public prosecutor and the court, advising them on a fitting punishment and suitable form of professional help
-   The Board ensures professional help is initiated
-   The Board coordinates the imposed community service
-   The Board monitors coordination of the activities of all agencies concerned with the child.

4.1   The inquiry

The inquiry is conducted by an associate of the Board: the Board investigator. The Child Protection Board maps out the situation of the child and the family. When there are problems in the family, or personal problems, then the Board investigator will seek a solution together with the parents and the child. The Board investigator makes decisions in consultation with others. Board methods and procedures have been formally laid down.

When a minor is subject of a police report or is remanded in custody, this is reason for the Child Protection Board to institute a systematic inquiry into the child and his/her circumstances.

A significant part of the inquiry is an interview with both the parents and the child. The purpose of the interview is to get to know more about the personal circumstances of the child. As a rule these interviews are based on a detailed questionnaire.

The Board investigator also speaks with other people who can inform him about the child, like a teacher. Usually these interviews suffice for the Board investigator to obtain an accurate impression of the child.

4.2   Follow-up inquiry

In some cases more inquiries are needed, for instance because the Board still has insufficient information or because there are problems. Moreover, the Board or the court may decide to have the child examined by a special expert, like a psychologist or psychiatrist. This is called a personality examination.

133

4.3   Problems

Sometimes indictable conduct signals specific problems. A child may suffer personal problems or things are not going well at home or at school. The Board therefore investigates whether the child has such 'underlying problems', purpose being to initiate, if necessary, professional help for the child and thus to prevent reoccurrence of his/her indictable conduct.

4.4   Consultation

In the course of his inquiries, the Board investigator has regular consultations with his supervisor and other Board associates such as a behaviourist and a legal expert. He therefore never takes decisions alone and his recommendations are always prepared in consultation with others.

4.5   The report

An inquiry is concluded with a report in which the Board investigator states conclusions and the sentencing advice of the Child Protection Board. The report describes the course of the inquiry and includes information supplied by others. Moreover, the Board investigator will include the views of the parents and the child. The report also contains the conclusions drawn by the Child Protection Board. The report concludes with a sentencing advice to the public prosecutor and possibly the court.

The Board forwards a copy of the report to the public prosecutor and if necessary to the court. The parents and the child also receive a copy at home, to which they can both give their comments. If it contains inaccuracies they can say so. Their comments are added to the final report or sent afterwards to the public prosecutor or the court.

4.6   The sentencing advice

The Child Protection Board issues a sentencing advice to the public prosecutor and to the judge. The intention of the Board with this sentencing advice is to achieve a situation whereby the child refrains from committing another indictable offence. If applicable, recommendations are also made to resolve personal or family problems.

The inquiry report of the Child Protection Board is intended for the public prosecutor and if necessary the court. This is the advice of the Board concerning punishment best suited to the child in pedagogical terms. After all, the child must learn something from his/her punishment so that he/she will behave better in future. The report may contain advice about further inquiries or about required counselling for the child, which may include calling in the juvenile probation service.

The public prosecutor and the court include the advice and recommendations in their considerations. However, they are independent officials free to accept or ignore Board advice.

The inquiry may show a situation involving serious upbringing or family problems. In such cases, the Board can petition the court to order a so-called 'child protection remedy', like Custodial Control of the child. The Board will only make such a drastic request when it is evident that the parents are not (any longer) capable of voluntarily coping with things, and the development of the child is gravely jeopardised by the situation.

4.7   Other activities
During the course of the child's punishment, the Child Protection Board monitors the activities of all agencies and persons involved in the case of the child, in this way ensuring proper coordination of all activities.

When the child is required to perform community service, the Board coordinates its implementation. The Board provides a fitting community service for the child and informs the public prosecutor on its progress.

5.   Participation of ethnic parents
The Penal Unit of the Child Protection Board deals with minors between the ages of 12 and 18 years who have committed an offence. The Child Protection Board does research about the minors, and reports and advises the Prosecutor and Juvenile Judge from a pedagogical point of view. The social workers of the Board are looking for explanations for the criminal behaviour and for possible problems. The Board is also responsible for the execution of community services. These community services are divided into working- and learning sentences.

The recruiting of new working projects and the development of new learning programmes are also the task of the Board. The progress and the final results of the community services are reported to the Prosecutor.

The project *Participation of Ethnic Parents* was preceded by a number of developments in society and thereby in the organisation. Fifteen years ago the average age of the youngsters committing an offence was approximately 16 or 17 years. Now we see more and more a movement towards a younger age. Youngsters of 12 years committing an offence are not exceptional any more.

There has also been a change in society towards the position of youngsters in the last ten to 20 years. Twenty years ago we looked towards youngsters as independent, grown-up, making their own decisions, etc. Nowadays we worship the role of parents again, we see that growing up is a process which develops gradually. To an increasing degree we, as a society, hold parents responsible for the behaviour of their children. We see this not only in Holland but also abroad. In England this is shown in court orders, etc.

These changes in society also influenced our vision on juvenile delinquency and especially the role of the parents in this matter. Our vision was also influenced by scientific research of one of the staff members of the Child Protection Board in Zwolle, the Netherlands. One of the conclusions of this research (*Passen en Meten*,

Herman Klein 2001) was that the community services of ethnic juveniles are finished less successfully than the community services of Dutch juveniles. In the years 1999 and 2000, respectively, 8% and 5% of the community services of Dutch juveniles failed; for ethnic juveniles the failure percentages were 28% and 29% in these same years.

The Child Protection Board who is responsible for the execution of the community services has started to improve its work by focusing on a central finding of a follow-up analysis: the lack of social control in the ethnic groups in comparison with the Dutch. The idea of participation of ethnic parents is that parents who are aware of the importance of a successful community service and who are better informed will stimulate their children to perform and finish the community service successfully.

With this new idea, we looked at our primary working processes and changed these where necessary. In the new approach, in the first investigation after the police has made up a warrant, the executive employees from the Penal Unit:

- Have a outreaching methodology and stimulate the empowerment of parents
- Inform parents about the criminal-law-chain
- Inform parents about the importance of a successful community service
- Discuss with parents the importance and necessity of participation in the execution of community service
- Advise parents about bringing up children in Holland, in a different culture
- Advise parents about the importance of involvement with your children by being there and being informed
- Invite parents for the start and end of the community service, and during the intake the rules are explained to the youngster and his/her parents. Parents may mention their learning aims for their child or participate in training or therapy. Parents are equally responsible for the appointments made
- Use official interpreters if parents do not speak the Dutch language well enough. The use of children or other family members as an interpreter is not longer accepted.

The participation of parents depends on the project. The work projects have been informed and are prepared to meet the parents. Parents are invited for the introduction at a work project. In the learning projects parents are invited for the introduction, evaluation and the final conversation. The community service and the role of the parents are made to measure, and parents will be activated as much as possible. The probation officer will also participate. If a youngster breaks any rules the parents are informed. A yellow card, an official warning, will be talked through with the youngster and the parents. The police, the Prosecutor and the Judges are informed of this way of working and also stimulated to involve the parents.

In order to create a common understanding and support for this methodology in the ethnic groups, we invest strongly in contacts and information meetings. In these meetings we inform the parents and discuss matters like the work of the Child Protection Board, and especially the Penal Unit, our working method, the participation of parents, raising children and integration in the western society. These meetings also give us new information and inspiration to coordinate our products even more to the diversity of the modern society.

The first results of our new methodology are good. The percentage of failed community services of ethnic juveniles has reduced drastically. These results will be the subject of further scientific research.

Equal opportunities for ethnic juveniles are created by an unequal approach.

Child Participation:
A Way to Prevent First-Time Offending

Carine Le Borgne

1.   Introduction

Child participation is a strong tool, a strong way, to fight first-time offending. The aim of this article is to show that child participation, with the full participation of young people, will make them more involved in the community and more integrated in society.

Juvenile delinquency is an ongoing issue in society. Despite the numerous investments in prisons, in rehabilitation measures, delinquency is still growing. Such investments are not an adapted answer to the question of how to reduce first-time offending.

Adults do not see children as a partner in the society's development. Some young people are still invisible to adults and their views are not taken into account. These young people are not integrated in society, and they feel angry because they are not being listened to. Adults do not involve them in the decision-making processes of issues that directly affect them. Some adults notice young people more through their misbehaviours, rather than the positive actions they bring to our society.

The late events in France are a good example. The French media showed young people burning cars, and an atmosphere of fear was created between adults and those young people. According to the young people, the only way to express themselves was to misbehave. The events highlighted the tensions between wealthy big cities and their grim ghettos, *les cites*, where young people do not feel like they belong or can participate in society, and therefore feel excluded.

Professionals working with and for children should be more sensitive to child participation. They should have knowledge on how to implement full child participation programmes that prevent first-time offending. In this regard, it is important to look critically at the nature of the participation of children, and to avoid manipulation, decoration and tokenism.

2.   Why develop child participation programmes to prevent juvenile delinquency?

2.1   The UN Convention on the Rights of the Child and the United Nations Guidelines for the Prevention of Juvenile Delinquency

Article 12 of the UN Convention on the Rights of the Child sets out the right of children to express their opinions and to have these opinions taken into account when decisions are being made that will affect them.

Article 12 provides a wonderful opportunity for children to become involved in decisions affecting their lives. This scope for children's involvement in decisions affecting them is a positive step towards empowering children, protecting their interests and building their future capacity. Moreover, it encourages adults to be more receptive to the insights and understanding of children.

In the United Nations Guidelines for the Prevention of Juvenile Delinquency (The Riyadh Guidelines), children are fully-fledged participants in society. Article 3 states that:

> *A child-centred orientation should be pursued. Young persons should have an active role and partnership within society and should not be considered mere objects of socialization or control.*

In the same direction, Article 10, which is essential for all areas of socialisation, states:

> *Due respect should be given to the proper personal development of children and young persons, and they should be accepted as full and equal partners in socialization and integration processes.*

Article 2 reflects:

> *Prevention of juvenile delinquency requires efforts by the entire society to ensure the harmonious development of adolescents, with respect for and promotion of their personality from early childhood.*

The conclusion can be drawn from these article that developing child participation programmes leads to work with young children and their families to reduce the risks of crime and anti-social behaviour. Parental involvement and interaction with their children form a potential factor against the development of offending. For example, a parent listening to his or her child's views may benefit family functioning and improve a young child's chance of never offending. Developing child participation programmes contributes to enhancing children's skills like confidence, self-esteem, and communication, and they feel more valued. It should be emphasised that children's participation has an impact on their socialisation within the family and society, and facilitates better integration. Children should be recognised as citizens who have a right to express their opinions and to have their views given due consideration. The participation of children in decision-making processes makes them partners in society.

2.2 The snowball effect theory on child participation in tackling juvenile delinquency

The snowball effect theory shows that child participation is a necessity in tackling juvenile delinquency. The snowball effect means that child participation can be a key factor for a better integration of children in society and, thus, in the prevention of first-time offending.

The snowball effect theory can be explained in the following way. If young people are listened to by adults, if they are able to participate in the decision-making processes regarding their issues, they will feel recognised as actors of their families or communities. Therefore, they will involve themselves in projects which build their personality and future. They will feel like actors of their life. They will feel responsible and will start understanding what is right from wrong. They will know that they do not need to misbehave to be heard since they can share their ideas. They will know that they will be respected, and therefore they will respect others. Therefore, young people need to be involved in their families' lives, and integrated in their communities to prevent first-time offending.

To illustrate this theory, let us return to the French riots of 2005. We notice that parents are giving up on their roles. Young people have poor parental supervision, and discipline. Children do not have support or protection from their parents any more. Most of the time, these children drop out of school and become involved in drug/alcohol or criminal environments. They do not have a family or societal frame. They become marginalized. Young people living in the *cites*, where the conditions of living are grim, become closed in the *cite* which is their world, without hope to get out. They are faced with a society that avoids or ignores them. They are in a situation where they are often unable to express their views in any other way than through acting out behaviour, including aggression. In this case, young people decided to be heard and taken into account by burning vehicles. Interaction with bad behaviour can be an indication of vulnerability and distress. Young people feel angry because adults are not listening.

Rosenczveig, a president of a juvenile court in Region Parisienne, says, "To destroy everything around them is not a suicide act for those young people because they are already dead". (*"tout détruire autour d'eux n'a rien de suicidaire pour ces jeunes puisqu'ils sont déjà morts"*). These words are strong but it reveals how young people feel about themselves, how integrated they feel in the country.

Those young people were not listened to. They could not express their miseries, how down they were feeling. They were left to themselves. They were not participating in any constructive activities or projects that involved their opinions and commitment. Their parents had no influence on them any more.

From the French case, we can realise that young people need to feel empowered, to play an active and positive role in their communities. Moreover, it is essential that parents and communities recognise the potential of young people to enrich daily life, to see young people as partners. In this way, children will become actors of change and improve their own lives. Furthermore, citizenship practice should be learned through the lived experience of belonging, being listened to, and speaking of their views. Enhanced democratic processes help children to become more active members of their community, and to protect children from violence.

3. How to develop child participation programmes to prevent first-time offending?

3.1 Working with professionals working with and for children

The starting point is to build a 'culture' of participation by training professionals with and for children. Child participation must be seen as part of the working society and not considered as some isolated, marginalized activity.

Before implementing any projects in child participation, all the actors in the process, at all different levels, must think about the needs and expectations that a child participation project demand. For example, some NGOs that have already implemented child participation projects have to go back to their drawing boards to ensure that all the staff have the same understanding of a child participation project: the bottom line of the project and how to get to it. Moreover, professionals need to listen to what young people have to say as a pre-condition to implement child participation projects.

It is not because you are organising a participation event that you are making children participate at 100%. Some events are organised more through the point of view of the professionals than that of the children. It could be considered as manipulation, decoration, tokenism and not participation. It is important to look critically at the nature of children's participation.

To do that, all actors in child participation projects have to share the same definition of participation and know each actors' strengths and weaknesses. A way of thinking has to established on the role of the adult and the role of the child in the discussion. Most of the time, adults have a certain approach to the child's role and do not consider them as partners. To establish effective child participation, adults must have more confidence in children. They need to know more about children and their needs. Professionals need to learn how to be a mentor to the children, how to listen to them, instead of manipulating their opinions.

Moreover, professionals have the role to spread information about the right of the child to participate to children, families and communities. To do it, they have to promote positive parent-child relationships, make parents sensitive to the problems of children and young people, and set up a place where the children can express their views and influence decision-making.

For example, to avoid first-time offending, professionals linked with the juvenile justice department should explain the law to children through educational activities. Children should learn what the law is, should understand it and what its purpose is, to integrate them in society and to show them that they belong to it with the respect of their rights and duties.

Furthermore, the work of the professionals is to be a facilitator, to organise workshops, to understand child participation and how to develop communication skills of the participants. Youth organisations should be created and strengthened at the local level. Professionals should accompany children to develop peer educators' programmes helping young people in need of assistance.

It could be interesting for professionals who want to develop their skills in child participation to join a participation network. For example, in the United Kingdom, there is an organisation called 'Participation Workers Network for England', which provides opportunities to adults for whom participation is part of their daily work to share new ideas and learn more about participation practice (www.participationworks.org.uk).

3.2   Working with young people and adults

Young people must also be trained on child participation to acquire some skills in communication. They need to receive all the information to be part of the decision-making process. Moreover, even if the children's wishes are not followed, they are more likely to collaborate if they feel that their views have been heard and the reasons for rejecting these views have been explained.

Adults commonly fail to grasp the reality of children and young people's lives. Young people have to be seen as partners to solve the issue. Adults have to consider the views of children and young people, and involve them in decision-making processes. Indeed, young people could effectively identify the problems they face. They have the skills to identify and resolve their own problems, frequently at no cost.

3.3   Some examples of activities with young people

Initiatives should be promoted to prevent youth offending, such as consultations, discussion groups and workshops. For example, young people need to be informed about the law, their rights and responsibilities. They could be trained to act as judge, jury, prosecution and defence of their peers. The goal is to be trained in legal processes, and to learn to judge their peers fairly and refer them to services when necessary.

Peer educators' programmes should be developed on the promotion of positive behaviour and young people should be trained to become facilitators.

Parenting programmes should be developed that provide necessary support and improve parent/child relations.

More cities should be involved in the child friendly cities initiative of the UNICEF Innocenti Research Centre in Florence (www.childfriendlycities.org). A city is where the voices, needs, priorities and rights of children are an integral part of public policies, programmes and decisions. A child friendly city promotes the active participation of children, ensuring children's freedom to express their views, and that their views are given due weight in all matters affecting them. By participating in local decision-making processes, children learn how to grow into citizens who are aware of and can exercise their rights and responsibilities from a young age.

4.   The results of developing child participation projects

The result of developing child participation projects is to promote a new status for children in society. It is necessary to create a new relationship between adults and children in the families, communities and schools. It is a learning process where the children become actively involved in decision-making concerning their own living environment. Child participation has an impact on their sociali-sation within the family and society. It helps them to better integrate. Professionals should facilitate and not manage the meeting of the children. It is a process that needs time, with the will of both the adults and children.

The role of professionals is to raise children to become citizens, to portray the positive contribution of children, of young persons, as active and effective partic-ipants. To implement it, adults and children have to understand the process of full participation, and the best way to understand it is by being trained.

Another result is to build a culture of participation, to create a natural, ongoing process of children's participation, not just a process that serves a particular need at a particular time.

5.   Conclusion

To refer back to my statement at the beginning, "Child participation is a strong tool, a strong way, to fight first-time offending." I believe that child participation demands a change of minds by adults about children. It is a learning process. Adults and children have to learn about it and practice it on a daily basis. The goal of child participation programmes is to encourage and facilitate children to under-stand their situation, decide what the priority problems are, and suggest solutions. Children become actors of social change.

Child participation programmes are one of the solutions to prevent juvenile delinquency. They benefit children's development, and improve the relationship between adults and young people.   Indeed, child participation has a snowball impact in preventing first-time offending. The fact that they can participate at programmes and be involved in projects gives young people the opportunity to feel that they exist and that they are essential to the community.

The aim of my article goes far beyond the prevention of juvenile delinquency. The goal is to develop a society where children will be seen as partners, can express their views on all issues that affect them and be part of the solution. Moreover, child participation programmes are a long process. The outcomes are not visible in the short-term. It is also a cross-cutting programme, which can be used to create opportunities for awareness-raising and implement other rights of children.

The key message is to adopt a participative approach to all of the topics linked with children. The first step has to come from the adult to work in a participato-ry way: a shift of culture towards recognising that all children have rights and may require support.

Emergency Powers for Child Protection

Judith Masson

1.   Introduction

Child protection systems include complex mechanisms to balance the rights of parents and children, to protect families from intervention which is not justified by law, and to ensure that state agencies are accountable for their actions. However, most systems have also made provision for responding immediately to children at risk without reliance on the family's cooperation. Children can be 'apprehended' or taken to a 'place of safety'. In Scotland they can be made subject to a 'child protection order' (Children (Scotland) Act 1995, ss. 57-62; McGhee and Francis, 2003), which is very similar to the 'emergency protection order' (EPO) in England and Wales (Children Act 1989, ss. 44-45B) or Northern Ireland (Children (Northern Ireland) Order 1995 ss. 63-64). These are all 'emergency' powers: they override the normal rules for intervention. Like emergency relief, they provide a rapid response to a crisis and, like emergency medical treatment, they secure only short-term remedies. They enable children to be removed or detained away from their families for days or weeks on limited evidence and without following the procedures normally required for state intervention. For example, social workers can remove children without court approval in many Canadian provinces (Blenner-Hassett, 2004; *Winnipeg Child and Family Services v KLW* [2000] SCC 48), in Spain (Picontó-Novales, 1998) and in some Scandinavian countries (Oppedal, 1999). In New Zealand, with the approval of a magistrate or the police, intervention can occur before a family group conference (Atkin, 2000). Similarly, in each of the countries of the UK, both the courts and the police can authorise removal or detention of children for their protection. Procedures for court approval are simple and perfunctory, often amounting to little more than a formal request, and permitting applications without notice to the parents (Masson, 2004).

This paper describes and discusses the circumstances in which these emergency child protection powers are used in England. Using data from two major empirical studies, it explores what constitutes a child protection emergency, necessitating the use of these powers, and considers the implications for service provision and for the new Safeguarding Boards. In doing so, it examines the concerns expressed about the use and misuse of these powers and whether these reflect practices recorded in the research.

2.   Emergency protection research

The research which provides the basis for the article involved two linked, multimethod, quantitative and qualitative studies, funded jointly by the Nuffield Foundation and the NSPCC. The first focused on police protection (Masson et al, 2001) and the second on emergency protection orders (EPOs) (Masson et al,

2004). No other studies since the implementation of the Children Act have examined these processes although they were considered during the Climbié Inquiry (Laming, 2003).

The Police Protection Study examined a random sample of records of incidents in 1999 where children were taken into police protection in eight of the 43 police forces in England and Wales. The sample included 311 incidents, involving 420 children. Interviews were conducted with officers who took the action and their supervisors. Twenty-four officers and 33 'designated' officers were interviewed. Social services child protection managers and emergency duty team (EDT) staff were interviewed in six local authorities. The EPO Study took place in the areas covered by three of the eight forces and involved six local authorities, six shire counties and six unitary authorities. Court records for all EPO applications made in these authorities in a 12-month period between 2001 and 2002 were examined.[1] There were applications in respect of 127 children from 86 families. Local authority social services and/or legal department files were read for 56 of these cases and over 80 interviews were conducted with social workers and social work managers, local authority lawyers, solicitors in private practice, magistrates' legal advisers (magistrates' clerks) and magistrates. Children's guardians on the three local panels completed a questionnaire. In both studies, records data was analysed using SPSS, and interviews were tape recorded and fully transcribed. Both studies also involved a telephone survey to provide a wider practice context for the more detailed research. This covered officers in charge of Child Protection Units in 16 forces and a magistrates' legal adviser with special responsibility for public family law proceedings in each of the 42 magistrates' courts committee areas.

3.   Emergency powers in the Children Act 1989

Social workers in Children's Social Care Authorities have three alternatives when seeking to secure immediate protection for a child. They can persuade the parents to agree to a protective arrangement voluntarily, for example to allow their child to be accommodated under Children Act 1989, s.20. Where agreement is not an option, they can either request that the police take the child into police protection under s.46 or they can apply to the magistrates' court for an emergency protection order under s.44. The new edition of *Working Together* states, "Police powers should only be used in exceptional circumstances where there is insufficient time to seek an Emergency Protection Order or for reasons relating to the immediate safety of the child" (DfES et al, 2006, para. 5.51).

It was clear from the research that voluntary arrangements were generally preferred. Social work managers wanted to avoid making emergency applications wherever possible and local authority lawyers knew that courts would not grant orders where the parents would agree to their children being looked after. In the EPO study, orders were sought in 17 cases after the breakdown of such agreements and were not granted in almost 10% of cases (7) because an agreement was made at or before the court hearing. A similar picture is apparent in the national statistics which show about 90% of application resulting in orders (DCA, 2005). Both local authority lawyers and social workers generally agreed that it was not appropriate to bypass the court by asking the police to use their powers. However, urgency and time pressures, the unwillingness of some courts to hear cases without notice, and the lack of an out of hours court service in courts and legal departments meant that there was considerable reliance on the police (Masson, 2005). In a third of cases (29), the local authority had arranged for the child to be taken into police protection before applying for an EPO. In another ten cases, the police had used their powers independently and the local authority followed police protection with an application for an EPO (Masson et al, 2004).

Police protection is used in a wider range of circumstances, including where children are lost or have run away. In the police protection study, only a third of cases were referred to the police by health or social services. The main referrers were parents (mothers) and the children themselves. In addition, police officers identified cases during the course of their duties, for example when attending a 'domestic dispute'. In just over half the cases, children taken into police protection were known to have been accommodated by the local authority, another 20% went to stay with relatives and only 20% returned to their own home. A quarter of cases from three forces were known to have been followed by an EPO application (Masson et al, 2001).

4. Concerns about the use of emergency protection powers

Emergency child protection powers have been the cause of considerable concern. In 1987, in Cleveland, England, the use of place of safety orders to remove and detain in hospital or foster care over a 100 children who were thought to be victims of child sexual abuse provoked an outcry, led to a public inquiry, and was instrumental in both law reform and practice development (Butler-Sloss, 1988; Parton, 1991). The wide publicity for this 'scandal' served to identify social workers as people who took children away, and did so without adequate justification, two issues which are discussed below. More recently, the European Court of Human Rights has considered whether emergency protection practices in five countries comply with the European Convention of Human Rights (Masson, 2006), and the Canadian Supreme Court has also considered them in the light of The Canadian Charter (Masson, 2004).[2]

Concerns about the use of emergency powers have focused on four issues. First, their existence may undermine good practice in child protection. Since the 1990s, emphasis has been placed on working in partnership with families, with open communication of social workers' concerns in order to reach consensus about the action required to safeguard children (Thoburn, 1995). Where workers have wide powers to act without involving parents, this can create a barrier between them and the family. Parents may assume that workers will use their powers, not trust them but act defensively, concealing their difficulties and failing to engage. Lacking cooperation, workers may become increasingly concerned as appointments are missed or access to children is denied, and resort to emergency powers. Secondly, the simple procedures provided to allow action in a crisis may make it 'too easy' to use powers and separate children from their families. Decisions may be taken to remove children without proper consideration of their future care.

Rather than identifying a suitable placement, the focus is on finding a bed. Also, poorly planned removal can be traumatic for both child and parents, and make future work with the family more difficult. Thirdly, without a thorough examination of the basis for intervention, there is a danger that action will be taken inappropriately. Social workers may resort to emergency powers instead of placing cases before the courts for scrutiny, leading to unnecessary disruption of families and long periods of separation before mistakes are rectified. Finally, the fact that emergency powers have been used may lead to assumptions about the inadequacy of the family and the need for intervention so that cases are never properly scrutinised and initial mistakes are confirmed, a process referred to in American socio-legal literature as 'sequentiality' (Cooper Davis and Barua, 1995; Chill, 2004).

5.   The use of emergency protection powers

There are no national figures for the use of police protection. The Home Office does not require forces to report this information. Not all forces collate their own records. Statistics were available for only 13 of the 16 forces surveyed for the Police Protection Study. From this material it was estimated that each year police protection powers were used in approximately 4,500 incidents, relating to 6,000 children in England and Wales, excluding London. Use by the Metropolitan Police is believed to be higher than in all other forces combined (Masson, 2002). Published statistics for EPOs are based on incomplete returns from courts. Figures obtained during the research indicated that approximately 3,000 EPOs are granted each year (Masson et al, 2004).

There are wide variations in use of police protection between forces, and in resort to EPO by different local authorities, both in terms of numbers and circumstances. Between the highest and lowest using forces there was a nine-fold difference in the use of police protection per 10,000 under the age of 18. Police protection powers can be used by any officer, but in two of the forces there was comparatively little use except by officers from the specialist Child Protection Unit (Masson et al, 2001). In the EPO study, the use of police protection at the request of social services was linked to difficulties in accessing courts for EPOs without notice. There are also wide variations in use of care proceedings between authorities. On the census date, nationally 54 children per 10,000 were looked after with 64% the subject of care orders. Figures vary between authorities with highs of 135 and above 75%, and lows of 29 and under 40% (DfES, 2005). There is also variation in the proportion of care proceedings preceded by an EPO, with the highest user authorities obtaining EPOs in over 40% of care cases compared with only 5% in the lowest (Masson et al, 2004).

6.   Who are the children made subject to emergency powers?

Police files contained little information about the children taken into police protection, other than their age and gender. Officers make a brief record of the circumstances in which they used the power. The researchers generally had more information about children where EPO applications were made, but mainly because they followed up the cases through later proceedings and in social services files.

Emergency intervention largely concerns young children. Approximately a third of the children taken into police protection were under the age of five years, and only one-sixth were 14 years or older; the majority of this older group were girls. Children made subject to EPOs were younger: 60% were under the age of five and one in eight was a new born baby. There were only ten children over the age of ten years in the EPO sample of 127, reflecting the more limited use of care proceedings for older children and perceptions that risks of immediate harm are lower for them.

Three quarters of the incidents in the studies concerned the use of emergency powers for one child only, but 14% of EPO applications and 8% of police cases involved action relating to three or more children. Only one in three EPO cases concerned an only child. A sixth of families had children already subject to a care order and another sixth had children living elsewhere, usually with their other parent. These existing family arrangements have implications for decisions about placement and contact.

6.1 Family involvement with social services

Long-term involvement with social services was a major feature of the families in the EPO study. Seventy per cent of the families had been involved with social services for more than a year and half of these had been involved for more than five years. In just under a half of the families, the child who was subject to the EPO was on the child protection register. In many of the families there were serious child protection concerns. Overall 59 children were currently included on the Child Protection Register and at least another ten had been registered previously.[3] Over 40% of families where there were other children they had been involved in earlier care proceedings. A local authority had previously obtained an EPO in respect of children from 11 families. There were only five families who were not known to social services before the incident which precipitated the EPO, and another five where the social services department had had no previous involvement with the children. All the EPOs in relation to previously unknown families were in response to non-accidental injury identified by medical staff. Such action was not automatic. Even in the case of very serious injuries, social workers might agree a voluntary arrangement with cooperative parents.

7. The decision to use emergency powers

In all six local authorities, the decision to apply for an EPO had to be agreed by a manager, at least at the level above team leader, and approved by a local authority lawyer. Strategy discussions, usually conducted by telephone, established what should be done in response to an incident or referral. There was a child protection case conference before the EPO was obtained in half of the cases (44). These included cases where the plan did not include bringing proceedings, 'planned emergency' cases involving pre-birth cases conferences, and seven cases where the application was made within three days of a conference and appeared to have resulted from decisions or actions there. In 20 cases, the EPO was sought a week or more after the case conference, and in another 20 a child protection conference was only held after the EPO had been obtained.

Emergency protection orders were rarely used to remove children from their parents. Of the 86 cases in the study, only 18 involved applications to remove children from their parents, and in another four, children who were left without a suitable carer were removed from their homes (see figure 1). It was more common for children to move from home by agreement or police protection, and for the EPO to be obtained if a parent threatened to remove the child, or would not agree to continue out of home placement after police protection expired. Not all children removed by the police and not returned home became subject to EPO applications. Indeed, the status of arrangements and any subsequent social services action was sometimes unclear, especially where children had identified relatives who would care for them (Masson et al, 2001).

Figure 1: Location of child when protective measures taken

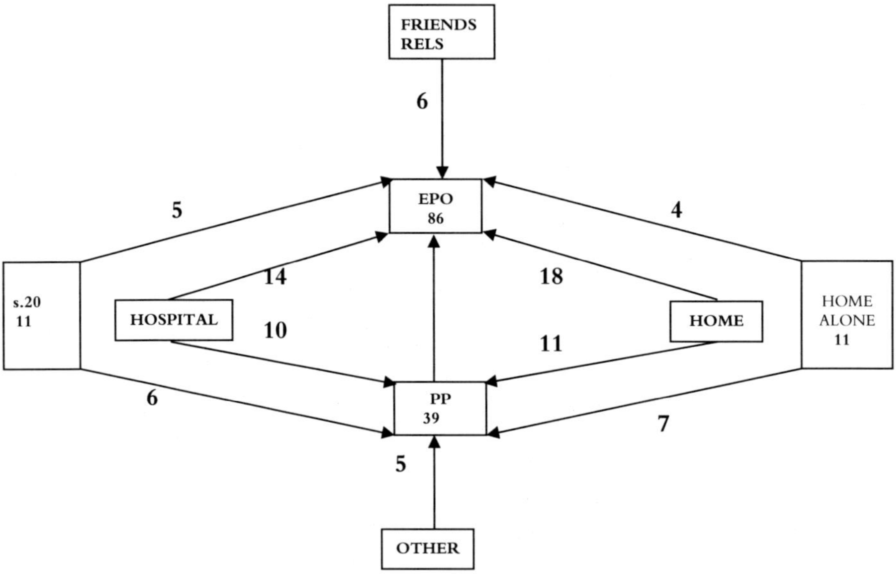

8.   The use of emergency powers

An EPO can be granted or a police officer may exercise protection powers where "there is reasonable cause to believe that a child would otherwise be likely to suffer significant harm" (Children Act 1989, ss. 44(1), 46(1)). This is not a difficult standard to meet. A local authority solicitor and a magistrate referred to it as 'a low threshold'. Similarly, police officers regarded it as a matter for their own judgment about the safety of the child and were less concerned about being challenged for using the power than for failing to do so. Both social workers and police officers focused on the current situation, but social workers generally knew more about the family, their circumstances and the child's previous care.

8.1   Planned emergencies

At first sight the concept of a 'planned emergency' may seem strange, with a clash between the ordered notion of planning and an emergency, an unheralded event which requires an immediate response. As one solicitor who acted for parents said, "An EPO should be used where there is an unexpected child protection issue." However, *Working Together* acknowledges that emergency action can and should be planned, with a strategy discussion immediately before action is taken wherever possible (D.H. et al, 1999). The fact that one day's notice is normally required before an EPO hearing also suggests some degree of planning. However, over 40% of courts in the national survey usually heard EPO application without notice.

There were two types of cases in the study in which emergency intervention was planned: 'certain events', which would occur at an unknown time, and 'uncertain events'. In these cases, alternative protective action, such as starting care proceedings by giving notice and obtaining an interim care order was considered to leave the child unprotected for too long, even though courts were prepared to shorten the notice period to three days.

The most common example of the first type was the birth of a baby to a mother who was considered to be incapable of providing care, even with support. There were 16 cases where pre-birth case conferences were held, and in 13 of these the baby was removed at or shortly after birth, although in two of these cases other protective measures had been planned. In three other cases there were pre-birth but the decision to remove was only taken subsequently, after a period of neglect. Even though emergency intervention was planned, action could not be taken before the child's birth.[4] Rather than wait until the parent sought to discharge the child, action was usually taken shortly after the birth. In case 73 where this was not done, the mother discharged herself and the baby, and went to an unknown address. The local authority then had to obtain an EPO and a warrant, and enlist police assistance to find the baby. Both police protection and EPOs were used for protection at birth. Police powers allowed immediate protection and were followed by EPO proceedings with notice to the parents.

The second type of case involved a decision to use, or to consider using, emergency powers if the parent acted in a specific way, asking the local authority to accommodate the child or breaching a child protection agreement. For example, where a parent resumed a relationship with an unsuitable partner they had agreed not to see, or asked for the child to be returned from foster care. In these cases, the local authority intended to use its compulsory powers but was content to let matters rest until a crisis occurred. Such a delay was unlikely to be in the interests of the parents and child, at least if they were separated and work was not being done to progress plans for the child's future.

8.2 Action without notice to parents

Parents have a right to be involved in decisions about their child's care, but the European Court of Human Rights has accepted that the need to protect a child can justify consulting parents only after emergency powers have been obtained (*P. C and S. v. UK* [2002] 2 FLR 631). Local authorities sought both police protection and without notice EPOs in order to secure children's protection without a prior warning to parents. Although they took such action in over half the cases

(46), this commonly occurred only after parents had refused to agree to accommodation, were threatening to remove their children from accommodation, had left children without a carer and could not be contacted, or in cases of removal of babies at birth.

Fears that, if parents were notified of the local authority's intention to remove, children would be put at greater risk because parents might abscond with them (or worse) led social workers to act in secret. Such fears were not imaginary. Out of 86 cases there were three where pregnant women moved to avoid social services' attention, and a further seven cases where action had to be taken to find the child after the EPO had been taken. Social workers were concerned because of what they knew about parents – previous moves, mental health difficulties and threats – or because they knew little about them. In the case of the planned removals of babies, there were also concerns about managing the birth and not damaging the mother's health by putting her under additional stress. In these cases parents were excluded from pre-birth case conferences and had no opportunity to suggest alternative means of protection.

8.3   Immediate crises

Some cases simply demanded immediate action: the baby found in a car with two unconscious adults had to be looked after; as did the children, all under four years old, found home alone without food; and the child whose father was threatening to kill her and commit suicide. Not all cases were life-threatening. For these a combination of three factors – current harm to children, additional stress on parents if care proceedings were commenced, and risks for the worker and agency if a child died (Ferguson, 2003; Scourfield, 2004) – meant that social workers wanted to use emergency powers and respond immediately. Where the police responded without a social services referral, their inexperience and difficulties in contacting social services could mean that children were taken into police protection when they might have remained at home with social work support. For example, the police removed a nine year old who had threatened the foster carer. The placement was disrupting but a social worker might have obtained the carer's agreement to keep the child for another night and avoided the child going first to the police station and then an emergency placement.

Social workers who resorted to emergency powers felt that children could not just be left at home even though objectively the child's condition might appear little worse than on previous visits. Their assessment of the situation, particularly the parents' ability to cope, left them acutely anxious. Where children were safe in hospital or with carers, concerns focused on protecting them against removal and clarifying the position for hospital staff and carers. Longstanding concerns about the quality of the parents' care were common in most cases where an EPO was sought to remove a child but cases were generally presented on the basis of a recent incident. This fitted with the name of the order and helped to justify to the court why it was being sought. Even a relatively minor incident brought to the worker's notice and the parents' reaction to this could precipitate action in the context of existing concerns. For example, in case 115 the social worker made a planned visit to the home and found the mother not yet dressed, and the children, who should have been in school, locked in their bedroom. In case 68, police protection was used because the parents would not allow access to a home where children were known to be neglected. These incidents were not necessarily the first occasions when the social worker had approached her manager or the legal department to request that emergency action be taken. Nor was it always more serious than previous incidents, but as the 'last straw' it triggered formal intervention because it was taken to indicate that the parents could not be relied on to adequately care for the child. And even in these cases social workers might seek to get agreement for accommodation, only resorting to formal action if agreement was not forthcoming, or if an earlier agreement was breached.

8.4   Other cases

Although almost all of cases fitted within at least one of the three categories above, there were a few where the need for an order arose from parental reaction to a social services intervention rather than in response to the initial risk of harm. These cases may be considered as 'manufactured emergencies', as both the family and social services contribute to their construction. In case 2, the violent interruption by family members of a discussion with a girl who alleged sexual abuse by a relative resulted in her being taken into police protection and an EPO being obtained. Breach of an agreement could precipitate the use of emergency powers, even though objectively the risk to the child was low. For example in case 10, the grandmother agreed that her daughter would not be left alone with her child. When the social worker returned later that day she found the mother and child alone. A visit the following day led to an argument and an application for an EPO. The social worker saw the grandmother as in breach of the agreement. She did not recognise that the grandmother had made a judgment about the safety of her grandchild.

9.   Outcome

Out of 86 cases, 75 resulted in an EPO, three in an interim care order and one in an interim supervision order. In seven cases, the EPO application was withdrawn because of an agreement. No applications were refused. Care proceedings were initiated in 77 cases, including four cases where the EPO had been avoided by an agreement. All but four of these cases continued to a final hearing. Of the remaining nine cases, five cases moved to private law proceedings and two had further public law proceedings.

Use of emergency powers by social services was largely a means of starting care proceedings with immediate protection for the child. Cases were generally expected by lawyers and social workers to lead directly to care proceedings. Indeed, some lawyers drafted the care application at the same time. However, it should be noted that only a minority of care proceedings were started in this way. It was more common for parents to be given notice of the proceedings. This contrasts with the position prior to the Children Act where almost all care commenced with the child being removed under a place of safety order (Social Services Select Committee, 1983).

10. Service Issues

Earlier use of care proceedings could avoid some emergency action but there will always be cases where formal protective measures have to be taken before an interim care order is obtained. Imposed arrangements to protect children are not voluntary and so it is not surprising that parents renege on them. It is also not clear that arrangements to keep cases out of the courts long-term are necessarily in parents' or children's interests. Where there are care proceedings, assessments of parents and plans for children are scrutinised by professionals acting for parents and for children, a process which leads to different proposals being accepted (Hunt and Macleod, 1999; Clark and Sinclair, 1999). At the very least, parents presented with an 'offer' of accommodation as an alternative to proceedings should have access to advice and advocacy services. Such support could encourage parents to work with social services (and vice versa) and therefore help to develop partnerships. There was some evidence that lawyers acting for parents in EPO and care proceedings helped parents to move away from the high levels of conflict with social services which had often prompted the application.

There are other measures (thorough assessment, access to suitable services and supervision for social workers) which may reduce crises, improve decision-making and reduce the extent to which child protection cases are driven by response to incidents. This is not to discourage any response, but to avoid situations where work in child protection is only about responding to crises. Local authorities and the police should monitor their use of emergency powers and seek to identify whether they are making too much or too little use of such measures. The creation of Safeguarding Boards provides an impetus to the development of policy, procedures and practice in the use of emergency powers. Such work is squarely within the remit established in the regulations.

Lord Laming was critical of the reliance placed on police protection. He recommended that local authorities should have access to legal advice 24 hours a day and that social work action in cases of deliberate harm should only be taken after legal advice has been obtained (Laming, 2003, rec. 36). Improving access to legal advice will not reduce reliance on the police if the current procedure for obtaining EPOs remains, nor will it improve social work services out of normal working hours. Resources need to be provided for Out of Hours services so that cases can have a social work response and the police are not left to handle cases on their own or for social services.

Close working with the police has given social worker access to police powers and allowed them to secure protection for children much more quickly and simply than through the courts. Giving power to the police rather than social workers provides a check on social work action. However, duty inspectors to whom these requests are generally made often lack sufficient knowledge of child protection to enable them really to assess the appropriateness of the action. Better decision-making and accountability might be provided by giving a power to remove or detain children for their protection to the Director of Children's Services or a named nominee, and requiring authorities to monitor and report their use of these powers.

154

Given that a high proportion of cases, especially where babies are removed at birth, involve families who have had children removed previously, consideration needs to be given to the services provided for these failing families, to prevent them from repeatedly experiencing care proceedings.

11.   Conclusions

Most social workers' use of emergency powers is in relation to families well-known to social services, where potentially harmful care and lack of parental cooperation are considered by workers and their managers to leave no other options. These are very serious cases where care proceedings are required. Emergency powers were used in these cases because of a failure to establish partnership with parents. There were relatively few high risk cases where social workers resorted to powers without trying to find an alternative approach.

There is substantially less resort to emergency powers as a preliminary to care proceedings than occurred before the Children Act 1989. However, it seems that forced 'agreements' are used for this purpose, with emergency powers relied on as a secondary measure. This conflicts with the notion of working in partnership just as much as resort to emergency powers. The research did not provide evidence that local authorities were taking action inappropriately, nor were they frequently using these powers to remove children from their parents. Rather social workers were securing arrangements for children who were already away from home or had been left home alone.

Social services generally obtain good cooperation from the police, and rely on the police where obtaining a court order would take too long, and out of normal working hours. There are a few cases where police would make better decisions, and removal of children from home might be avoided, if they had better access to social work assistance. Overall the use of emergency powers justifies more attention from those developing policy and practice than it has had in the past.

★ The author acknowledges the support of the NSPCC and the Nuffield Foundation for the research studies which provide the basis for this article, and the assistance of Maureen Winn Oakley, Senior Research Fellow, Kathy Pick and Deborah McGovern, research fellows on the two projects.

Bibliography

Atkin B (2000), Child abuse in New Zealand, in Freeman M D A (Ed), *Overcoming child abuse: A window on a world problem*, pp 305-328, Aldershot: Ashgate.

Blenner-Hassett D (2004), K.L.W. and warrantless child apprehensions: sanctioning gross interventions in private spheres, *Saskatchewan Law Review* 67, pp 161-204.

Butler-Sloss E (1988), The Report of the Inquiry into Child Abuse in Cleveland 1987 (1988 Cm 412), London: HMSO.

Clark, A and Sinclair, R (1999), *The focus on the Child*, London: National Children's Bureau.

Chill P (2004), Burden of proof begone – the pernicious effect of emergency removal in child protection proceedings, *Family Court Review* 42, pp 540-548.

Cooper Davis P and Barua G (1995), Custodial choices for children at risk: bias, sequentiality and the law, in University of Chicago Law School Roundtable Symposium: *Domestic Violence, Child Abuse and the Law*, pp 139-159.

DCA (2005), *Judicial Statistics Annual Report 2004* (2005 Cm 6566), London: TSO http://www.dca.gov.uk/jsarlist.htm.

DfES (2005), *Statistics of Education, Children looked after by local authorities*, London: DfES www.dfes.gov.uk/statistics/.

DH et al (1999), *Working Together to Safeguard Children*, London: TSO.

Ferguson H (2003), *Child protection in time*, Basingstoke: Palgrave Macmillan.

Laming H (2003), *The Report of the Victoria Climbié Inquiry* (2003 Cm 5730), London: TSO.

McGhee J and Francis J (2003), Protecting children in Scotland: examining the impact of the Children (Scotland) Act 1995, *Children and Family Social Work* 8, pp 133-142.

Masson J (2002), Police protection – protecting whom?, *Journal of Social Welfare and Family Law* 24, pp 157-174.

Masson J (2004), Human rights in child protection: emergency action and its impact, in Lodrup P and Modvar E (Eds), *Family Life and Human Rights*, pp. 457-476, Oslo: Glydendal Akademisk.

Masson J (2005), Emergency intervention to protect children: using and avoiding legal controls, *Child and Family Law Quarterly* 17, pp 75-96.

Masson J (2006), Fair trials in child protection, *Journal of Social Welfare and Family Law* (forthcoming).

Masson J, Winn Oakley M and McGovern D (2001), *Working in the Dark*, Warwick:Warwick University School of Law.

Masson J, Winn Oakley M and Pick K (2004), *EPOs court orders for child protection crises*, www.nspcc.org.uk/Inform/Publications/Downloads/EPO_pdf_gf25456.pdf.

Oppedal M (1999), *Rettssikkerhet ved akutte vedtak etter barnevernloven*, Institutt for offentlig retts skriftserie nr 6/1999, Oslo: Juidisk fakultet, Universitetet i Oslo.

Parton N (1991), *Governing the family*, Basingstoke: Macmillan.

Picontó-Novales T (1998), The application of Spanish child welfare law, *J. Law, Pol and Fam* 12 (2), pp 180-201.

Scourfield J (2003), *Gender and child protection*, Palgrave Macmillan: Basingstoke.

Social Services Select Committee (1983), *Second Report 1983-4, Children in care* (1983-4 H.C. 360).

Thoburn J (1995), *The Challenge of Partnership in Child Protection: Practice Guide*, London: HMSO.

Endnotes

1   All applications were made by local authorities. A national telephone survey of magistrates' court legal advisers established that applications by others were almost unheard of.

2   Finland, Italy, England and Wales, The Netherlands and Germany.

3   This information was not available for the police protection sample, but this should not be taken as indicating that the police did not carry out appropriate checks.

4   An unborn child cannot be the subject of court proceedings: *Re F (in utero)* [1988] Fam 122.

Intercountry Adoption:
Do the Existing Instruments Work?

Aukje Mens

1. Introduction

A hundred years of child protection, a hundred years of understanding that children should have specific rights, and that these rights must be protected and established in laws. In the Netherlands, adoption was introduced in 1956 as a means of child protection.[1] Since then, adoption has become a worldwide phenomenon. Intercountry adoption started to develop at the end of World War II, primarily as a humanitarian response to the large number of war orphans.[2] However, "from its initial purpose of providing a family environment for children, adoption has now become more demand-driven."[3] There exists an 'adoption market' nowadays, wherein children have become subject to the law of supply and demand.[4] Sometimes, the purpose of adoption seems to be no longer providing a child with a family, but rather providing a family with a child.[5] I do not object to intercountry adoption as an alternative means to create a family. However, the ardent desire to acquire a child may lead in the end to serious violations of the most basic rights of the child.[6] These violations are often justified by the thought that a child will somehow always be 'better off' in a materially rich country.[7] In other words, the end justifies the means.[8] I strongly object to this point of view. Although the adopted child may grow up happily within his or her adoptive family, this cannot be a reasonable justification for obtaining a child illegally, for instance without the consent of the birth parents.

Intercountry adoption is regulated by various legal instruments. At the international level, the Hague Adoption Convention 1993[9] is the most recent and most important international convention concerning intercountry adoption. At national level in the Netherlands, intercountry adoption is provided for by the 'Act regulating the conflict of laws regarding adoption'[10] and the 'Act concerning the placement in the Netherlands of foreign children with a view to adoption'.[11] The general purpose of these instruments is to ensure that intercountry adoptions are made in the best interests of the child and to prevent abuses.

Are the existing instruments effective in achieving this goal? What are the obstacles? In other words, do the existing instruments work? This article focuses on some of the questions and problems related to the existing instruments, in particular the Hague Adoption Convention 1993.

Here below, a summary is given of the most important international and national instruments concerning intercountry adoption, and their purpose, scope and importance are discussed. Furthermore, some of the existing obstacles are pointed out, and possible solutions are suggested. The focus is on the Hague Adoption

Convention 1993, but some of the other instruments concerning intercountry adoption are also reviewed. Although the Hague Adoption Convention 1993 provides for an essential legal framework with regard to intercountry adoption, it suffers from a number of shortcomings, such as its limited scope and the burden of responsibility on States of origin. Finally, in the conclusion, an attempt is made to answer the question whether or not the existing instruments concerning intercountry adoption work.

To conclude this introduction, I would like to explain my position with respect to intercountry adoption. Following Mason, I reject both the alternatives of a free market and a complete ban on intercountry adoption.[12] I am not an abolitionist, nor a promoter of intercountry adoption.[13] I consider myself as a pragmatist, because I accept the need for regulating intercountry adoption as a way of eliminating abuses, protecting the interests of children, and improving standards in a practice that will continue.[14]

2. National and international instruments concerning intercountry adoption

This section addresses the most important national and international instruments concerning intercountry adoption. It starts with a short introduction to the Hague Adoption Convention 1993. Afterwards, it goes briefly into a few other international instruments. Finally, it discusses the two main national instruments concerning intercountry adoption.

2.1 The Hague Adoption Convention 1993

The internationalisation of the adoption process in the seventies gave rise to the need for a new approach. Because of the explosive increase in intercountry adoptions since the late sixties, and insufficient existing domestic and international legal instruments, a framework for international standards and co-operation had been needed to combat and prevent abuses in intercountry adoption.[15] This perception resulted in the realization of the 'Hague Convention on the Protection of Children and Co-operation in Respect of Intercountry Adoption', concluded 29 May 1993.[16] The Hague Adoption Convention 1993 entered into force in the Netherlands on 1 October 1998.[17]

The Hague Adoption Convention 1993 is not a classical 'private international law instrument'.[18] The convention does not deal with conflict of laws, nor does it provide for rules on international jurisdiction. The convention does, however, contain rules on the recognition of intercountry adoptions (recognition by operation of law, article 23).

The focus of the Hague Adoption Convention 1993 is on the international co-operation between so-called sending and receiving States (articles 4 and 5), through the establishment of Central Authorities (articles 6-13). Each intercountry adoption is the joint responsibility of the State of origin and the receiving State.[19] Furthermore, the Hague Adoption Convention 1993 provides for the essential minimum standards and key principles to be taken into account in every intercountry adoption (articles throughout the convention). However, the Hague Adoption Convention 1993 is not a uniform substantive law instrument.[20] It does not try to establish a uniform international law of adoption.[21] Van Loon has described the Hague Adoption Convention 1993 as a 'multi-dimensional instrument',[22] because it contains elements of 'human rights law', 'private international law', and provisions for 'judicial and administrative co-operation'.

The Preamble and article 1 contain the basic principles of the Hague Adoption Convention 1993. The 'best interests of the child' are of paramount consideration. According to the Preamble, one of the principle objectives of the convention is, "to ensure that intercountry adoptions are made in the best interests of the child and with respect for his or her fundamental rights, and to prevent the abduction, the sale of, or traffic in children". Another principle which is recognised in the Preamble is the 'principle of subsidiarity', "each State should take, as a matter of priority, appropriate measures to enable the child to remain in the care of his or her family of origin, … intercountry adoption may offer the advantage of a permanent family to a child for whom a suitable family cannot be found in his or her State of origin". Intercountry adoption must be considered as a 'last resort', in the sense that national adoption takes precedent over international adoption. This is a widely accepted view. The principle of subsidiarity clearly expresses the focus on child protection in the Hague Adoption Convention 1993: "The subsidiarity principle is the key to making intercountry adoption a service for children rather than for prospective adopters".[23]

Article 1 contains the three key objectives of the Hague Adoption Convention 1993. These objectives were formulated because of the existence of a wide range of social and legal problems, and of malpractice and abuse.[24] The first objective in article 1 is, "to establish safeguards to ensure that intercountry adoptions take place in the best interests of the child and with respect for his or her fundamental rights as recognized in international law" (article 1, section a). The second objective is, "to establish a system of co-operation amongst Contracting States to ensure that those safeguards are respected and thereby prevent the abduction, the sale of, or traffic in children" (article 1, section b). The third objective of the convention is, "to secure the recognition in Contracting States of adoptions made in accordance with the Convention" (article 1, section c). Many States refused to recognise foreign adoptions, resulting in many adopted children living in a 'legal limbo'. The only solution was re-adoption.[25] Therefore, the Hague Adoption Convention 1993 provides for recognition by operation of law, on the condition that the adoption has been made in accordance with the convention. This recognition by operation of law is justified because of the guarantees the Hague Adoption Convention 1993 offers.[26]

Besides the Hague Adoption Convention 1993, there are a number of other (international) instruments which specifically deal with intercountry adoption.

2.2   Other international instruments

The Hague Adoption Convention 1993 was not the first attempt to realise an

159

international convention concerning intercountry adoption. On 15 November 1965 the Convention on Jurisdiction, Applicable Law and Recognition of Decrees relating to Adoptions was signed.[27] This convention is, in contrast to its successor, a classical instrument of private international law, concerning the three questions on jurisdiction, applicable law and recognition. However, the Hague Adoption Convention 1965 has not been very successful. When the Hague Adoption Convention 1993 entered into force, the Hague Adoption Convention 1965 was denunciated. Before that, only three States (the United Kingdom, Austria, and Switzerland) had ratified this treaty, and the Hague Adoption Convention 1965 thus had a very limited scope. Moreover, factors, such as its mere focus on intercountry adoption within Europe and the lack of provisions concerning international co-operation, contributed to the ineffectiveness of this convention.[28]

Similar to the Hague Adoption Convention 1965, the Inter-American Convention on Conflict of Laws concerning the Adoption of Minors 1984 also concentrates on questions of private international law.[29] However, this convention sets a greater focus on the welfare of the child than the Hague Adoption Convention 1965.[30] The Inter-American Convention applies to a number of Central and South American countries.[31]

The United Nations Declaration on Social and Legal Principles relating to the Protection and Welfare of Children, with Special Reference to Foster Placement and Adoption Nationally and Internationally 1986 is a non-binding instrument. It contains universal principles to be taken into account in cases related to foster placement or adoption of a child, either nationally or internationally.[32]

At the European level, there has been the European Convention on the Adoption of Children 1967 of the Council of Europe.[33] The aim of this convention is to harmonise the substantive national adoption laws of the Member States and to avoid conflict of laws.[34] The European Adoption Convention 1967 does, in general, not deal with the international aspects of adoption.[35] The European Adoption Convention 1967 has been ratified by 18 European countries.[36] The Netherlands has not ratified this convention. Currently, the Council of Europe is working on a revision of the European Adoption Convention 1967.[37] According to the Draft Explanatory Report,[38] revision is necessary because many Member States of the Council of Europe revised their laws on adoption due to the social and legal changes in Europe since the late sixties. Consequently, certain provisions of the European Adoption Convention 1967 have become outdated over the years. The Draft Explanatory Report continues that the revised convention as a whole will exert an important influence on international adoptions. It will provide an effective complement to the Hague Adoption Convention 1993, by ensuring that adoptions which are not covered by the Hague Adoption Convention 1993 are regulated in such a manner as to comply with the underlying aims of any adoption, which must be child centred, in the child's best interests and should provide him or her with a harmonious home.

2.3   Dutch instruments

At the national level in the Netherlands, the 'Act concerning the placement in the Netherlands of foreign children with a view to adoption'[39] provides administrative rules for allowing a child to enter the Netherlands for the purpose of adoption. This act contains aspects of child protection and immigration law.

The 'Act regulating the conflict of laws regarding adoption'[40], which entered into force in the Netherlands on 1 January 2004, is the first codification of Dutch private international law concerning adoption. Until 2004, Dutch international adoption law was based on case law. This act contains rules on conflict of laws (articles 3 and 4), and the recognition of foreign adoptions which fall outside the scope of the Hague Adoption Convention 1993 (articles 6-8).

3.   Bottlenecks, loopholes, and other shortcomings in the existing instruments concerning intercountry adoption, and possible solutions

A lot has improved in the field of intercountry adoption since the Hague Adoption Convention 1993 entered into force. This convention provides the basic principles that are to be taken into account and the essential international co-operation between sending and receiving States. Nevertheless, the Hague Adoption Convention 1993 suffers from a number of shortcomings.

3.1   Non-convention adoptions

In the first place, there is a problem with non-convention adoptions. A considerable number of foreign adoption children come from countries which have not ratified the Hague Adoption Convention 1993. In my opinion, adoptions from non-convention countries bear greater risks of malpractice and abuse than convention-adoptions. Because no Central Authority and authorised adoption agencies are involved, non-convention adoptions lack essential international co-operation and control. This is also recognised by the Dutch legislature. According to the Dutch Minister of Justice, convention-adoptions are carried out more carefully than non-convention adoptions.[41]

Bearing this in mind, it is very important that as many countries as possible join the Hague Adoption Convention 1993.[42] This seems to be a logical assumption, but more has to be done to reach this aim. The Parliamentary Assembly of the Council of Europe also believes the Hague Adoption Convention 1993 must be better publicised,[43] and calls on the Committee of Ministers to conduct information campaigns.[44] The Parliamentary Assembly also calls on the Committee of Ministers to give a clear indication of its political will to ensure that children's rights are respected, by immediately inviting the member states to ratify the Hague Adoption Convention 1993 if they have not already done so, and undertake to observe its principles and rules even when dealing with countries that have not themselves ratified it.[45]

This last sentence emphasises that, in addition, we must apply as far as possible the principles of the Hague Adoption Convention 1993 in non-convention cases. This is also the view of the Hague Conference on Private International Law:

> [T]he Special Commission recommends that States Parties, as far as practicable, apply the standards and safeguards of the Convention to the arrangements for intercountry adoption which they make in respect of non-Contracting States.[46]

"Although it would be difficult to implement all of the Convention provisions which involve co-operation at an administrative level where only the receiving State has established a Central Authority and a system of accredited agencies", Duncan believes a number of conditions and controls could be applied in non-convention cases.[47]

Finally, regulation of intercountry adoptions from non-convention countries by bilateral agreements could be an option.[48] Article 21, paragraph e, of the UN Convention of the Rights of the Child encourages the establishment of multilateral as well as bilateral agreements. The Parliamentary Assembly of the Council of Europe recommends bilateral agreements, too.[49]

3.2 Recognition of non-convention adoptions by operation of law?

A second problem, related to the first one, is the question of recognition of intercountry adoptions from non-convention countries. Articles 6 and 7 of the 'Act regulating the conflict of laws regarding adoption' deal with this issue. The Dutch legislature has opted for a system which distinguishes between intercountry adoptions whereby all persons involved have their habitual residence in a foreign country, and intercountry adoptions by adoptive parents having their habitual residence in the Netherlands.

The first category of adoptions is recognised by operation of law (article 6). The ratio of this article is that in cases where both the adoptive parents and the child live outside the Netherlands, the Dutch legal system is hardly involved, if at all.[50] Therefore, these adoptions should be accepted as *fait accompli*.[51]

The second category is intercountry adoption by adoptive parents having their habitual residence in the Netherlands. These adoptions are not recognised by operation of law (article 7). In these cases, the prospective adoptive parents have to go through a recognition procedure in the Netherlands. This choice is motivated by the thought that adoptions from non-convention countries could be carried out in a less careful way.[52]

The question is whether the above-mentioned distinction is justified, and whether or not we should recognise foreign adoptions from non-convention countries by operation of law.

On the one hand, recognition by operation of law benefits the legal status of the adopted child, because the child will automatically become a legitimate child of the adoptive parents. In this way, certain rights of the child, for instance his or her right to a name, nationality and rights of succession, will be secured directly.

On the other hand, should we automatically recognise foreign adoptions from countries which do not have to apply the provisions of the Hague Adoption Convention 1993? Is it desirable to give immediate effect to adoptions from countries which do not have a Central Authority that controls the intercountry adoption process, and whose internal requirements and procedures can considerably differ from those of the Hague Adoption Convention 1993? As mentioned above, precisely these guarantees of the Hague Adoption Convention 1993 justify recognition by operation of law. This is also the opinion of the Dutch legislature. According to the Dutch legislature, we should be extra cautious with non-convention adoptions.[53] Of course, the 'Act concerning the placement in the Netherlands of foreign children with a view to adoption' provides for rules on child protection. However, this act lacks the element of international co-operation, which is, from my point of view, crucial for the careful regulation of the intercountry adoption procedure.

Should we recognise non-convention adoptions by operation of law, or should we provide for a recognition procedure in non-convention cases whereby the foreign adoption will be examined thoroughly by the court? Is the choice our legislature made within the articles 6 and 7 of the 'Act regulating the conflict of laws regarding adoption' a fair one? I do not have an answer yet to these questions. All I wanted to do for the moment was to point out a dilemma, which should be taken into account in considering the recognition of non-convention adoptions.

3.3   Independent adoptions versus agency adoptions

A third issue concerns the so-called 'independent' or 'private' adoptions, which, in contrast to agency adoptions, take place without the involvement of an authorised or permitted professional adoption agency.[54] In these cases, the prospective adoptive parents work directly with individuals or agencies in the country of origin.[55] The main reason people choose independent adoption rather than agency adoption is to avoid bureaucracy, financial obligations, restrictions, waiting lists and other procedural delays.[56]

Independent adoptions have frequently been a topic of discussion, and during the negotiations for the Hague Adoption Convention 1993 it had to be decided whether or not the convention should outlaw independent adoptions.[57]

Eventually, the negotiating partners reached a compromise within article 22 of the Hague Adoption Convention 1993. Under article 22, non-accredited persons or bodies may perform the functions of the Central Authority. In the United States, for instance, independent adoption is very common.

Although there is no hard evidence, and child trafficking should not necessarily be associated with independent adoption, there is a widespread feeling that independent adoption opens the door to abuses much more easily than agency adoption.[58] I share this feeling. Independent adoptions bear a considerable risk of abuse, because of the lack of regulatory measures and control.[59] 'Agency to agency adoptions' are preferable.[60] I support the following statement made by Mason, "good practice is more likely to be achieved by public bodies and well-regulated non-profit agencies than by intermediaries in the business of adoption".[61] I conclude with another statement by Mason, "thus the success of the Convention – wide application – may be its ultimate failure if it facilitates risky, private adoptions and leads to their general acceptability."[62]

3.4   An indirect convention (i.e. a lack of criminal sanctions)

Another important shortcoming of the Hague Adoption Convention 1993 is the indirect way it works against abuses of intercountry adoption.[63] The convention only focuses on the civil aspects of intercountry adoption. It does not cover the criminal aspects, nor does the convention require States to outlaw baby selling or to punish baby sellers.[64] The reason the convention does not deal with the criminal aspects is that this field falls outside the scope of the Hague Conference on Private International Law.[65]

With article 33, the Hague Adoption Convention 1993 has created the possibility of taking 'appropriate measures' when the convention has been, or is likely to be, violated.[66] Although this article provides for a reporting system, it is essential in my point of view to impose criminal sanctions on the national level against people who violate the terms of the convention.[67] Kennard has expressed this opinion too, "while the Convention cannot mandate that states adopt penalties for breach of its terms, it is crucial that states take the initiative to do so."[68]

Under article 3 of the Optional Protocol to the Convention on the Rights of the Child on the Sale of Children, Child Prostitution and Child Pornography, States are obliged to cover certain acts and activities under their criminal or penal laws. Article 3 includes, "improperly inducing consent, as an intermediary, for the adoption of a child in violation of applicable international legal instruments on adoption".[69] The Optional Protocol clearly regards illegal adoption as a form of child trafficking.[70] Thus, each State should ensure that illegal adoption is covered under its criminal law.

In the opinion of the Dutch legislature, implementation of article 3 of the Optional Protocol is provided by article 273a of the Dutch Criminal Code, together with articles 27 and 28 of the 'Act concerning the placement in the Netherlands of foreign children with a view to adoption'.[71]

However, these articles do not sufficiently tackle the problem of illegal adoption. In the first place, articles 27 and 28 of the 'Act concerning the placement in the Netherlands of foreign children with a view to adoption' only cover violations of some of the provisions of this act. In addition, 'illegal adoption' seems to fall outside the scope of article 273a of the Dutch Criminal Code.[72] In my opinion, the Dutch legislature should deal with the criminal aspects of intercountry adoption more adequately. The Dutch legislature could do so by specifically including child trafficking for the purpose of illegal adoption and violations of the Hague Adoption Convention 1993 in the Dutch Criminal Code.

3.5   Lack of clear definitions?

Some commentators are of the opinion that the terms and definitions used in the Hague Adoption Convention 1993 are too vague and unclear.

For instance, Van Leeuwen thinks, "a weakness in the present Hague Convention is the absence of clearly outlined definitions of some of its key terms",[73] because "definitional differences are left to the discretion of the individual signatories to the Hague Convention".[74] She notes that the convention, for instance, "fails to define what constitutes the best interests of the child"[75] and also "fails to define key words … such as 'abandonment', 'orphan', 'special needs', and 'exorbitant cost'".[76] Another major loophole in the treaty she mentions is, "the authorization given to states to refuse to recognize an international adoption where the state finds it to be 'contrary to public policy'".[77] "Because public policy is not defined, an infinite number of political, social and cultural reasons might be made to refuse to recognise an adoption."[78] Van Leeuwen concludes that without clear definitions, the Hague Adoption Convention's implementation will fail to provide the uniformity so urgently sought to regulate the intercountry adoption process.[79]

Kennard is of the same opinion. Although she acknowledges that it seems unlikely that the text of the convention could have provided more language than it did on, for instance, the requirements of adoptability and consent, she points out that the convention does not seem to address situations which appear to meet these requirements but still are similar to baby selling.[80] In her opinion the Hague Adoption Convention 1993 fails to define 'non-profit objectives' in article 11, and 'improper financial gain', 'reasonable', and 'costs and expenses' in article 32 of the convention.[81] As does Van Leeuwen, Katz also criticises the 'veto power' to nullify an adoption on the basis of public policy.[82] She feels this opportunity allows each country to exercise discretion in determining the boundaries of public policy and to authorise only those adoptions that meet its own standards.[83] However, she recognises that States could never agree upon a treaty that purports to control all substantive issues.[84]

Stein believes the consent requirements in the Hague Adoption Convention 1993 are not strong enough to prevent baby selling. In his opinion, the Hague Adoption Convention 1993 should be modified to include the consent provisions of the Uniform Adoption Act.[85] One of the suggestions made by Stein is to include in the Hague Adoption Convention 1993 the requirement of a third party to witness the birth parent's signature on the consent form.[86]

Kleem takes a different view with regard to the necessity of defining the terms and standards in the Hague Adoption Convention 1993. In his opinion, "the rules set out in the Convention to prevent financial exploitation by adoption professionals are necessarily vague and undefined".[87] He believes that exact definitions of these standards in the convention might have caused considerable disagreement and debate, and he thinks a degree of discretion allows each country to apply them according to their already established notions.[88]

I agree with Kleem. It is simply impossible and not even necessary to define all of the terms and standards the Hague Adoption Convention 1993 uses. For instance, what exactly is meant by 'the best interests of the child'? This concept is impossible to define in my opinion. A certain degree of discretion is needed, to decide in each individual case what constitutes 'the best interests of the child'. The same applies to other terminology, such as 'reasonable' or 'improper'. Again, it has to be decided in each individual case whether the costs and expenses charged for an intercountry adoption were 'reasonable' or 'improper'. However, some clarification of convention terms such as 'improper financial gain' and 'costs and expenses' is desirable. During the Second Meeting of the Special Commission on the Practical Operation of the Hague Adoption Convention 1993 that took place from 17-23 September 2005,[89] some experts expressed their need for proper information and transparency to combat over charging by accredited bodies.[90] It was suggested that the Permanent Bureau of the Hague Conference on Private International Law could centralise the information provided by the States. Although this would only give an insight into the costs and expenses, it would at least one of the first steps to unify and limit the costs and expenses charged for intercountry adoptions.

With regard to the consent requirements in the Hague Adoption Convention 1993, I believe article 4 provides for sufficient tools to deal with consent in a proper way. However, the suggestion of a 'third party' made by Stein seems to be a good option. This requirement would help to reduce the chance of forgery.

In the opinion of Van Leeuwen and Katz, the term 'public policy' in article 24 of the Hague Adoption Convention 1993 should be restricted, or at least defined. Of course the latter would be impossible, because the precise 'public policy' of each State differs from the others. Public policy is that part of the national legal order which serves national interests, and those national interests vary among different States.[91] Moreover, I believe we should hold on to this 'veto power',[92] because we should not give up the possibility of excluding the application of foreign rules of law or to refuse recognition of foreign judgements which conflict with the fundamental principles of the national legal order.[93] However, as usual in private international law, we should apply article 24 of the Hague Adoption Convention 1993 exceptionally.

3.6 Burden of responsibility on the State of origin[94]
A few authors, in particular Duncan, emphasise that the main burden of regulating and controlling the intercountry adoption process is placed upon the States of origin.[95] Duncan states that, "much is expected of States of origin, most of which are struggling with serious economic problems, many of which will have only small budgets available".[96] He also mentions the considerable discretion of the States of origin with regard to the practical implementation of the principles and

frameworks of the convention.[97] He notes, "the success of the Convention will depend in part upon how wisely and effectively individual States of origin apply flesh to these Convention bones".[98]

Wittner criticises the Hague Adoption Convention 1993 in the same sense. She feels that, "the Hague Convention is ineffective because it puts the bulk of the burden associated with intercountry adoption on the sending country",[99] and it is, "infeasible for developing countries to implement".[100] She also believes that since sending countries tend to be developing countries they lack the stability and financial means to effectively implement the provisions of the convention.[101]

In the view of Duncan, there is a moral as well as a practical obligation on the more wealthy receiving States to lend assistance to States of origin, by ensuring that initial measures of implementation, both legislative and administrative, are realistic and as comprehensive as possible.[102]

The Parliamentary Assembly of the Council of Europe also calls on the Committee of Ministers to help countries of origin to develop their own adoption laws, and to train the relevant personnel in public authorities, properly accredited agencies and all other professionals involved in adoption.[103]

I fully agree with this point of view. Developed countries, such as the Netherlands, should lend assistance to those countries of origin which have neither the money nor the means to implement the Hague Adoption Convention 1993 in a proper way. The following statement of the Parliamentary Assembly of the Council of Europe expresses this view too:

> We must help developing countries of origin to set up Central Authorities with sufficient personnel and resources to perform their functions effectively, because it's clear that the implementation of the convention depends upon their effectiveness.[104]

3.7   Limited scope of the Hague Adoption Convention 1993

The Hague Adoption Convention 1993 only applies to 'intercountry' adoption cases in which a child is moved from a Contracting State to another Contracting State (article 2, section 1), and which create a 'permanent parent–child relationship' (article 2, section 2). Therefore, a number of situations associated with intercountry adoption fall outside the scope of the convention.

One example is the case of refugee or internationally displaced children. Because these children are adopted in the State of their habitual residence, there is no further movement of the child for the purpose of adoption and the adoption would be completely internal.[105] The Hague Adoption Convention 1993 does not cover these cases.

The same applies to arrangements which do not create a permanent parent–child relationship but rather a long-term alternative care arrangement, such as the

Islamic institution of 'kafalah'.[106] These arrangements fall short of the convention definition of adoption, even where they are 'intercountry'.

In the view of Duncan, these cases have international dimensions which call for special protection of the child and demand a very cautious approach.[107] He emphasises that the same risks which are present in intercountry adoption will continue to be present in many of the cases which fall outside the scope of the Hague Adoption Convention 1993.[108]

With regard to the case of refugee children, the Hague Conference on Private International Law established in April 1994 a Working Group to study the application to refugee children of the Hague Convention of 29 May 1993 on Protection of Children and Co-operation in respect of Intercountry Adoption.[109] In October 1994, the Special Commission of the Hague Conference on Private International Law on the implementation of the Hague Convention of 29 May 1993 on Protection of Children and Co-operation in respect of Intercountry Adoption has thereupon recommended that States should consider the application of certain convention principles to adoptions not covered by the convention, such as adoptions from refugee and other internationally displaced children.[110]

Duncan suggests that serious consideration will have to be given to the possibility of an extension in the scope of the convention to these extra-convention cases.[111] I support this point of view. The principles and safeguards of the Hague Adoption Convention 1993 should achieve the widest possible application.[112]

3.8   What's next? A European (Union) perspective

Last, but not least, let us consider intercountry adoption from a European (Union) perspective.

The European Union has adopted several Regulations on private international (family) law issues.[113] The Brussels II-bis Regulation, concerning jurisdiction and the recognition and enforcement of judgments in matrimonial matters and matters of parental responsibility, is the latest example of unification of private international (family) law within the European Union.[114] Furthermore, Regulations on international divorce law[115], international succession law[116], and international matrimonial property law[117] are being prepared at the moment.

Intercountry adoption is not included in Brussel II-bis. The European Community has not (yet) taken any action in this field. However, it is to be expected that the European Community will include intercountry adoption in its policy in the near future. In my opinion, there are sufficient indications that intercountry adoption will not stay behind.

The progressive 'communitarisation' of private international law, in particular of international family law[118], supports this presumption. Furthermore, the 1996 Resolution of the European Parliament[119], which insists on improving the law and co-operation between Member States on the adoption of minors and calls on ratification of the Hague Adoption Convention 1993, indicate the interest of the European Union in this subject.

Starting from the idea that the European Community will draw up a 'European Adoption Regulation', what should be the nature of such an instrument? Should it cover only private international law aspects of intercountry adoption, or should it include substantive law requirements too? The Hague Adoption Convention 1993 deliberately does not answer questions related to jurisdiction and applicable law. Unification of conflict of laws was regarded impossible because of the existing differences between the various countries.[120] Does not the same argument apply to a European Adoption Regulation? Is unification of international adoption law within the European Union necessary and feasible?[121] Considering the fact that almost all European countries are a party to the Hague Adoption Convention 1993,[122] what is left for Europe?[123] What is the advantage of special community rules concerning intercountry adoption beside the Hague Adoption Convention 1993? Do we have to repeat at the European level the work that has already been done on a worldwide scale?[124] Why re-invent the wheel?[125]

On the other hand, however, one could say that intra-European adoptions and adoptions from third countries require special community rules (of private international law), because they differ from adoptions that take place entirely outside Europe. It could be argued that the particular status of the European Union, the regional integration and the mutual trust between the Member States of the European Union require uniform (international) adoption rules within the European Union. It could also be argued that there is a clear need for special community rules of private international adoption law just because the Hague Adoption Convention 1993 does not regulate jurisdiction and applicable law in intercountry adoption cases.[126] Here, the European Community could play a part. However, the question whether such a private international law instrument is necessary and feasible still remains.

These questions should be considered in drafting a European Adoption Regulation and are also the main subject of my thesis, which I hope to finish by the end of 2008.

In conclusion, although the Hague Adoption Convention 1993 offers an essential international legal framework for intercountry adoption, there are still a number of obstacles and questions to be dealt with.

4.   Conclusion: do the existing instruments work?

The main question addressed in this article has been whether the existing instruments concerning intercountry adoption achieve their goal of protecting children in the intercountry adoption process. The focus of this paper was on the main shortcomings of some of these instruments, in particular the Hague Adoption Convention 1993.

Intercountry adoption is subject to the law of supply and demand these days. Intercountry adoption is a demand-driven process and in practice the best interests of the child sometimes seem to be pushed into the background. I definitely do not object to intercountry adoption as an alternative means to create a family. However, this market environment may lead to abuses and malpractice.

The Hague Adoption Convention 1993 tries to combat illegal adoption practices and makes clear that intercountry adoption is a means of child protection. It is clearly stated in the preamble that intercountry adoptions must take place in the best interests of the child and with respect for his of her fundamental rights, and that the abduction of, the sale of, or traffic in children must be prevented. The Hague Adoption Convention 1993 is definitely an essential – and for the moment the best available – international legal framework to regulate intercountry adoptions. Therefore, as many countries as possible should join the Hague Adoption Convention 1993.

However, this article demonstrates that the Hague Adoption Convention 1993 suffers from a number of shortcomings, such as its limited scope, its focus on the civil aspects and not the criminal aspects, the possibility of independent adoption, and the burden of responsibility on the States of origin. Moreover, some of its key terms, such as 'improper financial gain' and 'costs and expenses', could be made transparent. This article has also raised the question whether or not we should recognise non-convention adoptions by operation of law. Finally, intercountry adoption from a European perspective has been discussed. Is a European Adoption Regulation necessary, feasible, or even desirable? I hope that I will have found an answer to this last question by the end of 2008.

Bibliography

K. Beevers (1997) Intercountry adoption of unaccompanied refugee children, *Child and Family Law Quarterly*, pp. 131-147.

K. Beevers (1995) Intercountry adoption of refugee children: the Hague Recommendation, *Child and Family Law Quarterly*, pp. 10-17.

Th.M. de Boer (2002) Jurisdiction and enforcement in international family law: a labyrinth of European and international legislation, *NILR*, pp. 307-345.

K. Boele-Woelki (2002) Divorce in Europe: Unification of Private International Law and Harmonization of Substantive Law, in H.F.G. Lemaire en P. Vlas, Met recht verkregen. Bundel opstellen aangeboden aan Mr. Ingrid S. Joppe, Deventer: Kluwer, pp. 17-28.

A. van den Borne en C.J. Kloosterboer, Inzicht in uitbuiting: handel in minderjarigen in Nederland nader onderzocht, Amsterdam: Stichting Defence for Children 2005.

R.A. Bouwer, Bespreking van het Haagse Adoptieverdrag 1993. Adoption: a means of giving a child a family, not giving a family a child, Groningen 1994.

N. Cantwell, 'A flying start. Towards a convention on inter-country adoption', *International Children's Rights Monitor* 1990, p. 11-12.

I. Ceschi, Adoption ausländische Kinder in der Schweiz: Aufname, Vermittlung und Pflegeverhältnis, Zurich: Schultess Polygraphisches Verlag AG 1996.

Defence for Children International, International Terre des Hommes, International Social Service, 'Preliminary findings of a joint investigation on independent adoption', Geneva: Defence for Children International 1991.

Defence for Children International, International Social Service, 'Romania. The adoption of Romanian children by foreigners. Report of a Group of Experts on the implementation of the Convention on the Rights of the Child regarding inter-country adoption', Geneva. Defence for Children International 1991.

W. Duncan, 'Hague Convention on the Protection of Children and Co-operation in Respect of Intercountry Adoption (29 May 1993)', *International Family Law* 1999, p. 31-34.

W. Duncan, 'Intercountry adoption. Some issues in implementing and supplementing the 1993 Hague Convention on the Protection of Children and Cooperation in Respect of Intercountry Adoption', in: J. Doek, J.H.A. van Loon en P. Vlaardingerbroek, Children on the move. How to implement their right to family life, Den Haag: Kluwer Law International 1996.

W. Duncan, 'Regulating intercountry adoption – an international perspective', in: A. Bainham, Frontiers of Family Law, London: Chancery Law Publishing 1993.

Adviesbureau Montfoort, Evaluatieonderzoek Wobka. Een evaluatieonderzoek naar de Wet opneming buitenlandse kinderen ter adoptie, 2004, http://www.adoptie.nl/pdf/Wobka.pdf.

L. Frohn, 'De Wet conflictenrecht adoptie: het sluitstuk van de regelgeving inzake interlandelijke en internationale adoptie', *FJR* 2003, p. 242-247.

Hague Conference on Private International Law, Proceedings of the Seventeenth Session, Tome II, Adoption – co-operation, 10 to 29 May 1993

Hague Conference on Private International Law, Actes et Documents de la Dixième Session, Tome II, Adoption, 1964.

B. von Hoffman, European Private International Law, Nijmegen: Ars Aequi Libri 1998.

B.M. Hubing, 'International child adoptions: who should decide what is in the best interests of the family?', *Notre Dame Journal of Law, Ethics and Public Policy* 2001.

International Social Service, Internal and intercountry adoption laws, The Hague/London/Boston: Kluwer Law International 1996.

D. van Iterson, 'Op weg naar een nieuw Haags Adoptieverdrag', *NIPR* 1990, p. 147-154.

M. Jänterä-Jareborg, 'Unification of international family law in Europe – a critical perspective', in: K. Boele-Woelki, Perspectives for the Unification and Harmonisation of Family Law in Europe, Antwerpen – Oxford – New York: Intersentia 2003, p. 194-216.

L.M. Katz, 'A modest proposal? The Convention on Protection of Children and Cooperation in Respect of Intercountry Adoption', *Emory International Law Review* 1995.

H.C. Kennard, 'Curtailing the sale and trafficking of children: a discussion of the Hague Conference Convention in Respect of Intercountry Adoptions', *University of Pennsylvania Journal of International Business Law* 1994.

C. Kleem, 'Airplane trips and organ banks: random events and the Hague Convention on Intercountry Adoptions', *Georgia Journal of International and Comparative Law* 2000.

K.F. Kreuzer, 'Zu Stand und Perspektiven des Euopäischen Internationalen Privatrechts. Wie europäisch soll das Euopäische Internationale Privatrecht sein?', RabelsZ 2006, p. 1-88.

M. van Leeuwen, 'The politics of adoptions across borders: whose interests are served? (A look at the emerging market of infants from China)', *Pacific Rim Law and Policy Journal* 1999.

J.H.A. van Loon, 'Het Haagse Verdrag van 29 mei 1993 inzake de internationale samenwerking en de bescherming van kinderen op het gebied van de interlandelijke adoptie: achtergronden en krachtlijnen', in: P. Senaeve, Actuele vraagstukken van interlandelijke en inlandse adoptie en van verlatenverklaring, Leuven/Amersfoort: Acco 1995, p. 73-95.

J.H.A. van Loon, 'International co-operation and protection of children with regard to intercountry adoption', *Recueil des Cours* 1993 (VII), p. 191-456.

J.H.A. van Loon, Report on intercountry adoption, Permanent Bureau of the Hague Conference on Private International Law, The Hague, 1990.

G. Marquez, 'Transnational adoption: the creation and ill effects of an international black market baby trade', *Journal of Juvenile Law* 2000.

J. Mason, 'Intercountry Adoption: A Global Problem or a Global Solution?', *Journal of International Affairs* 2001, p. 141-166.

S.A. Munson, 'Independent adoption: in whose best interest?', *Seton Hall Law Review* 1996.

J.A. Nota, De adoptie. Rechtsinstituut in ontwikkeling, 1969.

G. Parra-Aranguren, Explanatory Report on the 1993 Hague Intercountry Adoption Convention, 1994, http://hcch.e-vision.nl/upload/expl33e.pdf.

Parliamentary Assembly of the Council of Europe, Doc. 10617, Motion for a Recommendation on international adoption, 28 June 2005, http://assembly.coe.int/ main.asp?Link=/documents/workingdocs/doc05/edoc10617.htm.

Parliamentary Assembly of the Council of Europe, Doc. 10226, Motion for a Resolution on the establishment of a European Adoption Agency/Monitoring Centre, 22 June 2004, http://assembly.coe.int/main.asp?Link=/documents/workingdocs/ doc04/edoc10226.htm.

Parliamentary Assembly Recommendation 1443 (2000), International adoption: respecting children's rights, http://assembly.coe.int/Main.asp?link=/Documents/AdoptedText/ta00/EREC1443.htm.

Parliamentary Assembly of the Council of Europe, Doc. 8600 (opinion), International adoption: respecting children's rights, 21 December 1999, http://assembly.coe.int/ main.asp?Link=/documents/workingdocs/doc99/edoc8600.htm.

Parliamentary Assembly of the Council of Europe, Doc. 8592 (Report), International adoption: respecting children's rights, 2 December 1999, http://assembly.coe.int/ main.asp?Link=/documents/workingdocs/doc99/edoc8592.htm.

M. Pestman, 'Verdrag over de bescherming van kinderen en samenwerking bij interlandelijke adoptie', *NJB* 1993, p. 1186-1190.

W. Pierce, R.J. Vitillo, Independent adoptions and the "baby market", in: E.D. Hibbs, Adoption: international perspectives, Madison Conecticut: International Universities Press 1991, p. 131-152.

F.J. Pilotti, Intercountry adoption: trends, issues and, policy implications for the 1990's, in: Childhood, Instituto Interamericano del Nino, Montevido, 1993, p. 165-177, www.innfa.org/InforEspe/BibliotecaVirtua/TEXTOS/00-10630.htm.

C. Saclier, 'Adoption and the Best Interests of the Child', in: P. Selman, Intercountry Adoption. Developments, trends and perspectives, London: BAAF 2000, http://www.iss-ssi.org/Resource_Centre/selman.PDF.

S.J. Schaafsma, 'Kroniek van het internationaal privaatrecht', *NJB* 2005, p. 478-484.

S.J. Schaafsma, 'Kroniek van het internationaal privaatrecht', *NJB* 2004, p. 513-519.

J.G. Stein, 'A call to end baby selling: why the Hague Convention on Intercountry Adoption should be modified to include the consent provisions of the Uniform Adoption Act', *Thomas Jefferson Law Review* 2001.

Unicef, Intercountry Adoption, Innocenti Digest, www.unicef-icdc.org/publications/pdf/digest4e.pdf.

P. Vlaardingerbroek e.a., Het hedendaagse personen- en familierecht, Deventer: Kluwer 2004.

P. Vlas, 'Naar een EG-Verordening IPR-Erfrecht?', *WPNR* 2002, p. 391-393.

A.P.M.J. Vonken, 'Legislatieve ontwikkelingen rond interlandelijke adopties. Verkaveling van de regelgeving inzake adoptie', *NIPR* 2004, p. 133-147.

K.M. Wittner, Curbing child-trafficking in intercountry adoption: will international treaties and adoption moratorium accomplish the job in Cambodia?', *Pacific Rim Law and Policy Journal* 2003.

Endnotes

1   Act of 26 January 1956, Stb.1956, 42. This act entered into force in the Netherlands on 1 November 1956.
2   Vlaardingerbroek 2004, p. 217; Pilotti 1993, p.13; Van Loon 1993, p. 214, 229; Van Loon 1990, p. 54; Unicef, p. 2.
3   Saclier 2000, p. 3.
4   Saclier 2000, p. 3; Parliamentary Assembly 1999, Doc. 8592, p. 1-2, 6-7, 11; Ceschi 1996, p. 43; ISS 1996, p. vi-vii; Van Loon 1995, p. 94; Katz 1995, p. 6; Kennard 1994, p. 2; Pestman 1993, p. 1186; DCI 1991b, p. 9; Unicef, p. 3.
5   Ceschi 1996, p. 44; ISS 1996, p. iv; Van Loon 1995, p. 94; Bouwer 1994.
6   Unicef, p. 6; ISS 1996, p. iv.
7   Unicef, p. 6; Parliamentary Assembly 1999, Doc. 8600, p. 3.
8   An example of abuse in intercountry adoption is the situation in India. In May 2001, an article in the newspapers headed: '*Adopting babies in India costs 5 guilders*' ('Adoptiebaby's in India kosten vijf gulden', Brabants Dagblad, 2 May 2001). A few months later: '*Trafficking in Indian babies for adoption is lucrative business*' ('Handel in Indiase baby's voor adoptie is lucratief', Volkskrant,15 August 2001). Both articles point out the criminal network in India, which set up a big business in adopting babies.
9   Hague Convention on the Protection of Children and Co-operation in Respect of Intercountry Adoption, concluded 29 May 1993. This convention entered into force in the Netherlands on 1 October 1998.
10 Act of 3 July 2003, regulating the conflict of laws relating to adoption and the recognition of intecountry adoptions (Wet conflictenrecht adoptie), Stb. 2003, 283, in force in the Netherlands from 1 January 2004.
11 Act of 8 December 1988, containing rules concerning the placement in the Netherlands of foreign children with a view to adoption (Wet opneming buitenlandse kinderen ter adoptie), Stb.1988, 566, as amended by the Act of 14 May 1998, Stb.1998, 302.
12 Mason 2001, p. 142.
13 Mason 2001, p. 148-149.
14 Mason 2001, p. 149.
15 Van Loon 1990, p. 6.
16 Hague Conference on Private International Law 1993. See for the text of the Hague Adoption Convention 1993: http://www.hcch.net/index_en.php?act=conventions.text&cid=69. See also Parra-Aranguren 1994.
17 Trb. 1993, 197; Rijkswet van 14 mei 1998, houdende goedkeuring van het op 29 mei 1993 te 's-Gravenhage tot stand gekomen Verdrag inzake de bescherming van kinderen en de samenwerking op het gebied van de interlandelijke adoptie, Stb. 1998, 301.
18 In contrast to the Hague Convention on Jurisdiction, Applicable Law and Recognition of Decrees relating to Adoptions, 15 November 1965 (p. 4/5). See for this characterisation of the Hague Adoption Convention 1993: Vonken 2004, p. 133.
19 Van Loon 1990, p. 336.
20 In contrast to the European Convention on the Adoption of Children, 24 April 1967 (p. 5).
21 Duncan 1999, p. 31.
22 Van Loon 1993, p. 337-338.
23 Mason 2001, p. 157.
24 Duncan 1999, p. 31.
25 Duncan 1999, p. 31.
26 Ceschi 1996, p. 111; Van Loon 1995, p. 92; Pestman 1993, p. 1190.
27 Hague Conference on Private International Law 1964. See for the text of the Hague Adoption Convention 1965: http://www.hcch.net/index_en.php?act=conventions.text&cid=75.
28 Ceschi 1996, p. 79-81; Van Loon 1995, p. 78; Nota 1969, p. 122.
29 See for the text of the Inter-American Convention: http://www.oas.org/juridico/english/treaties/b-48.htm.
30 Van Loon 1993, p. 309.
31 See for a list of ratifications: http://www.oas.org/juridico/english/sigs/b-48.html.
32 See for the text of this UN Declaration: http://www.un.org/documents/ga/res/41/a41r085.htm.

[33] See for the text and Explanatory Report of this convention: http://conventions.coe.int/ Treaty/en/ Treaties/Html/058.htm, and: http://conventions.coe.int/Treaty/en/Reports/ Html/058.htm.

[34] Cheschi 1996, p. 74.

[35] Van Loon 1995, p. 77. One has to keep in mind that the articles 11 and 14 of the European Adoption Convention 1967 do relate to international adoption.

[36] See for a list of ratifications: http://conventions.coe.int/Treaty/Commun/ ChercheSig.asp?NT=058&CM=8&DF=4/19/2006&CL=ENG.

[37] The Draft European Convention on the Adoption of Children, the Draft Explanatory Report, and other Working Documents can be found on the website of the Council of Europe: http://www.coe.int/t/ e/legal_affairs/legal_co-operation/family_law_and _children%27s_ rights/Activities/Meetings%20GT1 .asp#TopOfPage.

[38] Document CJ-FA-GT1 (2006) 2 Rev 2.

[39] Act of 8 December 1988, containing rules concerning the placement in the Netherlands of foreign children with a view to adoption (Wet opneming buitenlandse kinderen ter adoptie), Stb.1988, 566, as amended by the Act of 14 May 1998, Stb.1998, 302.

[40] Act of 3 July 2003, regulating the conflict of laws relating to adoption and the recognition of intecountry adoptions (Wet conflictenrecht adoptie), Stb. 2003, 283, in force in the Netherlands from 1 January 2004. See for the Dutch text of this act: http://www.recht.nl/doc/stb2003-283.pdf?RNL SESSION=. See for comment on this act: Vonken 2004 and Frohn 2003.

[41] Kamerstukken II 2001/02, 28 457, nr. 3, p. 7.

[42] Hubing 2001, p. 27; Cheschi 1996, p. 117.

[43] Parliamentary Assembly 1999, Doc. 8592, p. 11.

[44] Parliamentary Assembly Recommendation 1443 (2000).

[45] Parliamentary Assembly Recommendation 1443 (2000).

[46] See the Report and Conclusions of the Special Commission on the Practical Operation of the Hague Convention of 29 May 1993 on Protection of Children and Co-operation in Respect of Intercountry Adoption, 28 November – 1 December 2000, p. 28-31, http://hcch.e-vision.nl/upload/scrpt33e2000.pdf.

[47] Duncan 1996, p. 5-7.

[48] Parliamentary Assembly Recommendation 1443 (2000); Parliamentary Assembly 1999, Doc. 8592; Cheschi 1996, p. 76-78, 199; Van Loon 1990, p. 174-178.

[49] Parliamentary Assembly 2005, Doc.10617.

[50] Kamerstukken II 2002/03, 28 457, nr. 6, p. 4; Kamerstukken II 2001/02, 28457, nr. 3, p. 13.

[51] Kamerstukken II 2002/03, 28 457, nr. 6, p. 4; Kamerstukken II 2001/02, 28457, nr. 3, p. 13.

[52] Kamerstukken II 2001/02, 28 457, nr. 3, p. 7.

[53] Kamerstukken II 2002/03, 28 457, nr. 6, p. 1-2; Kamerstukken II 2001/02, 28 457, nr. 3, p. 7.

[54] Ceschi 1996, p. 53; Van Loon 1995, p. 86/87; Duncan 1993, p. 53; Pestman 1993, p. 1189; Unicef, p. 8; DCI 1991a, p. 4.

[55] Van Loon 1990, p. 68.

[56] Parliamentary Assembly 1999, Doc. 8600, p. 6; Ceschi 1996, p. 57-58, 60; Van Loon 1995, p. 86; DCI 1991a, p. 9; Van Loon 1990, p. 68.

[57] Duncan 1999, p. 33.

[58] Stein 2001, p. 16; Parliamentary Assembly 1999, Doc. 8600, p 5; Ceschi 1996, p. 58, 118; Munson 1996, p. 10; Kennard 1994, p. 7; DCI 1991a, p. 11, 18; Cantwell 1990, p. 12; Unicef, p. 7.

[59] Kamerstukken II 2004/05, 28 457, nr. 20, p. 6; Marquez 2000, p. 5; Evaluatierapport Wobka 2004, p. 168, http://www.adoptie.nl/pdf/Wobka.pdf.

[60] Ceschi 1996, p. 61; van Loon 1990, p. 150.

[61] Mason 2001, p. 165; see also in this sense: Pierce & Vitillo 1991, p. 141; DCI 1991a, p. 10.

[62] Mason 2001, p. 154.

[63] Mason 2001, p. 151; Stein 2001, p. 16; Marquez 2000, p. 10; Parliamentary Assembly 1999, Doc. 8592, p. 9; Katz 1995, p. 22; Kennard 1994, p. 11.

[64] Mason 2001, p. 151; Stein 2001, p. 16; Marquez 2000, p. 10; Parliamentary Assembly 1999, Doc. 8592, p. 9; Katz 1995, p. 22; Kennard 1994, p. 11.

65   Parliamentary Assembly 1999, Doc. 8592, p. 9; Kennard 1994, p. 11.

66   Article 33 of the Hague Adoption Convention states: A competent authority which finds that any provision of the Convention has not been respected or that there is a serious risk that it may not be respected, shall immediately inform the Central Authority of its State. This Central Authority shall be responsible for ensuring that appropriate measures are taken.

67   Wittner 2003, p. 3; Marquez 2000, p. 10.

68   Kennard 1994, p. 12.

69   Van den Borne & Kloosterboer 2005, p. 58.

70   Van den Borne & Kloosterboer 2005, p. 76.

71   Kamerstukken II 2003/04, 29 291, nr. 3, p. 10-11, 21.

72   Van den Borne & Kloosterboer 2005, p. 3.

73   Van Leeuwen 1999, p. 11.

74   Van Leeuwen 1999, p. 11.

75   Van Leeuwen 1999, p. 12.

76   Van Leeuwen 1999, p. 12.

77   Van Leeuwen 1999, p. 13.

78   Van Leeuwen 1999, p. 13.

79   Van Leeuwen 1999, p. 15.

80   Kennard 1994, p. 9.

81   Kennard 1994, p. 9-10.

82   Katz 1995, p. 26.

83   Katz 1995, p. 26.

84   Katz 1995, p. 26.

85   Stein 2001, p. 17.

86   Stein 2001, p. 18.

87   Kleem 2000, p. 18.

88   Kleem 2000, p. 18.

89   See for the Conclusions and Recommendations of the Second Meeting of the Special Commission on the Practical Operation of the Hague Convention of 29 May 1993 on Protection of children and co-operation in Respect of Intercountry Adoption, 17-23 September 2005: http://www.hcch.net/upload/wop/concl33sc05_e.pdf.

90   See Report of Meeting No 10.

91   Von Hoffman 1998, p. 23.

92   As Katz describes the 'public policy exception' of article 24 of the Hague Adoption Convention 1993.

93   Von Hoffman 1998, p. 24.

94   Duncan 1996, p. 1.

95   Duncan 1996, p. 1.

96   Duncan 1996, p. 1.

97   Duncan 1996, p. 2.

98   Duncan 1996, p. 2.

99   Wittner 2003, p. 9, 14.

100   Wittner 2003, p. 13.

101   Wittner 2003, p. 18.

102   Duncan 1996, p. 10; Duncan 1993, p. 60.

103   Parliamentary Assembly Recommendation 1443 (2000).

104   Parliamentary Assembly 1999, Doc. 8592, p. 9.

105   Duncan 1996, p. 7.

106   Duncan 1996, p. 9.

107   Duncan 1996, p. 7.

108   Duncan 1996, p. 1.

109   See for the text of the Report of the Working Group of 12-14 April 1994: http://www.hcch.net/index _en.php?act= publications.details&pid=932& dtid=2; see also Duncan 1996, p. 8.

110   Recommendation concerning the application to refugee children and other internationally displaced children of the Hague Convention on Protection of Children and Co-operation in respect of Intercountry Adoption, 21 October 1994 (Annex A). See for the text of this recommenda-

175

tion: http://www.hcch.net/index_en.php?act=publications.details&pid=934&dtid=2. This recommendation has been criticised by Beevers: Beevers 1997 and Beevers 1995.

111 Duncan 1996, p. 1, 8.

112 Duncan 1996, p. 10.

113 For instance, Council Regulation (EC) No 44/2001 of 22 December 2000 on jurisdiction and the recognition and enforcement of judgments in civil and commercial matters (the Brussels I Regulation), Council Regulation (EC) No 1206/2001 of 28 May 2001 on cooperation between the courts of the Member States in the taking of evidence in civil or commercial matters, Council Regulation (EC) No 1348/2000 of 29 May 2000 on the service in the Member States of judicial and extrajudicial documents in civil or commercial matters, Council Regulation (EC) No 1347/2000 of 29 May 2000 on jurisdiction and the recognition and enforcement of judgments in matrimonial matters and in matters of parental responsibility for children of both spouses (the Brussels II Regulation), and Council Regulation (EC) No 1346/2000 of 29 May 2000 on insolvency proceedings. See for an overview of European Community Regulations concerning private international (family) law matters: Schaafsma 2005 and Schaafsma 2004.

114 Council Regulation (EC) No. 2201/2003 of 27 November 2003 concerning jurisdiction and the recognition and enforcement of judgments in matrimonial matters and the matters of parental responsibility, repealing Regulation (EC) No 1347/2000 (the Brussels II Regulation). The Brussels II-*bis* Regulation entered into application on 1 March 2005. See for the text of this Regulation: http://eur-lex.europa.eu/smartapi/cgi/sga_doc?smartapi!celexplus!prod!DocNumber&lg=en&type_doc=Regulation&an_doc=2003&nu_doc=2201.

115 Green Paper on applicable law and jurisdiction in divorce matters, http://ec.europa.eu/justice_home/doc_centre/civil/doc/com_2005_082_en.pdf.

115 Green Paper Succession and wills, http://ec.europa.eu/justice_home/doc_centre/civil/doc/com_ 2005_065_en.pdf.

117 Council and Commission Action Plan of 3 December 1998 on how best to implement the provisions of the Treaty of Amsterdam on the creation of an area of freedom, security and justice (Vienna Action Plan, http://eur-lex.europa.eu/LexUriServ/LexUriServ.do?uri=CELEX:31999Y0123(01):EN:HTML); Tampere European Council Presidency Conclusions of 15 and 16 October 1999 (http://www.europarl. europa.eu/summits/tam_en.htm#c); See also Boele-Woelki 2002, p. 23-24.

118 See for the communautarisation of private international (family) law: Schaafsma 2005 and Schaafsma 2004.

119 European Parliament Resolution on Improving the Law and Co-operation between the Member States on the Adoption of Minors, 12 December 1996, *OJ* 1997, C 20, 20.1.1997, p.176. See for the text of this Resolution: http://europa.eu.int/abc/doc/off/bull/en/9612/p105006.htm. See also the 1999 European Parliament Resolution on the illegal trafficking of babies coming from Guatemala (*OJ* 1999, C 104, 14.4.1999, p. 113), the 2005 European Parliament Resolution on the trafficking of children in Guatemala (Bulletin EU 7/8-2005), and a motion for a Resolution on the establishment of a European Adoption Agency/Monitoring Centre, Parliamentary Assembly 2004, Doc.10226.

120 Van Loon 1995, p. 84-85; Pestman 1993, p. 1188; Van Iterson 1990, p. 153-154.

121 Comparative law research is necessary to answer this question.

122 Except for Greece, all Member States of the European Union are a party to the Hague Adoption Convention 1993. The Hague Convention of 25 October 1980 on the Civil Aspects of International Child Abduction is the only Hague Convention that has been ratified by all Member States of the European Union and thus belongs to the 'acquis communautaire', see Kreuzer 2006, p. 211.

123 See also in this sense: Vlas 2003, p. 392-393; Jänterä-Jareborg 2003; De Boer 2002, p. 335-337.

124 Vlas 2003, p. 393.

125 Vlas 2003, p. 392.

126 In contrast to the Hague Child Abduction Convention 1980, which includes rules on jurisdiction, conflict of laws, and recognition and enforcement. Here it could be argued that the need for special community rules is less clear.

Valuing Children, Valuing Parents

The Role of the Family in Protecting Children and Fighting Poverty

Beatriz Monje Barón

*Poverty is having all the same dreams for the future that everyone else has,
but no way on earth to make them come true*

*Poverty is everyone thinking that they have the right to have an opinion about me,
just because I ask for a bit of help*

*Poverty is being told that I have nothing to offer my own child,
and believing it − then.*

Parents from the UK working on definitions of poverty.

1.   Child poverty

The European Commission's first joint report on social inclusion confirms that the fight against poverty and social exclusion remains a priority for the European Union.[1] It recognizes that 18% of the EU's population (over 60 million people) are threatened by poverty and around half of them live in conditions of long-term poverty.

Across Europe, child poverty has become a major concern. In 1996, 21% of children − around 17 million - in the EU were living in a low-income household. In the UK alone 3.5 million children live in poverty. Petra Holscher, on a transactional study commissioned by the European Commission stated:

> *Economic poverty is often only one aspect of the deprivation that affects poor children, limiting their development and their chances of participation. Children growing up in low-income households are at risk.*

At both national government and European level, initiatives of all kinds have been adopted with the aim of improving children's lives. In 1999, UK Prime Minister Tony Blair committed his government and country to eradicating child poverty within one generation (20 years). But child poverty is inseparable from the poverty of their family. In other words, generally speaking, there are no poor children in rich households, and there are no rich children in poor households. As stated by the *Coordinadora de Barrios* in Madrid (Spain):

Children's needs are the needs of their families. When families are protected and supported financially, and in terms of housing, work, health, education, etc... the children's lives improve dramatically. That should be the focus of policies and investment.[2]

Ways to forward in the fight against child poverty must think in terms of 'family groups' or 'family dynamics.' First of all, they need to reflect the desire of parents living in poverty to do their best for their children and to remain key players in contributing to their children's future well-being. Yet, parents experiencing poverty and deprivation are often viewed as constituting a risk from which children may need to be protected.

2. Poverty and child protection

The link between poverty and child protection is a complex one and there is no comprehensive data available across the EU. However, in the UK's last National Action Plan on Social Inclusion, re-registration on the child protection register was used as an indicator of child poverty.

Valuing Children, Valuing Parents identifies the following factors as making practitioners and policy makers reluctant to acknowledge the link between poverty and child protection intervention leading to care measures: the link breaks national and international law; it leads to social powerlessness; the differing perceptions of poverty; the risk of labelling poor parents as abusive parents; and a lack of reliable information.

In the same paper, a small overview from Europe reveals interesting results. A children's services director in Belgium noted that of the 140 families it worked with, only 19 received work related income – the rest were in receipt of benefits or had no income. In Italy, the *Instituto degli Innocenti* found that economic reasons or serious housing problems relate to 51% of cases where children are placed with a foster family. And in the UK, a study by Bebbington and Miles[3] found that children from poor backgrounds were 700 times more likely to be placed in care than their peers from a non-poor background.

The experience of ATD Fourth World supporting very poor families bears this out. A mother of two in London stated:

The worst thing about being poor is the fear of having your children taken away. I will never forgive myself if my children end up in care. I went through that, I will never allow anyone to do that to them.

This is the fear of most parents supported by ATD Fourth World in the UK and all around Europe – but is also their repeated experience.

In London I have been supporting a young mother of three. Having being taken into care as a child she wasn't given the strength to break out of poverty. At the time of leaving care she didn't have any qualifications, any place to live, any means to make her living, but worst she did not have any self esteem or sense of identity left. As she explains:

> *You are like an onion and gradually every skin is peeled off you and there is nothing left. All your self-esteem is gone. You are left feeling like nothing and then your family feels like that.*

Her first child was taken into care because of concerns about neglect and was consequently adopted without her consent. During her second pregnancy she carried the pain and the fear of everything happening again, but found the courage to approach Social Services to ask for support. She said she would do everything they told her to do, but nobody told her what to do. She then told me, "I think they think I am OK," and carried on looking and finding her own ways to overcome difficulties. A social worker visited her for the first time once the baby was born. Care proceedings were initiated because of neglect – specifically the mother not offering enough stimulation to the baby and a stable environment in which to grow up. She was 20 years old and was genuinely trying her best to meet her baby's needs. But she was also fighting poverty and fighting her own feelings of worthlessness. She was living with very little money, taking all the necessary steps to have a stable place to live, and dealing with the Social Services assessment. At the same time – like any other mother – she was loving her child and enjoying their time together, but her second child was finally adopted, again without her consent. On her third pregnancy, she again approached Social Services. She had to go through an assessment again, but no plans were made on how to help this mother make improvements in her life. The child was taken into care at birth and is now adopted.

In the UK, social workers are allocated to the child, not to the whole family. For this mother – like for many other parents – this meant that she did not have contact with Social Services between pregnancies or even during pregnancies. Despite her wish to understand Social Services' concerns and her will to work with them, she was not offered any support after her children were taken into care and no plans were made for the future.

This mother never abused any of her children. With the means she had, she offered her best to her children and was as caring as any other young mother. Her children were not being neglected; they were children born in a poor family.

3. Overexposed parenting

Parents in poverty experience overexposed parenting and children in poverty are over-represented in the care system. A lawyer representing parents on care proceedings told me recently, "In ten years of practice only once I had a client from a professional background, all others were poor parents. Most of them are accused of neglect or emotional abuse." Let us take this as an illustration of the research carried out by Professor June Thoburn,[4] concluding that 98% of families whose children were considered to be at risk of emotional maltreatment or neglect were characterised by the poverty of their material environment.

Valuing Children, Valuing Parents calls for recognition that intervention by child protection services is mainly directed at children living in poverty. The paper emphasises that debates on child welfare must take into account the poverty factor – not to blame parents, but to take collective responsibility in providing poor parents with the means to offer a good start in life to their children or, in other words, to take collective responsibility in eradicating poverty.

4.   Parents living in poverty protecting children

Parents in poverty have to fulfil their role and responsibility as parents just like any others. They enjoy pleasures and have aspirations and fears, but in circumstances which are far more difficult than those of most parents. The general situation and the particular circumstances they find themselves in put a strain on their families and expose weaknesses much more than is the case for parents can who draw on networks of support, both economic and personal.

These parents, like any others, want to protect their children from any kind of harm. They exert tremendous efforts ever day to protect their children from the violence of the streets, and from harm and illness even when housing conditions are bad, to make sure that they go to school, have proper clothing and food, to comfort them when they are bullied, to assure them that they are lovable and loved. Concentrating only on vulnerability when looking at families experiencing poverty and deprivation leads too often to the view that they constitute a risk for their children.

But it is not parents in poverty that constitute a risk to children; it is poverty. To practice social work as if parents were the risk is both unfair and useless.

This approach leads to parents staying away from services, of course to protect themselves from the suffering of losing their children, but mainly to protect their children from the suffering of being separated from their family. To stay away from services – in poor parents' experience – is one child protection measure.

Let me illustrate this with an example that struck me recently. During an ATD Fourth World outing with families, a four year old boy bumped his head while playing with one of our volunteers. In seconds, a bad bruise appeared on his head. When the mother realised what happened, she became very angry and then looked at me very upset and said, "I am going to have Social Services on my back!" This mother is doing well and none of her children are in care, but she has learned from her background that any 'mistake' can become a turning point, the beginning of an exhausting relationship with Social Services. It took a long conversation with us for this mother to find the courage to take her son to school on the following Monday.

A father explains this event: "You hide when you are living in poverty every time you hear a knock at the door. It is either the money-lender, the housing officer or the social worker."

Parents experiencing poverty are not just poor but unequal: unequal financially, but also unequal within the context of social services departments. Parents often explain their feelings of powerless and hopelessness.

5.   A solution-focused approach
If these parents are offered ways to share their knowledge, to use their determination to meet their children's needs and the value of their life experience is recognised, their collective experience can guide both child protection policy and practice.

An important way of achieving this is to enable people with experience of poverty and bringing up children to shape social work training, ensuring that family support and child protection teams are fully equipped with the motivation, knowledge and skills to deal with the poverty of the families with whom they work, and better support parents to protect their own children.

By working closely with front line practitioners – social workers and others – we are well aware that understanding families in poverty as a source of strength in the protection and well-being of children is often understood in contradiction with the paramountcy of children's well-being.

However, *Valuing Children, Valuing Parents* – among many other studies – looks at innovative practice in child protection that suggests the strength of this approach. This is in fact a 'solution-focused' approach to practice, based on the development of an effective partnership with children and their families. This approach underlies that all families have strengths and capabilities. If we take the time to identify these qualities, to build on them, attempting to develop a true partnership rather than focusing on the correction of skills deficits or weaknesses, children would – with their parents – overcome the effects of poverty. By empowering parents in poverty in their wish to ensure their children's well-being, we will protect children experiencing poverty better. We will be working towards eradication of poverty and respecting human rights.

6.   Final recommendations for protecting children living in poverty

6.1   Involve children and their families in the research and evaluation of policy and practice against poverty
In order to develop successful policy and practice against child poverty, we recommend that:
- Research on child poverty is developed in terms of 'family groups'.
- Work is carried out to understand and promote the conditions required for a real partnership between people in poverty and the other parties involved in the fight against poverty and social exclusion.
- Research has qualitative and participatory dimensions.
- New indicators on child poverty are developed in partnership with families living in poverty.

- Children and parents become partners in building a better understanding of the most important features in the child's life and how to guarantee these features for all children.

6.2 Understand the links between child protection intervention and poverty

In order to gain a deeper understanding of the links between poverty and child protection policy and practice, we recommend that:

- Research and statistical analysis is carried out to identify the socio-economic factors of children and families affected by child protection intervention.
- Research on experiences and outcomes for children and families affected by care orders – particularly those experiencing poverty and social exclusion – assesses the suitability and long-term efficacy of existing child protection measures.
- Research is carried out to establish the impact on child protection systems of parents' fear of services.
- Child protection practices are evaluated using a human rights framework.

6.3 Supporting parents in poverty in safeguarding their children

In order to protect children in poverty better, we recommend that:

- Professionals are trained to understand and capitalise on the ways families in poverty protect their children from harm, so child protection systems and practice become more effective.
- Innovative 'solution-focused' approaches to child protection practice are developed. New approaches should take the time to identify strengths and capabilities, to build on them, attempting to develop a true partnership with families rather than focusing on the correction of skills deficits or weaknesses
- People with experience of poverty and bringing up children provide training to professionals working in family support and/or child protection teams
- Budgetary decisions reflect the need to create a stimulating environment for professionals, with provision for innovation, experimentation and research on family support and child protection fields.
- High priority is given to the search for alternatives to separating children and parents experiencing poverty and social exclusion.

Valuing Children, Valuing Parents is a discussion paper produced by ATD Fourth World, exploring the role of the family in protecting children and fighting poverty. This paper brings together some elements from *Valuing Children, Valuing Parents* as well as my own experience of supporting families in poverty in London.

Bibliography

ATD Fourth World (2005) *Valuing Children, Valuing Parents*, ATD Fourth World Publications, Paris.

ATD Fourth World (2005) *Getting the right trainers: enabling service users to train social work students and practitioners about the realities of family poverty in the UK*, ATD Fourth World Publications, Paris.

Bebbington and Miles (1989) *The background of children who enter local authority care*, British Journal of Social Work.

Department of Health (2001) *The Children Act now – messages from research*, The Stationary office, United Kingdom.

Thoburn et al (2000) *Permanent Family Placement for Children of Minority Ethnic Origin*, Jessica Kingsley Publishers.

Thoburn J, Wilding J and Watson J (2000) *Family Support in Cases of Emotional Maltreatment and Neglect*, London: Stationery Office.

Thoburn J, Lewis A and Shemmings D (1995) *Family Involvement in the Child Protection Process*, London: HMSO.

Endnotes

1. European Commission and Council (2001) *Joint Report on Social Inclusion*, Brussels.
2. ATD Fourth World (2005) *Valuing Children, Valuing Parents*, Paris.
3. Bebbington and Miles (1989) *The background of children who enter local authority care*, British Journal of Social Work, 19, 349-368.
4. Thoburn et al (2000) *Permanent Family Placement for Children of Minority Ethnic Origin*, Jessica Kingsley Publishers.

Guardianship of Foster Children

Carol van Nijnatten & Nanneke Quik-Schuijt

1.   Introduction

In the Netherlands, foster care is a major kind of child welfare. Only a few Dutch children are adopted nationally. During the period 1999-2004, the number of placements in a foster family rose from 10,000 to 16,000 children a year (*Landelijke Voorlichting Pleegzorg*). More than 10,000 children live in a foster family. Since the last decade, the number of new placements more than doubled to more than 5,500 children a year.

Most children prefer a foster family to a children's home. Raising a child in a family is generally considered to be the best guarantee for a balanced development. A foster family is a better alternative for most of the children than residential home care, which is often discontinuous by the working hours of the employees and the frequent transfers of the children and the employees. Children who live in a foster family have better relations with their caretakers than children who receive residential care (Bates; English & Kouidou-Giles, 1997). Foster care may also prevent hospitalisation of the child (Punselie & Nijon, 1999). Governmental administrators see that foster care is inexpensive compared to the care that is offered in children's homes. Foster parents do not receive a salary but do qualify for reimbursement of daily expenses. A majority of Dutch foster parents is favourable to paid foster parenthood (Robbroecks & Tamrouti-Makking, 1998).

In the Netherlands, only a few foster parents are also guardian of their foster children. Psychologists in the field of Dutch foster care plead that the foster parents of children with a long-term perspective in their family should obtain guardianship. Especially for young children, it may support their chances to the development of a good attachment (Weterings, 1998). Legal scholars think that guardianship should follow the child's residence (Quik-Schuijt, 1998).

Obtaining guardianship has always been possible but foster parents lost their right to reimbursement when they became guardians. So, only few foster parents took this step. Since 2001, foster parents who are guardians retain their right to reimbursement of costs of daily living. But still few of them asked for guardianship. Why is that? We presented this question to foster parents. In the Dutch national journal of foster care, we put an advertisement in which we asked foster parents to inform us about their main arguments, pro and con, to start a legal procedure for guardianship.

In this article, we will first explain the Dutch legal context of guardianship for foster parents. Then, we will go into the psychological and pedagogical relevance of 'foster guardianship', and the views of Dutch foster parents into the pros and cons of obtaining guardianship. We will finish with some recommendations for foster care policy.

2. The legal context of Dutch foster care

For Dutch children who cannot live with their parents, foster care is the only real option to live in a family. Dutch law does not provide for confidential adoption and open national adoption of children by adoptive parents is rare. Adoption has other legal consequences than foster care, as it results in cutting off the family ties between the child and his or her birth parents. The child becomes a legal child of the adoption parents and this has major consequences for descent, succession, the child's surname, etc. Foster care does not involve these changes: the child remains legally the child of his or her parents; keeps the parent's surname; and remains the inheritor of his or her parents.

In the Netherlands, there are three types of foster care:

(1) Voluntary placement

When children are placed voluntarily in foster family, the children's parents keep their parental say. There is no legal possibility for parents themselves to transfer their parental authority to foster parents. The Child Protection Board has the monopoly to submit the question of removal of parental authority to the judge and in this case it can only be granted if the parents agree.

If parents want their child back after he or she has stayed more then one year in a foster family, the foster parents have to agree. They have the so-called right of blockade: if they do not agree with the parents' decision to have the child returned to them, the parents need permission of the juvenile judge. In that case, foster parents can ask for removal of parental authority and if granted then they will obtain the guardianship themselves.

(2) Placement while the child is under family supervision

Family supervision is a child protection measure which limits parental say. It is pronounced when the child's development is seriously at risk, and voluntary help has failed or will most probably fail. It can only be ordered for a year at a time but it can be prolonged until majority. In case of family supervision, the juvenile judge can also give a care order for a year or shorter. As long as the family super-vision order continues, the care order can be renewed until the child is 18 years old.

After a placement in a foster family or in an residential home for more then a year and a half, the Child Protection Board can submit the removal of parental author-ity and placement in the foster family can be granted, even when the parents do not agree.

(3) Placement when parents are relieved of their parental authority
Removal of parental authority usually results in institutional guardianship. According to the law, foster parents can be appointed guardian but in the most cases an agency is appointed. This agency may request to deliver the guardianship to foster parents whenever they think this is in the best interests of the child.

In the three situations just mentioned, foster parents who care for a foster child are entitled to a reimbursement on basis of the real costs of food and clothing. In the past, foster parents lost that reimbursement when both or one of them were appointed guardian. Since 2001, it is possible for single foster parents to become guardian and retain the reimbursement. However, when both foster parents are appointed guardian, they still have no right to reimbursement of the costs of daily life they make for their foster children. The idea is that a foster couple with guardianship has so much resemblance to adoption, that the foster parents should be treated equally to adoptive parents and to all biological parents. In the Netherlands, every parent is entitled to child benefit, but that is far less than the basic needs that are reimbursed to foster parents.

In reaction to this rule, many foster parent couples who want to obtain guardianship decide that one of them will ask for guardianship, in order to maintain the reimbursement. In case of more foster children, the one parent can obtain guardianship of the one child and the other foster parent of the other child(ren).

3. Conditions for foster guardianship
Guardianship of foster parents may be in the best interests of foster children. The foster parents have everyday responsibility and have proved to be trustworthy caretakers. The daily care for children often requires decisions that can best be taken by the people who have a realistic overview of the child's conditions and the consequences of certain decisions. It causes frustration for many foster parents when they have to ask the institutional guardian permission for daily decisions regarding education, medical care, visit arrangements with the biological parents, holidays abroad, etc.

Yet, guardianship by foster parents is not the best solution in every case. In our view, foster guardianship in only wise in certain conditions. If these conditions are not fulfilled, it may be better to maintain the neutral institutional guardianship. The aim is to improve the situation of the child by foster guardianship. The conditions are discussed below.

3.1 Long stay perspective
The placement in the foster family has a long stay perspective. Only if the child's perspective is to stay in the family for the rest of his or her childhood, is obtaining guardianship a wise step. If the child will only be placed for a short time and if there is a realistic possibility that the child will return to his or her biological parents, obtaining guardianship is not preferable.

3.2   A good timing of the transfer of guardianship

As we saw before, obtaining guardianship is only possible after the parents are relieved of their parental authority. In case of a voluntary placement or if parents agree with the removal of their parental authority, it is wise to wait for a year or so, because parents may regret and take the child back home. In case of a baby, it may be recommended that foster parents accept the guardianship as soon as possible for reasons of attachment.

When parents do not agree, they can only be relieved of their parental authority after 18 months placement in the context of a family supervision order. Usually, the child was living in the foster family all that time. Even then it may be wise to appoint an institutional guardian, because the parents may be very mournful and cross because of the loss of what they consider their last tie with their child.

In the eyes of many of the foster parents, the institutional guardian may be a neutral buffer between biological parents and foster family. Sometimes, the child lived in a residential home before being placed in a foster family. Just after the child was placed in the foster family, or after the court decision with regard to parental authority, it may be difficult for parents to accept that foster parents will be appointed legal guardian.

Foster parents tell that the performances of institutional guardian agencies leave much to desire. They have little confidence in institutional care because there is hardly any continuity in care (one of the foster children in our study had 11 institutional guardians). The guardians often visit the family only once a year, and sometimes are far from neutral and choose the side of the biological parents.

Since 2005, Dutch foster parents who are appointed guardians can no longer rely on a specialised foster care worker as buffer between them and the child's parents when there are problems because of the access regulation. Many foster parents indicate that the loss of this buffer is a major reason to not start a foster guardianship procedure.

3.3   The feelings and opinions of the child

The feelings and opinions of the child are relevant. In the first place, the child should be informed about any plans of the foster parents to obtain guardianship. Any child, no matter how old he or she is, has the right to be informed about the crucial decisions that are planned to be taken and that regard him or her (Van Nijnatten, 2005). Any child should be informed about what is happening to him or her and about the plans for the future. Moreover, foster parents should only raise this subject as a possibility and give the child maximal space to talk about it and give any comment. Any objection should be taken very seriously.

Questions about agreement or disagreement with obtaining guardianship are not to be answered just like that. Foster children find themselves in an ambiguous position, between positive experiences in the foster family and their faithfulness towards their parents. They often feel that a choice for staying in the foster family and supporting the idea of foster guardianship is a choice against their birth parents. The feelings of loyalty of children for their birth parents are existential and deep (Boszormeny-Nagy, 1987) and are a serious threat for a prosperous development in the foster family. Any opportunity to improve the relationship between birth parents and foster parents will be in the best interests of the foster child. Guardianship for foster parents may imply working at a better relationship between foster parents and biological parents. Most children do not want to lose good contact with their birth parents by making a choice that may be seen as disloyal. Recent studies show that children grow up better if they have the possibility to meet their biological parents on a regular basis (Butler & Charles, 1999). It is also known that most foster children want to keep in touch with their parents (Greene & Pilowsky, 1994), and that poor contact with their parents and siblings is a major cause of foster children's unhappiness (Barber & Delfabbro, 2004).

The best interests of the foster child is the starting point for acquiring guardianship. Negative feelings of the child, no matter how incomprehensible they seem to be for outsiders, have to be taken very seriously. If the child considers obtaining foster guardianship as a move against his or her birth parents, and sticks to this negative position, it may be better to cancel the plans or the procedure.

Hence, it is important that foster parents and welfare agencies look for parental consent, and to convince them that the procedure for foster guardianship is an effort to improve the daily situation of their child and not a decision against them. It is crucial to convince the parents that accepting the fact that they will not be able to give their children the everyday care they need, does not mean that they stop to be important for them. Objections of the biological parents against the transfer of guardianship should be taken seriously, but *never* can be decisive. Other arguments may be more important in the frame of the best interests of the child.

3.4 Financial facilities

Having guardianship has financial consequences. Though, since 2001, foster parents do not lose the right to reimbursement of daily costs, they have to pay medical care and a contribution in educational costs, and they no longer have the financial advantages that child welfare children have (a bicycle every five years). Furthermore, only single parents, as opposed to couples who together have guardianship, get an allowance. The motivation to become a foster parent differs. Economic reasons are hardly ever principal, but neither are unimportant (Andersson, 2001). Economic independence has become a dominant value and the number of families with a single breadwinner is decreasing rapidly. Because of this, in the future, foster unpaid parenthood may be less attractive (Punselie & Nijon, 1999).

The most common argument by foster parents against asking for foster guardianship is the financial one. Although, since 2001, foster parents are entitled to a reimbursement, many foster parents say that they still have to pay many costs of the foster child out of their own pocket. Obtaining guardianship would mean that their costs would rise and many parents say that they would not be able to afford that.

4.   Problems

4.1   No periods specified by law

Most foster care placements start in the frame of a family supervision order. Birth parents keep their parental authority and the social worker tries to help them to improve their family situation in order to place the children back at home. When this attempt fails it is in the best interests of the child that a long-term perspective is guaranteed in a foster family (Hermanns & Horn, 1999; Weterings, 1999). As we said before, according to Dutch law, foster parents can only obtain guardianship if the birth parents have been relieved of their authority. This is only possible after an assessment of the Child Protection Board reveals that they are not and will not be able to raise their child. The law does not give specified periods. The decision to ask for such an inquiry of the Child Protection Board is often postponed time and again (Jonkers & Van Nijnatten, 1997). Sometimes the family supervisor waits three or more years before starting this legal procedure. By then, the mother may have a new partner and a new baby, enjoying a new family together. In this kind of case, the judge has fewer arguments to relieve parental authority because the parents are showing their ability to raise the other children well. The juvenile court will decide that the child can return to his or her mother. This, however, is against the best interests of the child when he or she lived in the foster family for many years.

4.2   Foster parents themselves have no access to the court

The Child Protection Board has the monopoly to start a legal procedure for removal of parental authority (together with the Public Prosecutor in exceptional cases).

The Child Protection Board often waits a long time before making a request for relief of parental authority. In our view, decisions about babies should be made within nine months, because that might help a secure attachment in the foster family (Weterings, 1998). Decisions about older children should be made within two years.

4.3   Other problems

Foster parents show in their answers that they are afraid to have little access to child care when their foster child needs it (and this is often the case). This is partly true, but it is surely more complicated to get it or to have it paid. Child care workers have professional entrance and more contact with their colleagues making it easier for them to arrange things.

Even if the child cannot go back to his or her parents, the foster parents are never certain the child will stay because the social worker can withdraw the child and place him or her in another foster family without authorisation by the judge, and then foster parents cannot ask to place the child back in their family. A family supervisor and an institutional guardian have the power to place the child somewhere else; foster parents can do nothing against it.

Even when the parents have lost their parental authority it is not easy for foster parents to acquire guardianship, because the practice is to appoint an institutional guardian and institutions are reluctant to give up the guardianship.

5. Conclusion

Only five percent of the guardianships that are pronounced go to the foster parents. This should be far more. It is an unique possibility to reduce institutional child welfare in favour of civil enterprise.

Even more important is that long-term perspectives in foster care will be guaranteed. Birth parents should be relieved of their parental authority earlier than now in daily practice of Dutch child welfare. In all foster care placements with a long-term perspective, removal of parental authority should be considered and appointing the foster parent(s) guardian should be the first option. Family supervisors and institutional guardians should not have the power to terminate a foster care placement without authorisation of the juvenile judge.

To promote foster guardianship, we have the following recommendations:
- Provide for mandatory judicial authorisation to remove a child from his or her foster family.
- Grounds to relieve parental authority according to the child's needs rather than the parents' shortcomings.
- Formulation of deadlines in the family supervision order to achieve that the perspectives of the child to stay in a foster family are known earlier.
- The right for parents to apply for relief of parental authority and foster guardianship.
- Complete allowance and reimbursement of expenses for foster-guardian, and access to specialised care and good and free admission to any further help.
- Abolishment of the rule that for foster couples there is no right to reimbursement of the costs, and no comparison to adoption parents.

Bibliography

Anderson, G. (2001). The Motives of Foster Parents, Their Family and Work Circumstances. *British Journal of Social Work, 31*, pp. 235-248.

Barber, J., & Delfabbro, P. (2004). Children's adjustment to long-term foster care. *Children and youth services review, 27*, pp. 329-340.

Bates, B.; English, D. & Kouidou-Giles, S. (1997). Residential treatment and its alternatives: A review of the literature. *Child and Youth Care Forum, 26*, pp. 7-51.

Boszormenyi-Nagy I. (1987), *Foundations of contextual therapy. Collected Papers.* New York: Brunner/Mazel.

Butler, S. & Charles, M. (1999). The past, the present, but never the future: thematic representations of fostering disruption. *Child and Family Social Work, 4*, pp. 9-19.

Greene, B. & Pilowsky, D. (1994). The Abused and Neglected Foster Child: Determinants of Emotional Conflict and Oppositional Behavior. *Journal of Social Distress and the Homeless, 3*, pp. 283-297.

Hermanns, J. & Horn, T. (1999). Pleegzorg in revisie. *Nederlands Tijdschrift voor jeugdzorg, 3*, pp. 3-9.

Jonkers, J. & Nijnatten, C. van. Ondertoezichtstelling of ontheffing. *Tijdschrift voor Familie- en Jeugdrecht, 19*, pp. 73-78.

Punselie, E. & Nijon, S. (1999). *Arbeid en pleegzorg in de 21ste eeuw. Discussienota.* Den Haag: Nederlandse Gezinsraad.

Quik-Schuijt, A.C. (1998). Het juridisch kader doet ertoe. In: T. Weterings (Ed.) *Pleegzorg in balans. Bestaanszekerheid voor kinderen* (pp. 27-48). Leuven/Apeldoorn: Garant.

Robbroeckx, L & Tamrouti-Makking, I. (1998). *Profielen in de pleegzorg. Een onderzoek naar de karakteristieken van pleeggezinnen.* Nijmegen: Katholieke Universiteit, Instituut voor Orthopedagogiek.

Singer, E. (1996). De bestaans(on)zekerheid van pleegkinderen. *Tijdschrift voor Orthopedagogiek, 35*, pp. 342-351.

Weterings, T. (Ed.) (1998). *Pleegzorg in balans. Bestaanszekerheid voor kinderen.* Leuven/Apeldoorn: Garant.

Weterings, T. et al. (1999). *Pedagogische criteria.* Den Haag: Ministerie van Justitie.

Serious Delinquency of Children Not Liable Under Criminal Law in Germany

Should Family Courts Intervene More?

Kirsten Scheiwe

1.   Introduction

Since children under the age of 14 are not liable under criminal law in the Federal Republic of Germany,[1] juvenile courts have no competencies to intervene in these cases. No procedure under penal law is possible. After a police investigation, the case will be dropped since a child under the age of 14 is irrefutably presumed to be criminally incapable. However, if the offence is not trifle, it should be reacted upon without too much delay. But who reacts? If parents contacted by the municipal youth office do not react adequately or do not voluntarily accept the advice or support offered to them, the penal court has no competencies. The last resort is then the family court. Acting in the 'best interests' of the child, family courts have competencies to intervene, in cases of repeated criminal offending or a grave crime by a child, but the procedure addresses the child's parents. The fact that repeated or grave offences have been committed by the child may be taken as an indicator of the parents' failure to educate the child properly, thus endangering the child's 'best interests'. The Court may therefore initiate family law proceedings against the parents who endanger – with or without intention – the child's welfare.[2] The family court could arrange for or even impose different measures of support or intervention or restrict parental authority rights. Therefore, in the name of child protection, family courts could intervene in serious cases of child delinquency with the purpose of protecting the welfare of the child by preventing future criminal behaviour. However, these competencies of family courts are rarely used – this may lead to the problem that nobody reacts.

2.   Delinquent children below 14 years – competencies to intervene under German law

Since children under the age of 14 are not liable under criminal law – due to the *doli incapax* presumption (para. 19 Penal Code, para. 1 sec. 2 Juvenile Courts Act) – no procedure under penal law is possible, and the Juvenile Courts (*Jugendgerichte*) have no competency in these cases. It should be added that in Germany there is nothing like the French or Belgian Juvenile Court,[3] with broad competencies for orders related to youth welfare measures or child protection, the old 'Chicago model',[4] where the court has competencies for children and youth not liable under penal law. Germany follows a 'two-tracks'-model of split competencies between the family court and the juvenile court.[5] If the youth welfare office has been informed of a case of serious or repeated child delinquency and tries to get in touch with the child and the family, but the family does not react, refuses to cooperate or is unwilling to accept any kind of help or pedagogical intervention on a voluntary basis, the family court is the only authority that can intervene in the name of the child's 'best interests' and initiate preventive measures to protect the welfare of the delinquent child.

3. Child delinquency – institutional competencies and communication problems

The competencies of different institutions in cases of child delinquency are quite clear-cut, but in practice communication between the different institutions is often a problem. Law in the books and law in practice often differ, as is well known.

The police is usually the first authority informed about a case of child delinquency. The police will gather information in such a case, but since no penal procedure and prosecution against a child under 14 is possible, police competencies during the police investigation are more limited than in the case of criminally liable young persons or adults. Controversies about police competencies during police investigation in preliminary proceedings, and the reproach that the restrictions regarding criminally not liable children were not respected properly,[6] were to a large extent settled, at least at the normative level, when the internal guidelines for the police on how to handle youth cases[7] were reformed in 1995. Police investigation is only permitted to find out whether: older persons who are criminally responsible are involved; persons with parental responsibility have seriously infringed their duty to care and educate and considerably endangered the physical or psychical development of a young person under 16 (punishable under para. 171 Penal Code); or the person with parental responsibility is drug or alcohol dependent or has incited the child to commit a crime. The police has to transfer the file with collected records to the public prosecutor.

The police also has to take a decision about whether or not to inform the youth welfare office. This should be done immediately, if already during police investigation it becomes evident that youth welfare measures may be indicated.[8] In all other cases, the youth welfare office should be informed at the latest when the police transfers the file to the public prosecutor and the welfare of the child seems to be at risk.[9] The police guideline PDV 382 gives examples to specify this. Child welfare may be endangered if a young person is suspected to have committed a crime, especially in a group or repeatedly – here the police has a certain margin of discretion. Child welfare is endangered definitely – and information has to be forwarded to the youth office and possibly to other institutions – if a serious crime has been committed in a gang with intensive planning and involving particular cruelty. How the police interprets the condition that 'child welfare is at risk' and how the margin of discretion is used should be subject to further empirical research, since very little is known about it.

Once the full report including all available information is handed over to the public prosecutor by the police, he/she is the authority which has the most information. The public prosecutor has to terminate the procedure if the offender is not yet 14 years old and therefore not liable under criminal law. But he/she is obliged to investigate to whom information has to be passed on directly, especially to the youth welfare office and/or the Family Court (or maybe even to the school).[10] The public prosecutor has to decide if a procedure should be started against the person responsible for supervision of the child. According to the legal guidelines, the public prosecutor has to inform the family court in cases which require family court intervention to prevent a serious danger from the minor person.[11]

If the police informs the youth welfare office, the adequate reaction (or none) has to be established by the youth welfare office team. In severe cases where they consider the child welfare to be at risk and where the family contacted is unwilling or unable to cooperate, they have to apply to the Family Court to intervene.[12]

The Family Court is obliged to investigate each case in which an endangerment of child welfare is reported to the court (independently of whoever may have reported it to the court: this could just as well be a school or the neighbours). As a first step the court asks for a report by the Youth Welfare Office (it may take up to six weeks or so to get a report). In procedures based on para. 1666, 1666a German C.C., the Youth Welfare Office has to be heard in court[13] and to give a report.

A recent reform of the Children and Youth Support Act[14] has explicitly stressed the necessity for the youth welfare office to offer support to persons with parental responsibility in cases where child welfare may be at risk. Furthermore, NGOs involved in supplying youth support measures are obliged to report cases where the help actually given may be insufficient to counteract the risk.

3.1 Some empirical insights on how cooperation between different authorities works in practice

There is very little empirical research investigating how these procedures work in practice and inquiring how communication between the different actors and bodies involved takes place. An outstanding exception is an empirical research project in Berlin (Bindel-Kögel/Heßler/Münder 2004). It was based on interviews and file analysis in 14 of the 23 communal Youth Welfare Offices in Berlin between 1999 and mid 2000. It involved the records of about 1000 cases of child delinquency reported by the police to the Youth Welfare Office. Since in cases involving child delinquency the police and the public prosecutor are the key authorities possessing the most detailed information, it is interesting to know how often the police and the public prosecutor inform youth welfare offices and family courts. The Berlin research project found out that the police informed the youth welfare office in about every fourth case of child delinquency. According to internal police regulations,[15] cases which are more severe and may endanger child welfare should be reported. But this guideline is not mirrored by the cases forwarded in practice, which involve mainly first-time offenders, while the police did not focus sufficiently upon multiple offenders (Ibid. p. 273). Furthermore, there was a considerable time lag in reporting. In two thirds of the cases involving particular cruelty or violence, such as robbery or bodily injury, more than two months passed before the police information reached the Youth Welfare Office.

In cases where the youth office received information on child delinquency from the police, how did they react? The Berlin research project found out that they reacted in about 40% of the cases, while police information remained without reaction in nearly 60%. Often the intention was to de-dramatise the case in less serious cases. This coincides with the fact that in cases involving violence or serious offences reaction was more frequent. In 42.6% of the cases involving bodily injury, in 58.6% of grave bodily injury, in 62.5% of burglary, and in 68.5% of robbery or blackmail of children, the Youth Welfare Office reacted (Ibid. p. 275). However, the main criterion determining whether or not the Youth Welfare Office reacted was not the gravity of the act, but whether they had already collected other information about the family in the past. They reacted sooner if they had already been in contact with the family before.

When did the Youth Welfare Office apply for family court intervention? Generally, family court intervention into parental authority is requested by the Youth Welfare Office[16] only at a rather late stage in cases where far-reaching measures limiting parental rights (such as placement of the child outside the family) are intended, not earlier.

The practice and problem consciousness of authorities dealing with child delinquency was subject of another research project[17] of the German Youth Institute (*Deutsches Jugendinstitut (DJI)*) in 1999. Seventy interviews with representatives of the police, schools and youth welfare offices were performed (family courts, however, were not included as relevant institutions in this research project). The main focus was on how families reacted to police information about child delinquency. But police interviews included questions on what the first contact with the family was like, and when the youth welfare office was informed. The youth welfare offices' staff were also asked how much time passed between the delinquent act, information by the police and a reaction of the youth welfare office.

Another research project which investigated child delinquency in Bremen between 1996 and 1998[18] found out that, in about one third of all cases where the Youth Welfare Office contacted the parents of seriously delinquent children (defined as children who had committed at least two acts involving violence or four other delinquent acts), the parents categorically refused the help and assistance offered because they did not wish any intrusion into the family by public authorities (Karl 1999:194). This shows the extent of the problem and the potential space for family court intervention – however, the project mentioned above does not tell us anything about family court intervention.

4. Delinquency endangering child welfare? Family Courts hardly ever intervene in cases of child delinquency

The conditions in which the family court judge may issue orders are laid down in para. 1666, 1666a German C.C. Basically, the court may take action to avert the danger to the child's welfare if the parents are unwilling or incapable to do so. In such cases it has considerable space for manoeuvre. When a child commits serious or repeated offences, hence no trifles, this may be taken as an indicator of 'parental failure' and of endangering the child's welfare. Committing similar offences in the future or even a 'criminal career' of the child must look probable. The other condition for the family court to interfere is that the parents are not capable or unwilling to avert the danger. If so, the family court judge may, within the bounds of the proportionality principle, take all measures which seem to be appropriate and adequate to protect the child's welfare. But note that the family court has no punitive measures at hand. The procedure is not directed against the child, but focuses on the parents and the child as part of the family system. All measures provided by the Children and Youth Assistance Act (Social Code Book VIII) are available, ranging from supervision and care within the family, participation in social training groups or counselling services, to placing the child in care.

There are hardly any published cases related to delinquent children where family courts intervene. And even in the legal literature and comments the question is rarely mentioned. Empirical research on the subject is widely missing. One research project of the TU Berlin on the subject of institutional responses to child delinquency (Bindel-Kögel et.al. 2004) touched upon the issue, but only briefly. The researchers wanted to interview family court judges in two Berlin family courts (Berlin Tempelhof/Schöneberg and Pankow/Weißensee) but the Court Presidents informed them that there were too few cases involving child delinquency. So they ended up interviewing only two judges, who reported that child delinquency played no particular role in their cases protecting child welfare, but was sometimes part of the package related to multi-problem-families where they had to place the child outside the family.

The findings of this research – that family courts intervene in cases where the welfare of the child is endangered only at a late stage, when far-reaching measures such as the placement of the child in foster care or institutional care or serious restrictions of parental authority are at stake – have been confirmed also by other authors. The family law judges interviewed in the Berlin research project clearly expressed their view that earlier intervention is the task of the youth welfare office. Another Ph.D. researcher, and lawyer, Esther Rosenboom, came to the same conclusion in a study on family courts in Hamburg. The youth welfare office applies to the family court mostly (and only) if the intention is to restrict parental authority rights extensively.[19] The family court is hardly ever called upon to push parents towards a change of the daily living arrangements and the education of the child.

But the problem is that earlier intervention of the Family Court in cooperation with the Youth Welfare Office might help, especially in those cases where parents are reluctant or unwilling to accept measures offered to them or the child on a voluntary basis. The intervention of the family court, and bargaining in the shadow not only of the law but also in the shadow of court authority, might help to overcome some parental refusals and improve the protection of the child's welfare. Some authors therefore claim that the Family Court should make more use of its authority to arrange matters with the family on issues of daily life, school participation, leisure time, drug prevention, etc. (Ostendorf 2005: 1520). The family court of Kerpen has developed an intervention strategy leading in this direction in cases where young persons repeatedly refuse to visit school (Raack 2003). However, this is a single and contested case.

More often, the family court is overlooked as a potential ally in projects aiming to prevent youth delinquency. Various projects in Germany related to juveniles who had committed repeated or serious offences did not tackle the potential role of family courts.[20] A handbook in English on *Prevention of Youth Crime in Germany: Educational Strategies* of the DJI of 2004[21] mentions family courts only once and takes it for granted that the family court intervenes, "only exceptionally, in cases in which more members of the family and others are held to be at risk, are the Family Courts asked to intervene, so that decisions can be taken even against the will of the parents" (Holthusen/Schäfer 2004: 15). This may be a correct description of the most frequent practice, but not of the legal rules regulating family court intervention for children 'at risk', and the potential role of family courts.

5. Should family courts make more use of their competencies?

Child protection means that measures should be taken to prevent a 'criminal career' of a child through family courts, if parents are unwilling or unable to do something against this risk – already at an earlier stage and on a lower level than court intervention to place the child in institutional care or take it out of the family. If parents do not respond to attempts of the youth welfare office to get in touch with the family and refuse cooperation, it often turns out in the court hearing that there are serious family problems, and that the child's repeated serious delinquency is a symptom of family problems. The court's authority and threatening potential can push non-cooperating parents and the child to participate. Family Court procedure is less stigmatising and more informal than a penal procedure before the Youth Court, and flexible and differentiated reactions and measures are possible. However, the Family Court should not act without, but in cooperation with, the Youth Welfare Office and the professional competency of social workers.

6. Controversies and potential problems of Family Court interventions – preventive measures to protect child welfare, or punitive tendencies?

Family court intervention in cases of child delinquency is contested, since some favour a sort of a punitive approach to the parents and the child. This was the case with a draft law proposed by the Land of Bavaria[22] that the family court should have the competence to impose educational measures upon parents and the child and to enforce these measures through fines (similar to the Juvenile Court's competence in penal proceedings against juveniles). But this draft law was rejected and did not find a majority in parliament. Family court intervention under German law differs therefore from a more repressive approach underlying the introduction of 'Antisocial Behaviour Orders' or 'Parenting Orders' under English or Scottish Law.[23] It has to be admitted that there is a danger of a 'law-and-order'-mentality and punitive tendencies, which might be reinforced by the lack of adequate pedagogical training of judges. Furthermore, the family court procedure entails a pedagogical dilemma (you 'blame the parents to address the child'). Another trap envisaged by some is a lack of respect by the family court towards the Youth Welfare Office's collaborators' competencies and professionalism, and that the family court might tend to 'order around' the representatives of the Youth Welfare Office involved in the court proceedings.

One central issue in the German legal debate is the competence of the family court to make legally binding orders if these orders involve educational measures or social services to be provided by and within the competence of the Youth Welfare Office (involving also financing obligations), for example to order that the child is obliged to attend a social training course, that the family accepts pedagogical family support or a family therapy, that the child should attend after-school care or a social training course or that a young person should have a supervisor. Can the family court make these kind of orders which bind the Youth Welfare Office to grant these social benefits (and pay for them), or is it up to the Youth Welfare Office to decide in an independent procedure (which implies that it could refuse to grant the benefits or offer help of another kind)? For non-Germans this controversy in legal literature[24] may be somewhat difficult to understand. One issue at stake is the independence of the youth welfare office as part of the municipal administration, which has to decide itself if and what social benefits and services – which they finance – are granted to families. In a recent amendment of the Children and Youth Welfare Act, this issue has been clarified by the legislator: even in case a family or juvenile court judge has obliged the parents or the young person to take part in a youth support measure, the municipal administration, as the competent body, has to finance such measures only if it has taken the decision in a proper procedure (respecting the parents' right to choose).[25] Thus, it is emphasised that the decision has to be based on the professional competence and decision-making process of the Youth Welfare Office and also has to involve the parents. Despite the ongoing debate, the direction should be clear: the Family Court should cooperate with the Youth Welfare Office (YWO), accepting the professional competence and views of the multi-disciplinary team, and not 'order them around'. This can be done within the court hearing, since the YWO has to be heard and give a report in all cases based on para. 1666, 1666a German C.C., or in general through broader cooperation to develop special programs for delinquent children or parent groups. Another procedural solution resolving the competence problem between the family court and the youth welfare office in cases of conflict between them is that the family court appoints a guardian *ad litem* for the delinquent child, who has the limited task to apply for and arrange youth support measures, possibly even in the administrative court if the municipal youth welfare office refuses them. It seems that there is sufficient space to improve the cooperation and communication between the Family Court and the youth welfare office with regard to child delinquency.

7.   What a Family Court could do

It must be emphasised that the aim of family court intervention in the name of the child's best interest is not to sanction parental behaviour, but to prevent future damages to the child and to avoid that the child's deviance develops into a 'criminal career'. For that, a prognosis is necessary: court intervention presupposes that there is a high risk that the future development will bring about serious damages to the child's welfare if no intervention takes place.[26] Another requirement is that the parents are unable or unwilling to prevent the risk. Negligence means inactivity of the parents − if parents are prone to accept support by the youth office or willing to take part in measures or activities to prevent the risk and these activities are appropriate, there is no space left for court intervention.

In these cases, the Family Court may take the appropriate measures, for example:
- Make orders regarding the daily life and education, school or training of the child
- Appoint a guardian (*Ergänzungspfleger*) for the child who has to arrange for youth support measures instead of the person with parental rights, or to decide about the whereabouts of the child (this may be not only residence, but also relate to schooling or training of the child, etc.)
- Give one parent more rights to take decisions on behalf of the child than the other parent
- Oblige child and parents to participate in a special programme or course (in cooperation with the Youth Welfare Office present at the court hearing).

In conclusion, Family Courts should make more use of their competencies to intervene in cases of serious child delinquency, possibly already at an earlier stage than at present. This requires improved cooperation between the Family Court and the Youth Welfare Office, but also better communication between the different authorities involved. There have been various programmes developed over the last years which have the goal to prevent delinquent children from getting on a 'criminal career' track, or to strengthen family competences, but family courts have usually not been part of the networks and cooperations established.[27] Family Courts should not focus on punitive measures, but exercise their task to protect the child welfare not only in cases where serious interventions into parental authority are at stake, but also when parents are unable or unwilling to act in cases where a child commits repeated and serious offences. Maybe consistent bargaining in the shadow of the law and use of the court's authority can help families already at an earlier stage than is the case at present. More empirical research and international comparison would be welcomed to highlight these issues.

Bibliography

Arbeitsgemeinschaft für Jugendhilfe (2003), Kinderschutz und Kinderrechte zwischen Jugendhilfe und Justiz, Dokumentation des 11, Treffens der Arbeitsgemeinschaft für Jugendfragen, Freiburg: AGJ-Verlag.

Arbeitsstelle Kinder- und Jugendkriminalitätsprävention, dji (Hrsg.) (2004). Prevention of Youth Crime in Germany: Educational Strategies. Trends, Experiences and Approaches, Munich: dji, http://cgi.dji.de/bibs/Bd_8_prevention.pdf.

Bindel-Kögel, G./Heßler, M./Münder, J. (2004), Kinderdelinquenz zwischen Polizei und Jugendamt, Münster: Lit Verlag.

Cleland, Alison/Tisdall, Kay (2005), The challenge of antisocial behaviour: New relationships between the state, children and parents, International Journal of Law, Policy and the Family 19 (2005), 395-420.

Coester-Staudinger, Kommentierung § 1666 BGB, in: Staudinger, Kommentar zum BGB, Buch 4 Familienrecht, §§ 1638-1683, Berlin/New York: Gruyter.

Deutsches Jugendinstitut (ed.) (1999), Strafverdächtige Kinder und ihre Familien – Problembewusstsein zuständiger Institutionen, Dokumentation zweier Workshops und einer Befragung von Fachleuten, Projektgruppe Delinquenz von Kindern – eine Herausforderung für Familie, Jugendhilfe und Politik, München/Leipzig, http://cgi.dji.de/bibs/27_347_kidokumentation_okt99.pdf.

Deutsches Jugendinstitut – Arbeitsstelle Kinder- und Jugendkriminalitätsprävention (Hg.) (2000), Wider die Ratlosigkeit im Umgang mit Kinderdelinquenz – Präventive Ansätze und Konzepte, München: dji.

Deutsches Jugendinstitut – Arbeitsstelle Kinder- und Jugendkriminalitätsprävention (Hg.) (2001), Schnelle Reaktion – Tatverdächtige Kinder und Jugendliche im Spannungsfeld zwischen beschleunigtem Verfahren und pädagogischen Hilfen, Munchen: dji.

Deutsches Jugendinstitut – Arbeitsstelle Kinder- und Jugendkriminalitätsprävention (Hrsg.), Evaluierte Kriminalitätsprävention in der Kinder- und Jugendhilfe, Erfahrungen und Ergebnisse aus fünf Modellprojekten, München, 2003.

DVJJ-Journal: Zeitschrift für Jugendkriminalrecht und Jugendhilfe – Mitgliederrundbrief der Deutschen Vereinigung für Jugendgerichte und Jugendgerichtshilfen e.V.

Frehsee, D. (1988), Strafverfolgung' von strafunmündigen Kindern, Zeitschrift für die gesamte Strafrechtswissenschaft (ZStW) 100, 290-328.

Hefendehl, R. (2000), Täter und Opfer bei kindlicher Gewaltkriminalität, JZ 2000, 600-608.

Hübner, G.-E./Kerner, S./Kunath, W./Planas, H., Mindeststandards Polizeilicher Jugendarbeit, in: DVJJ-Journal 1997, p. 26 ff.

Höynckh, Theresia/Soisson, Robert/Trede, Wolfgang/Will, Hans-Dieter (ed.) (2002), Youth care – youth punishment: approaches to juvenile delinquency: a European perspective, Frankfurt: IGfH.

Holthusen, Bernd/Schäfer, Heiner (2004), Youth crime prevention and the law: support, social education and punishment, in: Centre for the Prevention of Youth Crime (Arbeitsstelle Kinder- und Jugendkriminalitätsprävention, dji) (Hrsg.). Holthusen, Bernd/Schäfer, Heiner, Prevention of Youth Crime in Germany: Educational Strategies. Trends, Experiences and Approaches, Munich: dji, 157-167, http://cgi.dji.de/bibs/Bd_8_prevention.pdf.

Holthusen, Bernd (2004), Modellprojekt: Kooperation im Fall von jugendlichen Mehrfach- und Intensivtätern, Abschlussbericht der wissenschaftlichen Begleitung, Munich, http://cgi.dji.de/bibs/170_4142.pdf.

Mayer, Markus (1990), Die Vernehmung von Kindern als Beschuldigte im Rechtshilfeverfahren nach dem Europäischen Übereinkommen über die Rechtshilfe in Strafsachen, GA 1990, 508ff.

Müller, Siegfried/Peter, Hilmar (Hrsg.) (1998), Kinderkriminalität, Opladen.

Münder/Mutke/Schone (2000), Kindeswohl zwischen Jugendhilfe und Justiz, Münster: Votum Verlag.

Ostendorf, Heribert/Hinghaus, Matthias/Kasten, Alexandra (2005), Kriminalprävention durch das Familiengericht, Zeitschrift für das Gesamte Familienrecht no. 18/2005, 1514-1520.

Ostendorf, Heribert (2000), Kommentar Jugendgerichtsgesetz, 5th ed., Munich.

Ostendorf, Heribert (ed.) (2004), Effizienz von Kriminalprävention – Erfahrungen im Ostseeraum, Lübeck.

Raack, Wolfgang (2003), Schulschwänzen – Familiengerichte mit ins Boot, Das Jugendamt no. 11/2003, 505-507.

Steindorff, Caroline (1992), Der französische Jugendrichter im Zentrum der französischen Jugendgerichtsbarkeit. Mainz.

Thomas, Karl (1999), Der Kinderdelinquenz Einhalt gebieten – aber wie?, Zeitschrift für Rechtspolitik (ZRP) 193-196.

Verein für Kommunalwissenschaft e.V. (Hrsg.) (2004), Die Straftat als Hinweis auf erzieherischen Bedarf? Pädagogik und Konsequenz im Umgang mit Kinderdelinquenz, Berlin.

Weber, Victor/Matzke, Michael (1996), Jugendvertrag als jugendkriminalrechtlicher Verfahrensabschluß, Zentralblatt für Jugendrecht 83 (1996), 171-175.

Endnotes

1   According to para. 19 of the German Penal Code (*Strafgesetzbuch*), persons under 14 are incapable of guilty intent (the *doli incapax* presumption). Therefore, the Juvenile Courts Act (*Jugendgerichtsgesetz*), which regulates the penal procedure and measures against minors and young adults up to the age of 21 (educational measures, disciplinary measures or youth punishment), is only applicable to persons above the age of 14.

2   The legal basis of this procedure before the family court is para. 1666, 1666a German Civil Code (BGB) – or para. 1631b German C.C.

3   The French Juvenile Court has competencies to decree punitive orders as well as youth support measures (Steindorff 1992). The Belgian Juvenile Court is responsible for all minors whose health, safety or morality is endangered. As a rule, criminal liability starts only at the age of 18 (with very few exceptions).

4   The idea of a 'great family court', as it was institutionalised in Chicago in 1899, encompassed wide competencies of the court in matters of divorce, guardianship, maintenance and support, personal status and also all youth court matters. In Germany, the German lawyers assembly (*Deutscher Juristentag*) in 1928 demanded the introduction of such a 'great family court, but without success. Nowadays, competencies are split between family courts, introduced in 1977 (for family law matters), and juvenile courts (for penal law procedures against young persons above the age of 14).

5   However, in a case against a minor over 14 the juvenile court can also take over the tasks of the family court (para. 34 Juvenile Courts Act), but in practice this hardly happens. The other possibility is that the Juvenile Court transfers the decision on educational measures to the family law judge (para. 53 JGG), but this is a provision which is hardly ever applied. In 1997 only in 0.02% of all cases before the juvenile court – which means 18 times in 1997. The maximum was 0.1% of all cases in 1973 and 1974 (Ostendorf, JGG-Kommentar, Grdl zu § 53 Rn. 4).

6   It was contested how far compulsory measures under the Penal Procedure Act (*Strafprozessordnung*), such as forced identification measures, are permitted against children (see Frehsee 1988 and Mayer 1990 for an overview).

7   Police Instruction no. 382 (*Polizeidienstvorschrift* = PDV 382) 'Handling of youth cases', see DVJJ-Journal 1/1997 (no. 155), p. 5-21.

8   PDV 382, point 3.2.7 (DVJJ-Journal 1997: 10).

9   PDV 382, point 3.2.7 and 2.2 (DVJJ-Journal 1997: 10, 7-8).

10   The public prosecutor is obliged to check whether information has to be passed on to any other institution which should be involved in case that no penal procedure takes place due to the lacking criminal responsibility of the minor (based on para. 1 Juvenile Courts Act and the implementing decrees RiStBV and guidelines to the Youth Court Act).

11   Information on penal proceedings (*Mitteilungen in Strafsachen*) no. 31 and 37, quoted by Bindel-Kögel et.al. (2004: 204).

12   Now para. 8 sec. 3 of the amended Children and Youth Assistance Act.

13   Para. 49a sec.8 of the statute regulating the procedure in family court (*Gesetz über die freiwillige Gerichtsbarkeit*).

14   Amended § 8a SGB VIII, in force since 1 October 2005.

15   Internal Police Guideline (*Polizeiliche Dienstvorschrift*) 382 ('Handling of youth cases'). This guideline regulates also the proceedings concerning children who are not criminally responsible (see Bindel-Kögel et.al. 2004: 273).

16   We know from another empirical research project on child protection cases before family courts that in the vast majority of cases the family courts are called upon by the Youth Welfare

Offices (Münder/Mutke/Schone 2000). But this interesting empirical research on the practice of family courts and youth welfare offices did not grant particular insights into cases involving child delinquency, since it encompassed all cases of family court intervention where the 'best interests' of a child were at risk (based on para. 1666, 1666a German C.C.).

[17] A summary report of the project group *Child delinquency – a challenge for families, youth help and politics* was published in 1999 (Deutsches Jugendinstitut 1999).

[18] Project *Child delinquency – occurrence, causes, prevention.* The main results are summarised by Thomas (1999).

[19] Esther Rosenboom in an interview with the German Youth Institute (dji) of December 2005 (www.dji.de).

[20] See the overview of model projects and cooperation involving different institutions by Bernd Holthusen, German Youth Institute (dji) in the final report of a project on juvenile multiple offenders and severe offenders (Holthusen 2004: 11ff.).

[21] Not even in an article giving an overview on youth crime prevention and the law by Holthusen and Schäfer, in: Arbeitsstelle Kinder- und Jugendkriminalitätsprävention/Centre for the Prevention of Youth Crime (Hrsg.), Prevention of Youth Crime in Germany: Educational Strategies. Trends, Experiences and Approaches, Munich 2004, 157-167.

[22] Draft Law of 26 February 1998 (*Bundesratsdrucksache* 645/98).

[23] See the article of Cleland and Tisdall (2005) for an overview of legal developments. They make the point that court-enforced 'anti-social behaviour orders' mark a shift in state intervention from focusing on children's welfare and need to focus on their behaviour, and displace the welfare-based children's hearing system as the primary decision-making forum.

[24] Cp. Ostendorf (2005: 1517 ff. m.w.N.).

[25] Amended para. 36a sec. 1 Children and Youth Help Act, in force since 1 October 2005.

[26] Coester-Staudinger, BGB-Kommentar, para. 1666 C.C., no. 62; 79.

[27] Different projects and initiatives are described for example in Arbeitsstelle Kinder- und Jugendkriminalitätsprävention (2003), Arbeitsstelle Kinder- und Jugendkriminalitätsprävention/dji (2004), Holthusen (2004), Verein für Kommunalwissenschaft e.V. (2004), Ostendorf (2004).

The Interface between Child Protection, Child Justice and Child Labour via Convention 182 on the Elimination of the Worst Forms of Child Labour

Julia Sloth-Nielsen

1. Introduction

The inclusion of Convention No. 138 among the seven core ILO conventions – the ratification of which was promoted – affirmed this body's commitment to the eradication of child labour.[1] However, Convention No. 138 remained the least ratified of all core conventions and the attempts to increase ratifications of Convention No. 138 succeeded only partially.[2] Especially the African and Asian countries have not yet acceded in large numbers to Convention 138, and it is in this context that the ILO drafted a convention on the eradication of the worst forms of child labour.[3]

On 17 June 1999, the International Labour Conference of the ILO unanimously adopted the Convention Concerning the Prohibition and Immediate Action for the Elimination of the Worst Forms of Child Labour, known as Convention 182. This Convention is one of four fundamental labour conventions of the ILO. To date, 157 of the world's countries have ratified Convention 182, with South Africa being one of the first countries to do so.

The mandate of the Convention is clear. It requires ratifying countries to take "immediate and effective measures to secure the prohibition and elimination of the worst forms of child labour as a matter of urgency."[4] Recommendation 190, which accompanies the Convention, calls for the immediate implementation of the programmes of action referred to in Article 6 of the Convention.[5] According to the Recommendation, such programmes should take into consideration the views of the families and the children who are involved in the worst forms of child labour.[6]

In the world we are living in today, unacceptable forms of exploitation of children exist and persist, but they are particularly difficult to research due to their hidden, sometimes illegal or even criminal nature. Slavery, debt bondage, trafficking, sexual exploitation, the use of children in the drug trade and in armed conflict, as well as hazardous work are all defined as 'Worst Forms of Child Labour' under Convention 182.[7]

Before starting any analysis, it is of importance to point at some inherent ambiguities pertaining to the issue to be dealt with here. For the purpose of clarity, the notion 'children used by adults to commit crimes' is one category of a worst form of child labour dealt with in Convention 182. However, the first reference to children being used to commit crime is made in the United Nations General Assembly (GA) Resolution 43/121 of 8 December 1988 on the use of children in the illicit traffic in narcotic drugs and rehabilitation of minors addicted to drugs. This resolution was followed by the much broader General Assembly Resolution 45/115 of 14 December 1990 on the instrumental use of children in criminal activities. It is also important to recognise Article 33 of the Convention on the Rights of the Child (1989), which provides that:

> *States Parties shall take all appropriate measures, including legislative, adminis-trative, social and educational measures, to protect children from the illicit use of narcotic drugs and psychotropic substances as defined in the relevant international treaties, and to prevent the use of children in the illicit production and trafficking of such substances.*

The idea of children being used to commit offences does raise some conceptual and definitional issues.[8] For instance, ILO Convention 182 does not use the exact wording of General Assembly Resolution 45/115, which mentioned the instru-mental use of children in criminal activities. Rather, the Convention refers to "the use, procuring or offering of a child for illicit activities, in particular for the production and trafficking of drugs". From consultations and discussions that were undertaken at the commencement of the research and implementation project described here, it appeared that the extent and scope of the meaning of the notion of children 'used' by adults to commit crimes could be unclear. This is because the term could be construed more widely or more narrowly, depending on how the word 'used' is interpreted. A narrower construction would revolve around direct and active instrumentalisation of children in the commission of offences, such as where they are recruited to climb through small windows to commit housebreaking, or act as drug couriers. A wider interpretation of the word 'use' would include a more extensive array of indirect forms of adult involvement. Indeed, various forms of facilitation of criminal activity could be drawn in, depending on how widely one is prepared to consider the use of children by adults or older children. An example is adults being prepared to buy (already) stolen goods from children, or providing them with transport to or from a poten-tial crime scene. For the initial purposes of the project described here, a wider interpretation was adopted.[9]

This chapter will detail the findings of a research study that was undertaken in South Africa over the period of December 2004 until September 2005 to imple-ment the provisions of ILO Convention 182 on the Elimination of the Worst Forms of Child Labour. As one form of child labour that has been identified for specific intervention in South Africa,[10] the chapter will in particular explain the link between juvenile justice and child labour. The findings of the study and some theoretical and practical challenges are further explored. A conclusion and rec-ommendations for actions for role players wrap up the discussion.

2.   Child labour, child protection and juvenile justice: the nexus

Although there is a body of knowledge, data and documentation on child labour, there are also still considerable gaps in understanding the variety of forms and conditions in which children are exploited or work. This is especially true of the worst forms of child labour, which by their very nature are often hidden from public view and scrutiny.

As one of the worst forms of child labour, the issue of children used by adults to commit crimes is not an exception to the general rule that there is a considerable gap in understanding the nature and magnitude of child exploitation. Not only does it often occur in private, but since the children are themselves vulnerable to criminal prosecution, there are considerable disincentives to disclosure. Hence, the need for further research to better understand this phenomenon.

The issue of children used by adults to commit crimes and its connection with child labour is a relatively new concept for people who are directly or indirectly involved with children in the criminal justice system.[11] Thus, as much as it is a child labour issue, it also concerns the juvenile justice system because generally, after children are used by adults to commit crimes, police involvement is virtually assured. Therefore, how the police react to such children provides the initial intersection between the two issues. Furthermore, how these children are dealt with by probation officers and members of the judicial and prosecutorial authorities, and how programmes such as diversion, prevention and alternative sentencing interventions address the instrumentalisation of children in the commission of offences, constitute a key nexus between the criminal justice system and our research which was undertaken through a child labour lens.

3.   Overview/description of the study

The Programme Towards the Elimination of the Worst Forms of Child Labour (TECL) is a technical assistance project to the Department of Labour (DoL) and is essentially an executing agency for the Child Labour Action Programme (CLAP).[12]

The research which was commissioned involved three phases. The first was a rapid assessment. The rapid assessment phase involved a report on an initial national stakeholder analysis conducted with relevant national and provincial government departments as well as members of civil society, such as NGO service providers in the child protection and juvenile justice spheres, criminologists, crime intelligence and policing specialists, and academics. It included qualitative and quantitative research to determine an initial assessment of the nature, causes and extent of children used by adults to commit crimes. Very little of concrete value was, however, unearthed. A literature survey scanned the applicable policy and legislative environment, including a detailed analysis of the development of the Child Justice Bill, 49 of 2002, which seeks to establish a separate juvenile justice system for South Africa. The rapid assessment also helped identify four potential pilot sites for the following phases of the research.

Following the rapid assessment was a parallel child consultation process to explore the experiences of children directly, and a baseline study to deepen the initial research concerning the nature and causes of the phenomenon, and to finalise the two sites for programme implementation.

The child consultation process was conducted over a period of three weeks in August 2005. There were 542 children involved in this process, mainly children who were alleged or proven to be in conflict with the law and a control group from ordinary secondary schools. Many of the children were awaiting trial in Secure Care Facilities (SCFs). The facilities were selected on the basis of the degree of accessibility of the children and the level of cooperation offered by the centres.[13] The child consultation process identified factors that would place children at risk of being used by adults to commit crimes (more generally), as well as providing information relevant to the design of the programmatic interventions to be implemented in following phases.

The child consultative process explored several key themes relating to children being used by adults or older children to commit crimes. These included background profiles to the children themselves,[14] general information about children's economic activity (legal and illegal)[15] and the use of money, how children become involved in crime, how adults are involved when children commit crime, who the adults are and what should be done. It also enquired into what kinds of things adults expect children to do and whether children are really coerced to commit the crime or whether they are willing participants, and then ended with conclusions and recommendations for intervention.

The consultation demonstrated that from the children's perspective, adults and older children using younger children to commit crime occurs widely and is a commonplace experience in the lives of children, especially those who are in conflict with the law. This was illustrated in many ways through the study, and is clearly indicated by the fact that 46.7% of the children in SCFs who took part in the child consultation process stated that they were co-accused with an adult in relation to their current charges. Of concern is not only the high reported engagement in illegal activities, but also the finding that a significant number of respondents of the total group and of the SCF group spend their money on drugs and alcohol. Of the total group 43.7% and of the SCF group 48.8% reported that they spent their money on drugs and alcohol. Adolescents' desire for fancy goods (branded clothing, jewellery and the like), rather than basic survival needs, emerged as a key theme in the study. Apart from financial drivers, one third of the groups noted that abuse and neglect by parents, parents' abuse of alcohol and drugs, children having to take care of themselves, and the lack of parental advice and supervision lead to children's involvement in offending. The active influence of friends and peer groups in recruiting children into criminal life was revealed to be pervasive.

At the same time as the child consultation process was underway, the baseline survey was being conducted. The intended result of this was to provide more detailed qualitative and quantitative research at the four identified potential pilot sites to inform the design of the pilot projects as well as to finalise the selection of two pilot sites.[16]

Initially, the baseline study attempts to provide a summary of the rapid assessment on which it builds. Furthermore, the baseline study provides for a review of international literature and South African legislation pertaining to children used by adults to commit crimes. It also explains the national and provincial stakeholder analysis that was undertaken as part of the research.

What is of more interest in the context of juvenile justice is the insight of the baseline study in four areas. In relation to the way in which the South African police deal with children used by adults, the baseline study dealt with divergent aspects of the research. As regards the involvement of the police, the survey recorded the results of meetings with legal advisors of the South African Police Service (SAPS), results of investigations at the level of individual police stations and, lastly, a brief discussion of Metropolitan Police Departments (MPDs).

As to probation practice, the baseline study focused on whether the evaluation process that is supposed to occur after the arrest of a child could be employed to identify children used by adults to commit offences and the adults concerned. Also, the actual availability of assessment services and their contents in practice were explored.

Judicial and prosecutorial practice in relation to children used by adults to commit crimes was also examined more narrowly. Magistrates and prosecutors were consulted about what avenues the juvenile justice system should follow when an instance of a child used by an adult to commit crimes is picked up.

The fourth issue dealt with in the baseline survey pertained to the issue of diversion and prevention interventions, and whether for example they include sessions which deal with peer pressure, aspirations for material goods and so forth. An attempt was made to look into the availability of diversion and prevention interventions, in order to locate potential partners for programmatic implementation in the next phase.

Finally, the baseline study provided a local site analysis in order to motivate clearly for the choice of the final sites. Recommendations as to how implementation with role players should be effected concluded the baseline study.

4.   Findings of the study and some theoretical and practical challenges

Seen as a composite, the findings of the three activities described above call for closer scrutiny. This section discusses some theoretical and practical challenges and dilemmas that may have to be faced in dealing with children who are used by adults to commit crimes. Critically, the responses of the children consulted in relation to this project enrich and augment earlier debates.[17]

As mentioned, it now seems that the phenomenon of adults using children to commit crimes is not unusual. Through their responses, all 41 focus groups provided information that indicated that this phenomenon is common, and showed clear and direct examples of how adults are involved when children commit crime.[18] The study notes both the role of coercion, where children describe being 'forced' to commit crime, as well as 'guidance', with adults showing children what to do.[19] Children even reported threats and the use of physical violence to coerce them into committing crime, such as torture, beatings, rape and the use of guns. Children stated the following:

- They have guns and they are gangsters and they force you to do things
- Some torture you, they beat you or threaten you
- They threaten you with a gun
- They rape you
- They threaten to stab you
- Adults abuse children – they beat them up and threaten them with further violence to make the child commit crime
- Sometimes an adult tells you to do it
- Fathers of the neighbours tell them to do it
- Adults pull you into it
- Older people with a lot of experience guide you about what to do
- You walk with adults and they use you. Then they see that you can do it
- Older people force you.

It was previously mentioned that one of the initial role players is the police. In relation to children used by adults to commit crimes, some of the findings from the baseline study related to the investigative and detective techniques and methods used by police, as well as the specific legal environment governing their conduct.[20] The central point is the finding that no police follow-up currently occurs where children are used by adults in illegal activities. There are a range of reasons for this.

An obvious difficulty relates to the fact that the police (SAPS) fear civil claims for damages for alleged wrongful arrest if they proceed to effect arrests of adults simply on the basis of what a child has disclosed during police investigation. It was reported, for instance, that it would frequently be the child's word against the adult's word and independent proof of the adult's role is not generally available from the child.[21] Another reason why adults who use children to commit crime or who facilitate their involvement in illicit activity are not brought to book is due to the socio-economic conditions in the relevant communities.[22] This is because sometimes it is the criminal adults themselves who provide some of the members of the poor families with basic necessities, and communities and the relevant families then protect their identities.

It was intimated that, at best, any information concerning children used by adults to commit crimes flowing to SAPS members would have to be dealt with as crime intelligence. In this regard, the onus would then rest on crime intelligence officers[23] to collate and collect information so as to be able to build further profiles of the adult's use of children, and in order to assess whether a police investigation[24] and consequent 'sting' operation to bring the adult to book are deemed warranted.

Another related challenge posed is the fact that once the children are remanded to court and diverted there,[25] the police docket would be regarded as closed and therefore no further investigation would ensue. Therefore, SAPS would remain unaware of the fact whether or not a child had been used by an adult to commit crimes. As no complainant would exist, no grounds for opening a further docket for investigation of possible adult perpetrators behind the child's offending would arise.

The research showed there is presently a poor police understanding of their potential role in relation to adults using children to commit crimes. The main recommendations that appeared from the consultations with police were that there is a need to try and secure prosecutions of adult co-accused when a child co-accused admits guilt. The possible use of section 204 of the Criminal Procedure Act[26] for children who disclose adult perpetrators should also be considered, although calling such children as state witnesses may be risky to them. It was also highlighted that the use of children as traps to catch adult perpetrators could be considered, although the morality and appropriateness of this approach for children has also been questioned by children's rights activists.

Finally, as it could fairly be inferred, police might lack the necessary awareness and skill in handling cases of children who are used by adults to commit crimes. Rule 12 of the Beijing Rules, which deals with police, requires that police who deal regularly or exclusively with children in conflict with the law receive specialised training and instruction. This is not the case in South Africa at present. Accordingly, a specialised training and instruction tailored specifically to the issue at hand may be called for. Although the rapid assessment had proposed that police reaction might be governed by a standing order or national instruction to set out specific procedures to be followed where it is identified that children have been used by adults to commit crimes, what emerged during the research was that no formal standing order (National Instruction)[27] was likely to be developed or implemented prior to the finalisation of the Child Justice Bill, 49 of 2002, in Parliament.[28]

Probation practice and pre-trial assessment of children used by adults to commit crimes is another relevant issue that the baseline study covered. Probation services are currently integral to the management of children in conflict with the law.[29] Not only are these services of importance once the child enters the criminal justice system, but they are also critical to prevention.[30] Through an assessment, it is the probation services that devise the most appropriate recommendations, for example concerning diversion to a programme before the matter of an alleged child offender goes to trial.[31] Probation officers are additionally required to fulfil a role following conviction by providing the court with a pre-sentence report prior to the imposition sentence.[32] A probation officer who is a trained and qualified social worker carries out the assessment.[33]

Through this research, it was established that, although many of the probation officers have encountered cases of children used by adults to commit crimes, formal records of this do not exist and there is no follow-up of the issue by the probation officer. Had probation officers followed up where there was disclosure of a child being used by an adult to commit a crime, it could have informed prosecutorial withdrawal of charges, the diversion programme content, or resulted in this factor being considered in mitigation of sentence. Where the child appears to be in need of care and protection, a recommendation for conversion of the criminal proceedings to a welfare hearing could be proposed and the case transferred to a Children's Court.[34]

The identification by the probation officer of a case involving children used by adults could also have serious implications with regard to the placement of the child in the care of his or her parents pending any trial. This is because some parents themselves are allegedly the adults who use the children to commit crimes. Although the focus groups in the child consultation process provided a wide range of responses in relation to the general question which adults use children to commit crimes, parents and caregivers are among the list.[35] As the child consultation process reported, "participants in the groups noted that sometimes parents say, 'if you are a man, you will do this' – the children want to do this (commit a crime) to impress their parents."[36]

This indicates the parents' involvement in the crime. This clearly shows that the issue of children used by adults to commit crimes is an important issue that needs to be considered by probation officers before the child can be placed with his or her parents or any other caregiver as the case may be.

The failure of probation officers to follow-up leads to the possibility of the continued use of these children for crimes by adults. This is because, when children are diverted or released with very insignificant repercussions, and no follow-up ensues on the adults who used them, it fuels the cycle of crime in the future.

The study concluded that the current assessment forms were not structured to identify cases of children used by adults to commit crime appropriately. It recommended that an instruction, directive or a guiding tool should be developed to assist probation officers to identify cases of children used by adults and to refer such children appropriately. Otherwise, the lack of follow-up by the probation officer of the fact that the child was used by an adult to commit a specific crime would negatively affect the way in which the child is dealt with, making a mockery of the whole process and the rights of the child.

An interesting and challenging area that the baseline survey highlights relates to judicial and prosecutorial practice in relation to children used by adults to commit crimes. This is partly because of the theoretical and practical challenges posed by identifying children who commit crimes at the behest of adults as victims of the worst forms of child labour.[37] What the children reported was that the involvement of adults was both direct and indirect. As the child consultation process indicated:

> *In terms of direct involvement of children by adults in crime, which was noted by 30 of the groups, this related to engaging children as accomplices in the commission of crimes. This included committing crimes together, children acting as lookouts, adults taking children to crime scenes, adults overseeing the commission of the crime, and adults paying children for the commission of crime. This also involved using children to sell drugs.*[38]

As regards indirect involvement, all the focus groups referred to children being offered rewards and incentives, such as the use of money, drugs, and other things as a means of luring, bribing or goading them into criminal activity or into a general criminal lifestyle. Participants also described children being drawn in by adults through deception, indebting the child to the adult in some way in order to get the child to commit crime.

As regards rewards, the following examples were cited:
- Adults are afraid to get their hands dirty. They pay kids off to do things
- Adults like the Nigerians give youth drugs, they show kids how much money they can have if they do some things
- Adults say that you must go and steal, and they will give you money or drugs
- They bribe you with dagga, drugs and alcohol, and girls
- If you are addicted, you don't have a choice
- Some just get drugs, not money
- They sometimes bribe you with a gun and money
- They show you lots of money – they show you R10 000.00 but you will only get R500.00
- Old criminals see that children and youth are in need
- They buy them branded clothing.

Deliberate deception was a common theme, and one which gave rise to anger on the part of the children that they had been made to bear the brunt of the consequences of the offence:
- We get tricked by these adults
- They say they will give you a lift, but they take you to do a crime
- They say, *"ons gaan net saam loop"* (we will just walk with you a bit) but adults take you along to commit a crime
- He tells you to rob people. The people see you but the adult doing this and when you get arrested he forgets about you. You must then stand alone for this case
- You go together to commit crime – they tell you that you won't go to jail.

During the justice sector part of the research, almost all the magistrates (except for one magistrate) as well as the all the consulted prosecutors indicated that they have come across cases involving children used by adults to commit crimes. Magistrates have also encountered many cases where children were co-accused with adults. One magistrate stated that although he assumed that the child could have been used by an adult to commit the crime, he never really asked the child whether he or she was influenced by the adult or used by the adult to commit the offence.[39]

The question as to whether the fact that the child might have been used by the adult or older child could possibly serve as a mitigating factor for the child during sentencing was also posed. The response of some was that they could only consider this as a mitigating factor if evidence to that effect was led during the trial or brought to the attention of the court by the probation officer in a pre-sentence report, while others thought that it should be considered a mitigating factor but that each case should be considered on its merits. Magistrates were unanimous that the criminal involvement of the child cannot be completely obliterated by the fact of adult involvement, and that these children cannot be viewed only as victims.

However, given the children's reports of threats, inducement and even violence as noted above, the fact that children have been led into crime by adults to commit crimes should be considered at least as mitigating factor. Indeed, depending on the degree of influence and direct coercion, this should even serve in some instances to exclude criminal liability completely. Therefore, magistrates and prosecutors should be obliged as a mandatory step to consider whether children were used by adults to commit crimes, and, if so, to ensure that this serves as a mitigating factor when convicted children are to be sentenced.

In relation to prosecutors, the research indicated that prosecutors often find it difficult to establish adult involvement. Even in situations where they suspect that a child was used by an adult to commit a crime, it is difficult to prosecute the adult for his or her involvement. In the first place, children usually do not report that they were used by adults to commit the crimes. Occasionally, they disclose to legal representatives, but they would warn the legal representatives not to reveal for fear of reprisals and attacks on their families.[40] In addition, in situations where the prosecutor is aware that a child is being used by an adult to commit crimes, it has been alleged that the sole testimony of the child – who is also an accomplice – is not good enough evidence to initiate a prosecution. However, as will be pointed out in the concluding section, the aims and objectives of the implementation of the pilot project are indeed to put these assumptions to the test, and to initiate prosecutions against offending adults.

A further difficulty relates to the question as to what offence an adult may subsequently be charged with. The Child Justice Bill, 49 of 2002, which was tabled for Parliament in August 2002, was subject to numerous changes which were effected during deliberations by the Portfolio Committee on Justice and Constitutional Development. One such change included the elimination of the proposed substantive new criminal offence of inciting, persuading, inducing or encouraging a child to commit an offence.[41] Instead, members of Parliament suggested that reliance should be placed on the common law (and existing statutory) offences of incitement and conspiracy.

Incitement and conspiracy to commit a crime is punishable in terms of the Riotous Assemblies Act, 17 of 1956. Section 18(2) reads as follows:

> *Any person who… incites, instigates, commands, or procures any other person to commit any offence, whether at common law or against a statute or statutory regulation, shall be guilty of any offence and liable on conviction to the punishment to which a person convicted of actually committing that offence would be liable.*[42]

Conspiracy is also punishable under South African general criminal law, as the law provides that it is an offence for, "[a]ny person who… conspires with any other person to aid or to procure the commission of or to commit… any offence… shall be guilty of an offence…"[43]

A similar approach is adopted in the case of being an accomplice and being involved as an accessory after the fact.[44] A person is guilty of an offence as accomplice if he unlawfully and intentionally engages in conduct whereby he furthers the commission of an offence by someone else. The word 'further' includes any conduct whereby a person facilitates, assists or encourages the commission of an offence, gives advice concerning its commission, orders its commission or makes it possible for another to commit it.

The requirements for accomplice are:
- Accessory nature of liability – somebody else must have committed a crime as the accomplice's liability is of an accessory or dependant nature. The perpetrator need not be tried and convicted (Dettbarn 1930 OPD 188 191)
- Acts or omissions which further the crime – in order to be guilty as an accomplice, a person must commit an act which amounts to a furthering of a crime committed by somebody else. In respect of children used by adults to commit an offence and children selling stolen goods to a known 'fence', the buyer of illicit goods may be charged as an accomplice of the seller
- Unlawfulness – the act of 'furthering' must be unlawful, in other words, no justification ground must exist
- Intention – to be liable as an accomplice, a person must intentionally further the commission of a crime by someone else.

The prosecutors in the baseline survey indicated that they knew of no case where a case of a child used by an adult to commit a crime led to the prosecution of the adult on the basis of incitement or conspiracy. In order to prosecute the adult in these matters, respondents stated, the prosecutor would need to rely on the evidence of the child. This creates evidentiary hurdles as cautionary rules against a child witness and against a single witness come into play.[45] Unsurprisingly, the baseline study confirmed that prosecuting authorities are reluctant to separate the processes relating to the youth from those that ensue in relation to adults at criminal proceedings and it is difficult to convince them to abandon their well-established premise of joint prosecution, and the conception of shared criminal responsibility (co-perpetrators and accomplices). The proposals for action by prosecutors in the implementation of the pilot project attempt to address this reluctance, and suggest that where a child disclosed that he or she has been used by an adult or older child to commit a crime, the involvement of the adult should be fully explored whilst at the same time either referring the child back to probation officers for appropriate referrals, and referral of the docket to the investigating officer for further investigation into the role of the adult. Where a child has already pleaded, has been found guilty either on his or her plea or at trial, the prosecution should consider the fact of the instrumental use of the child as a mitigating factor in arguing for sentence. Using the child as a state witness against the adult could also be considered, but only if this does not jeopardise the safety and well-being of the child.

In some legal systems, it is argued that a substantial portion of the perceived increase in juvenile crime could be laid at the feet of flaws in parenting.[46] Therefore, a movement is afoot to hold parents criminally responsible for the delinquent acts of their children.[47] In this regard, an issue that could be posed in relation to children used by adults to commit crimes is the need to establish the criminal responsibility of parents for the offences of their children. As the child consultation process noted, "parents and families are either passively excusing or ignoring their children's criminal behaviors. In some cases, children described ways in which parents subtly rewarded behaviors as well."[48]

Arguably, in these exceptional circumstances whereby there is a clear case of irresponsible parenting leading to the use of children by adults to commit crimes, the potential of enforcing greater parental responsibility for juvenile crime to induce parents to undertake greater responsibility for their wayward children, and threatening increased legal sanctions if they fail, could be considered. This may well be achieved through the opening of children's courts' inquiries to establish whether the child is possibly in need of care due to his or her parents' *laissez faire* behaviour.

5.   Conclusion

According to ILO estimates, there are approximately 250 million children aged five to14 years old employed in developing countries.[49] ILO Convention 182 is addressed to those 50-60 million children who are involved in the worst and most abusive forms of child labour, which the ILO defines as modern types of slavery, sex work, illicit activities such as drug trafficking, and any other work likely to harm the health, safety and morals of children.[50] In defining the term 'the worst forms of child labour', Article 3(d) of ILO Convention 182 provides that it comprises, "the use, procuring or offering of a child for prostitution, for the production and trafficking of drugs as defined in the relevant international treaties." It is from these definitions that the notion of children used by adults to commit crimes emanates from, and forms a nexus with child protection and with juvenile justice, and the way in which these children are to be addressed in the criminal justice system brings this to the fore.

The findings of the study discussed above attempted to indicate the magnitude of the problem as well as the challenges and opportunities for intervention that can be identified. From the child consultation study, it appears that the phenomenon is multi-faceted and that, consequently, in the design of the pilot programmes, no single method can be relied upon to address this worst form of child labour. The plot projects therefore include programmes related to prevention, diversion and guidance for criminal justice stakeholders to follow-up and record instances of adult involvement. This can only be facilitated by greater awareness of the issue at grassroots level amongst the various criminal justice role-players, coupled with a drive to get behind the child's involvement to the adults concerned. A key aspect of the implementation of the pilot phase therefore hinges on training of these officials at local level, and the setting up and testing of protocols to guide follow-up and action. The assessment process was identified as the initial stage at which a child might disclose the involvement of adults, and for this reason indicators have been developed to assist probation officers in identifying these children.[51] A further component of the project design was the development of a guidelines booklet on the management of children who are used by adults to commit crime. The purpose of this booklet is to provide information and awareness on the issue of CUBAC, and further to advocate and sensitise professionals working with children that children who are used by adults to commit crime should be seen as victims rather than as perpetrators. Finally, the implementation phase will include material to be added into existing diversion and prevention programmes currently on offer in the pilot sites that have been selected to try to identify and prevent children from being lured into criminal activity by adults.

In conclusion, there are considerable challenges posed by the intersection between child protection, on the one hand, and child labour, on the other, in this sphere. They relate to procedure, prosecutorial practice, the structure of criminal law, and factors relevant to communities and to children themselves. The issues involved are new and will benefit from further debate and research. We need to begin to conceptualise the ramifications of the notion that children used by adults to commit crimes are necessarily to be seen as victims of the worst forms of child labour.

Endnotes

1   K Hanson and A Vandaele, "Working children and international labour law", (2003) 11 *The International Journal of Children Rights*, 113.

2   As above.

3   As above.

4   Article 1 of ILO Convention 182.

5   Article 2 of Recommendation 190.

6   Article 2 of Recommendation 190.

7   Article 3 of ILO Convention 182.

8   One of the few published papers on ILO Convention 182 (Noguchi Y, "ILO Convention 182 on the worst forms of child labour", (2002) 1 *International Journal on Children's Rights,* 355-369) does not explore the definitional issues discussed here in detail.

9   An earlier discussion of this issue it to be found in: J Sloth-Nielsen, "Let not the sins of the fathers (and their brothers and uncles and tjommies… Exploring the child labour/juvenile justice intersection)", unpublished paper presented at the 4th World Congress on the Rights of Children and Youth, Cape Town, March, 2005.

10 The other three identified country-specific categories being children having to carry water under onerous circumstances which prevents their attending school, children involved in commercial sexual exploitation, and trafficking of children. Similar projects are being undertaken by the Programme Towards the Elimination of Child Labour in the neighbouring countries Botswana, Lesotho, Namibia and Swaziland, in respect of each of which different focus areas have been identified.

11 For instance, during the baseline survey, a prosecutor from Mamelodi expressed, "surprise at the notion the children used by adults to commit crimes are victims of a worst form of child labour." (See *Baseline Survey*, 80). However, the child consultation process described in more detail below concluded that the case of adults using children to commit crimes is not unusual. Through their responses, all 41 focus groups provided information that indicated that children being used by adults to commit crimes is a common phenomenon. All 41 focus groups provided clear and direct examples of how adults are involved when children commit crimes. See *Child Consultation Process Report*, 18.

12 The CLAP was adopted by Cabinet in 2003, and endorsed by a wide range of government departments, including those responsible for justice, social development, labour, education, safety and security, and local government, as well as by other agencies.

13 This created some limitations for the study, one of which was that it was not possible to include young women awaiting trial.

14 For instance, less than a third of the participants had been living with both parents prior to the interview, and this figure was less than a quarter for those children who were deprived of their liberty in SCFs. The most common charges against the detained children were burglary, robbery and murder, which together accounted for 60% of the charges.

15 The respondents were asked whether they had ever done anything to earn money, and if so to describe what it was. The data was categorised into three broad categories, namely 'Not economically active', 'Legal activities' and 'Illegal activities'. Of the total group, two thirds had in the past engaged in some activity that earned them money, and there were significant differences between the school group and the SCF group. Two thirds of the school group stated that they had never done anything to earn money compared to only 25% of the SCF group. Roughly 37% had engaged in some legal activity to earn money. In terms of illegal activities, just more than 30% of the total group and 38% of the SCF group reported engaging in illicit activities to earn money. In contrast, only 2.5% of the school group reported that they have engaged in illegal deeds to earn money.

16 The final two pilot sites will be the locations at which the actual programmatic interventions will be implemented during 2006.

17 See "Let not the sins of the Fathers" (note 9 above).

18 Children's Rights Project, *Report on the child consultation research process regarding children used by adults to commit offences* (hereafter *child consultation process report*) (2005), 16.

19 Although the groups provided responses to indicate that children were often threatened and coerced into committing crimes… they also noted that children were equally making decisions as to whether they commit crime. Thirty-nine of the 41 groups stated that children often com-

mitted crime willingly... Sometimes related to necessities, but mostly to the acquiring of clothes and other possessions that, in their view, enabled them to gain esteem and worth in the eyes of others... There will inevitably be situations where the child has exercised his or her own choice, and acted accordingly, and where the sole fact that an adult is involved in the commission of a crime would not necessarily come to their rescue.

20 The relevant international rule guiding police practice is Rule 10 of the Beijing Rules, which requires the police to respect the legal status of the juvenile and promote his well being and avoid any harm. Within the context at hand, practically speaking, this requirement includes investigating a case of a child used by an adult to commit crimes, and, if so required, taking positive or negative measures which would ensure that the child would not fall into the same trap of being used again by the same adult or by another one.

21 This was mentioned in Mitchell's Plain, a particularly crime ridden and gang infested part of the Cape Metropole.

22 By far, poverty (and in some cases, unemployment) was noted as the most pervasive condition leading children to offend, with 20 of the 41 groups raising this as an issue. Children in the focus groups stated:
   - They commit crime for food
   - Children come from a hard environment, they have a poor family
   - Parents stop giving you money. You have to help yourself
   - There is no food at home
   - Maybe you don't get any food and then you steal
   - There are no jobs
   - You don't get money at home and you go out and rob people.

23 Evidently such an official has been identified at each police station.

24 Given scarce resources within the SAPS.

25 Or the case otherwise finalised.

26 This is a state witness, where an accused person gives implicating evidence against a co-accused or other person in exchange for the withdrawal of charges against him or her. However, the test is whether the evidence given is reliable and credible for the section 204 benefits to accrue.

27 These are policy instructions to inform police officers about the manner in which they should execute their duties.

28 It would, the researchers were told, be contrary to good governance to develop delegated legislation on a matter on which the primary law was still not in final or approved form. Further, the policy within the Department was not to develop standing orders (National Instructions) on a piece-meal basis, and to highlight children used by adults to commit crime via a standing order (National Instruction), without there being a general standing order on children in trouble with the law, would not synthesise with departmental objectives and procedures. However, the Department has agreed, as an interim measure whilst waiting for the Child Justice Bill to be finalised in Parliament, to issue a Circular highlighting the phenomenon.

29 The Probation Services Act, 116 of 1991, details the powers, functions and duties of probation officers.

30 J Sloth-Nielsen and J Gallinetti, *Child justice in Africa: A guide to good practice* (2004), Community Law Centre: Bellville, 130.

31 Assessment is an evaluation process occurring after the arrest of a child. It involves an evaluation of the child, his or her home circumstances and the circumstances surrounding the commission of the alleged offence with a view to formulating appropriate recommendations.

32 For a detailed discussion of the role of a probation officer as sentence recommendation officer, see J Sloth-Nielsen and J Gallinetti (note 30 above), 133. See also A Skelton "Children accused of crimes", in: S Padayachee (ed), *Children and the law* (2nd ed) (2004), Lawyers for Human Rights: South Africa, 189.

33 The Child Justice Bill, 49 of 2002, in chapter 4, makes a provision for an assessment by a probation officer to be carried out in respect of every child alleged to have committed an offence before such child appears in court. The Bill has not yet been passed in Parliament.

34 A Skelton (note 32 above), 196.

35 *Child consultation process report* (note 18 above), 26.

36 As above. Children also mentioned the role of parents and families in not teaching children right from wrong, not providing appropriate examples for children, and, particularly, exhibit-

ing inappropriate and criminal behaviour, which was noted by the children to as permissible. The following examples were noted by children:

- Parents say, "if you are a man, you will do this" – the children want to do this too
- They see their parents doing crime and get influenced
- They are lazy to get jobs and then influence children to commit crimes
- Parents don't tell you right from wrong
- When a car or other things are being stolen – the adults don't discourage it
- The parents take the child to the tavern when they go drinking.
- They commit crime in front of them; they discuss their crime in front of children.

Another set of responses related to parents and families either actively or passively excusing or ignoring their children's criminal behaviour, overlooking the possession of stolen goods. In some cases, children described ways in which parents subtly rewarded behaviour as well.

[37] J Sloth-Nielsen (note 9 above), 7.

[38] *Child consultation process report* (note 18 above), 19.

[39] *Baseline survey*, 74.

[40] Admittedly, the lawyer-client relationship privilege would require the defence counsel not to disclose information against the instruction of the client. However, it is arguable that in situations where the child is a victim and has been exploited it would be necessary for the legal representative to communicate to the court or prosecutor that his or her client is a child used by an adult to commit crimes. This may serve the best interests of the child in the particular case and also help the prosecutor charge the adult involved.

[41] Clause 117 (3) of the Child Justice Bill, which also determined that the offence was only punishable if committed by an adult, and that this was an offence in addition to any other offence for which the adult concerned may be charged. The proposed penalty upon conviction was a fine or imprisonment not exceeding two years.

[42] S v Nkosiyana 1966 (4) SA 655 (A) held:
- An inciter is one who reaches and seeks to influence the mind of another to the commission of a crime
- It is immaterial whether the incitee is susceptible to persuasion
- The means used to influence the incitee are also immaterial
- The incitement may be explicit or tacit
- The emphasis is on the intention and conduct of the inciter and not of the incitee
- Incitement may also be committed even where the inciting statement is made in response to a question first asked by the incitee.

[43] Section 18(2)(a) of the Riotous Assemblies Act 17 of 1956.

[44] For a discussion of accomplice and accessory after the fact, see C R Snyman, *Criminal Law* (4th ed) (2002), Butterworths publishers: Durban, 269, 274.

[45] These obstacles faced by prosecutors were also echoed by a member of the National Prosecuting Authority at the workshop held on 2nd August 2005.

[46] J H Difonzo, "Parental responsibility for juvenile crime", (2001) 80 *Oregon Law Review*, 1.

[47] As above.

[48] *Child consultation process report* (note 18 above), 22.

[49] D Stone, *Policy Paradox: The Art of Political Decision Making* (1997), 63, as cited in: M G Davidson, "The International Labour Organization's latest campaign to end child labour: Will it succeed where others have failed?", (2001) 11 *Transnational Law and Contemporary Problems*, 203.

[50] M G Davidson (note 49 above), 205.

[51] They are as follows:
- The fact that an older co-accused is involved in the commission of the offence
- The child is a member of a gang
- The involvement of the child in any gang-related activities
- The fact that the child is living on the street
- The type of offence for which the child is charged, e.g. possession or dealing in drugs, housebreaking and theft and dealing in liquor or firearms
- Whether the child had existing avenues open to him or her to dispose stolen goods, e.g. a regular 'fence' for stolen property
- Whether the child could give any further information e.g. addresses for the acquisition of drugs.

Organisation of Youth Care:

New Trends and Experiences in Bulgaria and Romania

Velina Todorova

1.   Introduction

This article provides a comparative research on child care reforms in Bulgaria and Romania. The research covers three areas: (1) historical background of the development of policies towards children; (2) current situation of child and youth care services; and (3) development of the institutions and legislation. The analysis is based on available documents, in particular previous researches, official reports, statistical data and legislation. The main focuses of this article are: driving forces of the reform in child care in the two states, which differ, though bearing some similarities; the major problems in carrying out the reforms; and strategies to overcome them.

Both Bulgaria and Romania have started their child care reforms, though officially called 'Child Welfare Reforms', comparatively recently, on fairly equal grounds, under similar conditions. They are developing the same services based on equivalent foreign technical assistance, in response to one and the same needs.

The reforms of concern here, which focus on individual services, need to be regarded as an effort to modernise the previous systems of child care. The two states have inherited a social policy that, although quite generous in some respects, proved to be inadequate from the perspective of today's actual needs of its beneficiaries. Both countries lack tradition in services' provision as well as a culture of demand for services. Strong professional communities are also missing to support and advocate for reforms. Therefore the state remains the main agent of the change and the society is not so much involved.

The current reform in the child care system coincides with the overall political, economic and social transformation in the region. That change caused a massive erosion of children's welfare and a decrease in political attention paid to children and youth. Therefore the start of the reforms in child care had to compete with many other issues, such as unemployment, poverty, reforms in education and health care, in order to be tackled by governments as a matter of priority. In such a context, the aspiration of Bulgaria and Romania to accede the European Union (EU) and, consequently, the negotiation process for accession were certainly the key factors for the start of reforms.

2. The policy for children and youth in Bulgaria and Romania before the fall of 'Iron Curtain'

The policy and the practice in child care before 1989 in the states behind the 'Iron Curtain' have common features, but they also differ, mainly due to the variations in their historical development and traditions before World War II. Many – mainly Western –commentators have defined some topical features of the social policy of that time in the countries of Central and Eastern Europe to include:

- Labour market orientation of the policy towards women and the family
- The 'welfare' system comprises universal benefits for children in combination with limited number of services for families, women and children, which are mainly enterprise based; and
- Generous child day care, free education and healthcare.[1]

Bulgaria and Romania, unlike other countries of Eastern Europe (for instance, the Czech Republic and Hungary), do not have a close 19th and early 20th century association with welfare traditions of Central and Western Europe. In addition to the above-listed features of their social policy, Bulgaria and Romania have experienced aggressive pro-natalist agendas. Cultural factors such as the role of extended family in family support and child upbringing, as well as the prevailing patriarchal attitudes to family and children that were common for the region,[2] had a considerable impact on the child care policy of the two countries.

The aggressive pro-natalism and women's 'liberation' after World War II are considered as key factors for marking the pathways of social policy in Romania and Bulgaria.[3] These are rooted in the accelerated industrialisation that has imposed a demand for labour force. Generous child care was provided to guarantee full participation of women to the labour market.

To a great extent, the official active pro-natalist agenda has exhausted the policies towards children and the family in both states.[4] While in Bulgaria this policy was implemented by 'soft' measures,[5] Romania undertook extreme ones, via the widely known ban on abortions and some increased allowances for large families as well as day care for children.[6]

The focus on natalist policies predetermined the social construct of childhood before 1989. Children were regarded mostly as a resource for the future of the nation (labour force) rather than as children or human beings, or as family members. Therefore the link between the child and the state, with its role to educate children, was given more importance than the role of the family to bring up the child:

> In both the education and child protection systems, the child was seen as individual in relationships with the state rather than as a member of a family. Consequently, families were often blamed rather than supported, and not infrequently state institutions were considered preferable.[7]

The ideology that the state is better than the family in child upbringing was materialised in the well-established system of residential public care for children abandoned by their parents, instead of developing a family type of care. This model changed only in the late 1990s when the concept of foster care was introduced in the region.[8]

Furthermore, the active natalist policy emphasised the quantity of the children's population, but not the quality of children's lives. This is a serious problem, which is being reproduced today.[9] The general public and a large segment of the academic community still explore the problems of children and childhood from a quantitative perspective – from the standpoint of the deteriorated demographic structure and the decreasing child population.[10] Therefore, no tradition has been established to research the quality parameters of childhood. This gap is especially visible as regards the research on the 'negative aspects of childhood'. Officially, in the past, children's daily life was presented in a socially desirable form.[11] The existence of many social problems was either denied or defined as a product of individual pathology – deviation from the state approved behaviour. An example to this end was 'the concealment' from society, both in the physical meaning and in terms of information, of the 'different' children: children with disabilities, children placed in institutions and children with deviant behaviour.[12] This generated public ignorance and insensitivity to these groups of children. Only in the mid-1980s, the first national survey on the situation of children in Bulgaria was conducted, and 'children in especially difficult circumstances due to health or social reasons' were identified as an object of concern.[13]

The absence of a national tradition to research the child and childhood before 1989 has two consequences from today's perspective. First, drop-back was effected in humanitarian sciences, which by definition need to 'inform' the policies on children and families. Concepts, such as individual care, best interests of the child, professional specialised assistance, needs based services and others, remained underdeveloped at the national level.[14] Thus, the transition from institutionalised care to the de-institutionalisation of child care was not possible in both countries based on national ideology, model and efforts. Secondly, no professional communities (of social workers, children's psychologists and psychiatrists, judges and lawyers) were established that could advocate for a change in the policies addressing children. For instance, social work as a subject with content similar to the Western traditions is hardly present in the university curriculum in Bulgaria. Academic researches in this area are scarce, not only due to limited resources but also due to the lack of interest and/or demand. Active in this field are mainly NGOs under projects supported by foreign donors (such as UNICEF, World Bank, EU).[15]

3.   Services for children and youth before the fall of 'Iron Curtain'
In general, in both countries, until the fall of 'Iron Curtain', only services were offered to families for which there was low or no risk. These services included financial assistance, free and almost universal health care, day care for children and education that usually is granted to all families.[16] The deterioration of the economic conditions after 1989 resulted in a serious collapse of those services.[17]

Only for a small proportion of children who were exposed to serious risk of abandonment, and for whom no appropriate form of help in the family environment existed, services were offered to replace their family, mainly in the form of adoption or placement in large residential institutions. Placement in institutions was also the most frequent service provided for children who demonstrated so-called 'delinquent behaviour'.

The consequence is the increased need for various forms of assistance, such as help in child upbringing, consultation, training of parents, assistance for disabled people, youth centres and emergency services, social work in the municipality. In brief, there is an increased need for differentiated services that are considered as the foundation of a modern child welfare system.[18] Such services are not offered in both countries.

The institutional care[19] in Bulgaria and Romania dates back to the 1950s. It is not an invention of these countries, but for many reasons Bulgaria and Romania became examples of misuse of that type of care for children after the fall of the 'Iron Curtain'.

The residential care of today's type was created in response, first, to the need for post natal care of babies born with high medical risk and, second, to combat the high early child mortality from 1950 to 1960.[20] Gradually the number and the grounds for placements enlarge and the two states intensively utilise the pedagogic concept of 'collective child socialisation'.[21] Factors of demand and supply type are equally significant for the growth of the system that remained dominant until 2000, and even until today in Bulgaria.[22] This led to the following four developments.

A. High rate of child abandonment – as a means to resolve a family problem (sometimes related to the care of children).[23]
During the 1970s and 1980s, the number of children in state care in Romania rose, reaching more than 100,000.[24] Only a tiny minority of children in state care – currently estimated at just 3% – are there because they have no living relatives. In Bulgaria a research of 1991 shows that 65% of children placed in institutions have their own families.[25] By 1990 institutions were used as an alternative to the missing individual services. Some social or cultural norms were also 'push' factors for placement, such as disability, out of marriage births, etc.[26]

After 1989, the two countries faced a new increase in the number of placements as well as new reasons for this increase. The number of children in institutions almost doubled in Bulgaria over a period of 10 years: from 18,000 in 1991 to 35,123 in 2000. It is one of the highest shares of institutionalisation across Europe: 1.78% (of the entire children's population).[27] Only 1% of these children are orphans. The situation in Romania is similar.[28] The number of institutionalised children has remained basically the same as in 1989, despite the sharp drop by half a million in Romania's overall population during the same time period (in large part due to emigration and decreased birth rates).[29] In accordance with a survey carried out by the Observatory of Child Growing in Europe, the estimated rate of abandonment is of 1.7 abandoned children per 100 live births. The main reasons for the abandonment/placement are poverty of the family and family problems.[30] The ethnicity, in combination with poverty, is a considerable factor: the Roma group is over-represented among children in institutions[31] in the region. Today, in terms of rate of institutional placement of children, Bulgaria and Romania are leading (together with Russia) in child institutionalisation, with 10 to 20 children per 1,000 living in residential institutions.[32]

B. The existence of many large institutions with improper living conditions.
The service of 'institutional placement' has gradually established not merely the culture of child abandonment,[33] but also the 'industry' of abandonment, through the expanded supply of the service.[34] Institutions were interested in the growth of the number of placements and have used different means for the recruitment of children. This was important to maintain the staffing and the support for the institutions from the state budgets. Even until recent years, parents were attracted by media announcements for placing their children in institutions. Institutional interest is maintained by an open system for placement, which feeds the system.

C. A child protection system inappropriate for child development.
By 1990, the main factor for institutionalisation was not poverty or an absent parent, but rather the need to resolve a family problem (sometimes related to the care of children).[35] Institutions substitute the missing individual services, which resulted in underdeveloped capacity in delivering services other than institutionalisation.

D. Public opinion is ignorant on the effects of institutionalisation, and its alternatives, and supports institutions.
Today in Bulgaria, the public opinion is to a large extent neutral to the reform underway that is aimed at setting up alternative services. The public is more inclined to discriminate rather than to be considerate to children in institutions.[36]

4.   The difficult start of child care reforms: 1990–2000
The heavy burden of the pre-1989 policies of child care determined the difficult start and the slow progress of the reforms of today in the two countries.

By the mid-1990s, the two states did not attach importance to services as an alternative of institutions. The lack of reforms is effected by the lack of not only political will, but also resources for the reform. It became clear that any development of services for children and youth is unquestionably related to the process of de-institutionalisation and the dismantling of the monopoly of that (only) service.

This period is marked by the high external pressure aimed to generate internal political commitment for reforms. It is focused mainly on Romania. It started in the early 1990s, when the Western media discovered the situation in child care institutions there, and culminated in 1998 when the European Commission made the child welfare reform (CWR) a precondition for Romania's entry into the

European Union. One of the two principal conditions for the opening of negotiations for Romania in 2000 was, "...that the...government have taken effective action...to provide adequate budgetary resources and to implement structural reform of child care institutions before the end of 1999."[37] The Commission highlighted the fact that child care is a matter of human rights, and they would not initiate negotiations until this issue was dealt with. Therefore it could be argued whether the reform started based on a genuine concern for children, or due to the internal political ambition for accession to the European Union.

The same argument is valid for Bulgaria. Unfortunately for Bulgarian children, the country did not experience external pressure similar to that in Romania. A Mission of World Bank of that time (1999-2000)[38] resulted in the first Government Strategy and Action Plan for Childcare Reform of 2000.[39] For the first time, that Plan made explicit to the problems in this area, such as: over-institutionalisation (2,15% of the children's population); super-centralisation and subordination of child care to five ministries; and low effectiveness and high cost from the perspective of public costs and children's rights. However, reforms in child care did not become a political priority in Bulgaria until now. No doubt, the missing international pressure is one of the reasons, if not the major one, for that.

In conclusion, during the 1990s, the efforts in the region were directed at the development of child care, rather than family focused services in view of setting up alternatives for the institutions. At that stage, the reform in services was not perceived as an effort for setting up a comprehensive model for child welfare, as needed in a democratic society. The reforms in the two countries were initiated from the top, which resulted in drawbacks and omissions.

5. The actual start of the reforms in services

5.1 Romania

Romania is the unquestionable leader in the reform, with its start in 1997 and with its achievements today. Bulgaria started later and is still falling behind.[40] In 1997, Romania initiated two important steps, it created the specialised administration and decentralised the child care institutions.[41] The management of the child protection system was delegated from the central government (several different ministries) to 41 county councils. Forty-one County Directorates for Child Protection were set up and charged with operational and financial responsibility, both for children in need and institutions within their counties. The new decentralised approach aimed to: prevent institutionalisation by providing assistance to families at risk; close down old style institutions; and create alternative forms of care for children. However, the decentralisation in responsibilities was not paralleled by a decentralisation in the financing of services.[42] This resulted in a financial crisis and generated risk for the children. Thereby, the financing planned for the de-institutionalisation was used in 1998-2000 for financing the system. In this way, the modernisation of the system was made possible.

5.2 Bulgaria

According to Bulgarian commentators, the beginning of the reform in the country should be associated with the adoption of the Child Protection Act in 2000. Similar to Romania, in Bulgaria the adoption of the Law was followed by the setting-up of a central and local administration with the functions similar to those of the parallel authorities in Romania

However, passing of the modern law on Child Protection could not secure the success of the reforms. Bulgaria was congratulated for its efforts in the field of legislation but was equally criticised for the laws not being equipped with the necessary resources to be implemented properly. Neither the institutions nor the funding of services were decentralised. The centralised funding of residential institutions did not change either, which was criticised by the European Commission in its Regular Report for Bulgaria's accession of 2004: "the number of children placed in institutions continues to determine the funds allocated to these structures which does not provide the necessary incentives for de-institutionalisation." Still no methodology has been adopted for the financing of private services provided, for example, by NGOs.

6. The services today: the successes and the shortcomings

6.1 Legislation on services

Bulgaria and Romania apply different approaches in their law making in the field of social services.[43] While Bulgaria starts with a relatively comprehensive law defining new policy targets (e.g. priority of family type of care, best interests principle, development of services, child participation, social work, judicial control, etc.), Romania begins with fragmented legislation regulating separate services.[44] This process culminated in a comprehensive law on Protection and Promotion of the Rights of the Child that was passed in 2004.

While Romania concentrated on the development of services in practice, Bulgaria put efforts in legislation. A bulk of secondary legislation to the Child Protection Act was passed in 2003. This actually gave the only ground for some positive comments by the EU Commission: "as regards children's rights, the government has shown its commitment through various strategies, action plans (including a new programme for child protection, adopted in December 2004) and legislation." Each international monitoring report on Bulgaria starts with recognising the progress made in this area.[45]

There are some common features of the legislation passed in the region:
- The 'best interests of the child' principle and the right of the child to express his/her views are incorporated.
- The access of children to services depends on their needs. The needs' assessment is a responsibility of the social worker from the Child Protection Department (Directorate in Romania). The needs' assessment should lead to setting up an individual plan for care that could suggest the type of the service.[46] The social workers have to manage each case according to specific common rules and time limits.

227

- Each placement of the child out of the biological family is based on a court order. Placement in institution is a measure of last resort.
- The services are public and private. Public services are financed by the state budget, while the state, the municipality or the private provider could fund the private ones.
- The social entrepreneurship is encouraged for public and private agencies and persons.[47]
- A licensing (accreditation in Romania) and registration regime exist for private social service providers for children.[48]
- Criteria and Standards have been passed by the Government for provision of community-based social services and services in specialised institutions, which are binding for all providers, irrespective of whether they are state-owned, municipal or private.[49]
- A monitoring of the quality of social services is envisaged.

6.2   Priority list of services

As mentioned above, the two countries were pressed to develop as a matter of urgency certain types of services, in particular services for child protection, which mostly address problems of care and the risk of abandonment of the child. These services are: services to prevent abandonment (e.g. counselling, financial support, mother and baby units, day care, rehabilitation); services for reintegration in the biological family (counselling, placement with the extended family, day care, financial support, schooling); and services providing alternatives to the family – adoption, placement in the extended family, foster care, small group home.

Services to strengthen the capacity of the family and its members are just emerging (e.g. family therapy, contact services, mediation, psychological counselling of the child).

Services to address the needs of some groups of vulnerable children, such as street children, victims of trafficking and children with deviant behaviour, are being developed by NGOs mostly.[50]

6.3   The 'old' institutions

Institutions still remain, now provided by the law as a last resort for placement in public care. However, in Bulgaria, institutions still exist in practice as the most available service. According to the government's own recent assessments,[51] the number of children in some specialised institutions has remained more or less constant in the period 2001-2004, though the legal definition for institution was changed not to cover the special boarding schools for children with special educational needs. At the end of 2004, out of the 1.48 million children in Bulgaria, 12,612 are living in residential-type institutions. This represents 0.84% of the child population. Quite logically, the Comprehensive Monitoring Report of October 2005 concludes that, "progress in de-institutionalisation remains very limited and falls behind the Bulgarian plan to reduce by 10% the total number of children in specialised institutions in the period 2003-2005."[52]

In Romania, based on agreed methodology for their closure, around 100 institutions have been closed.[53] However, 86 large institutions remain (with over 100 children each), in which 40% of the children in the residential system are being cared for. At the end of 2004, of the 4.9 million children living in Romania, 82,902 are in the care. This represents 0.75% of the total number of children in Romania.[54]

6.4   Services for prevention of abandonment

Preventing the child from being separated from his/her family by supporting mothers at risk has been a major part of the government's strategy in the region. In the Mother and Baby Centres/Units, the mother is provided with shelter and food, and has the chance to remain with her child for some months. During that period, social work is carried out with her to support her independent life. Day-care centres for children and day-care centres for disabled children have been established to provide rehabilitation facilities, and social and educational opportunities for such children, as well as support to their families. A practice has been established in Bulgaria to open day-care centres within the facilities of some institutions. This is considered as a stage in the transformation of the institution.

Reintegration of children in their biological or extended families is a priority wherever possible. The legislation and practice in the two countries utilise the traditionally existing strong ties within the extended family. Placement with the extended family has been legalised as one of the family type services with a mixed nature: prevention of institutionalisation or reintegration.[55] In Romania, in 2003, the number of children to which this measure was applied was 25,922, almost twice the number of children placed in foster care. In 42% of the cases, children came to the extended family from institutions.[56]

The placement with relatives/extended family is the most efficient and popular service in Bulgaria so far. In 2002-2004, 4,162 children were placed with their relatives mostly as a measure for prevention of abandonment.[57] That the biological tie guarantees the success of the placement is taken for granted could be a problem, however. The relatives who take the child could receive financial support on a monthly basis depending on the age of the child, as well as counselling.

6.5   Foster care

Romania has started to provide foster care as a professional service[58] (maternal assistant), in the frame of both specialised public services and private organisations authorised in the field of child protection.[59] The number of placements considerably increased from 3,058, in 1999, to 15,682, in 2004. Foster placement and placement with the extended family are reported to be the measures that changed the structure of the numbers of children in public care. Research shows that: 66% of the children placed in foster care come from the institutions; 13% come from some other form of family placement (some other foster care or placement with extended family); and 8% are new cases when they are brought to the foster family).

There is a poor take-up of foster care in Bulgaria. Only 29 children are placed with foster parents, to the end of 2004, and the number of trained foster carers is 45.[60] The service is not professional, which is considered as one of the reasons for the bad start,[61] together with the lack of capacity and proper financing.

It appears that family values and social norms also have an impact on the unpopularity of this service in Bulgaria. A recent sociological survey[62] revealed that the attitude towards foster care, in general, is negative. The majority of the participants in the focus groups discussions has declared unwillingness to become foster parents. Their grounds are as follows:

- Economical difficulties – the support of the child is costly, and that is a problem related to the low living standards in general. In addition, it appeared that the social norm of parents being responsible for economic security, even of grown-up children upon whom they can rely in their old age, is still strong. People think that such type of relationships cannot be established with the foster child and this creates resistance to foster care.
- Psychological problems – they are not certain whether they could manage. The foster child is an additional stress factor.
- Emotional problems – the return of the child (if he/she will not be adopted) will create emotional discomfort.
- Lack of skills and fear of taking care for a problematic child. Lack of confidence in social workers to provide the necessary support.

The attitudes listed above highlight the need of value oriented awareness raising campaigns. They should focus on the importance of the child and the role of the family beyond patriarchal dependencies.

Commentators discuss the following problems of foster care, common for both counties: insufficient training for the foster carers; insufficient professional assistance for each case (for the child, for the foster parent(s), for the natural family); lack of clarity about whether this is a temporary service or a long-term one, and what the consequences and measures would be for each option, particularly in view of maintaining contact with biological family.[63]

6.6   Adoption

National adoption was the only traditionally well-developed service in the region before the fall of 'Iron Curtain'. It was regulated within the Family Law as a service for adults rather than for children. The whole system was built on that perception. Before its court stage, the adoption was a private arrangement between the prospective adopters and their lawyers, who were supposed to have good contacts in the child care institutions. Children suitable for adoption were selected by the directors or directly by medical doctors in the hospital to match the aspirations of adopters. Termination of adoption was widely available.

The change in 1989 found the two countries with poorly developed legislation and practice for international adoption. The new regulations had to be shaped under the pressure of an increasing demand for international adoptions and the criticism from international organisations for 'selling children abroad'.[64] Therefore, international adoption, particularly in Romania, became the most controversial issue of child care reform. It is worth noting that the first pieces of child legislation passed in the two countries after 1989 were regulations on international adoption. Romania changed its regulations several times, under the pressure from countries demanding children for adoption, on the one side, and the EU – requiring reforms, on the other. Thousands of children were adopted abroad, which lead to the moratorium on international adoptions in 2001. The new Romanian Law on Adoption enacted in 2005 made the service of international adoption very restrictive.[65]

Bulgaria also changed its legislation on adoption in 2003, following the ratification of the Hague Convention on Protection of Children and International Co-operation in Intercountry Adoption in 2002.[66] The new regulation is based to a large extent on the 'best interests of the child' principle. The pre-adoption phase was regulated to include social work for the assessment of adoptability of the child. Registers were created to encompass the adoptees and prospective adopters. Commissions match the child and the candidates based on the child's interests. In the first year after the change, the number of international adoptions fell and the domestic adoptions increased.[67] It is too early to know whether this is a long-term trend, or whether the reduction is due to the transitional period in which the old system ended and the new system was not fully established. It is therefore important that this is closely monitored.[68]

In conclusion, although positive, the changes in legislation need a continuation. It could be questioned whether the severely restricted system in Romania corresponds to the best interests of the child if the child cannot be properly placed in the country (as provided by the UN Convention on the Rights of the Child). The Bulgarian system ought to apply the 'best interests principle' in both domestic and foreign adoptions. Capacity building is needed.

6.7   Services for child victims of trafficking

The most recent report on trafficking in children in South-eastern Europe[69] states that both countries are countries of origin, a transit country for trafficking in persons and, to a lesser degree, countries of destination. Children have been trafficked for the purposes of sexual exploitation, labour, begging, delinquency and adoption. Some victims have also been exposed to dual forms of exploitation while trafficked. The currents laws in Bulgaria and Romania provide for services for victims, such as shelters for temporary accommodation, and crisis centres to provide shelter, social, medical and household servicing, and psychological assistance, and social and legal counselling, and medical support. A referral system for child victims of trafficking was currently agreed upon among relevant governmental agencies in Bulgaria. Children are entitled to receive all the protection envisioned by the laws for child protection/rights. However, in spite of well designed legislation, the services are developing slowly, the NGOs are still the main provider, and reintegration of victims via education and employment is a problem.

6.8 Services for disabled children

The system includes residential institutions in Bulgaria and Romania for the care of children with severe disabilities and special boarding schools as part of the education system for children with special educational needs.[70] The care of children with disabilities in the two countries is now handled at local authority level, but the central government still has the responsibility for financing and monitoring of the standards of care. Increased benefits were introduced, as well as day care services to support families taking care of disabled children. There is still a social stigma attached to mental disability in both countries and parents will often seek to conceal it by placing the child in an institution.

The education laws changed to incorporate the concept of integrated education for children with special educational needs. However, children with disabilities continue to face obstacles to their participation in the mainstream education system. Persistent problems include: lack of accessible school buildings; widespread failure to develop appropriate, individual educational plans; and an insufficient number of professionally trained resource teachers – all of which are pre-requirements for ensuring inclusive education practices.[71] The resistance coming from parents and other children is also a serious obstacle.

At present, a number of alternatives to residential care for children with disabilities exist: Day Care Centres within some institutions; specialised kindergartens; and a number of Day Care and Rehabilitation Centres run by the municipalities and NGOs.

6.9 Children in conflict with the law

The system dealing with children in conflict with the law is outdated and still repressive.[72] Bulgaria established a separate system for juvenile justice in the early 1960s.[73] The Juvenile Delinquency Act (JDA) of 1958, even after its last revision of 2004, defines the behaviour of children that places them in the juvenile justice system very broadly, thus mixing criminal with other types of behaviour – so called 'antisocial' or deviant. The legal definition stipulates that, "the 'anti-social act' is any conduct which is socially dangerous and against the law or against the moral and good mores." The 'anti-social acts' cover (art. 35 JDA) a wide variety of activities, such as running away from home or school or institution, wandering, prostitution, alcohol and drug addiction (not all would be criminalized in other countries).

The law does not offer services but rather sanctions: the so-called 'correctional measures' that are 'alternatives' to sanctions. The major method to address children is placement in specialised institutions: Socio-Pedagogical Boarding Schools (SPBS);[74] Correctional Boarding Schools (CBS) (both to the Ministry of Science);[75] and Homes for Temporary Placement of Minors and Juveniles set up by the Ministry of the Interior.[76] The common features of these establishments are:

- The 'correction' takes place basically through educational and qualification programmes and activities. The JDA even provides for compulsory

vocational training for delinquent children above 16 who previously dropped out.[77]
  - Despite the clear legal prohibitions, corporal punishments are used.
  - Victims and offenders could be mixed in some institutions.
  - The establishments' main function is to protect the society from these children and not to help the children.

After severe criticism from national and international organisations, such as the Bulgarian Helsinki Committee[78] and Human Rights Watch,[79] some changes of the system were undertaken. However, these changes are still partial, and the system needs a profound modernisation in line with the UN Convention on the Rights of the Child and other UN standards on juvenile justice. It should be linked with the system of child protection, and children should benefit from services for prevention and rehabilitation. The system desperately requires capacity building.

7. Roma Children

Children of Roma origin in the region are over-represented in institutions, international adoption as well as in facilities for delinquent children. Members of ethnic minorities are particularly vulnerable to trafficking for the purposes of sexual exploitation, labour, begging, delinquency and adoption.[80] Roma children face discrimination and are more likely to end up in segregated schools, or in special schools with mentally and physically impaired children, with little education and career prospects.

A consensus exists in the region and internationally that failure to attend school is the main problem among Roma children.[81] Poverty, unemployment of parents, child labour and domestic violence are correlated with low attendance in school. Parents sometimes actively discourage their children from attending school. Children from minority communities face barriers including language proficiency and geographic isolation. Cultural traditions also influence participation in education. Girls from some Roma communities often marry early and do not continue their education. Respecting the traditions of the Roma community, however, requires that they in turn respect the law. A public debate is needed on this issue in the two countries.[82]

Many programmes have been adopted in the two countries to improve access of children to school. Roma social workers and foster families have begun to emerge in some provinces of Romania. Pre-school education was made compulsory and free of charge for all children (in order to lower the language proficiency barrier for minorities) in Bulgaria, and helped teachers start to work at primary school. The CMR/2005 for Bulgaria however is severely critical on this subject. It says, "the strategic documents and programmes on the educational integration of children from the Roma minority have not significantly changed the situation on the ground."

8. Conclusions

8.1 Services: a priority among competing issues?

Due to the deficit of political will for the start of reforms in both countries for almost ten years after the fall of 'Iron Curtain', the pressure from outside has been crucial. It should have come in place of the missing pressure from professional groups and public opinion within the countries.

Romania started successfully to develop social services for children and families to a large extent due to the high political pressure from the EU that generated political commitment of the Government in 1999. That promise was supported by significant technical and financial support from abroad. For the first eight years Romania received 39 million Euros from EU pre-accession funds and 54.5 million USD from donors such as USAID, the British Government, UNICEF, the Netherlands, the Department for International Development (DFID), France, and the World Bank. The Romania Comprehensive Monitoring Report (CMR) 2005 does not identify problems in this area any more.

By contrast, children in institutions have never been high on the agenda of EU accession discussions for Bulgaria. Only in the fourth EU-Bulgaria Accession Partnership (AP) in 2003 specific mention was made of the need to reform children's institutions with a general commitment to, "systematically reduce the number of children in institutional care." It was 1999 when Romania AP included a short-term priority to, "guarantee adequate budgetary provisions for the support of children in care and undertake a full reform of the childcare system." No High Level Group for Bulgarian Children has ever existed. Despite AP commitment, and a series of EC Annual 'Regular Reports on Bulgaria's Progress Towards EU Accession', which noted every year since 2001 the need for reform in child welfare, the October 2004 Regular Report stated that, "there is no comprehensive approach to the closure of institutions on the basis of agreed criteria and to develop and promote alternative forms of care." And the CMR in 2005 concluded that the, "…real progress…remains limited and action should be taken urgently." This confirms that political will in the country needs further strengthening.

8.2 Resources are limited and not well managed

At the level of policies, the two countries seem very well equipped with different action plans and legislation.[83] The problems arise when they have to be implemented in practice. Financing of the policies is a big issue for both countries. Budgetary resources are as a whole very limited, but it is also true that even the available ones are not well managed. Romania is again leading with established de-centralised funding of services and with responsibilities both of the central and local governments to commit funds for children in the budgets.[84] For example, the Romanian National Authority for Child Protection could launch its own national-level development policies through the Programmes of National Interest. There is concern though that, when the money from foreign donors expire, it will be difficult to sustain and replicate the achieved results.[85]

The reform in Bulgaria to a large extent relies on local resources that are also limited. For the first three years, the reforms received technical and financial assistance to the amount of 3.18 million euros from the pre-accession funds and around 20 million USD from donors such as the British Government, UNICEF, Governments of Japan and Switzerland, the Netherlands, and the World Bank.[86] The local resources, however, are still not used properly. As many commentators suggest, including the State Agency for Child Protection (SACP), the material factor for the domination of institutional care in social services is the guaranteed funding for the institutions in contrast to the community-based services.[87] The funding of institutions on the per capita base nurtures the interest for keeping them, while no mechanism exists for the state to provide funding for services at the level of the municipality or at least at the regional level, as experts currently suggest.

8.3 The institutions remain obstructive

The resistance to the change of institutions themselves but also of the politicians linked to their locations is enormous, at least in Bulgaria. The causes are twofold – lack of constructive ideas for alternative employment for their staff (the development of professional foster care is an option) and little support to the staff from the new administration to turn the services.[88]

8.4 Lack of capacity

Another issue of concern is the lack of capacity of: the new specialised administration; the municipalities; and service providers. On one hand, the local structures (CPDs) as a whole are understaffed, at least in Bulgaria. The lack of tradition of local government management and administration is also a problem.[89] The limited expertise of the local institutions results in controversial interpretations of social services. This discords at the local level results in dividing the children into 'municipal' and 'state-owned', which hampers the establishment of a market for social services, and also impairs the links between the children and their families. Problems exist on the level of legally defined mandates and subordination between local structures and the central bodies in Bulgaria.[90] This leads to overlapping institutional roles and responsibilities.

Improvement of professional capacity in the system requires systematic efforts. Social work is a very new profession in the region and the environment for its development is still not supportive. There are no academic traditions,[91] no established schemes for training and supervision of social workers, no professional forums and discussions to build the professional confidence of social workers. Probably some time is also needed for other professions such as lawyers and medical doctors to recognise the profession and to start working together.

9.   Recommendations

Close monitoring and support are needed for the progress of reforms in the two countries.

The development and provision of social services need co-financing from their own resources and encouraging donors' involvement

New social services have to be started in cooperation with the interested parties and in a good coordination at local level.

Urgent de-centralisation of institutions is needed, as well as a unified methodological guidance by the SACP and the CPD in their funding in Bulgaria. It is worth noting that municipalities undertaking the responsibility for the social services does not create a market in itself. Still, in the two countries, there are no solvent clients and financially stable municipalities. At this stage this is a quasi market, which is not able to function without guaranteed (at least partially) state financing. Standards should be developed for financing community services to guarantee the optimal financing of the state-delegated activities in the municipalities.

A clear division of the mandates of central and local administrative bodies is needed regarding managing the policies for children.

And last but not least, strengthening the expert and the coordination capacity of the structures is vital for the success of the reforms. The academic community must take its responsibility and the burden of the reforms. Media should also raise its own capacity in order to send a clear and correct message to the society at large.

Endnotes

1   Tobis, D. (2000), Moving from Residential Institutions to Community-based Social Services in CEE and the former SU, The World Bank, Washington. See also Pringle, K. (1998), Children and Social Welfare in Europe, pp. 109 et seq.

2   In Vrasmas, E., Family and Education, at http://www.crvp.org/book/Series04/IVA-14/introduction.htm.

3   See further Zhekova V. and Kotzeva T., Demographic Policy in Bulgaria until 2004, in Atanasov, A. and Ivanov, M. (eds.) (2005), Demographic Development of Bulgaria, Sofia, pp. 185-190; Belcheva. M. (2004), Social-demographic Researches and Analyses, pp. 24-28; National Analysis of the Situation of Bulgarian Children and Families, Bulgarian National Committee for UNICEF, 1992.

4   Ibid.

5   The pro-natalist policy in Bulgaria was predominantly *incentive-based* through: provision of universal benefits for children starting from 1968 onwards; generous package of paid child birth and maternity leave with secured re-employment; a package of incentives for young women, mainly university students, for early child birth; a wide access to day care for children – nurseries, kindergartens, and in kind support (free summer camps, canteens and medicines); and soft abortion policy. These policy measures aimed to create a family pattern such as early marriage, early child birth (during the time of university graduation of the woman) and early entry to the labour market with already two children born and placed at state day care facilities. Thus, employment was made the main access route to child care and related services. See also: UNICEF (1999), Women in Transition, MONEE Project Regional Monitoring Report No 6, pp. 42-43; National Analyses of the Situation of Bulgarian Children and Families, Bulgarian National Committee for UNICEF, 1992.

6   The ban on abortions was introduced by a Governmental Decree of November 1966 that reflected the intention of politicians to increase the population from 23 to 30 million by the year 2000. See The Situation of Child Abandonment in Romania, UNICEF, MLSSF and MCCI, 2005, at http://www.unicef.org/romania/resources_1551.html and at http://www.childrights.ro/child_care_system.htm.

7   UNICEF (1999), Women in Transition, p. 44.

8   For Bulgaria, it was the Child Protection Act of 2000 that provided the framework for its development.

9   See the National Strategy for Demographic Development of Bulgaria – 2006-2020, which was passed in 2006.

10 See Sociological research of ASSA M, at http://www.assa-m.com/.

11 See Balkanski, P. and Kulanov, D. (1991), Children in the Social Crisis, p. 23. Similarly in Pringle, K. (1998), op. cit., p. 110.

12 It is well known that the child care institutions were placed in remote villages or small towns with dual functions: not only to provide care for children but also to create employment in those settlements for their survival. In Social Assessment of Child Care in Bulgaria, 2000.

13 By the Ministry of Public Health and Social Protection and the National Statistical Institute (1980-1986). In: Belcheva, M. (2004), Social-demographic Researches and Analyses; National Analysis of the Situation of Bulgarian Children and Families, Bulgarian National Committee for UNICEF, 1992.

14 Re-organising the International Adoption and Child Protection System, Independent Group for International Adoption Analysis, Romania, Final Report, March 2002.

15 The initiatives of new administrative authorities for child protection that were created after 2000 in both countries are excluded from this statement.

16 See more in: UNICEF (1999), Women in Transition; Zhekova V., Kotzeva T., op. cit., pp. 185-190; National Analysis of the Situation of Bulgarian Children and Families, Bulgarian National Committee for UNICEF, 1992.

17 See more about the status of child welfare in the region during the transition period in Stubbs, P., Rights and Crisis in Transition: Developing a Children's Agenda in South Eastern Europe, at http://www.seecran.org/resources/publications/doc/rights_in_crisis.PDF.

18 In: Twinning – Road Map for Setting Up a System for Child Welfare in Bulgaria, 2003; Twining Project 'Reform for increasing the child welfare in Republic of Bulgaria', UNICEF, 1997; Children at Risk in Central and Eastern Europe: Perils and Promises, MONEE Project,

Regional Monitoring Report No 4.

[19] Relevant literature pays attention to the difficulties in terminology and in gathering statistics for the analysis of institutional type of care. The definition of 'institution' varies with societies and cultures (Children at Risk in Central and Eastern Europe: Perils and Promises, pp. 63 et seq.). In Western societies, 'institution' is associated with one type of public care provided for children. According to the established model in Central and Eastern Europe – operational long after the fall of the Iron Curtain – the term 'institution' has actually reflected the only type of public care. For the purposes of this analysis, 'institution' will mean 'an establishment of residential type for rearing and upbringing of children where the latter are permanently separated from their family environment'. This definition is applied by the Child Protection Act in Bulgaria, too.

[20] In 1950 Bulgaria experienced a high rate of child mortality, 100 per 1000 births, which was a reason for the network of institutions to start to enlarge. In 1952 there are 13 homes with 800 places. Medical reasons are the main grounds for placement of children, including low weight, premature birth, sickness and disability. See Doichinova, A., A Brief Observation on the Creation and Development of the 'Mother and Baby' Homes in Bulgaria, in Banova, V. (ed) (1999), To Grow Up without Parents, pp. 99-102. Similarly in Child Care System Reform in Romania, UNICEF/NACP, 2004, p. 13. See also the Law 3/1970 abrogated by Emergency Ordinance 26/1997 in Romania.

[21] In Re-organising the International Adoption and Child Protection System, Independent Group for International Adoption Analysis, Romania, Final Report, March 2002.

[22] Bulgaria 2005 Comprehensive Monitoring Report, European Commission, SEC, 2005, 1352.

[23] The regulation of placement of children in Bulgaria makes it possible on various grounds, starting from a health or behavioural problem of the child, or health, social, personal or family problems of the parent. The Regulation for Placement of Children in the 'Homes for Children and Adolescents' of 1967 even views the placement as a privilege for some categories of parents (communist activists). They did not need to refer to specific grounds when applying for placement of their child.

[24] At http://www.un.ro/unicef.html#program.

[25] Reports on the situation of institutions for child care in Bulgaria, State Agency for Child Protection, 2004, at: www.sacp.government.bg.

[26] Therefore, social indicators for placement were introduced alongside medical ones. Placement was provided mostly for children of single mothers (very often underage) and children with disabilities. In Belcheva, Ì., op. cit., pp. 185-198.

[27] UNICEF, UNDP, World Bank (2000), Social Assessment of Child Care in Bulgaria.

[28] The statistics are a little confusing. The sources suggest that at the end of 1980s the number of children in institutions was 100,000. Suddenly, 10 years later, it is reported that this number halved, although the trend reported is to increase. The possible explanation is that this figure does not include the number of institutionalised children with disabilities. In 1990, there were 47,405 children in social care institutions. Since 1998, the number has diminished to 38,597 as a consequence of promoting alternative forms of family type protection. At the end of 1999, the number of children in public placement centres reached 33,350. In Family and Child in Romania, National Institute of Statistics, National Authority for Child Protection, 2001, pp. 32 et seq.

[29] Matschullat, B., Government Strategy Concerning the Protection of the Child in Difficulty – Romania's New Child Welfare Reform Effort: Will It Make a Difference? at http://www.factbook.net/countryreports/ro/Child_protection.htm. See also http://www.un.ro/unicef.html#program.

[30] Poverty per se is not explicitly envisaged as a ground for placement in the regulations. Children are not officially placed because their parents are poor. However, the grounds listed in the regulations suggest social reasons that are linked or could lead to poverty, like sick parents, mentally disabled parents, disabled parents, etc. In: Social Assessment of Child Care in Bulgaria, 2000; Children and Families, Report by Richard Carter on the evaluation of the projects of European Children's Trust implemented in Plovdiv and Haskovo, 2003, p. 10.

[31] See Belcheva, Ì. (2004), op. cit, p. 198.

[32] Gudbrandsson B., Final Report for Working Group on Children at Risk and in Care, Children in Institutions: Prevention and Alternative Care, CDCS, DG III – Social Cohesion, Council

of Europe. See also UNICEF (2000), A Decade of Transition, MONEE Project, Regional Monitoring Report No 8.

[33] Including via the legislation which has enlarged the entry to institutions in Bulgaria even more. See the Regulation on the Mother and Baby Homes, which was passed in 1980 and cancelled the previous regulation of 1964.

[34] See The Continuing Misuse of Children in Institutions in Bulgaria, Save the Children, 2003, at www.savethechildrenbg.org

[35] The Regulation for Placement of Children in the 'Homes for Children and Adolescents' of 1967 even views the placement as a privilege for some categories of parents (communist activists). They did not need to refer to specific grounds when applying for placement of their child.

[36] The Sociological Survey of Alpha Research, 'Public attitudes and factors influencing the development of foster care in Bulgaria' (2005) (not published), revealed that the respondents perceive these children as 'second quality' ('second class') individuals with unacceptable manners and bearing.

[37] European Commission, A Composite Paper: Reports on Progress towards Accession of the Candidate Countries, 1998.

[38] See Project Appraisal Document for Child Welfare Reform Project (2001), Rep No 21012 – Bul.

[39] Governmental Decision of 8 December 2000.

[40] Bulgaria 2005 Comprehensive Monitoring Report, European Commission, SEC, 2005, 1352.

[41] The Romanian Government opened the way for decentralising state child protection services through Emergency Government Ordinance 26/1997. The restructuring of the child protection system was accompanied by the process of administrative decentralisation, through implementation of the Law on Local Public Administration 24/1996 and the Law on Local Public Finance 189/1998.

[42] For example, the methodological norms establishing the share of local community funding for child protection activities were published as late as June 2000, although the institutions had been transferred to the local level two years earlier. As a result, local administrations did not allocate sufficient funds to the Child Protection Departments and an unprecedented financial crisis occurred in 1998. In Stephenson P., Anghelescu C., Causes of Institutionalisation of Children in Romania, FICF, UNICEF, 1997 p. 27.

[43] See Bulgaria: National Report on Social Services, in ILO (2004), Good Practices in Social Services Delivery in South Eastern Europe, pp. 167-203.

[44] See the implementation methodology for Emergency Government Ordinance of 1997, published on 12 March 1999, and the methodology for coordinating activities for the protection and promotion of national-level child rights.

[45] Explanatory memorandum by Mr Hancock to the Council of Europe, 2004.

[46] Article 20 of the Implementing Regulations to the CPA.

[47] Article 42 of the Social Assistance Act in Bulgaria.

[48] As per procedures under the Application Rules of the Social Assistance Act and the Child Protection Act.

[49] State Gazette 68 of 2003.

[50] The community social services for street children, children dropping out from the school system, the work in the Roma neighbourhoods, the work with drug addicted children, the prevention of drug addiction, etc. are not fully developed in the regulatory framework. Systematic financial support by the state for these vulnerable groups of children is lacking.

[51] Assessments of homes for medical/social care of children and homes for children deprived of parental care at www.sacp.government.bg.

[52] EU Commission, Comprehensive Monitoring Report on Bulgaria, October 2005.

[53] Explanatory memorandum by Mr Hancock to the Council of Europe, 2004.

[54] Childcare System Reform in Romania, 2004, UNICEF/NACPA.

[55] Regulation No 181, dated 1 August 2003, and Chapter Five of the Implementing Regulation of the CPA.

[56] Childcare System Reform in Romania, 2004, UNICEF/NACPA, pp. 54 et seq.

[57] Annual Report of the SACP/2004 at: www.sacp.government.bg.

[58] UNICEF (2002), Social Monitor, MONEE Project.

59   See Child Care System Reform in Romania, 2004.
60   Save the Children UK, Alternative Comprehensive Monitoring Report on Bulgaria, 2005, p. 9.
61   See Annual Report of the SACP/2004 at www.sacp.government.bg.
62   A Qualitative Research on Public Attitudes and Factors that Influence the Foster Care, Alpha Research, 2005.
63   Child Care System Reform in Romania, 2004, pp. 60 et seq. Annual report of the SACP/2004 at www.sacp.government.bg.
64   See further: Dickens, J., Inter-country Adoption: Policies and Paradoxes, Information Romania, Issue No 57, February 2001; Overview of the Romanian Child Care System: A Look to the Past, at www.childrights.ro/child_care_system.htm.
65   See further at http://www.jcics.org/JCICSPressInformationRO.pdf.
66   The new Bulgarian legislation on inter country adoption (in English and French), including statistics, at http://www.mjeli.government.bg/structure.aspx?page=17.
67   Save the Children UK, Alternative Comprehensive Monitoring Report on Bulgaria 2005, p. 13.
68   Ibid.
69   Surtees, R. (2005), Second Annual Report on Victims of Trafficking in South Eastern Europe, IOM, Regional Clearing Point, pp. 163-165.
70   Social Assessment of the Childcare in Bulgaria 2000.
71   Save the Children UK.
72   In Bulgaria it is based on the Juvenile Delinquency Act, which was passed in 1958.
73   Children in Conflict with the Law and Juvenile Justice in Bulgaria, UNICEF, 2003.
74   Regulations of the Socio-Pedagogical Boarding Schools of the Ministry of Education and Science (MES) of 1999 and JDA (Art. 28) changed in 2004.
75   Article 13, paras. 1, 13, and Article 21, paras. 1-2, of the JDA, and Articles 61 and 64 of the Penal Code.
76   Under the Law of the Ministry of the Interior (Art. 34), the JDA (Art. 35) and the Regulations issued by the Minister of Interior (1998, amended in 2003).
77   Article 32, para 4.
78   Assessment of the CBS and SPBS, 2003, BHK.
79   Children of Bulgaria: Police Violence and Arbitrary Confinement, Human Rights Watch, 1996.
80   Surtees, R. (2005), op. cit.
81   Explanatory memorandum by Mr Hancock to the Council of Europe, 2004. see also World Bank Poverty Survey, 2000.
82   Ibid.
83   Bulgaria in particular. See www.mlsp.government.bg.
84   Explanatory memorandum by Mr Hancock to the Council of Europe, 2004.
85   Ibid.
86   Project Appraisal Document for Child Welfare Reform Project (2001), Rep No 21012 – Bul.
87   SACP/ASA/Save the Children.
88   Agency for Social Analyses (ASA), Bulgaria – Study on the Provision of Social Services to Children and Families, 2003.
89   Working Group for the Cooperation on Children at Risk, Council of the Baltic Sea States: Priority Paper for the Work of WGCC, 2002, at http://childcentre.baltinfo.org/news/ifid2457.html
90   Twinning Project, and ASA, Bulgaria – Study on the Provision of Social Services to Children and Families.
91   The underdeveloped market for social services is, to a great extent, due to the lack of knowledge of the essence of social services. This is valid for almost all representatives of the interested parties, including at national and local levels. The knowledge gaps, the incomplete and unclear visions of clients, providers and interested parties are due to insufficient information and to the lack of a support system for staff training and qualification. See also ASA's Study, op cit.

Invest Now in Kids or Pay Later for the Last Resort: Misspent Youth, Crime and Kids Behind Bars

Irvin Waller

The offender is responsible for the harm done but we are responsible for the harm done because we do not use our knowledge to prevent crime.

1.   One clear lesson from 100 years of child protection

There is one clear lesson from 100 years of child protection. Investment in services that assist kids at risk from becoming offenders are in the interests of the kids, the potential victims and taxpayers. Yet the UN Convention on the Rights of the Child (CRC) and the follow-up meetings ignore these facts to the serious detriment of all.

The CRC is the most ratified UN instrument. It is cited as the benchmark of all that is good for children in rich and poor countries alike, but Article 37(b) is its Achilles heal that causes 'misspent' youth, crime and kids behind bars. Article 37(b) states that, "the arrest, detention or imprisonment of a child… shall be used only as a measure of last resort and for the shortest appropriate period of time."

But the CRC and the follow-up meetings never defined what was meant as last resort. It assumes somehow that legislators as well as police, lawyers and judges – enlightened or not – will avoid putting kids behind bars. This is a pipe dream that misses the most fundamental understanding of how legislators, law enforcement and criminal justice work.

Let me clarify. Some young people get in conflict with the law – a phrase that papers over a combination of theft, robbery, vandalism, sexual assault, and more with the old status offences of homelessness, street kids and so on. Governments and their voters expect their law enforcement agencies to do something about children in conflict with the law who commit crimes. This is not unreasonable as these kids inflict injury, trauma and financial loss on their victims. Governments and their voters are not so clear on status offences, but it is also not unreasonable to expect some action in relation to kids who are in difficulty and on the street where they also create fear and divert business.

In most countries, the lack of investment in prevention of these problems and services to take care of the children at risk in the community leaves law enforcement and lawyers with no choice but to use incarceration as the measure of last resort. In the USA, 100,000 kids are behind bars on an average day following judicial processes and the rule of law consistent with the CRC. As bad in many developing countries, thousands of kids are behind bars in abdominal conditions of overcrowding, sexual exploitation, and lack of access to schooling and family despite legislation that also makes incarceration the measure of last resort. In fact, their legislation may make matters worse by inadvertently leaving the police to covertly incarcerate – detain is the polite word – and punish many young persons because there is no other solution.

These outrageous situations occur because of the lack of interest of many policy makers and advocates for what goes on behind locked doors, as well as their ignorance of the knowledge and norms that have been established in the last decade. The implications of this undiscovered and overlooked crisis are for better planning of prevention and setting limits on the use of incarceration that allow this situation. The report of the UN Special Rapporteur on children in places of last resort must cry out to governments to use our knowledge and international norms to prevent kids from getting in conflict with the law and so being placed behind bars.

While the intent behind Article 37(b) may have been to limit the use of incarceration, much more specific language and action is needed. Incarceration must be limited to those who are dangerous or have committed particularly serious acts. This cannot be left to the application of vague legal criteria. Standards must be set that limit the use of incarceration for kids to never exceed a fixed number of children – perhaps 10 children per 100,000 of the total population for poor developing countries who may have difficulty finding the funding to prevent, and less than one child per 100,000 for rich countries who misspend their funds for incarceration for kids.

States must invest now in parenting, families, schools and so on to avoid kids growing up to be delinquent or homeless. The costs of procrastination are immense, including the costs to many kids who will lack positive futures, people who will be victims of crime and taxpayers whose funds are misspent.

Defence for Children International has launched a global campaign to stop kids being put behind bars by promoting the preparation and implementation of national action plans that are aimed at reducing the number of children deprived of their liberty. In order to bring about a shift from the use of detention, the National Action Plans should focus on the necessary measures for the full implementation of Articles 37 and 40 of the CRC, and other relevant international instruments. In particular, the National Action Plans should provide for measures to implement the standard that, "the arrest, detention or imprisonment of a child shall be in conformity with the law and shall be used only as a measure of last resort and for the shortest appropriate period of time", including measures to ensure:
  - The adoption of effective measures to prevent juvenile delinquency
  - The use of diversion
  - The use of alternatives to detention, as well as restorative justice

- The collection and analysis of national data on children in conflict with the law
- The improvement of conditions for children deprived of their liberty.

An important step in monitoring the success of the campaign is to improve the collection and analysis of national data on children in conflict with the law, particularly those deprived of their liberty.

The preventive programs must include programs to reduce family violence by helping parents avoid violence in their own relationships and also against their children, which is one of the prime risk factors for kids to leave home for the street as well as kids being in conflict with the law.

2.   Deterrence for at risk kids is a myth – what not to do
Rapid urbanisation, extremes of poverty and affluence, unemployment, ineffective policing and other ills from globalisation are just some of the forces that have made cities less safe from crime. Yes, but the real cause of crime and violence is our insistence that police and lawyers can solve these problems, particularly through deterrence and retributive justice. Crime is too important to be left to police and lawyers. We must invest in preventive strategies that are proven. We must get tough on risk factors that cause crime, not tough on young criminals.

The fallacy in the lawyers' arguments that juvenile justice is the way to stop crime is illustrated with some staggering facts about the use of incarceration in the USA for adults and so the failure of the deterrence model to deter. Between 1975 and 2005, the US increased the number of people incarcerated by a factor of more than three – going from 200 per 100,000 to 700 per 100,000 persons incarcerated on an average day. There are now two million people incarcerated in the US today. That is one in four of all people incarcerated across the globe. If deterrence and retributive justice worked, then the numbers incarcerated should have gone down but they did not – the reverse happened.

Nevertheless, scientific analyses of the impact of incarceration on the crime rates suggests that about 30% of the reduction of crime in the 1990s came from incapacitating many young adults by incarcerating them. But the $100 billion needed to achieve this extra-ordinary rate of incarceration could have been used much more effectively to prevent crime than for the 300,000 extra police officers and the additional one and a half million incarcerated on an average day, which is extravagantly expensive to taxpayers, wasteful of the lives of the young men and costly to the many persons who suffer as victims before the offenders are caught.

Think what they could have done with $100 billion and more each year in terms of preventing violence at home, helping kids to complete school, training them for the job market, mentoring of difficult teenagers, reducing bullying, teaching conflict resolution skills and so on. My recent book – *Less Law, More Order* – gives more details of how this $100 billion could have been spent on prevention while avoiding incarcerating kids and saving taxes. I will give you some of the headlines.

The taxpayers deserve to have their money used to reduce crime effectively – not misspent on increases in these big buck cops, courts and corrections whose cost effectiveness is questionable. Of course, behind the statistics is a continuously growing industry promoting the importance of corrections in the US but also across the world. They even influence political parties. If you look at financial contributions to the political campaigns in California, you will see not only the prison construction industry, but also the prison unions, who are a much bigger contributor than even the National Rifle Association. So the deterrence and incapacitation folk are a major challenge to getting our children treated decently, and making our homes, streets and schoolyards safer and more caring.

The world press has given us the impression that Mayor Giuliani decimated violence in New York City by making the police more accountable, recruiting a police commissioner who put CompStat in place and by using a theory called 'Broken Windows'. It is possible that each of these made some contribution to crime rates that had already plummeted by 40% before Mr. Giuliani was even elected.

However, the evaluations of Giuliani's methods suggest that it may not have caused more than 5% of the reduction in crime rates that were already plummeting in New York City as in most cities in the USA for other reasons. Andrew Karmen has done a detailed analysis of all the possible explanations (Karmen, 2001). His conclusions show many factors contributing. Indeed, his strongest conclusion is that the increases in the number of youth going onto college were probably the strongest explanation.

But it is George Kelling who provides the most damning assessment of Giuliani's hyperbole. Kelling, the co-author of the Broken Windows article that speculated about what would happen by cleaning up broken windows, was also an advisor and collaborator with the Giuliani efforts to reduce crime. His analysis of the contribution of broken windows was actually an analysis of how misdemeanour arrests contributed to the decrease in crime. His conclusion was that 5% of the reductions were due to the increased misdemeanour arrests. So let us get some perspective and some sanity into the discussion of the Giuliani effect and particularly the potential for tough on kids to prevent victimisation.

The end result of these increases in incarceration and policing and also lawyers is that the average American tax payer has to pay proportionately more for cops, courts and corrections. In fact, they pay twice what a Canadian tax payer pays and British taxpayer puts out. The US, British and Canadian rates were nearly equivalent 30 years ago. Ironically, it is Americans who are most anti-government. Do you want to use your taxes to build prisons for your young men instead of help them complete school and find jobs? Do you want to take money from schooling and job creation for young persons to pay for more police?

3. Prestigious Commissions conclude on what works

Now not all the US money on crime and criminal justice was being 'misspent' on more police, prisoners and judges. The Americans have been very generous because they have done so much wonderful research for us all to use on evaluations of projects to prevent criminal violence. It is generous of the Americans because it is available to us here, in Canada or in developing countries but they themselves make little use it for any of their policies to reduce crime.

At the level of the World Health Organization and governments in Western Europe and North America, there are more than a dozen prestigious commissions, who have reviewed all this research and then developed conclusions and often actionable recommendations.

Those commissions show that standard North American or European ways of using cops, courts and corrections are not succeeding other than very partially in the USA through the exaggerated use of incarceration (see particularly: Audit Commission, 1996; National Research Council (US), 2004; Waller, 2006).

Yet those commissions are clear on what does work:
- Be tough on risk factors that cause crime
- Use what has been proven to work
- Get police agencies to solve problems strategically
- Plan ways to lower rates of crime involving schools, police services, public health and so on.

For me these prestigious commissions are unanimous in saying that governments must shift from reactive and expensive law enforcement to being smarter at mobilising different social and economic programs to tackle the risk factors. They must shift from using Rambo tactics to react to crime and instead use knowledge and intelligence to drain the swamp. Avoid billions of dollars in loss, harm and trauma to victims and communities and ensure that taxes are used to invest in youth and communities.

Prestigious commission after prestigious commission have reviewed all the evaluations of what works and what does not. So the work is done and easily accessible. Just look at the list – organisations that have earned trust on other issues: The World Health Organization, the US Surgeon General, the British Audit Commission, the International Centre for Prevention of Crime, the US National Research Council, the National Institute of Justice for the US Congress, the British Inspectorate of Police and so on.

**Prestigeous agencies agree clear
evidence on what reduces crime**
- United Nations
  - Guidelines on Crime Prevention, (2002)
    - International Centre for Prevention of Crime, 1997/1999
  - World Health Organization, (2002)
- Blue Ribbon Agencies
  - Audit Commission, 1996 (UK)
  - Home Office and Treasury, 1997 (UK)
  - British Inspectorate of Police, 1998/2001 (UK)
  - Report to US Congress, 1997 (USA)
  - Surgeon General, 2001 (USA)

---

wallerirvin@msn.com   10

These commissions have identified which programs have worked to reduce crime and which have not, which are promising and even how these programs should be delivered by cities to achieve large reductions in crime and victimisation. In sum, they agree that tackling the multiple causes of crime requires multiple solutions – most of which invest in youth rather than outlaw them, keep teenagers in their families and communities rather than behind bars, and make policing smarter not bigger.

Let me emphasise that many of the citizen crime prevention programs exported willy-nilly from the USA have also been shown to waste taxpayers money and volunteers' time as they do not prevent crime. The most comprehensive study ever of crime prevention – done for no less a body than the US Congress – shows that some of the most popular programs, including boot camps, midnight basketball, neighbourhood watches and drug education classes in schools, have little impact. That is, Boot Camps, DARE, Neighborhood Watch and Scared Straight do not work to reduce crime. Another example is community policing – a popular phrase to embellish policing – but too often refers to public relations programs on the margins of police agencies rather than the strategies known as problem oriented and – often overlooked by researchers – first in aid to victims that reduce crime and treat victims fairly (Sherman et al., 2003).

4. Being smart about reducing offending?

From the prestigious commissions, we know a lot about how you can intervene on some of the social causes: inconsistent parenting, school abandonment, situational determinants and weak policing tactics. We also know that tackling the risk factors that cause crime and violence is more cost effective than current policing and judicial remedies, particularly prison practices.

This means that there should be a massive shift of resources in affluent countries from those areas into what I am going to call the secondary pre-crime prevention area. In developing countries, there should be proportionately a high percentage shift of their resources. The impressive thing about social prevention (for example keeping children in school, anti-bullying programmes, mentoring and so on) is that they not only reduce violence, but they also give other benefits. Children grow up to be better citizens. Some go on to be good parents, citizens and pay taxes.

Prestigious agencies confirm outcomes from tackling 'at risk' situations
- Reacting to crime, neighbourhood watch, DARE, and unfocused community policing do not reduce crime
- tackling particular social causes (inconsistent parenting, school abandonment, and so on) reduces offending
- tackling particular situational determinants (lack of surveillance, easy of turning into cash and so on) reduces victimization
- police agencies using strategy and partnerships to solve problems (hguns, gangs, GIS, compstat) reduce crime
- tackling causes is significantly more cost effective than current policing, judicial and particularly prison practices
- social prevention projects lead to additional benefits (school completion, jobs, paid taxes and so on)

For instance, if you look at the Incentives to Complete School Programme, you basically see a 62% reduction in involvement in crime. What is important here is not so much the specifics, but how large those percentage decreases are. Through prevention you can get huge reductions in all types of crime including violence. Of course this has to be used to get funding for those programmes. Dropping out of school is related to persistent offending, and working in partnership on this issue seems to be in the legislation here. It works but you have to make it actually happen.

Tackling causes of persistent youth offending (5% responsible for 55%) reduces crime by 50% or more

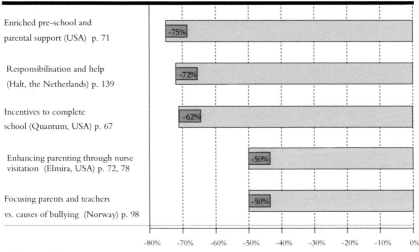

Enriched pre-school and parental support (USA) p. 71 — -75%

Responsibilisation and help (Halt, the Netherlands) p. 139 — -72%

Incentives to complete school (Quantum, USA) p. 67 — -62%

Enhancing parenting through nurse visitation (Elmira, USA) p. 72, 78 — -50%

Focusing parents and teachers vs. causes of bullying (Norway) p. 98 — -50%

wallerirvin@msn.com   17

Yes, we need to use what is proven where it is relevant to the causes of violence but we also need to pursue programs that are tailor-made to tackling those causes. Peer mediation maybe one of the most important activities to change the youth view that they can achieve things through violence. It is also a way of getting back to the issue of violence in the home. To explain the potential of peer mediation, I draw a parallel with smoking. Thirty years ago a child was told that smoking was bad, so he came back and he took the cigarette out of his mother's mouth. His mother said, "No, it's *my* business, you are too young to know about it", and she went on smoking, but eventually she started to change her views. Well it is exactly the same on violence. If you can get children to go home and say to Daddy, "It is not a good idea to beat up Mommy", and Daddy will say, "It's none of your business kid." But over time he will begin to think. This is maybe unproven, but it is something in which there has to be a much bigger investment.

The cost of those proven programmes above is way less than the cost of incarceration. If you look at California data, you can see what would be needed if you were going to reduce crime by 10%. If you invested in keeping children in school to achieve this crime reduction, the increase in taxes per family is about $35 US. It is not a lot. If you wanted to do it through incarceration, then it would cost over $200 US in extra taxes. The difference between the two is considerable. You basically have to pay about seven times as much to achieve crime reduction through incarceration as you do through the sorts of programmes that WHO has talked about. My title was, *An ounce of prevention is worth a pound of deterrence*. This is not actually true. An ounce is only worth about half a pound, but who cares. Even if it were only three times, it is a very convincing argument.

Reducing crime through prisons costs 7 times targeting youth at risk to complete school

Increases in taxes to achieve 10% reduction in crime (ICPC, 1999a)

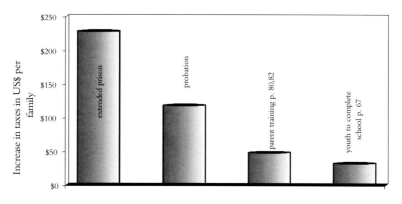

walderirvin@msn.com   8

I want to just give you a quick overview of what we know about policing. What we know is that large increases in policing like we have seen in the US or even England and Wales do not make a lot of difference to crime levels. Of course it also takes money away from what would work. We know that the way that modern – standard – policing, as it is organised in England and Wales or for that matter in Canada or the US or Australia, does not work. Devoting 40 or 50% or your resources to responding to calls – most of which are not urgent – to a national emergency number does not work. In fact, victims are increasingly not going to the police. Generally clearance rates are dropping.

So what has worked in policing? Let us look at an example from Boston. The interesting thing about this example is that it involves a joint police and university team. It involved the School of Public Administration of Harvard University and the Police Chief. Basically, they looked together at what were the causes of the sudden rise in youth homicide in Boston, and then they found a way of addressing those causes. All of this was evaluated. I want to repeat that evaluation is important. It is clear that this program reduced the number of youth homicides.

Problem Solving Policing – examples
- "Hot Spot" Analysis and Problem-solving (Edmonton, Canada)
  - use police crime data to identify local challenges and "hot spots"
  - engage high-risk neighbourhood in planning and i mplementing
  - Edmonton Police: reduces crime 41%, violence 31% over 4 years
- Strategic Approaches to Community Safety (Boston + SACSI)
  - joint police and university teams to analyse causes of violence
  - NB success of Operation Cease-Fire in Boston for youth homicides
  - Replications across USA and now piloted in Brazil
- Partnership between police and business (e.g., Netherlands)
  - reduce commercial robbery by improving situational prevention measures (limit access to cash, improve surveillance, etc.)
  - create a tracking system for robbery offenders
  - support community youth employment and educational initiatives
  - 26% drop in commercial robberies and doubled solved robberies
- www.popcenter.org
  - Internet site that gives many examples

There are some things that do work. For things like targeting traffic violations, everyone in this room knows that deterrence works to keep us below the speed limit or stopping at stop signs. However, this is because as employed, middle class people, we have something to lose. The same is true for intra-familial violence, where research proves that middle class men can be deterred by arrest but unemployed men are not.

What is overlooked is repeat victimisation. Often it is the same woman being battered every Friday night, and the same child abused. Responding one at a time to national emergency number calls loses this important information. Focusing on repeat victimisation therefore becomes very important. Crime mapping with police organised to solve problems through law enforcement or partnership with community agencies become critical to success.

5.   Investing in community services, avoiding misspent youth
There are other important ways to reduce youth offending. England and Wales is particularly interesting because of the careful and logical way it has addressed youth crime. In 1996, its Audit Commission – a national body that investigates whether taxpayers are getting value for money – looked at whether the current response to youth crime was money well spent. Its conclusion was no. Its conclusion was that using the police to react after the crime and paying for courts and corrections was misspending taxes because some of this money could have been invested in pre-crime prevention to reduce youth offending. Their report is poignantly entitled, *Misspent Youth – a play on misspending the lives of the youth and misspending taxes on youth* (Audit Commission, 1996).

If you wait until a young person attacks a victim, then you wait to see if the victims reports it, then you wait until the police decide whether they are going to prosecute, then you have already wasted huge amounts of resources. It is important to hold children accountable and it probably *is* up to a point. If your interest is in reducing crime, however, the Audit Commission makes it very clear that you should be spending your money *before* the children get involved in those levels of violence – on pre-crime prevention.

Pre-crime prevention, speedier justice, less offending

paradigm shift from only juvenile justice
- Example - Youth Justice Board, England and Wales
- Misspent Youth (1996)
  - British Audit Commission review of programs to tackle youth offending
  - Expenditures on policing, courts and prisons are misspending (on) youth.
- Youth Justice Board created by Crime and Disorder Act (1998) to prevent youth offending and improve justice for youth
  - permanent public body, independent of police, courts and corrections
  - power to persuade schools, housing, social services and police to collaborate
  - committed to use evidence on effective practice
  - business plan to achieve specific targets such as a 10% reduction in youth offending.

wallerirvin@msn.com   7

In 1998, just a year after Blair became Prime Minister, they passed the Crime and Disorder Act. This was not another piece of law introduced by lawyers to increase the work for lawyers. It was not another piece of legislation to increase penalties and punishment in the hope of incarcerating more young men for longer. It had several well-thought sections designed to reduce crime and disorder. One of these was the creation of an agency to prevent youth crime and reform the youth justice system – the Youth Justice Board (YJB). The most important thing about the YJB is that it was set up separate from the Home Office. Consequently, it did not get caught in the territorial wars between the police, corrections and research, which have neutralised so many of the efforts to drain the swamp. It was also given a mandate to actually use evidence in prevention. Because it controlled a lot of funding, it was able to implement and within a relatively short periods of time demonstrate success with a number of its initiatives.

The one of most interest here is called the youth inclusion program. They took a project that had been demonstrated scientifically to have reduced crime and then implemented it in 70 of the most deprived areas across England and Wales. The project is relatively simple. It focuses on the 50 worst kids in each project site. The kids are identified by police, schools and so on. The project then outreaches to the youth to invite them to come to a youth centre where there are sports facilities, assistance with homework, computers and adult mentors. The project is relatively inexpensive but does require salaries for the professionals working there and some equipment in the youth centre. They evaluated the results scientifically by comparing the rate of arrests before and during the program. This showed a 60% reduction. This is not just the 60% reductions in arrest rates that have been achieved by several US proven prevention projects but this was achieved across 70 sites.

Crime Concern meets challenge from Youth Justice Board to reduce youth arrests by 65% and general crime by 16%
   - Locates 50 most at risk youth aged 13-16 in each of 70 of the most difficult neighborhoods
   - 10 hours a week focused on sports, training in information technology, mentoring, help with literacy and numeracy, and coping with violence, drugs, gangs and personal health
   - cost about $5,000 per place per year

	Targets	Outcome
-	60% reduction in youth arrests	65%
-	30% general reduction in crime	16%
-	30% reduction in youth removed from schools.	30%

   - The Youth Justice Board used the results from the evaluation to expand the program to 140 neighborhoods and start an equivalent program with youth aged 8-13.

---

wallerirvin@msn.com   25

The Youth Justice Board was set up separate from the Home Office. It is not part of a Health or any other Ministry. It has an independent board bringing together experts from key sectors such as policing, law, social services, prison after-care, minority groups and so on. Because of its independence, its mandate and its requirement for transparency, it is inspiring for others who want to reduce crime and violence.

6.   Comprehensive planning by cities will reduce risk factors that cause crime

If we are going to make a difference to levels of violence, then we have to find a way of mobilising the agencies that can affect those causes and of getting them to focus on them. The actual, specific solutions are not so important. This diagram is the secret to successful prevention.

252

Bonnemaison – Crime will be solved through wise partnerships of schools, local government and policing to tackle multiple causes

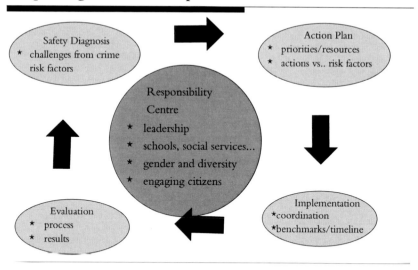

wallerirvin@msn.com   15

We know much about what causes young persons to grow up as persistent offenders from the longitudinal studies. Crime, as we are all aware, is highly concentrated. The offenders are concentrated, the victims are concentrated, and the places where they come together (in so called hotspots) are concentrated (ICPC, 1999a; Waller, 2006).

So if we are going to make a difference to violence then we have to be much more strategic to focus on those concentrations, and that is a money issue. You cannot just wait until crime occurs and have a police officer respond to a national emergency number in his fancy car with his fancy computer. We just cannot afford to go on doing it, and it does not reduce crime anyhow. We have to start seeing where we can strategically intervene to use our resources better.

The best example of this is the City of Bogotá. Two successive mayors decided to reduce violence in the city where it had reached dramatic proportions. As I mentioned, they established an observatory – a secretariat to analyse the causes of violent crime and propose solutions – better investments. Within ten years the rates of violence were cut in half. You are going to ask what did they do and I told you. Yes, they did not pass harsher criminal penalties and they did not just add more police, consult with Mr. Giuliani or introduce Compstat. The most important ingredient to their success was they organised to solve the problem at its roots.

Alcance realizado de la reducción del crimen – La comparación de tasas de homicidio de 1992-2001 en Bogotá y Colombia

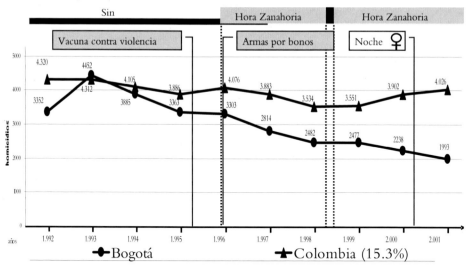

Restricción al porte de armas de fuego

We have seen that reaching for the Giuliani solution will give states little relief. Yet, there are solutions for which there is more hope. Governments should instead reach for the Warner solution. Warner was one of the architects of the Youth Justice Board in England and Wales. As its first chairperson, he implemented the Youth Inclusion Program (YIP) that demonstrated large reductions in youth crime through investment in pre-crime prevention. The YIP is basically a community centre for youth, where those most in need of care and supervision could be invited to enjoy positive attention from mentors, programs to help get homework done and so on (Jones, 2005; Waller, 2006; Waller et al., 2006).

If states are facing violence, then they should reach for the Mockus solution that used pre-crime prevention to drive murder rates down in Bogotá – maybe as much as 50%. More importantly, governments should reach to proven solutions, proven strategies and tackling the problems that lead to crime. If governments are serious about making streets, schools and homes safer than it is today in a sustainable way, then it is time for them to use facts and international standards not media headlines.

Less crime will be achieved affordably and in a sustainable manner through the leadership of local government, not policing, lawyers, judges or prisons. The mayor must look to his top officials, his planners, his epidemiologists, not just his police chief. The mayor must look to proven solutions not seductive political hype and media myths. He must establish the plan on how to be tough on causes instead of ratcheting up expenditures on policing alone. He must mobilise schools, youth services, urban planning and also police in a planning process that focuses separate and joint programs to tackle the causes of crime in the families, schools and neighbourhoods most at risk. That means a 'crime prevention investment office' that diagnoses the problems and proposes solutions. For Mockus in Bogotá, it was called an observatory, but it worked on actionable solutions reporting to the Mayor to analyse amenable causes, establish priorities on limited budgets, implement strategic solutions and monitor the results.

In the 1998 Crime and Disorder Act, the Blair government first required every Municipal Authority or Local Government Authority to develop a crime prevention plan through a committee called the community safety partnership. This requires a partnership of leaders of local government, police, health and other sectors to work together to analyse the extent and the causes of the crime problems in the city. They then develop a plan as to how they will separately and jointly work to tackle the causes of those crime problems within their budget priorities. You can read these plans on the Internet for cities such as Birmingham, Liverpool and Manchester. There are a lot of improvements that need to be made under the Crime and Disorder Act in 1998 to bring these partnerships in line with UN standards, but these programs are a very practical and logical way to address crime reduction – way ahead of spending more for more standard police courts and corrections.

More and more cities from Santiago in Chile to Birmingham in England – not just CompStat in New York City – have crime mapping which shows where crimes occur geographically. They can also be used to show how the rates of offending and victimisation are related to other factors such as poverty, broken families, lack of sports facilities and so on. In England, they are often available to community safety partnerships where local government, police leadership and others come together to plan out crime. They are also available to local residents over the Internet. These show not only crime maps but social deprivation maps. The fact that the local group do not really seem to use these yet in the best way is, in my view, irrelevant. Their potential for mobilising schools, housing, social services, police and others around the causes of crime across cities are critical for future efforts to reduce crime sustainably and cost effectively.

7.   Support and justice for victims of crime

I want to say something, briefly, about the victim issue because it is always overlooked. Basically, the system of justice that you have (and the one that I have in my country) does not do a whole lot for victims. So it is very good to see when people from the World Health Organization talk about placing an emphasis on victims. Even if you *do* drain the swamp, you do need to have some sort of response for victims. It is actually very much in the interest of the cops, courts, and corrections industry to start doing a lot more for victims. Relatively few victims report violent crime. Only about 45% of the average crime victims in European or North American countries go to the police. Once you look at sexual assault or wife battering that proportion drops even more. So please be cautious about the police statistics. We have been using police statistics as if they are very reliable. In the case of homicide they probably are, but most of them are very unreliable. It is very important when you come up with indicators that you use one that is independent. It is also important for the people in that industry to start doing more for victims.

Helping victims protect themselves is probably the one thing I would like to see the police do to reduce the relatively very high rates violence against women and children. I would like to see some sort of all female police stations. The developing countries do this. I have just come back from Tamil Nadu where the chief minister is a woman. There were 200 all female police stations there. They have a murder rate more or less the same as Canada. This sort of action encourages more women to come forward. People overlook how few victims go to the police about their victimisation. Therefore if you can increase the number of women going to the police you may see some impact, particularly if this results in the man going to a battering programme that is known to work.

Due to the yeoman work of the International Bureau of Children's Rights, the UN has recently endorsed the UN Guidelines on Basic Principles of Justice for Child Victims and Witnesses. These clarify in positive terms what practitioners, lawyers and experts should do to respect the needs of children. For their implementation, governments need to adapt them into national legislation and train professionals in their use.

8.   Delivering results

In England and Wales, they have some agencies engaged in skill development, which is essential to successful crime prevention. Just as lawyers need to go to law school and get certified according to agreed standards and police officers need to be trained and certified, so prevention managers and practitioners need the same. At this point, universities are beginning to offer programs so that graduate students can learn about prevention but we still need to develop standards. In the meantime, the work of the internationally renowned Crime Concern is critical in order to make progress. It is important when you come up with a violence prevention strategy for this country that there is a large investment in training and professional development. It is not easy to go from a basically reactive system of cops, courts and corrections to one where you are focusing on prevention, bringing different agencies together, using data comprehensively. And so, there has to be a very large investment in skill development and training to go along with that.

I must also emphasise the importance of having different sources of data, not just health and police data but also survey data. In many countries you have reliable data on crime collected independent of the police. In England and Wales, the British Crime Survey is a regular and large scale survey of 60,000 households to measure victimisation, reporting to police and attitudes to crime prevention and sentencing. It is conducted every second year and the respondents are asked if they have been victim of certain types of crime. They are asked if they reported this to the police, which more than 50% have not. It talks about attitudes to prevention and sentencing among other things. It is a very sophisticated survey. The US has a bigger one but the UK has a better one. These surveys provide a lot of information that could be very useful in trying to establish where you should be focusing to prevent violence and also to evaluate programs to prevent violence.

In many countries, you have longitudinal surveys which have been very much used by the World Health Organization and the International Centre for Prevention of Crime to develop and assess what is effective. These give information on the life experiences that occur before young persons become involved in frequent offending. These have identified several critical life experiences which include inconsistent and uncaring parenting, troublesome behaviour in primary school and dropping out of school as teenagers. These negative life experiences statistically predispose young persons to being involved in more and more serious offending.

9.   Actionable recommendations

So here are my actionable recommendations for the next 100 years for governments:

- Establish an independent national board to shift the focus from reaction by cops and corrections to pre-crime prevention using a fixed percentage of 5% of expenditures on cops and corrections.
- Require every local government to bring together the leadership of schools, housing, social services, police, youth and so on to identify and tackle the risk factors that cause youth violence.
- Invest in programs in the community for kids at risk, such as youth clubs, mentoring, assistance to complete school and job training.
- Provide all youth with courses to use conflict resolution and avoid destructive decisions while providing services for child victims and witnesses as required by international standards.
- Promote programs to help young persons avoid the excessive and illicit use of alcohol and other substances.
- Ban handguns and wanton media violence.
- Prevent child abuse by investing in parent training and support, respite and childcare, public health care nurse visitations, etc.

Further information

Audit Commission (1996). *Misspent Youth.* London.

Defence for Children International (2003). *Kids behind Bars: A Study of Children in Conflict with the Law: Towards Investing in Prevention, Stopping Incarceration and Meeting International Standards.* Amsterdam.

Goldblatt, P. & C. Lewis (1998). *Reducing Offending: An Assessment of Research Evidence.* London: Home Office.

HM Inspectorate of Constabulary (1998). *Beating crime.* London: Home Office.

Jones, Lauren (2005). *Can Ontario Deliver Effective Crime Prevention based on the Youth Inclusion Programme?* Ottawa: University of Ottawa. MCA Research Paper.

Karmen, Andrew (2001). *New York Murder Mystery: The true story behind the crime crash of the 1990s.* New York: New York University Press.

International Centre for Prevention of Crime (1999a). *1 Crime Prevention Digest II.* Directed by Irvin Waller. Written by Sansfaçon, Daniel, and Welsh, Brandon. Montreal.

International Centre for Prevention of Crime (1999b). *100 crime prevention programs to inspire action across the world.* Directed by Irvin Waller. Written by Gauthier, Lily-Ann, David Hicks et al. Montreal.

National Research Council (US) (2004). *Fairness and Effectiveness in Policing: The Evidence.* Washington, DC: The National Academies Press.

National Research Council (US) (2001). *Juvenile crime, juvenile justice.* Washington, DC: National Academy Press.

Newman, Graeme ed. (1999). *Global Report on Crime and Justice.* New York: Oxford University Press.

Sherman, Lawrence, David Farrington, Brandon Welsh, Doris MacKenzie (2002). *Evidence Based Crime Prevention.* New York: Routledge.

US Surgeon General (2001). *Juvenile Violence: A Report of the Surgeon General.* Washington, D.C.

United Nations (2005). *Guidelines on Justice for Child Victims and Witnesses.* New York.

Waller, Irvin (2006). *Less Law, More Order: Truth and Sense to Prevent Crime.* Westport: Praeger Imprint.

Waller, Irvin, Mel Bania, Mary-Anne Kirvan, Lucie Léonard (2006). *Handbook on Implementation of UN Guidelines for the Prevention of Crime.* Ottawa: manuscript in preparation for National Crime Prevention Centre.

Waller, Irvin (2004). *Crime Victims: Doing Justice to Their Support and Protection.* Helsinki: European Institute for Crime Prevention and Control affiliated with the United Nations.

Waller, Irvin, Daniel Sansfaçon (2000). *Investing Wisely in Prevention: International Experiences.* Washington, D.C.: US Department of Justice, Bureau of Justice Assistance. Monograph, Crime Prevention Series #1.

World Health Organization (2002). *World Report on Violence and Health.* Washington, D.C.

Restorative Justice in Reaction to Youth Offending

Added Value in the
Dutch Pedagogical Criminal Youth Law

Annemieke Wolthuis

1.   Introduction

In the Netherlands interest in restorative justice practices in relation to juvenile offending has grown in the last years. Experiments and projects have been set up with forms of Victim Offender Mediation and Family Group Conferences. They have taken place in the form of experiments. By the end of 2006 the Minister of Justice will decide on whether or not to go on with these projects and to integrate them in the existing reactions on crime. In this article an overview is given of restorative elements in the Dutch juvenile justice system, followed by some suggestions on what more can be done with restorative justice in reaction to juvenile behaviour. In relation to experiences with more severe cases, experiences in Belgium are described.

In the Netherlands methods with restorative justice for juvenile offenders or youngsters in conflict situations have been developed mainly since the 1990s. This went along with the growing victim protection movement. In many Dutch cities experiments and projects have been set up with forms of Victim Offender Mediation (VOM) and Family Group Conferences (FGCs), often based on real justice methods. These methods are currently still taking place in the form of experiments. Different initiatives occur by different organisations in different municipalities with different funding sources. No structural implementation and laws have been passed.

This article describes the main restorative justice developments for juveniles in the Netherlands. First a short introduction is given about the relevant international standards pleading for a separate and pedagogical juvenile justice system, including restorative justice. Then the main aspects of the Dutch juvenile justice system are explained, with special emphasis on alternative sanctions such as HALT. Emphasis is given on how restorative justice practices fit within international juvenile justice standards and in the Dutch juvenile justice system. In relation to Family Group Conferences concerning more severe cases, a description is given of the experiences of our Belgium neighbours. The article concludes with some ideas about how the Dutch practices could and should be strengthened.

2. Pedagogical dimension of juvenile justice

The UN Convention on the Rights of the Child (CRC) offers in articles 37 and 40 protection for the rights of juvenile delinquents, and provides obligations for the state to carry out a good administration of juvenile justice by a separate and pedagogical system. Article 37 CRC gives rules about punishment and for youth in detention. Article 40 CRC deals with the administration of juvenile justice and gives young offenders protection. In addition, there is a set of three documents that provide a more complete set of rules for juvenile justice: The *Beijing Rules* (1985) on the administration of Juvenile Justice; the *Havana Rules* from 1990 giving protection to youngsters in detention; and the *Riyadh Guidelines* (1990) focusing on prevention in a broad sense.[1] The Committee on the Rights of the Child considers these resolutions together with the CRC as the normative set for juvenile justice. The rules ask for a child friendly system.[2]

In light of the CRC states are obliged to set up a system in which the following principles should prevail:
- the best interests of the child should be the paramount consideration
- the system should be focused on integration and socialisation
- detention should be a measure of last resort
- diversion should be stimulated, which is where restorative justice comes in
- extra protection such as specialised professionals working with children (youth judges and public officers, but also within the police and the closed facilities).

At the same time it is important to invest in prevention. Detaining young people should really be a measure of last resort. In the closed facilities a pedagogical climate is important, focused on learning from mistakes and towards reintegration in society.[3]

3. Restorative justice for juveniles

Restorative justice is seen as a method in which a strong emphasis is put on the responsibility of citizens. Restorative practices are often inspired by ancient methods used by indigenous peoples on how to deal with conflicts within their group.[4] However, also in Europe, similar practices were active in the past.

In restorative justice the harm done towards a victim by a criminal offence is the central focus. The offender is invited to take responsibility for the harm that he has created. Restorative practices can take many different forms, but are often led by an independent third party, the mediator/coordinator. Examples are forms of Victim Offender Mediation and Family Group Conferences, where in addition to the offender and the victim also people from both social networks are taking part in the conference.[5]

Restorative justice practices can be used before, during or after a criminal process. Voluntariness is in most systems a central item. Also other principles such as proportionality and subsidiarity need to be taken into account. In most cases the result, an apology, a form of restoration or community care, is written down in an agreement or a contract. If the agreement is not carried out, another way of dealing with the case will be followed, which is in most cases a penal process. In principle, all cases are suitable for mediation, even severe violence or abuse cases. Many evaluations show positive views from offenders as well as victims who have taken part in restorative justice sessions. For youngsters it is often a very confronting method which gives an extra motivation not to re-offend.[6]

4.   The Dutch juvenile justice system

Special provisions relating to the treatment of juveniles under criminal law have been inserted into the Dutch code of criminal law and the code of criminal procedure. A start was made already in 1905, which results today in the celebration of 100 years of child protection laws. The original notion behind special provisions for juveniles under criminal law is the idea that any related punishment must be reformatory in nature. The notion of education and reform is pivotal. In 1995, a new amendment to juvenile criminal law was passed in the Netherlands. On one hand, the amendment reinforced the legal basis for alternative penalties which, in practice, had operated since the 1980s until then. At the same time, provisions relating to juvenile criminal law were also tightened up: the maximum period of imprisonment for juvenile delinquents was raised from one to two years and restrictions bearing the application of general criminal law to juvenile were eased.

Substantive law governing juvenile crime must be applied in cases where a juvenile is between 12 and 18 years of age at the time when the crime was committed. Children below 12 are deemed to be below the age of criminal responsibility. If any action is taken under civil law, such as the appointment of a legal guardian, then this is permitted only on condition that it will benefit the juvenile. Under certain conditions juveniles between 16 and 18 years of age may also be subject to the general provisions of the criminal code. This depends on the personality of the offender, the circumstances surrounding the case and the gravity of the offence. According to the former provisions of juvenile criminal law, all of these conditions had to apply. However, since 1995, simply the gravity of the offence can suffice for the general provisions of the criminal code to be applied. Nonetheless, the resultant legal proceedings are still bound by the provisions of juvenile criminal law. Juvenile criminal law may be applied to adolescents between 18 and 21 years of age if the personality of the offender or the circumstances surrounding the case makes this necessary. This can be the case if the juvenile displays signs of mental retardation.

During the last years, there has been a more punitive tendency in the Netherlands in relation to young offenders. The numbers of detained youngsters has increased and of youngsters who have been sentenced according to adult criminal law have increased. If you believe the media, young people in the Netherlands are becoming more and more aggressive and the number of criminal offences is increasing drastically. In-depth research has shown that this is not the case. When you look at most forms of criminal offences committed by juveniles, they have decreased, with the exception of offences using violence. Group offending and the amount of more serious crimes have increased. Another aspect of growing numbers is that of police, who is more active in tracking down offenders.

On the other hand, maybe as a reaction to calls for more severe punishment, some are voting for more alternatives, such as restorative justice. A growing feeling for a larger role of the victims (and their family) is one of the reasons. Furthermore, the procedures are lengthy, which results in uncertainty for the young offender. A related issue is the current lack of capacity of youth facilities. Both issues need more attention and money.

5.   Alternative sanctions

The Dutch juvenile justice system knows different forms of alternative sanctions – meaning alternatives for the formal justice system – at different levels. For instance, the police can refer to a so-called 'HALT arrangement', and the public prosecutor and the judge have the possibility to impose so-called 'task penalties' that consist of community service and learning schemes. With community services, the work should appeal to the young offender's sense of responsibility with regard to the offence that has been committed. The communal nature of the work should change his or her social behaviour for the better. The kind of jobs done under this scheme should promote the needs of society at large and be of educational value.

Learning Schemes are offered to provide practical and social skills. They are geared towards the provision of group work as well as one-on-one care. Depending on the nature of the offence that has been committed, the juvenile is required to go on different kinds of schemes which have been developed and made available throughout the Netherlands. The main ones are Focus on the Victim Learning Project, Sexual Education Learning Project and Social Skills Learning Project.

6.   Halt

One of the so-called alternative sanctions which contain restorative aspects in the Netherlands is Halt. Halt, short for 'the alternative', is a special sanction where the police can propose a project in which the young offender can be a participant. The youngster will be referred to a Halt-bureau where work or damage compensation is offered for a maximum of 20 hours. This can happen in cases consisting of vandalism, damage to property or petty theft.

Since 1995, the possibility of calling on the services of Halt-bureaus, which were set up in 1981, is embodied in the criminal code. Further details regarding the way these bureaus operate have been laid down in legal regulations and in the unitary guidelines of the state prosecution service. For example, a Halt-arrangement can only be initiated if the juvenile has already confessed and has not already participated in two other Halt-arrangements. Moreover, the juvenile must have been under 18 at the time the offence was committed. Charges are officially dropped after a successful Halt-procedure. The juvenile never reaches the level of prosecution and a criminal record is avoided.[7]

A Halt-arrangement is designed to deal with the following offences: vandalism causing up to 900 euro worth of damage; arson with danger to the public on objects; simple theft and receiving stolen goods; switching price tags; simple damage to property, including graffiti; despoilment of streets and disorderly conduct; unlawful entering of a restricted area; and firework misdemeanours. The juvenile is given the choice of having the charges dropped in exchange for his or her participation in a Halt-arrangement. A written offer is made to the juvenile with the reminder that he or she is not forced to participate in the scheme. If the juvenile is below 16 the parents must give their consent. If the juvenile agrees to the offer, the police draw up a protocol and send it to a Halt-bureau. The possible measures on offer are work, damage compensation, or a combination of the two. After the measures have been carried out, the police conduct a review with the Halt-team and subsequently decide whether further charges should be dropped. If the outcome of the Halt-arrangement is positive, the police inform in writing both the juvenile and the state prosecution service about the result. By doing so, further criminal proceedings are dropped. If the results are negative, a file for the instigation of preliminary proceedings is opened and passed on to the state prosecution service.

The Halt-procedure has as a second important task, the prevention of youth criminality. This is done by information lessons in schools, mainly focusing on youngsters aged between 10 and 14. Halt is also involved in prevention projects related to improving the safety of schools and/or communities. Of the approximately 50,000 youngsters who are arrested per year by the police, about 20,000 go to one of the 62 Halt-bureaus. The total number of youngsters that the police in 2005 sent to Halt was 24,163: 22,215 for a Halt-arrangement and 1,948 for a Stop-reaction. In particular, the HALT arrangements contribute to:
- empowering juveniles in conflict with the law
- promoting the participation of the youngsters in the resolution of their cases, as the application of the HALT procedure requires the juveniles' consent at different stages
- keeping youngsters out of the judicial system
- developing preventive approaches to youth offending
- promoting the link or cooperation with parents.[8]

7.   Current restorative initiatives in the Netherlands

In the Netherlands a search started in the 1970s for new alternatives in reaction to criminal offending by youngsters. The renewed interest in mediation is visible in the development of the victim movements and mediation projects. Only since the 1990s, experiments with restorative justice methods have been developed here. There are projects under different names, among them real justice (*echt-recht*), restorative justice, restorative mediation and (family) group conferences. Most of them work with the offender, the victim and family members or other persons from their social network.[9] Referrals come mainly from the police, Halt-bureaus and the Youth Protection Board.

Real justice conferences have spread throughout the country. The method is based on an American example, the principles of Real Justice developed by Terry O'Connel (Australia), and includes the provision of training to youth care workers. The method can be used separately from the penal procedure, also in school settings. Often police, justice authorities, HALT, the youth probation office and youth care are involved. A conference takes place after an incident has taken place where harm or pain is a result and restoration is needed. The well prepared meeting brings the victim and the offender together with family members and other persons that are important to them. The whole meeting is set up according to a plan and is led by the real justice coordinator. A training session with the organisation is a condition to become a coordinator. All participants get the chance to speak and explain what the incident has done to them. After that, one tries to find a solution on how this harm can be restored, which is then laid down in a contract to be signed by both parties. Currently there are projects in six cities of the Netherlands, which are funded by the Ministry of Justice and the province Overijssel. The Youth Protection Board in Zwolle now has five years of experience with the method and evaluations are positive. There are still relatively small numbers, but an increase is visible. In Overijssel in 2004, 16 restorative justice meetings took place. In 80 cases preparations were made to come to a meeting. In 2005 there were 24 meetings and in 120 cases steps were taken to set up a meeting. Sometimes other forms of restoration were met by writing an excuse letter for example. The total number of criminal cases with young offenders was 929 in 2005.[10] Since 1999 the police in Tilburg also works with mediation for youngsters who have come in contact with the police. They work with a method inspired by the Thames Valley Police in the UK. For certain cases (often Halt-like offences) an offer can be made to take part in a mediation session, in this case coordinated by a police man/woman who is trained to do so.

The use of restorative justice in detention centres is also increasing. 'Developing restorative skills for delinquent youth' *(Herstelopvoeding),* is a relatively new programme in a few closed facilities for young offenders in the Netherlands.[11] The method is especially focused on the population in the Judicial Correctional Institutions: youngsters who are in general not aware of the consequences of their behaviour and for that reason do not feel responsible.[12] Raising awareness about these consequences and the confrontation with the committed offence should contribute towards diminishing the chance of recidivism. It is a pedagogical reaction to give youngsters more clarity on the consequences of their behaviour and to let them take steps and responsibility for it. The programme consists of two elements: the first is training; and the second is a more individual restorative path, which can result in writing an apology letter or even in a group conference. In 2002 the Board of General Public Prosecutors launched a positive position paper in relation to restorative justice, on condition that it should be in line with the wishes of the victim and based on his or her willingness to participate.[13]

The Ministry of Justice has launched a five-year youth programme called '*Jeugd terecht*'[14]. Even though it stands for action and reaction, there is also room for some initiatives in relation to restorative justice methods. Six pilots throughout the country are part of it. By the end of 2006 the Minister of Justice will take a decision on whether or not to make restorative justice initiatives a country-wide reality.[15]

8.   From experiments to an obligation
At the European level restorative justice became mandatory. In 1999 the Council of Europe adopted Recommendation No. R (99) 19 of the Committee of Ministers to Member States concerning Mediation in Penal Matters and, in 2002, the UN noted the Basic Principles on the Use of Restorative Justice Programmes in Criminal Matters. In 2001, the European Union took another step to make certain actions mandatory for its member states and those who want to join the EU. The EU Council Framework Decision on the Standing of Victims in Criminal Proceedings is binding and calls for implementation of its articles on penal mediation by March 2006. It proposes ways to monitor this implementation.

This also means that the Netherlands should have regulated mediation in penal cases by 22 March 2006. In the policy paper of the Minister of Justice dealing with mediation in legal cases, nothing is said about using it in penal law. In April 2006 we can conclude that no concrete steps have been taken. There is more openness when is comes to using mediation programmes in relation to young people, some promises have been made, but so far there is nothing structural yet.[16] Our neighbours in Belgium seem to be further in this regard. They have been talking about a new law as a basis for restorative reactions for several years now and the latest proposal is very likely to be passed this summer. One of the working methods they use is looked at in more detail below.

9.   Mediation in more severe cases, examples from Belgium
Mediation between offenders and victims of criminal offences has been integrated in Belgium in the penal system, for both youngsters and adults. For youth there are currently two forms, restorative mediation and family group conferences, called *Hergo*. I will concentrate on the latter.

Since November 2000, for more severe cases, such as bag snatching with violence, aggravated theft, street fighting, the project *Hergo* (restorative group conference) has been active. It is used in five Belgium cities. Financial support comes from the Flemish Community. *Hergo* is based on the Family Group Conferences in New Zealand, inspired by the traditions of the Maori people and laid down in the Children and Young Persons Act. A *Hergo* is a meeting in the form of a circle with the offender, victim, family members and other related persons, coordinated by a mediator. The meeting takes place with the attendance of a police officer. To protect the rights of the child there is also a lawyer present. The session is focused on finding a constructive solution for the consequences of a criminal offence. Special is the attendance of the police officer. He/she is fulfilling the role of the person promoting the interests of the community ('*belangenbehartiger*'). A role which formally can only be carried out by a public prosecutor, but this is said to be practically not possible. Persons who have a trust relationship with the victim and offender are very important in the *Hergo*.

A referral can only be done by the juvenile judge and is limited to more severe cases.

The agreement can, in addition to doing restoration directly to the victim, also contain a proposal of, for example, carrying out a community service or a pedagogical course.

The agreement can only be carried out after the youth judge has approved it, whereby the motives of the youngster in the intention agreement are taken up in the judgment / sentence. Participation is voluntary.[17]

Hergos are carried out by non-governmental organisations in the field of youth care. Most of the time, these are institutions that also deal with community work and training for young delinquents. There is a structure and an umbrella organisation for the development of the content and methodology.

In 2002 in Flanders 1,604 youngsters were referred to mediations, and in 2003 1,542. The largest part was referred to restorative mediation and a small part to *Hergo*.[18] The first evaluations show good results. Most victims, offenders, mediators and others involved are positive in their reactions on the method. So far referrals were possible indirectly under the Youth Protection Law of 1965.[19] Since the 1980s several law proposals have been passed and discussed, also with a fully restorative approach. The last proposal which went through has its focus still on youth protection law, but restorative practices get a main place in it. This new law was approved by the Senate in May 2006.[20]

10. Conclusions

On the basis of the principles of the CRC and the additional UN principles governments have the obligation to make sure that young people do not make mistakes and fall into criminal behaviour, but the moment they do so the governments have to react in an adjustable and pedagogical way.[21] The Dutch criminal justice system is mainly a pedagogical system which started about 100 years ago. Recently we have seen reactions on crime which are harsher towards young people. At the same time more emphasis has been given to alternatives for imprisonment, such as Halt, community service and learning schemes, and new forms of restorative justice. Restorative justice offers an opportunity for both the young offender and the victim, as well as the community, to reach an acceptable solution in case of a conflict or a criminal offence.

Especially for young people the understanding of the caused harm is important. They can and should learn from their own mistakes. Evaluations show that restorative justice meetings result in less recidivism. For the victims it offers at the same time an opportunity to diminish feelings of revenge and to leave the matter behind. It can also create more acceptance and understanding in (local) society.

Referring back to the Dutch situation, the government is slowly recognising the possibilities of restorative justice initiatives, although there is no real structure or clear policy proposal yet. Looking at the international rules and especially the EU frame work decision, the Netherlands is obliged to do so. Municipalities can play a stimulating role. Implementation, research and evaluation are needed, as well as financial support. What is happening in the field of restorative justice for juveniles is encouraging but it is not sufficient. Especially in more severe cases there is an additional task for restorative justice methods such as conferencing. The method of *Hergo* in Belgium or Family Group Conferences in New Zealand, whereby the juvenile judge is referring youngsters to such a session, are examples that the Netherlands could and should follow. A hundred years after the child protection laws it is time for restorative action in reaction to crime committed by juveniles.

Endnotes

1 Beijing Rules (1985): United Nations Standard Minimum Rules for the Administration of Juvenile Justice, United Nations, General Assembly, UN Doc. /A/RES/40/33.

Havana Rules (1990): United Nations Rules for the Protection of Juveniles Deprived of their Liberty, United Nations, General Assembly, UN Doc./A/RES/45/113.

Riyadh Guidelines (1990): United Nations Guidelines on the Prevention of Juvenile Delinquency, United Nations, General Assembly , UN Doc./A/RES/45/112.

2 Mijnarends, E.M. (1999), *Richtlijnen voor een verdragsconforme jeugdstrafrechtspleging. 'Gelijkwaardig, maar minderjarig'* (diss. Leiden), Den Haag: Kluwer Rechtswetenschappelijke Publicaties 1999, p. 5.

3 Wolthuis, A. (2005), Van fouten kun je leren. IVRK geeft pedagogische invulling jeugdstrafrecht; lessen voor Nederland, *NJCM-Bulletin*, p. 717-734.

4 For example by the Maori in New Zealand, and the Indians/inuit in Canada. Conflicts in these societies are still settled among relatives and other concerned persons. Often the meeting (mediation) is led by an elder or another important person within the community.

5 Bazemore, G. & Walgrave, L. (ed.) (1999), *Restorative juvenile justice. Repairing the harm of youth crime,* Monsey, New York: Criminal Justice Press.

6 See for example: Maxwell, G. and A. Morris (2001), Family Group Conferencing and Re-offending, in: Morris, A. en G. Maxwell (eds.), *Restorative Justice for Juveniles, Conferencing, Mediation & Circles*, Hart Publishing, Oxford.

7 See for more information: www.halt.nl.

8 HALT year report 2005. See also: www.halt.nl; Wolthuis, A. (2001), *Moving Forward – Restorative Aspects in the Dutch Juvenile Justice System*, Amsterdam, DCI-NL.

9 Hokwerda, Y. (2004), *Herstelrecht in jeugdzaken, een evaluatieonderzoek van zeven experimenten in Nederland*, Den Haag, Boom Juridische uitgevers, p. 47-50.

10 Information given by the Centrum voor Herstelgericht Werken (www.eigen-kracht.nl).

11 De Winter, M., Meijnen, M., Goldschmidt, H.I.M. (2005), *Eindrapportage Herstelopvoeding. Een onderzoeksverslag van de pilot herstelopvoeding in JJI De Heuvelrug, locatie Eikenstein, september 2004 - mei 2005*, Utrecht: Universiteit Utrecht, Opleiding Pedagogiek.

12 See for example Weijers, I. (2005), *De pedagogische uitdaging van het jeugdstrafrecht*, Amsterdam: Uitgeverij SWP, oratie Universiteit Utrecht.

13 Berghuis, B. (2002), Strafrecht en Herstelrecht, OM-beleid in het licht van bemiddeling, *Tijdschrift voor Herstelrecht*, 2, p. 29-40.

14 *Jeugd terecht. Actieprogramma jeugdcriminaliteit 2003-2006,* Den Haag: Ministerie van Justitie. www.justitie.nl/jeugdterecht

15 Internal position paper of the Ministry of Justice, Directie Justiteel Jeugdbeleid, Den Haag, November 2005.

16 Ministerie van Justitie, Beleidsbrief Mediation en het Rechtsbestel, 19 april 2004, Den Haag.

17 Vanfraechem, I. (2003), Family group conferences in Vlaanderen: Herstelgericht groepsoverleg (Hergo), *Tijdschrift voor Jeugdrecht en Kinderrechten*, Kluwer, nr. 2003/3, p. 142-148.

18 Jaarverslag, Ondersteuningsstructuur Bijzondere Jeugdzorg, periode juni 2002 - juni 2003, Brussel. See also: www.osbj.be

19 Geudens, H. (2003), Verwerking gegevens herstelbemiddeling voor minderjarige daders m.b.t. 2002, *Tijdschrift voor jeugdrecht en kinderrechten*, Kluwer, December 2003, p. 269-283.

20 More information can be found at: www.dekamer.be. *Wetsontwerp tot wijziging van de wetgeving betreffende de jeugdbescherming en het ten laste nemen van minderjarigen die een als misdrijf omschreven feit hebben gepleegd., zittingsperiode 2004/2005, DOC 51 1467/001, aangenomen door de Kamer op 04.05.2006, art. 77 en de Senaat op 30.03.2006.*

21 Articles 37 and 40 CRC, in relation to the main principles laid down in articles 2, 3, 6 and 12.

Part III

Recommendations

Recommendations for the Future

Introduction

Children in need are the concern of parents, professionals, policy-makers, society, and last but not least of the children themselves. Children in need, including children who cause serious problems, are entitled to protection and help.

What is the future of child protection? In 1905, special laws on children and young people entered into force in the Netherlands, namely a law concerning the restriction of parental authority, a juvenile justice act and a law on child protection measures. In the same period, similar laws were adopted in other European countries. The Century of the Child, declared by Ellen Key, had just begun.

One hundred years later, it is time for retrospection and reflection. The Convention on the Rights of the Child is a relatively recent international human rights treaty, with standards and procedures that form the basis for the protection of children. During the International Conference '100 Years of Child Protection' (28-30 November 2005, Amsterdam, the Netherlands), there was an exchange of ideas, experiences, solutions and visions, concerning the past and the future, between East and West, and North and South. The principles and 22 action-oriented recommendations listed below reflect the new ideas, good practices and promising perspectives for the future that came out of the conference. They are relevant for everyone working to realise the protection of children, in particular competent authorities and bodies.

I.   Principles

A.   Principles on child protection

The United Nations Convention on the Rights of the Child (UN CRC) contains principles and provisions which govern child protection, and the relevant rights of the child and corresponding State obligations, in particular:

- General Principles: Articles 2 (non-discrimination), 3(1) (best interests of the child), 6 (right to life, survival and development) and 12 (respect for the views of the child); and
- Rights: Articles 3(2) (child's well-being), 3(3) (standards of protection), 4 (measures of implementation), 5 (parental guidance), 9 (separation from parents), 18 (parental responsibilities), 19 (abuse and neglect), 20 (children deprived of a family environment), 25 (periodic review of placement), 39 (recovery and reintegration).

They form the basis of the following 'UN CRC Framework for Child Protection':

1. Child Protection without discrimination.
2. Child Protection with participation.
3. Child Protection with sufficient resources.
4. Child Protection with quality.

1. Child Protection without discrimination.
   - Child Protection that provides all necessary assistance and services and is accessible to all children without exception (Art. 2).

2. Child Protection with participation.
   - Child Protection that allows every child to freely express his/her views in all matters affecting the child (Art. 12).

3. Child Protection with sufficient resources.
   - Child Protection that can provide the protection and care which are necessary for the child's well-being in all cases (Art. 3(2)).
   - Child Protection with sufficient financial resources to set up and maintain a good child protection system (Art. 4).
   - Child Protection that is available to all children in need of it at the time that they need it (Art. 4).
   - Child Protection with sufficient services and facilities for the assistance of parents, including working parents, and children (Art. 18).

4. Child Protection with quality.
   - Child Protection where the best interests of the child are the paramount consideration (Art. 3(1)).
   - Child Protection that provides adequate protection and care (Art. 3(2), Art. 19).
   - Child Protection that ensures the development of the child (Art. 6(2)).
   - Child Protection that takes into account the evolving capacities of the child (Art. 5).
   - Child Protection that takes into account the right of the child to maintain contact with both parents (Art. 9).
   - Child Protection that takes into account the ethnic, cultural and religious background of the child and his/her parents (Art. 20(3), Art. 30).
   - Child Protection that takes into account continuity in a child's upbringing (Art. 20(3)).
   - Child Protection that promotes the recovery and social reintegration of child victims of abuse, neglect and exploitation (Art. 39).
   - Child Protection with supervision (Art. 3(3), Art. 25).

B.   Principles on juvenile justice

The CRC contains principles and provisions which specifically govern juvenile justice, and the relevant rights of the child and corresponding State obligations, in particular:

- General Principles: Articles 2 (non-discrimination), 3(1) (best interests of the child), 6 (right to life, survival and development) and 12 (respect for the views of the child); and
- Rights: Articles 37(a) (prohibition of torture), 37(a) (prohibition of capital punishment and life imprisonment), 37(c)-(d) (children deprived of their liberty), 40 (administration of juvenile justice).

Other relevant United Nations instruments are: the 1985 United Nations Standard Minimum Rules for the Administration of Juvenile Justice (Beijing Rules); the 1990 United Nations Rules for the Protection of Juveniles Deprived of their Liberty (Havana Rules); and the 1990 United Nations Guidelines for the Prevention of Juvenile Delinquency (Riyadh Guidelines).

They form the basis of the following 'UN CRC Framework for Juvenile Justice':

1.   Best interests of the child as a paramount consideration.
2.   A pedagogical approach.
3.   Deprivation of liberty as last measure.
4.   Promotion of diversion and dispositions.
5.   Special safeguards.

1.   Best interests of the child as a paramount consideration.
- The establishment of a minimum age for criminal responsibility (Art. 40(3)(a)).
- The best interests of the child and the well-being of minors form the primary considerations during the entire process (Art. 3(1)).

2.   A pedagogical approach.
- The right to be treated in a manner which takes into account the desirability of promoting the child's reintegration in society and the child's assuming a constructive role in society (Art. 40(1)).
- The right to be treated in a manner consistent with the promotion of the child's sense of dignity and worth, and which reinforces the child's respect for human rights and fundamental freedoms of others (Art. 40(1)).
- The right to be treated in a manner which takes into account the child's age (Art. 40(1)).
- The continuation of education (Art. 40(1), Art. 4).

3.   Deprivation of liberty as last measure.
- The arrest, detention or imprisonment of a child shall be used only as a measure of last resort and for the shortest appropriate period of time (Art. 37(b)).
- Prohibition of capital punishment and life imprisonment without possibility of release (Art. 37(a)).

– Prohibition of torture or other cruel, inhuman or degrading treatment or punishment (Art. 37(a)).

4.   Promotion of diversion and dispositions.
–   The use of measures without resorting to judicial proceedings (diversion) (Art. 40(3)).
–   The use of dispositions and other alternatives to detention or institutional care (Art. 40(3)-(4)).
–   The use of restorative justice (Art. 40(3)-(4)).

5.   Special safeguards.
–   The right to prompt decisions on any actions (Art. 37(d), Art. 40(3)).
–   The right to a fair and just trial (Art. 40(2)).
–   The establishment of specialised authorities and institutions such as juvenile courts, judges, lawyers and police (Art. 40(3)).
–   The right to freely participate in the process (Art. 12, Art. 40(2)(b)(iv)).
–   The right to be informed and assisted in understanding their rights and duties (Art. 40(2)(b)).
–   The important role of parents and contact with family members (Art. 37(c), Art. 40(2)(b)).
–   The right to have his/her privacy respected at all stages of the proceedings (Art. 40(2)(b)(vii)).

II.   Recommendations

A.   General recommendations
–   A child rights approach should be the basis of all actions concerning children undertaken in the fields of child protection and juvenile justice.
–   All relevant international instruments, including the Convention on the Rights of the Child and the Hague Conventions on children, should be ratified and implemented by all countries.
–   All actions concerning children in the fields of child protection and juvenile justice should be taken *with* the participation of children, with respect for the views and dignity of the child, the views of the child being given due weight in accordance with the age and maturity of the child.
–   Prevention at all levels should be the primary focus in all societal sectors. This comprises ensuring the accessibility, availability and quality of basic services and facilities for the protection and care of children, including day care centres, schools and health care facilities.
–   All policies and programmes for children in the fields of child protection and juvenile justice should be evidence based and should be approved by national and/or international accreditation panels.
–   United Nations agencies should gather data on the numbers of children deprived of their liberty, whether based on civil, penal, health care, immigration or other grounds, and the reasons for the deprivation of liberty.
–   Governments should ensure that all persons working with children in the

fields of child protection and juvenile justice, including judges, prosecutors, police officers, social workers, have appropriate and regular training.
- The initial contact of the child with authorities in the fields of child protection and juvenile justice should start with an immediate, validated assessment specifically focusing on the needs of the child, in order to avoid unnecessary delay and inadequate measures for the care or protection of the child.

B. Recommendations on child protection

- In all cases where the protection of the child conflicts with the privacy of the parent(s), the best interests of the child should prevail. One of the means to ensure that the best interests of the child are the primary consideration is to provide the child with a legal representative or another third party.
- Adequate screening instruments for assessing children at risk should be available, taking due account of the child's ethnic, religious, cultural and linguistic background.
- In all cases where alternative care for the child, and in particular placement outside the family, is considered necessary, the quality of the alternative care provided to the child should in any case be better than the prior situation. The competent authorities should guarantee, monitor and review, at regular intervals, the alternative care provided to the child. Assessing a child's needs should, whenever possible, be done in full participation with the child and his or her parents, or others responsible for the child. All actions, including the child's treatment, should as a rule be extended to his or her family of origin.
- In cases where the child is removed from his or her family environment, foster placement should always come first. Adoption, both internationally and nationally, should, in policy and practice, always be the last resort. With a view to strengthening the position of the foster child, the legal status of foster parents needs to be improved. In any case, certainty about the child's stay in the foster family is necessary. The court should hold a favourable approach towards the transfer of parental responsibilities to foster parents. Foster parents should be afforded such an amount of financial compensation that adoption as well as institutional care will really be the ultimate resort.
- Separation of a child from his or her parents should not as a rule affect the legal status of the parents, but other restrictions of parental responsibilities are allowed, taking into account the best interests of the child.
- Any forms of violence within the family including corporal punishment of children should be forbidden by national law.

C. Recommendations on juvenile justice

- Capital punishment and lifetime sentences without parole for juveniles should be abolished by national law.
- International standards, such as the Beijing Rules, the Riyadh Guidelines, the Havana Rules and the relevant recommendations of the Council of

Europe, should be available in the national language(s), and should be fully implemented in national regulations and provisions.
- Boot camps or similar programmes can only be applied if they are part of a social programme and evidence based.
- Restorative justice should be the basic principle in the attitude towards juvenile delinquency, and should be promoted and used at all stages of the criminal proceedings.
- The UN Committee on the Rights of the Child should stimulate research and issue a General Comment concerning the minimum age of criminal responsibility.
- The pedagogical dimension of juvenile justice requires that, when juveniles have committed a criminal offence, they must, as soon as possible, be confronted with their criminal behaviour to build a bridge between their former behaviour and their new start for the future. A confrontation with the victim(s) can be part of this programme.
- During their detention period, probation services should be active to make it possible that the relationship with the family members of the juvenile is kept and stimulated, and they should work on programmes for the period after the detention to prevent the children to restart criminal activities. Educational and vocational programmes during detention and after release should be promoted.
- Special attention should be given to children who were involved in criminal activities of their parents, because there is a risk that children start as victims and then end up as perpetrators.

These recommendations for the future were formulated by a group of experts, taking into account the discussions at the International Conference '100 Years of Child Protection – Recommendations for the Future', which was held on 28-30 November 2005 in Amsterdam, the Netherlands.